Supporting Individuals with Autism Spectrum Disorder in Recreation

Phyllis Coyne & Ann Fullerton

SAGAMORE
PUBLISHING

Production Coordinator: Janet Wahlfeldt
Cover Design: Janet Wahlfeldt
Cover Photos Courtesy of: Top Photo—Patty McNary
                                   Middle Photo—Mt. Hood Kiwanis Camp
                                   Bottom Photo—Mt. Hood Kiwanis Camp

Library of Congress Catalog Card Number: 2003112439
ISBN: 1-57167-498-5

Printed in the United States

10 9 8 7 6 5 4 3 2 1

Dedication

We dedicate this book to the many individuals with
ASD who have been our teachers.

Contents

List of Figures

List of Tables

Acknowledgments

We would like to express our gratitude and appreciation to the various persons who contributed significantly to this book. First, we'd like to thank Jane Rake and Mary Lou Vandenburg for writing chapters in this book. Jane Rake's insights as a parent and a consultant to families bring the important voice of parents and siblings to the book. Mary Lou Vanderburg, as an author, autism specialist and master teacher, also brought the gift of her experience in the field of Autism Spectrum Disorder.

Our intention in planning this book was to provide foundational knowledge and best practices in Chapters 1 through 6 and then to show how those practices are actually used in various programs in Chapters 7 through 11. This would not have been possible without the important contributions of the directors and staff of these programs. These individuals provided, through interviews and other materials, extensive information about their programs. They offered important perspectives, methods, and many practical examples. We are deeply grateful to them for sharing their expertise and creativity with the readers of this book.

In Chapter 2, one program is briefly described. Thanks for providing this information:

- Patty Prather, CTRS, Community Inclusion Specialist, The Arc of Multnomah County, OR.

In Chapter 3, several families and/or parents contributed their experiences and insights. Thanks to these parents as well as members of the Portland Asperger's Network:

- Kendra Hogue
- Diane and Jeff Wills
- Katie Ripplinger
- Kathy Henley
- Dena Amend
- Dave, Mary, and Peter Krug
- Christine Bruno

In Chapter 4, we are deeply grateful to a group of young adults with Asperger's Syndrome who shared their experiences and views of leisure and recreation and offered ideas for recreation therapists and leaders. Thanks guys, you know who you are!

We also wish to thank Diane and Jeff Wills for sharing their experiences and ideas.

We'd like to especially thank Debbie Kelly for her many ideas and contributions to this chapter, and for her support of this book project. Debbie, thanks for being our teacher.

In Chapter 7, descriptions of special programs for individuals with ASD that have much to teach recreation providers about individuals with ASD were provided by:

- Jennifer Lingell, Site Director, San Jose, Jay Nolan Community Services, California
- Kelly Stone, CTRS and Recreation Therapist, Creative Living, Raleigh, NC
- JoAnne Seip, Director, and Kitty Doyle, Teacher with the Provincial Resource Program

In Chapter 8, three parks and recreation agencies and their staff offered practical ways to support individuals with ASD in community recreation programs. Our deep thanks to:

- Jan Book, CTRS and Kevin Mattias, Disabled Citizens Recreation, Portland Bureau of Parks and Recreation, Portland, OR
- Tracey Crawford, CTRS, Superintendent of Recreation, Dawn Schaefer, CTRS, Manager of Inclusion, and John McGovern, Executive Director of Northern Suburban Special Recreation Association (NSSRA), Northbrook, IL
- Molly Elliot, CTRS, Inclusion Coordinator and Specialized Recreation Programmer, and Dena Amendt, CTRS, Specialized Recreation Programmer; City of Eugene Recreation Services, Eugene, OR

In Chapter 9, three youth service organizations and their staff offered a variety of examples of how their organizations are supporting participants with ASD. We sincerely appreciate the information from:

- Jim Rutledge, State Program Leader & Department Head, 4-H Youth Development Education, Oregon State University
- Patty McNary, Morrow County 4-H leader and parent, Oregon Extension Service
- Sue Urrey, Tillamook County 4-H leader, Oregon Extension Service
- Helen Orloff, Disabilities Coordinator, Girl Scouts of the United States of America
- Sharon Cupp, Assistant Executive Director Membership, Girl Scouts—Totem Council, Seattle, WA
- Ruth Baccha, Girl Scout leader and parent, Girl Scouts—Totem Council, Seattle, WA
- Lisa Grimes, Girl Scout leader and parent, Girl Scouts—Totem Council, Seattle, WA
- Joy Lee, basketball coordinator and parent, Challenger Division, Lake Oswego, OR
- Janice Schmahl, baseball coordinator and parent, Challenger Division, Lake Oswego, OR
- Kathy Prenovost, soccer coordinator and parent, Challenger Division, Lake Oswego, OR.
- Marci Hammel, autism specialist and parent, Challenger Division, Lake Oswego, OR
- Sarah Peters, autism specialist and parent, Challenger Division, Lake Oswego, OR

In Chapter 10, several camp programs and their staff provided a wide array of creative approaches to creating a positive and joyous camp experience for individuals with ASD. We deeply appreciate the contributions of:

- Kevin Mattias, Director, Camp Kyowa, Portland Parks & Recreation, Portland, OR
- Allison Stewart, Program Coordinator of Operation Access Project and Professor, Department of Recreation and Leisure, San Francisco State University, San Francisco, CA
- Susan Hansen, Founder and Director, Camp Awareness, Indianapolis, IN
- Evelyn Coffey, Program Director and Gene Nudelman, Executive Director, Mt. Hood Kiwanis Camp, Portland, OR
- Edna Smith, Executive Director, Autism Asperger Resource Center, University of Kansas Medical Center and Kelly Tedbenkamp, Director, Camp Determination, Kansas City, MO
- Betsy Cable, Assistant Director, Camp Royall, Moncure, NC. Sponsored by the Autism Society of North Carolina, Raleigh, NC

- Kari Dunn, Autism Resource Specialist and Director, Camp Discovery, Courage North, MN. Camp Discovery is sponsored by the Autism Society of Minnesota, St. Paul, MN and serves its members

In Chapter 11, staff and parents from three programs that were started by parents provided examples of supports for success. We sincerely thank the following for their contributions.

- Marci Hammel, Supervisor and parent, and Sarah Peters, Assistant Supervisor and parent, ACAP (Autistic Children's Activity Program), Portland, Oregon
- Pat Fiske, Director, Stepping Out Program of the Cove Center, Groden Center, Providence, Rhode Island
- Michelle Kuepker, Founder and parent, Game Club, West Linn, Oregon

Lastly, we wish to thank our friends and colleagues who generously volunteered to review the manuscript. Thanks to Kari Dunn, Kelly Stone, Patty Prather, Dena Amend, JoAnne Seip, and Kitty Doyle for your feedback on content. We are also deeply grateful for the editing and word-crafting skills of Tom Boyer.

Thanks to Michael Bender for providing us an opportunity to propose this book to Sagamore Publishing and for reviewing the manuscript. Lastly, we wish to thank Douglas Sanders, General Manager and Janet Wahlfeldt, Production Manager at Sagamore Publishing for their support, suggestions, and commitment to bring the production of this book to fruition.

Phyllis Coyne and Ann Fullerton

Preface

Recreation is important to everyone's quality of life. This includes over half a million Americans with Autism Spectrum Disorder (ASD) whose lives can be enriched through leisure pursuits. With appropriate supports, many individuals with ASD can learn lifelong leisure skills through organized recreation programs. In fact, since most of these individuals do not easily develop skills through less formal means, organized recreation is one of the primary means to develop recreation interests and skills. These interests and skills may then continue to be pursued with a group or individually. Therefore, the providers of recreation services must recognize and accept responsibility for serving all people, including those with ASD.

Although ASD is one of the most common developmental disabilities, many professionals and family members are unaware of how it affects recreation participation and how they can effectively work with individuals with this disorder in recreation settings. Many agencies that provide recreation services have tried to include individuals with ASD with varying degrees of success. Unfortunately, many recreation service providers currently lack knowledge of effective ways to assist individuals with ASD in recreation activities.

A major factor limiting recreation opportunities for individuals with ASD appears to be the lack of awareness concerning the needs of individuals with ASD among recreation staff and the broader community. Until recently little has been known about how to effectively support individuals with ASD in recreation activities. While there is limited literature specific to ASD and recreation, there is considerable literature and research on the general problems, needs and effective interventions for individuals with ASD that provides a compass on how to support these individuals.

Difficulties with reciprocal interaction, self-initiation, motor planning, activity planning and sequencing, along with a restricted repertoire of interests and the behaviors that may result from these difficulties are all characteristics of ASD. This understanding of difficulties provides a framework for understanding why individuals with ASD may exhibit non-goal directed, nonfunctional, repetitive or other behavior out of context with the activity, if they are not provided with planned, positive experiences with appropriate supports.

This book was developed to assist recreation service providers, as well as families, to understand strategies for supporting individuals with ASD in community and school recreation programs. The ideas have many practical uses in generic and specialized recreation programs. A variety of audiences, including teachers, recreation service providers, Certified Therapeutic Recreation Specialists (CTRS), physical education teachers, adapted physical education specialists, occupational therapists (OTR), university students in the previous professions, program directors, residential staff, youth service workers, camp staff, autism consultants, families and advocates, will find answers to their questions regarding the challenges of supporting individuals with ASD in organized community and school recreation activities. Table 0.1 outlines subject areas about which professionals typically have questions. In addition, recreation service providers and families will learn about their roles and responsibilities in better serving individuals with ASD in community and school recreation programs.

Table 0.1
Answers for Recreation Providers and Family Members

Position	Answers Regarding:
Teachers	ASD, legal mandates, assessment and supports, collaboration, resources
Recreation program staff	ASD, assessment and supports, how other programs are meeting needs, resources
CTRSs	ASD, legal mandates, assessment and supports, staff training, program development, what selected programs are doing, resources
Phys. Ed teachers	ASD, assessment and supports
Adapted P. E. teachers	ASD, legal mandates, assessment and supports, staff training
Occupational therapists	ASD, assessment and supports, what selected programs are doing
University students	ASD, legal mandates, program development, assessment and supports, program examples, resources
Program directors	Needs, legal mandates, program development, staff training
Residential staff	ASD, assessment and supports, approaching service providers
Youth service workers	ASD, assessment and supports, how other programs are meeting needs
Camp staff	ASD, assessment and supports, effective approaches used by other camps
Autism consultants	Assessment and program development specific to recreation, examples of effective programs
Families and advocates	Legal mandates, examples of effective programs

The material in this book is designed to assist in the provision of more meaningful and enjoyable recreation services to individuals from age five through adulthood with all ability levels. Because of the continuity across autism spectrum disorders, this book addresses both the more narrowly defined disorder of autism and the broader range of ASD, including pervasive developmental disorder—not otherwise specified (PDD-NOS), Asperger's disorder, and childhood disintegrative disorder.

The level of functioning and degree of challenge of individuals with ASD are intentionally not specified in this book. Every person, regardless of level of functioning, should be supported to develop recreation interests and participation. All information and strategies are applicable to address the needs of those with any age or level of ability in specialized to generic programs. However, each individual with ASD is unique, so supports must be chosen to meet individual needs.

This book provides information on the impact of ASD on recreation participation, guidelines on how to support individuals with ASD, as we currently understand their needs, and examples of selected programs that are using promising practices to meet this challenge. Figure 0.1 shows the organization of this book. Understanding ASD, utilizing the individual's existing skills and interests, and providing appropriate supports in organized recreation programs are emphasized throughout the book.

Figure 0.1

Supporting Individuals with Autism Spectrum Disorder (ASD) in Recreation

Phyllis Coyne & Ann Fullerton

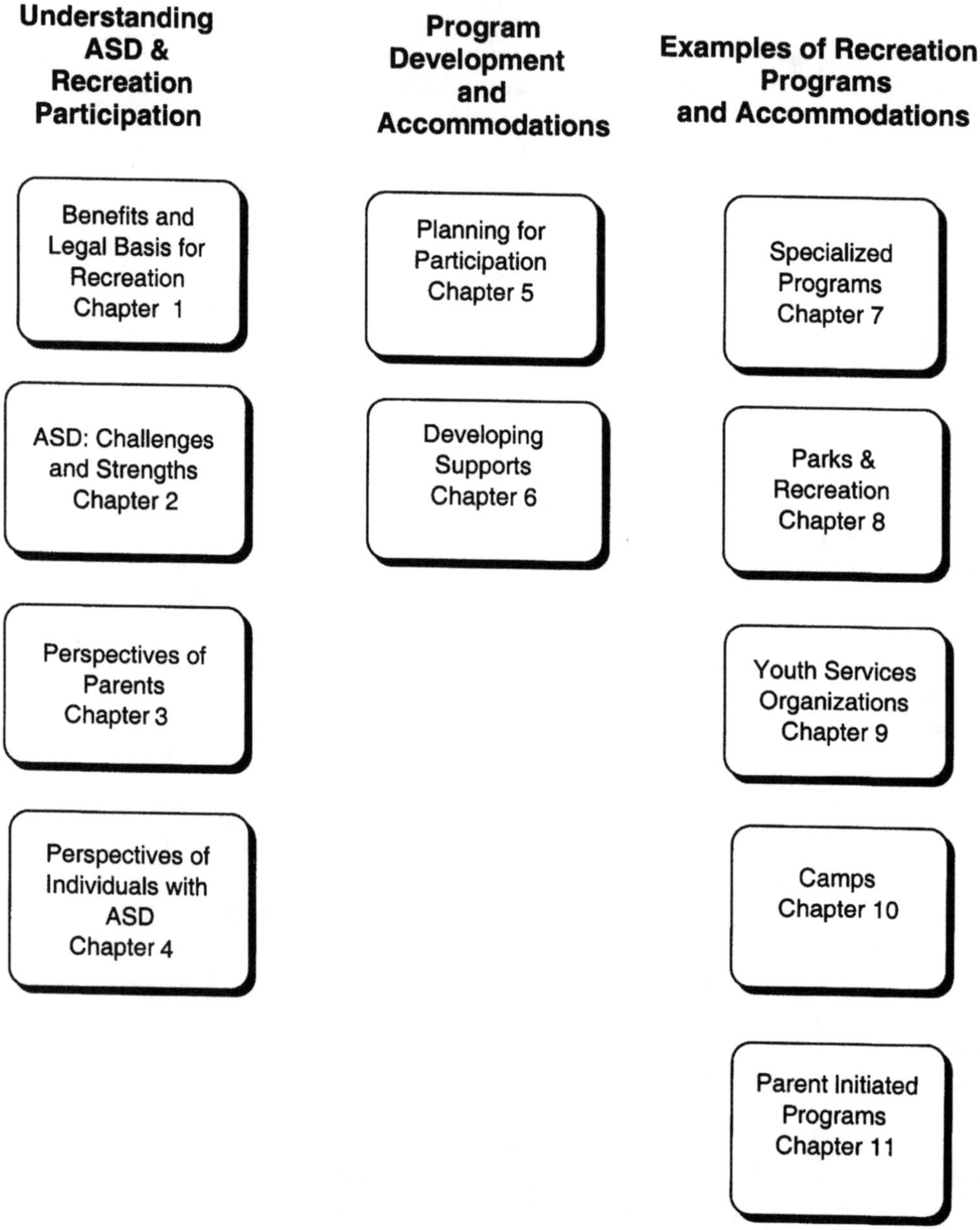

Understanding ASD & Recreation Participation

Benefits and Legal Basis for Recreation
Chapter 1

ASD: Challenges and Strengths
Chapter 2

Perspectives of Parents
Chapter 3

Perspectives of Individuals with ASD
Chapter 4

Program Development and Accommodations

Planning for Participation
Chapter 5

Developing Supports
Chapter 6

Examples of Recreation Programs and Accommodations

Specialized Programs
Chapter 7

Parks & Recreation
Chapter 8

Youth Services Organizations
Chapter 9

Camps
Chapter 10

Parent Initiated Programs
Chapter 11

In Chapters 7-11, success stories from around the country demonstrate that individuals with ASD can participate in community and school recreation programs, if sufficient support is provided, all are informed, and proven strategies are used. A variety of programs that represent a continuum of services in providing recreation options for individuals with ASD from specialized programs to generic programs are presented to illustrate key features that lead to program effectiveness. Challenges encountered along the way in selected existing programs are also illustrated. Although the examples provided are specific, the approaches described can be applied to most recreation settings.

Community and school recreation opportunities are provided by a variety of organizations. Typically community recreation opportunities are provided by parks and recreation departments, schools, interest groups, such as dog clubs and hiking clubs, community colleges, churches, private organizations, such as country clubs, YMCAs, and YWCAs, or youth service organizations, such as Boys and Girls Clubs and sports leagues. Establishments such as bowling centers, movie theaters, and arcades also provide many community recreation options. In addition to featuring selected programs in the areas of special programs, parks and recreation departments, youth service organizations, camps, and programs begun by parents, this book includes shorter examples from schools, private organizations, and commercial recreation establishments.

Group recreation activities may always be too uncomfortable for some individuals with ASD, but many uncomfortable situations can be avoided with careful planning and ongoing support. Even given exposure to various organized recreation programs, some individuals with ASD may chose to spend most of or all of their leisure alone. We respect the right of anyone to choose to spend most or all of our leisure alone when the choice is based on having had exposure to recreation options with appropriate support.

Terminology in this Book

Terminology related to ASD and recreation related areas has been used in different contexts in the literature. The identification of the most preferred terminology is a continuously evolving process. To prevent confusion by the reader, a description of how selected terms are used in this book is provided.

Autism Spectrum Disorder (ASD). Throughout this book, the term Autism Spectrum Disorder and/or ASD will be used. A number of years ago, the concept of Autism Spectrum Disorder was introduced to provide an umbrella term for autism and other disorders that include similar impairments in basic social skills, but vary in severity or the presence of communication delay and repetitive behaviors. Autism spectrum disorders are unique in the pattern of deficits and areas of relative strengths. The most important considerations in devising recreation programs for individuals with ASD have to do with recognition of the autism spectrum as a whole, with the concomitant implications for social, communicative, and behavioral development, along with the understanding of the strengths and weaknesses of the individual.

Because of the continuity across autism spectrum disorders, this book addresses both the more narrowly defined disorder of autism and the broader range of ASD, including pervasive developmental disorder—not otherwise specified (PDD-NOS), Asperger's disorder, and childhood disintegrative disorder. Rett's syndrome (i.e., its onset and pattern of deficits), is not specifically considered in this book. Individuals with Rett's syndrome, however, may require similar supports in some circumstances (National Research Council, 2001).

Individuals or participants with Autism Spectrum Disorder (ASD). Individuals or participants with ASD is used in this book, except where it is part of an organization's name or a quote, to focus on considering the person's uniqueness and worth first.

Leisure and Recreation. A wide range of terms related to leisure is commonly used by professionals in recreation, special education and Adapted Physical Education (APE), but even these professionals experience difficulties in clearly defining the differences among these terms (Rizzo & Davis, 1993; Schleien et. al., 1995). In keeping with common usage, the terms "leisure" and "recreation" will be used synonymously throughout this book to refer to activities or experiences of interest that people chose to participate in for fun, enjoyment, or enrichment during time free from obligations. Hobbies, sports, fitness activities, arts and crafts, music, dance, art, drama, nature experiences, and studying topics of interest are some of the recreation opportunities that are included in this category.

Organized recreation. Organized recreation, as used in this book, refers to community and school recreation programs and activities that are offered by any agency, organization, establishment or group.

Strategies and Supports. The terms strategies and supports are used interchangeably in this book to indicate techniques, tools, equipment and communication style that enables an individual with ASD to increase meaningful involvement in community and school recreation programs. These may also be referred to as modifications, accommodations or interventions. They are provided to enable the participant to be as successful and independent as possible.

Inclusion. As used in this book, inclusion refers to the participation of those with and without disabilities together in activities of choice. Complete inclusion is achieved when the supports are in place to allow social, mental and emotional inclusion of all participants. Inclusion is about ensuring choices, having support, having connections, and being valued. In the recent past, this process has also been called mainstreaming and integration.

Pronouns. The pronouns "he," "she" and "s/he" are used interchangeably in the text.

Chapter One

Introduction

Phyllis Coyne

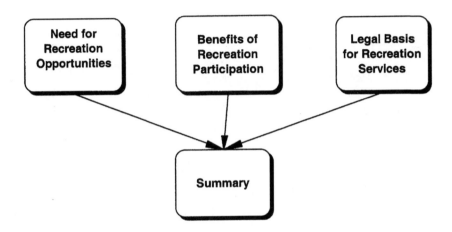

Recreation is an important aspect of quality of life for everyone and plays a major role in the lives of most of us. According to Edginton, Jordan, DeGraaf, and Edginton (1995), a growing number of us are participating in a multitude of recreation activities. We may eagerly wait for the times when we can engage in our favorite leisure activities. Our favorite activities may vary with our age and interests and can take place in many community and school settings.

- Six-year-old Michelle enjoys taking ballet classes at a community arts center operated by the city's department of parks and recreation.
- Eight-year-old Jamie enjoys taking classes in Tae Kwon Do at a private school for the martial arts.
- Nine-year-old Tyler enjoys caring for and riding horses as part of a 4-H Club.
- Twelve-year-old Mica enjoys playing trumpet in his school band.
- Fourteen-year-old Maya enjoys making beaded jewelry at a local YWCA and hopes to sell jewelry through an online crafts store.
- Sixteen-year-old Gordon enjoys being on a cross-country running team at his high school. His team voted him "Most Improved" last year.
- Nineteen-year-old Brent loves plants and is taking horticulture classes in a post-secondary program.

- Twenty two year old Derek took drama class as an elective in high school and continues to be in a community theater group.
- Twenty six year old Brandon started playing golf in an adapted physical education class in high school and continues to play at local golf courses.
- Thirty three year old Darrell enjoys auto mechanics and participating in a Classic Car Club.

Some people may be astonished to learn that the above examples are all individuals with Autism Spectrum Disorder (ASD). They may not know that individuals with ASD can enjoy or participate in community and school recreation activities, such as those listed above. Some people may erroneously believe that only individuals who are mildly affected by ASD could participate in these organized recreation activities. However, these examples represent individuals with the full range of ASD. In some cases, even people who knew these individuals with ASD in other environments were surprised by the competence that the participants demonstrated when the needed supports were provided for activities of interest.

Given appropriate opportunity and structure, individuals with ASD often enjoy the same recreation activities as others. Yet, many of the over half million citizens with ASD have been denied access to the full range of recreation opportunities within their communities, because of the misconceptions others have about them. Although ASD is one of the most common developmental disabilities, many recreation providers are unaware of how it affects recreation participation and how they can effectively work with individuals in recreation settings. Many recreation programs have tried to include individuals with ASD with varying degrees of success. Unfortunately, until recently little has been known about how to effectively support individuals with ASD in recreation activities. Many recreation service providers still lack knowledge and training regarding ASD and the necessary supports in recreation activities.

Supporting individuals with ASD in leisure pursuits is often an adventure with unexpected twists and many rewards. Many of the unexpected twists can be avoided when recreation providers understand ASD and effective strategies for supporting participation in recreation activities. Use of effective strategies and interests can help individuals with ASD develop their interests and skills.

Many people assume that everyone will automatically learn how to play and socialize. This assumption is not the case for persons with ASD. The individuals with ASD introduced earlier in this chapter participate in a variety of recreation activities and settings. However, the enjoyable and successful participation of these individuals did not develop automatically. Their successes are a result of focusing on ability and interest while providing structure and support. All of these individuals were previously described as having limited interests. They are at their best in their leisure pursuits, because they have been given the necessary support to develop leisure interests and skills, as well as to participate in activities that are understandable, comfortable and enjoyable for them.

- Michelle's successful participation in ballet may surprise those who have thought of her as being routine-bound, nonverbal, fearful, tactile defensive and inattentive to directions. Her ballet classes are successful because they utilize her desire to move, her excellent coordination, and need for routine, while the need to follow verbal directions are minimized for her.
- Jamie's avid pursuit of Tae Kwon Do belies his reputation as lethargic, rocking repetitively, being "tuned out," inadvertently hurting others, and persisting in his own agenda. He does well with the predictable routines, repetitive movements, and instructions that are precisely broken down into small steps for him.

- Those who have seen Tyler with horses find it hard to believe that he may be physically aggressive, isolated, anxious, resist touching 'dirty' objects and unable to cope with change in other situations. He is good at following the specific rules of horsemanship, as well as predictable routines. He loves the warmth and movement of his very gentle horse.
- Some people at school described Mica as being perfectionist, asking repetitive questions, reacting to noise and blurting out answers in class. The consistent routine of band allows him to demonstrate his natural talent in music. The band teacher does not see the behavior that other teachers describe.
- Maya is known for repetitively lining up objects, twirling, resisting fine motor activities, e.g. writing, and giggling for no apparent reason. She found an outlet for her desire to order things in patterns in making bead jewelry. When she is engaged in making jewelry, she does not twirl or giggle.
- Gordon is successful in cross-country running despite having been described as having limited safety awareness, hitting himself, not sharing and crying easily. Others like to be paired with him as a running buddy because of his exceptional ability to memorize courses and "run like the wind." They are happy to remind him to stop at streets and he responds well to their reminders. While cross-county running, he never engages in the behaviors that are a concern in other settings.
- Brent frequently irritates people by poking them and repetitively saying "Cock-a-doodle-do." Having his hands in the moist planting soil in a horticulture class helps Brent relax. He is focused on planting and any comment he makes is related to a common interest of the group, plants.
- Derek enjoys drama activities despite having been described as fearful of people, sensitive to light, overstimulated, and rote. At first he had a great deal of anxiety around the people. However, when he demonstrated his strong rote memory to learn scripts, along with an uncanny ability to mimic movements and voice intonation, he received many compliments and acceptance from the group. His intense focus on his part allows him to cope with the bright lights associated with theater.
- Brandon was described by those who knew him as crying when he lost a game, being rigid in routines, saying unkind words to people, disliking crowded environments, and persisting in his own agenda. Golf has allowed Brandon to play a game in which he can chose not to interact or compete. He can play as he wishes in a large open space, as long as it is within the rules of the course he is playing. Other golfers appreciate his focus and lack of idle talk.
- Darrell was known as a loner who unwittingly insulted others with his candidness and fixation on his favorite topic, cars. His incredible knowledge of cars and ability to fix anything makes him a valued member of the Classic Car Club. Many of the other members listen intently to his "pearls of wisdom" about cars. In this environment of shared interest, his perseverance with cars is appreciated.

Behind these success stories are careful planning, problem solving and ongoing support specific to the needs of each of the individuals. Without appropriate supports they would not have enjoyed these activities and would not have learned the necessary skills for participation. These leisure and recreation activities add to the quality of life that everyone deserves.

Need for Community and School Recreation Opportunities

It is a common claim in the literature that one of the major symptoms and problems that characterizes people with ASD is the lack of ability and lack of interest in becoming involved with leisure activities. Individuals with ASD often play with toys and other objects in a non-goal-directed and often unusual manner. Some individuals with ASD will spend hours on end on a repetitive activity, such as lining up objects. This often makes it difficult for others to involve them in meaningful activities. Their difficulties with reciprocal interaction, self-initiation, motor planning, activity planning and sequencing along with a restricted repertoire of interests are some of the conditions that contribute to this problem. The characteristics and behaviors associated with ASD have often limited opportunities for these individuals to access school and community recreation activities.

Unfortunately, recreation opportunities and leisure experiences have been given low priority in the education and preparation of citizens with disabilities (Fine, 1991; Dattilo & Schleien, 1994). Persons with ASD often have significantly more free time than those without a disability. They are often under- or unemployed and/or have not learned to use community or school facilities. Despite the growing number of individuals identified with ASD and their inordinate amount of free time, there is limited literature and information on ASD and recreation programming. Therefore, recreation professionals may not have any knowledge of how to provide supports to participants with ASD.

Benefits of Recreation Participation

All people, including those with ASD, need recreation in their lives and to benefit from having positive leisure experiences. Recreation and leisure fill a significant need in the lives of many. Although a primary focus is to have fun, the benefits from participating in recreation activities are multitudinous. Five major benefits of recreation participation are listed in Figure 1.1.

Figure 1.1
Benefits of Recreation Participation

- Quality of life
- Social relationships and acceptance
- Decreased inappropriate behaviors
- Physical well being
- Community skill development

There is general agreement that organized recreation activities are important to prepare individuals with ASD to pursue their free time and to achieve an enhanced quality of life. Some collateral benefits of recreation include developing social relationships and acceptance, decreasing inappropriate behavior, increasing physical well being, and developing skills for accessing one's community. Interactive social and communication skills, appropriate social behavior, and community living skills can be developed during "fun" recreation activities, which motivate the individuals to learn the necessary skills to perform the activities.

Quality of life

Quality of life is an amorphous concept. The Autism and Asperger's Syndrome Independent Living Association strongly supports:

"Promoting recognition of the need for inclusive recreation and leisure activities as an essential component of a quality life for people with Autism and Asperger's Syndrome." (www.amug.org/-a203/rec).

Participation in recreation activities:

- Can increase life and leisure satisfaction
- Can provide a sense of accomplishment or achievement
- Can enhance self-esteem
- Can provide joy
- Can increase choice and control
- Can enhance the quality of life of families and staff by easing some stress and reducing the need for constant, intense supervision.

Box 1.1

The parents of ten year old Joel have always had difficulty taking him to activities in the community. Joel screamed with gusto when events were new or different than he expected, when he was first asked to do almost anything, and when he was bored. His screaming embarrassed them. As a result, he had very restricted opportunities for community involvement, and his family underestimated his capacity for participation in recreation activities.

Recently, Joel's older brother got a snowboard and the family went to a local ski area. Joel's brother struggled with balance and coordination in this complex activity as the family watched his snowboard lesson. At the end of the lesson, Joel got on the snowboard and amazed everyone by executing the basics introduced in the snowboard class. He grinned broadly with apparent joy as he slid down the hill. Meanwhile, his family's shocked expressions transformed to grins as broad as Joel's. They all shared in Joel's accomplishment. At that moment, the whole family's quality of life was improved.

Social Relationships and Acceptance

Many recreation activities are done with others. Organized school and community recreation programs occur in groups and, therefore, provide a rich environment to develop and practice social skills. Participation in recreation activities:

- Offers significant opportunities for social development/skills (Schleien et. al, 1997)
- Can teach individuals to interact more capably with peers through games
- Can encourage social play among younger participants in the parallel, cooperative and competitive social levels of play
- Can help achieve relationships around mutual interests
- Can provide a way to meet others and form friendships that is more comfortable for people with ASD
- Can help people without disabilities learn that people, regardless of abilities, can participate if given an opportunity
- Can improve the level of awareness and level of acceptance by community members

In addition, research has shown that adults without disabilities perceive other adults with disabilities as more competent and more "normal" when they are participating in a typical age-appropriate leisure pursuit.

> **Box 1.2**
>
> Andy is a member of a chess club at school. He is one of the best chess players in the club. Everyone enjoys the challenge of playing against him and a number of the club members are studying his unique strategies. It does not matter to the chess club members that Andy does not speak and may make unusual sounds or movements.

Sometimes organizations or the community at large assume that the benefits of participation by individuals with ASD flow in one direction. However, typical participants frequently remark that they learn many important life lessons from participants with ASD.

Decreased Inappropriate Behavior

Behaviors, such as physical aggression, self-abuse and property damage, have been found to decrease when individuals are engaged in appropriate recreation and physical education activities (Favell, 1973; Schleien et. al., 1997; Voeltz et. al., 1982; Moon, 1994). Participation in recreation activities also:

- Can enhance self-control
- Can help calm and relax during times of anxiety
- Can reduce self-stimulatory behaviors (Favell, 1973; Watters & Watters, 1980; Moon & Bunker, 1987)
- Can help refocus through physical exercise
- Can reduce inappropriate behaviors while increasing alternate, incompatible behaviors (Schleien et. al., 1995)

Everyone in Ruth's life had been concerned about her picking her skin until it bleeds. This behavior increases during times of stress. Since she learned to make gimp keychains at camp, she spends much of her leisure making precisely patterned keychains. Everyone is relieved that this activity appears to relieve her anxiety and decreases the frequency of her picking at her skin.

Physical Well Being

According to the National Therapeutic Recreation Society (1990), leisure, recreation and play are inherent aspects of the human experience, and are essential to health and well being. Participation in recreation activities:

- Can provide outlet for physical energy
- Can develop higher levels of physical fitness and energy
- Can improve gross and fine motor skills

Tom enjoys swimming every day at a private athletic club. His family and teachers have noticed that he is less restless, better able to focus and sleeps better at night since he began this routine.

Skills for Accessing the Community

Individuals with ASD may have difficulty in accessing their communities, in part, because of a lack of skills. Many community skills can be acquired and/or practiced during "fun" recreation activities. Participation in recreation activities:

- Can promote independent functioning, community inclusion, and mastery of life skills applicable to recreation involvement
- Can prepare individuals to pursue their discretionary time independently
- Can help people with and without ASD to develop skills and attitude needed to live harmoniously in communities
- Can motivate the individuals to learn the necessary skills to perform the activities
- Can develop skills that can be used for a lifetime
- Can increase social and communication skills
- Can contribute to successful transition to adult life through development of lifetime recreation skills (Sherrill, 1993)
- Can alleviate forced and unfulfilling idle periods that occur due to unemployment, underemployment, and community adjustment problems (Dunn, 1996)
- Can result in job opportunities

Brent is taking horticulture classes because of his interest in plants. Through this interest he is advancing his skills in counting, following routines, following a calendar, planning, etc. He and his family are planning to use this leisure interest for his vocation. They dream of his owning and operating a small greenhouse business.

Legal Basis for Recreation Services in Community and Schools

"The child shall have full opportunity for play and recreation, which should be directed to the same purpose as education; society and public authorities shall endeavor to promote the employment of this right." (United Nations, 1948, Principle 7).

Individuals with ASD have experienced dramatic changes in how society views their place in their communities. In the past, society found places apart from the rest of us for people with disabilities to live, to be educated, to work and to recreate. In the mid 1970s a number of developments gradually brought people with disabilities into some community recreation programs. The reason for this can be traced to the deinstitutionalization movement and the passage of several landmark pieces of nondiscriminatory federal legislation, including the Rehabilitation Act of 1973 and the Education for All Handicapped Children Act of 1975 (Reynolds, 1993; Schleien & Ray, 1988). The civil rights movement for people with disabilities led to the passage of the American with Disabilities Act (ADA) in 1990. These legislative mandates specified the rights of individuals with ASD along with others with disabilities. These laws have been developed to ensure equal opportunity for all people. The current generation of children and adults with ASD are the first to experience these changes.

Rehabilitation Act Amendments (Reh. Act), PL 102-569

The Rehabilitation Act Amendments, which were first enacted in 1973 and reauthorized in 1992, affect a wide range of rights and services, including recreation services. Title V, particularly in Section 504, protects against discrimination in all federally assisted programs and activities. It mandates that federally assisted programs be made accessible to persons with disabilities. Section 504 requires public programs, including school interscholastic athletics and extra curricular activities, along with city and county recreation agencies, to allow qualified individuals the opportunity to participate.

Americans with Disabilities Act (ADA), PL 101-336

The Americans with Disabilities Act (ADA) extends the reach of Section 504 by making similar nondiscriminatory demands of both private and public entities. The ADA ensures equal opportunity for individuals with disabilities in both public and private sectors so that there is no discrimination based on one's disability in any aspect of living, including employment, housing, education, transportation, recreation and access to all public services. The ADA defines an individual with a disability as one who: 1) has a physical or mental impairment that substantially limits one or more major life activities, such as seeing, hearing, speaking, walking, caring for oneself, working, learning or participating in *recreation*. Due to the ADA, all private, public, and nonprofit agencies delivering recreation services to the public must supply accommodations and modifications within their programs to persons with disabilities as requested.

Schools, YMCAs, parks and recreation departments, private athletic clubs, and other organizations that provide recreation programs cannot exclude potential program participants from services, programs, or activities on the basis of disability. For instance, due to the ADA, school districts are required to provide nonacademic services and athletics in the manner necessary to afford students with disabilities an equal opportunity for participation in such services and activities (Gorn, 1997).

The ADA describes a potential program participant as a qualified individual with a disability, meaning that the person meets the essential eligibility requirements for program participation. These may include residency, ability to pay, willingness to abide by the rules of conduct for the program, and compliance with registration procedures.

The ADA requires the consideration of accommodations when an individual with a disability meets essential eligibility requirements. Programs cannot exclude individuals with disabilities unless their presence would pose a direct threat to the health or safety of others or require a fundamental alteration of the program.

Programs, services, and activities provided by community recreation agencies must be available in the most inclusive setting possible. Programs have to make reasonable modifications to their policies and practices to integrate participants with disabilities into their programs unless doing so would constitute a fundamental alteration. The organization must modify rules, polices, and/or practices, as necessary to enable an individual's participation.

Reasonable accommodations must be made to ensure that leisure is as effective for persons with disabilities as it is for everyone else. Programs must remove communication barriers to enable an individual's participation. This includes providing appropriate auxiliary aids and services needed for effective communication with persons with disabilities when doing so would not constitute an undue burden. Additional staff must be provided as needed. It is recommended that agency personnel and volunteers receive appropriate training on supports prior to use. Inservice training for personnel should include principles of ADA, use of sensitive language, awareness of attitudinal barriers, and adaptive techniques.

Providing accommodations in compliance with the ADA may on occasion be proven to be an undue burden under specific situations. These include when it constitutes a significant economic burden, when it constitutes a significant administrative burden, e.g., shortage of qualified personnel for implementing accommodations, or significant programmatic burden, e.g., it results in a fundamental alteration of the program.

Individuals with challenging behavior can be especially difficult to support. If a potential program participant has a severe behavior problem, such as a tendency to become physically aggressive toward other people, the agency must provide "reasonable accommodations." "Reasonable accommodations" could include: providing a 1:1 staff, providing training for staff so that they can structure activities in such a way as to avoid incidents that might escalate behavior, providing training that will enable staff members to reinforce the positive behaviors, and discourage the inappropriate behavior, consulting with autism specialists, behavior specialists and other professionals. If, however, accommodations for a person with a disability fail, and the safety of others is at risk, then a participant may be removed from the program.

Some people erroneously believe that the ADA requires that all individuals with disabilities are included in generic programs. Under the ADA, recreation agencies can still offer separate, specialized programs for individuals with disabilities, but these individuals also have the right to choose to participate in a general program. Recreation professionals have the unique opportunity to make compliance with the ADA a visible and positive statement for the entire leisure industry, and most importantly, for individuals with disabilities.

Individual with Disabilities Education Act (IDEA), PL 105-17

In 1972, the first of several class action suits was won establishing the right of children with disabilities to a public education. Some states and local communities had previously established services and policies for individuals with special needs, but these polices were limited and widely varied. Congress decided that a federal mandate was necessary to provide a more unified approach.

The first key federal legislation relevant to children with ASD was the Education of All Handicapped Children Act (PL 94-142) in 1975. The Individual with Disabilities Education Act (IDEA), the 1990 reauthorization of PL 94-142 (The Education for All Handicapped Children Act of 1975), and its subsequent amendments in 1997 (PL 105-117) mandate a free appropriate education in the least restrictive environment to be provided for all children with disabilities. The law guarantees public education services for children from birth through 21 years of age and requires that secondary students' Individualized Education Plans (IEPs) include transition plans starting at age 14. Autism was added as a new category to IDEA in 1990 and, therefore, children with ASD are guaranteed these services.

There are many behaviors that ordinary children learn without being taught, but that children with ASD may need to be taught (Klin, 1992). Educational goals for these students often need to address areas that are not part of the standard curricula. Under IDEA (34 C.F.R. 300.16(b)(9)) recreation is a related service that can be delivered as part of the IEP requirements for students with disabilities. Subpart B of the rules and regulations specifically identifies Therapeutic Recreation Specialists as qualified personnel to provide recreation as a related service if it is included in the IEP. Recreation as a related service includes assessment of leisure function, therapeutic recreation services, recreation programs in schools and community agencies, and leisure education.

Specially designed recreation programs do not necessarily mean separate classes. Programs can involve peer or adult assistance, rule modifications, or special equipment in inclusive settings. Interscholastic sports or other extracurricular activities listed on an IEP may be related services, although they are not expressly included in "recreation" under 34 C.F.R. 300.6(b)(9). The IEP team would have to determine that participation was a necessary component of a Free Appropriate Public Education (FAPE) for an individual student and include recreation participation as a specific component of the IEP for interscholastic sport or other extracurricular activity to be considered related services (Gorn, 1997).

Adapted physical education is also a related service in IDEA. These services are designed to help children develop gross motor and game skills that would enable them to participate in sports activities. Recreation participation is more encompassing and may include art, music, pets, plants and other activities, in addition to sports.

The IEP content requirements of the 1997 Amendments to IDEA (1414(d)(1) stipulate inclusion of a statement of supplementary aids and services necessary for participation in extracurricular and other nonacademic activities. "Nonacademic services and extracurricular activities" in IDEA include athletics, recreational activities, and special interest groups or clubs sponsored by the public agency. The Sections 504 definition is virtually the same (Gorn, 1997).

Inclusion of recreation services and activities in the educational program for a student with a disability is nonmandatory, but may be a part of a student's IEP (Gorn, 1997). One impartial hearing in Iowa in 1994 confirmed that each IEP team must at least consider whether recreation/leisure needs are priority areas for that student. If they are, recreation/leisure services must be provided. Unfortunately, many IEP teams do not include the interdisciplinary expertise of related services professionals knowledgeable in the assessment of leisure function, such as Adapted Physical Educators and certified Therapeutic Recreation Specialists (CTRS). Therefore, the leisure needs of students with ASD may go unaddressed in the school setting.

With the passage of IDEA and its subsequent amendments in 1997 (PL 105-117), a broader range of life outcomes has been included in the transition process. A recent survey indicated that 17 states identified leisure/recreation as one of the major domains in transition planning guides (Clark & Patton, 1997). However, even students from these states may not have substantial leisure-related goals. The Individualized Transition Plan (ITP) component of IDEA mandates that if recreation programs are needed by a student as s/he moves from school to adulthood then the providers of these services in the community must be invited to participate in the development of that student's IEP. Brannan (1999) proposed that education for leisure should be an essential part of the transition process for students with disabilities, and that special educators be key facilitators of leisure education in concert with other disciplines and the parents of the students involved.

During the recent past, some improvements have been made as a result of legislation, but many forms of discrimination still exist. There is a general failure to accommodate the needs of individuals with ASD. These laws clearly show us why we must be moving toward the inclusion of all people in recreation services.

Summary

- Leisure and recreation activities play a major role in the lives of most community residents. These residents include the over one-half million individuals with ASD in the United States.
- Individuals with ASD often enjoy the same recreation activities as others.
- Presently many professionals, volunteers, caregivers and family members are perplexed about how to facilitate successful recreation participation for persons with ASD.
- Persons with ASD need structured, organized programs with appropriate supports to discover their recreational interests and to develop leisure skills.
- Although one of the main goals is to have fun, the benefits from participating in these activities include enhancing quality of life, developing social relationships and acceptance, decreasing inappropriate behavior, increasing physical well being, and developing community skills.
- Recent legislative mandates have given rights to access recreation services to individuals with ASD along with individuals having other disabilities.
- Schools, YMCAs, parks and recreation departments, and other organizations that provide recreation programs cannot exclude potential program participants from services, programs, or activities on the basis of disability.

Chapter Two

Autism Spectrum Disorder: Challenges and Strengths for Recreation Participation

Phyllis Coyne

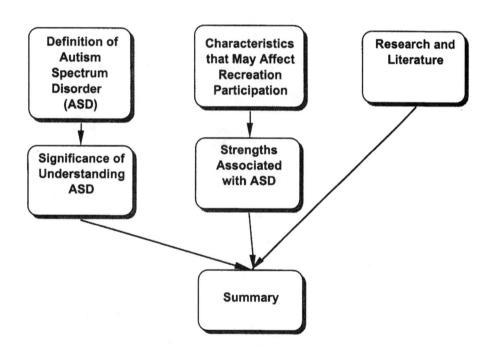

Autism Spectrum Disorder (ASD) seriously impacts how an individual participates in recreation. The impact is so great that the Autism Society of America (1998) listed leisure/play skills along with verbal and nonverbal communication and social interactions as the primary difficulties in ASD. In fact, leisure is one of the greatest challenges for individuals with ASD, as well as his or her family, caregivers, and professionals who seek to provide meaningful and enjoyable leisure services. However, leisure may also be a realm where individuals with ASD can demonstrate competencies and experience joy.

Those who facilitate recreation participation for individuals with ASD must understand the nature of the disorder and its impact on recreation participation. Without knowledgeable staff and advocates, individuals with ASD are often misunderstood and underserved.

Autism Spectrum Disorder

There are still many unknowns about ASD, but understanding of this complicated and variable disorder has grown tremendously since Dr. Leo Kanner, a pediatrician, first described it in 1943. ASD can have a major influence on an individual's understanding of the world and the ways in which they communicate with others. Some of the current beliefs regarding the nature of ASD are presented in Figure 2.1.

Figure 2.1
Current Beliefs about ASD

ASD is:
- A developmental disability that typically appears during the first three years of life
- A neurological disorder that affects the way information is processed, organized and integrated
- A spectrum disorder with various manifestations, such as severity of symptoms, age of onset, and the presence of various features, such as mental retardation and specific language delay
- Defined on the basis of behavioral and developmental features
- A unique pattern of deficits and areas of relative strengths that, when taken as a group, describe a syndrome
- Associated with unusual responses to sensory stimuli
- Represented by a wide range of IQs and verbal skills from profound mental retardation and severe language impairments to high intelligence
- Found throughout the world among individuals of all socioeconomic and racial groups
- Estimated to occur in one in 500 individuals (Center for Disease Control and Prevention, 1997) when PDD is included and as many as one in 200 individuals when PDD and Asperger's Syndrome are included (Bristol-Powers, 2002)
- Found in four times as many males as females
- In many cases genetically linked
- Sometimes helped by medication to treat associated behaviors such as hyperactivity, sleep disturbances, aggression, agitation, self-injurious behavior and seizure disorders
- Associated with unusual responses to sensory stimuli
- Associated with increased risk of developing seizure disorders throughout the developmental period
- A lifelong disability with a need for lifelong support in most cases
- Often misunderstood and misdiagnosed because those afflicted look normal to the casual observer

ASD is not:
- The result of emotional deprivation or emotional stress
- A willful desire to avoid social contact
- Due to parental rejection or cold parenting
- In any way related to socioeconomic class
- A psychological disturbance
- Misunderstood genius, although in a few circumstances some individuals have special abilities in narrow areas
- Curable, although improvements can be made in all cases

The understanding of ASD continues to expand through research. The personal accounts of individuals with ASD, additionally, help us to understand the experience behind what can be observed. Although there is still no cure for ASD, greater understanding of this spectrum disorder has led to the development of better coping mechanisms and strategies for the various manifestations of the disability. Careful planning and appropriate supports can reduce the impact of the disorder on leisure functioning. However, there is still much to be learned.

Definitions of Autism Spectrum Disorder

During the past six decades, many names and definitions have been given to autism. Terminology often still causes confusion, since there are two distinct systems with different purposes for identification in the United States. In addition, there are other systems that are used in other countries. One system used in the United States, the Diagnostic and Statistical Manual, Fourth Edition (DSM IV), uses criteria for medical diagnosis of related disorders under Pervasive Developmental Disorder to classify and watch for etiology and treatment. The other system, the educational system under the Individuals with Disabilities Education Act (IDEA) uses criteria for eligibility for special education services under only one category, Autism (Spectrum Disorder). A comparison of the DSM-IV and IDEA identification is shown in Figure 2.2.

Pervasive Developmental Disorder may be considered an umbrella term with specific subtypes. ASD also encompasses these subtypes.

These two classification systems have similarities and differences. One similarity is that both the medical and educational systems include the following broad characteristics, which is referred to as the triad of impairments:

- Qualitative Impairments in Reciprocal Social Interaction, for example appearing aloof and indifferent to other people;
- Qualitative Impairments in Communication (verbal and nonverbal), for example not understanding the meaning of gestures, facial expression or tone of voice; and
- Restricted, Repetitive, and Stereotyped Patterns of Behavior, Interests, or Activities, for example doing an activity in a rigid and repetitive manner.

The Individuals with Disabilities Education Act (IDEA) lists two additional characteristics that are often associated with Autism (Spectrum Disorder) as:

- Resistance to environmental change or change in daily routines, and
- Unusual responses to sensory experiences

Medical Diagnosis

In medical and psychiatric settings in the United States, the Diagnostic and Statistical Manual, Fourth Edition (DSM-IV) medical diagnostic criteria is most commonly used for diagnosis. The American Psychiatric Association (APA) publishes this manual to standardize the diagnostic criteria for mental and emotional disorders and to improve the reliability of diagnostic judgment and research. Every few years the manual is revised to incorporate new information and definitions may be changed significantly. This diagnostic manual lists criteria for specific subtypes of ASD under the category of Pervasive Developmental Disorder. In the DSM-IV, Pervasive Developmental Disorder is a general category of related disorders that are characterized by severe and pervasive impairment in several

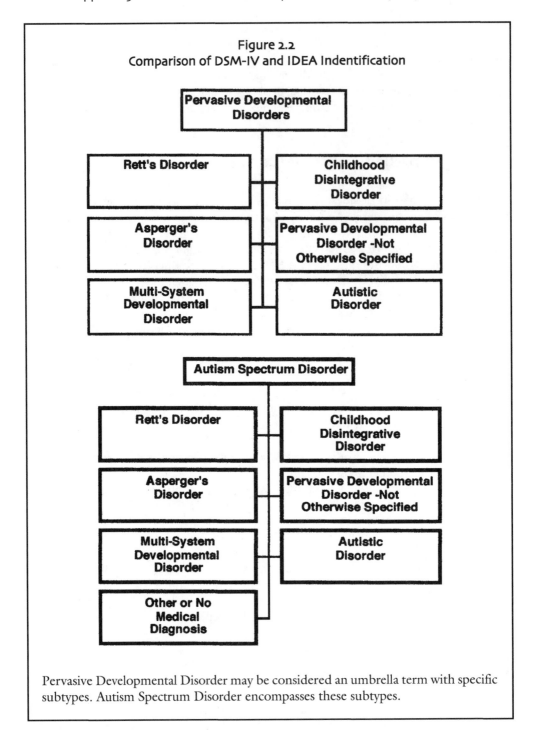

Figure 2.2
Comparison of DSM-IV and IDEA Indentification

Pervasive Developmental Disorder may be considered an umbrella term with specific subtypes. Autism Spectrum Disorder encompasses these subtypes.

areas of development (American Psychiatric Association, 1994). The DSM-IV includes five separate diagnoses under Pervasive Developmental Disorder: Autistic Disorder, Rett's Disorder, Childhood Disintegrative Disorder, Asperger's Disorder and Pervasive Developmental Disorder, Not Otherwise Specified (also called "Atypical Autism"). Medical researchers are exploring different explanation for the various forms of ASD.

Eligibility for Special Education Services under Autism (Spectrum Disorder)

The Individuals with Disabilities Education Act (IDEA) provides the regulations for identification of students who qualify for special education services. "Autism" is defined in IDEA (300.7) as "a developmental disability significantly affecting verbal and nonverbal communication and social interaction, generally evident before age three that adversely affects a child's educational perfor-

mance. Other characteristics often associated with autism are engagement in repetitive activities, resistance to environmental change or change in daily routines, and unusual responses to sensory experiences."

Some states further elaborate on autism as a spectrum disorder. For instance, the Oregon Administrative Rules for Special Education adds, "Autism may include autism spectrum disorders such as but not limited to autistic disorder, pervasive developmental disorder—not otherwise specified, and Asperger's syndrome" (OAR 581-015-0005). The single term Autism (Spectrum Disorder) is used in the educational setting, because there is not as much need to subcategorize. It is currently believed that the general strategies known to be effective with individuals with autism can be individualized to help those across the spectrum.

Some Characteristics of Autism Spectrum Disorder that May Affect Recreation Participation

ASD, with its associated strengths and limitations, seriously impacts how an individual participates in recreation. Although individuals with ASD differ from one another in many ways, as a group they face significant challenges in leisure, as illustrated later in this chapter. Their leisure is often expressed in ways that are uniquely their own. In Chapter 4, individuals with ASD describe their varying experiences with recreation opportunities.

There are great differences among individuals with ASD. The effects of ASD can range from mild to severe. The intellectual ability can range from gifted to severely cognitively impaired. ASD can occur along with other disabilities and conditions. Although individuals with ASD share common characteristics, they are unique in how they manifest. In addition, every person with ASD is an individual, and like all individuals, has a unique personality with a unique combination of interests, strengths and limitations.

No one characteristic defines ASD. While many of the behaviors typical of ASD are also typical of earlier stages of normal development, it is the combination or pattern of behaviors and the intensity and persistence of the behaviors that distinguishes this disorder. Participants with ASD are best served when the staff shares a common understanding of this disorder. If recreation providers do not understand the behaviors associated with ASD, the person with ASD will have limited opportunities to access school and community recreation.

Although many of the ways in which individuals with ASD participate in leisure may surprise us, some limitations are inherent in ASD and manifest in similar ways. The categories of challenges identified in the DSM–IV and IDEA are broad. These limitations are elaborated in the following section.

Qualitative Impairments in Reciprocal Social Interaction

Many recreation activities have social aspects. Significant problems in social interactions are pervasive in ASD and, thus, require special attention in programming. The reality for many individuals with ASD is that their behavior does not fit into others' perceptions of what is "normal." Unconventional attempts to socialize are frequently mistaken as signs of deviance or limited social interest. Individuals with ASD may be teased and taunted by intolerant participants or simply disregarded by good-hearted ones.

By definition, individuals with ASD demonstrate impairments in relationships with people, use of imitation, and symbolic or dramatic play. Their social interactions are characterized by low rates of both initiation and response. The social issues manifest in a variety of ways in different individuals with ASD. However, the extent of the difficulty in social-communication is profound.

Some individuals with ASD appear more "aloof" than others. They may distance themselves from others or act as though they are unaware of the presence of others. Without guidance or support, these individuals often remain isolated or on the periphery of groups. In addition, since they are not as "tuned in" to people, the social praise that helps motivate others is often ineffective with individuals with ASD.

> **Box 2.1** Dominique generally moves away from others in the room. He appears to be in "his own world" and does not even respond to praise given even by family members.

Some individuals with ASD tend to be more "passive" and follow along or watch what their peers are doing. Although this may be a problem, it can also be a source of enjoyment to the individual. It is their way of participating.

> **Box 2.2** Cody is not bothered by noisy crowds and enjoys being a spectator at the local WNBA games. It is the only time he appears to be engaged in a traditional recreation activity.

Social skills are generally immature at best. Basic skills, such as sharing and turn taking are often inconsistent.

> **Box 2.3** Unlike the other campers, Jeff does not automatically understand about waiting his turn to ride a horse at camp. He tries to push to the front of the line and starts to scream to get a turn immediately.

Imitation is generally an area that does not evolve naturally for individuals with ASD. They seldom learn through informal observation or imitation of others as other participants may. Well-organized recreation instruction and activities help to compensate for their difficulties in imitation, as well as their difficulty in initiation. In addition, clear, consistent, repetitive instruction minimizes the occurrence of challenging social behavior.

The social complexity of competitive team activities in which participants must take turns, cooperate as a team, play against another group and compete is confusing for many individuals with ASD.

> **Box 2.4**
> Scott grabs the ball from a teammate in basketball and throws the ball at the nearest hoop. He successfully makes a basket for the other team. He is pleased with himself and exclaims, "I won." Meanwhile, his teammates are upset with him.

Individuals with ASD have a general lack of social understanding. Difficulties conveying and interpreting social cues often interfere with their attempts to initiate and join in activities with others.

> **Box 2.5**
> During recess, Anthony runs after a group of boys while yelling about Power Rangers. Although they are playing tag, he thinks he is playing Power Rangers with them. All the boys, except him, know that they are playing tag. He lies down on the ground and cries when his peers tell him that they are not playing Power Rangers.

While individuals with ASD may want to interact with others, they are rarely very good at it. The attempts of individuals with ASD to socialize may be idiosyncratic, subtle, obscure or poorly timed.

> **Box 2.6**
> Although he can talk, Mel touches others to socialize. He is oblivious to how this aggravates his billiards partner who is about to shoot.

They have difficulty understanding what others feel, think and intend or that others even have feelings, thoughts or intentions that may be different than theirs. This is sometimes referred to as lacking "Theory of Mind" or "mindblindness." They often do not know the social consequences of their behaviors.

> **Box 2.7**
> Jarred hears the guys talking in the locker room in the gymnastics center about parts of women's bodies. Everyone laughs and seems to be having a good time. Jarred does not realize that this is "locker room" talk only and can be hurtful. He wants to be "cool" and repeats what he heard to a girl at the gymnastics center. He gets accused of sexual harassment.

Mesibov (1986) has described the social-communication experience of a person with ASD as being like getting off the plane in a foreign country without knowing the language, cultural gestures or cultural norms. One young man with ASD, who heard this explanation, reported that it is even more difficult than that. He said that it is more like being from a different planet and that he needs a social "manual for extraterrestrials." Since that time, Temple Grandin, an international author and speaker on her experience with autism, has described her experience as being like an "Anthropologist from Mars." The extent to which social situations can be confusing to individuals with ASD cannot be overestimated and the social confusion often results in heightened anxiety.

Qualitative Impairments in Communication (Verbal and Nonverbal)

Communication is important to all of us, but for many individuals with ASD, establishing an effective means of communication is a major challenge. Difficulties in verbal and nonverbal communication are a core challenge in ASD. Communication is often confusing. Individuals with ASD process and respond to information in unique ways. Most of the inappropriate behaviors exhibited by persons with ASD and desired behaviors not exhibited reflect a lack of understanding.

Individuals with ASD tend to be concrete and literal in their use and understanding of language. Sometimes recreation opportunities involve abstract concepts and experiences, which can be difficult for the person with ASD to comprehend; however, individuals with ASD may misinterpret even expressions that are commonly used.

> **Box 2.8** When the instructor in the drawing class asks everyone to sit down, Gary drops to the floor. Because the instructor understands ASD, she knows that Gary followed her directions literally and did not understand that she meant to sit in a chair at a desk. She adds, "Please sit at a desk with an empty chair."

Individuals with ASD often do not respond to instruction in the same manner as other participants. They often have difficulty following simple verbal directions or following directions out of the usual setting or routine. They may appear not to hear the directions. Even when directions are understood, they may have a delayed response time.

> **Box 2.9** In swim class, Jordan does not put his face in the water to blow bubbles with the rest of the class. Thirty seconds later, when the instructor is demonstrating a different skill, he puts his face in the water and blows bubbles.

Understanding gestures and facial expressions is also difficult for individuals with ASD. They are unlikely to process and comprehend the meaning of smiles or nods designed to reinforce good behavior, as well as stern expressions designed to curb behavior.

> **Box 2.10** Todd is talking loudly while the woodworking instructor is giving directions. The instructor looks at Todd with a scowl, puts his hand on his hip and clears his throat. Todd cannot interpret this nonverbal reprimand and continues to talk.

The attempts to communicate by individuals with ASD may be equally as challenging for us to decode as their attempts to decode our communication. Despite the fact that at least 50 percent of individuals with ASD display some functional speech and language skills (Lord & Paul, 1997), individuals with ASD often develop idiosyncratic, unconventional, subtle or inappropriate behaviors to communicate. They communicate through body posture, facial expression, where they stand in relation to the group, how and when they look at people, how they hold their hands, how they watch an activity and so on. They may briefly glance at something to show interest or make a request. They may take someone by the hand to an area as a request for a desired object or simply grab the object. They may point to what they want, when no one is looking. They may repeat words (echolalia) they have heard in a situation associated with the desired item thinking that others understand that this is how they are making a request. Aggression, tantrums and self-injury are often used, particularly when other means of communication have not been understood, to get attention, to escape from task or situation, to protest against change of schedule and routine, or to regulate interactions in a predictable manner.

> **Box 2.11**
>
> Jill takes the hand of the choir director and leads her to the door. Jill then says, "You want go home?" Jill is trying to let the choir director know that she has stayed in choir as long as she can that day. The choir director says, "No, it's not time to go home yet." Jill continues to say, "You want go home?", because it is the only means she has to say that she needs to leave, but the choir director does not understand her message. Jill finally throws herself on the floor and starts screaming.

Individuals with ASD may protest or reject an activity by screaming, bolting, scratching or saying, "No." They do this because they do not have the skills to communicate in more appropriate ways.

Those who talk may confound us even more, because the words they use do not always match their intended meaning. In addition, they may not understand some of the more sophisticated sounding words that they use.

> **Box 2.12**
>
> When the instructor asked the class what they had done for the weekend, Randy said that he had gone to the castles. The instructor thought that Randy must have an active imagination, since there were no castles in the area. However, when the instructor asked his parents about the castles, they told her that "castles" was Randy's name for a nearby city, because of its skyscrapers.

Restricted, Repetitive, and Stereotyped Patterns of Behavior, Interests, or Activities

The way individuals with ASD interact with the environment, materials, and others is often different than how others spend their leisure. Individuals, particularly children, with ASD are less likely to explore objects in unstructured situations (Kasari et. al, 1993; Sigman et. al., 1986). Another hallmark of ASD that can adversely affect participation in recreation activities is the limited, repetitive and sometimes stereotyped interests and use of materials. It may be difficult to find reinforcers or activities that will motivate participants with ASD. They may have a short attention span for some activities and not for others. They more readily learn things that are self-satisfying.

When left on their own, individuals with ASD tend to spend inordinate amounts of time in repetitive and unimaginative activities. Some individuals with ASD will spend hours on end on the same repetitive activity, making it difficult for others to involve them in meaningful activities. According to Libby et. al. (1998) and Stone et. al. (1990), more repetitive and immature play is seen in children with ASD than in children with other developmental delays matched to the same developmental level. Individuals with ASD often get stuck on one or a few activities reflecting earlier stages of development. They may engage with objects through simple exploration and manipulation, e.g., mouthing, banging, twisting, or elaborate routines and rituals, e.g., lining up objects according to size. Some individuals pursue particular obsessions or narrowly focused interests.

Box 2.13
Russell insists on lining up the members of his softball team by height before each game. The number 3 fascinates him. Every 3 on a uniform, 3 strikes or 3 balls, and 3 in the score all cause him to jump and flap his hands. He wants to play third base and bat third.

Some participants with ASD engage in repetitive actions with their bodies, such as rocking or hand flapping. However, while engaged in preferred leisure activities, these behaviors tend to decrease. At times variations of these movements may be incorporated into activities by leaders to develop other interests or as reinforcement. Introducing individuals to a wider range of options can broaden their repertoire and help them find new joys.

Box 2.14
Phil enjoyed using the rowing machine for exercise, because it incorporated both the rocking and arm motions that he engages in repeatedly.

Many individuals with ASD also have difficulty with the planning skills that enable others to occupy themselves productively. They often need to rely on others to provide them with the experiences and support needed to acquire and meet their leisure needs.

Resistance to Environmental Change or to Change in Daily Routines

Unstructured time, waiting, and change are all particularly stressful for individuals with ASD. They often do not develop new interests because an aversion to novelty can result in low curiosity and low exploration. Initially, participation in new activities may be difficult, because many individuals with ASD tend to avoid novel objects and prefer familiar objects or actions. They may react strongly to changes even if they are looking forward to an activity. Wearing different clothes for an activity, substitute instructors, and cancellations may all be very stressful. Without support, individuals with ASD are unlikely to explore new recreation options or feel comfortable in new activities.

Box 2.15
Renna enjoys the tap dance class she is taking at a community center. Because of construction, the class needs to enter by a side door. Renna stands by the side door entrance bouncing up and down for 20 minutes before she can enter by this alternative entrance.

Participants with ASD often memorize and understand rules in a rigid manner. They often do not tolerate any variation. They may become the "rule police," which includes tattling on others and correcting the instructor.

Box 2.16
When the instructor for the dog grooming class is demonstrating how to do a "puppy" cut, Sal interrupts with, "Actually" and proceeds to lecture on what he has read in a book on the subject.

Unusual Responses to Sensory Experiences

Many people love the excitement, activity and noise in community or school recreation settings. Many enjoy the sights, smells, tastes, touch, movement and close proximity of others. However, individuals with ASD can be over-stimulated by these same things.

The movement, crowding and reverberation of sound in an auditorium, multi-purpose room or gymnasium may cause extreme agitation or discomfort, if appropriate supports are not in place. The anxiety that results from sensory overload may lead to aggressive behavior that in turn results in a participant being excluded from a program. Therefore, it is vital to understand the sensory issues of individuals with ASD.

Although not presently part of the medical definition, it is generally accepted that the sensory system has a tremendous and often negative impact on individuals with ASD. However, the sensory and motor difficulties for individuals with ASD vary in the specific symptoms or patterns expressed (Dawson & Watling, 2000). Sensorimotor behaviors exhibited by individuals with ASD include both heightened sensitivities (hypersensitive) or reduced responsiveness (hyposensitive) across sensory modalities, such as visual, vestibular, proprioceptive, tactile, auditory, gustatory and olfactory sensitivities (Ermer & Dunn, 1998; Kientz & Dunn, 1997). Particularly when they are younger, they may explore the environment by licking, smelling, and handling objects. Sometimes the sensory issues are not obvious particularly as individuals with ASD mature. Therefore, the sensory issues are often missed and accommodations are not provided.

Box 2.17 Chris's instructor at computer camp accepts that he sits away from the group at a computer in the corner and initially attributes it to Chris's statement that he has a terror of people. During the second week of camp it occurs to the instructor that Chris also has his computer monitor adjusted so that it provides little light and that he always turns the light off in the area in which he sits even when he is reading a computer manual. The savvy instructor asks Chris if light bothers his eyes. Chris thinks for awhile and says that he does not know. Chris has no way of comparing his experience of light to that of others. The instructor asks his mother about how Chris reacts to light. After thinking for awhile, she notes that he has always sought out shade or wanted to stay inside when it is a sunny bright day, but that she had never really thought about it before. His mother is concerned with more intrusive aspects of his ASD. Chris's teacher at school says that he often turns the lights out in the classroom, but she thinks he does it for attention. Once his sensitivity to light is discovered, he is provided with glasses that adjusted to the amount of light in the environment. Chris and the people who know him notice that he no longer changes the environment to accommodate his sensitivity to light.

Visual system. Visual processing problems related to ASD can take many forms. Many individuals with ASD have sensitivities to bright light, bright colors, and fluorescent lighting. These individuals may prefer shaded areas outdoors or may keep their heads down. Sometimes they appear not to see objects that are right in front of them. A participant with ASD may not look at others directly in order to modulate sensory stimulation.

Motor skills. Although the basic motor skills of individuals with ASD are often reported to be an area of relative strength, numerous studies also provide evidence that motor problems may sometimes be quite significant. Hypersensitivity or hyposensitivity in an individual's vestibular and/or proprioceptive systems can impact many areas related to movement. Such difficulties could affect participation in a variety of recreation activities.

Vestibular system. The vestibular system is involved in movement, posture, vision, balance and coordination. Successful participation in sports, such as basketball, soccer, baseball, gymnastics and football requires an intact vestibular system. Rocking back and forth, moving constantly, as well as being clumsy are often signs of vestibular hyposensitivity. Rocking chairs, hammocks and swings may help a participant with ASD to calm down.

In addition, many individuals with ASD seek out sensory motor activity such as running, jumping, spinning, bouncing and climbing. When these are areas of strength, they may be appropriately directed to recreation activities that utilize these motions.

> **Box 2.18** Nels has stamina and well-developed gross motor skills. He enjoys directing his desire to jump, bounce and climb into his gymnastics class.

Avoiding movement, difficulty changing directions and a fear of feet leaving the ground can be signs of vestibular hypersensitivity.

> **Box 2.19** Julio is overweight, so his family decides to have him participate in track. Despite his best efforts, he is the last to start running after the whistle blows. He runs painstakingly slowly, but finally makes it to the finish line. However, when he gets to the finish line he does not stop and bumps into several others. His family realizes that his difficulties are related to more than his weight and take him to see an occupational therapist with expertise in sensory motor integration.

Proprioception. Proprioception, which includes righting balance and a sense of where one's body is in space, is also important to enjoyable participation in a number of recreation activities, such as riding a bicycle. Dropping objects, moving slowly and complaints of being tired can be signs of difficulties in proprioception.

Touch. Many individuals with ASD are oversensitive or undersensitive to tactile sensations. Those who are hypersensitive to tactile sensations may react strongly to certain textures and being touched unexpectedly. They may avoid certain textures, such as glue, velvet, or chalk. They may not be able to tolerate the labels or seams in clothing, the roughness of new clothing, or the knobby surface of a ball. They often stand away from others to modulate sensory stimulation.

> **Box 2.20** Rory loves plants and is a participant in a community garden run through a parks and recreation agency. His mentor notices that he goes to the hose to wash his hands after he has his hands in the soil every few minutes. Rory's hands are getting dried and cracked, which results in Rory picking at them until they are raw. The mentor suggests that Rory wear gloves, but Rory can not tolerate the feel of the gloves that he is given. Rory gets the job of watering the plants until they can go shopping for a pair of gloves that he can tolerate.

Individuals with ASD may respond to being touched, accidentally jostled or physically guided by hitting, scratching or dropping to the ground.

> **Box 2.21** One of Tip's friends bumps into him while they are playing soccer. Tip hits his friend and tells his coach what he mistakenly believes, "Chad hit me."

On the other hand, those who are hyposensitive to tactile sensations may not respond to touch, but use touch to explore the environment or seek intense sensory sensations. They may approach people very closely in order to use their sense of touch.

Auditory. Individuals with ASD may overreact and/or underreact to sounds as a result of problems in processing auditory information. Those with auditory hypersensitivity may respond to loud noises by screaming, covering their ears or biting themselves, because loud noise can be painful. They may have equally catastrophic reactions to every-day noises, such as vacuums, hairdryers, and garbage disposals. This hypersensitivity can be evident when participants are in busy or crowded areas, such as roller skating rinks. They may become preoccupied by quiet sounds that others may not hear.

> **Box 2.22**
>
> Ty is taking a yoga class at an athletic club. The room is very quiet and the class is doing downward facing dog. Ty suddenly jumps up and yells that the war has started. Everyone in the class wonders why he yelled that. Two minutes later a commercial jet flies over the building and Ty becomes more agitated. He had heard the jet well before anyone else could hear it and had associated it with an air attack.

On the other hand, they may be hyposensitive to sound and seem oblivious or not respond to their name being called.

Gustatory and Olfactory Systems. The gustatory system, sense of taste, and the olfactory system, sense of smell, can also be problems for individuals with ASD. The diverse smells in our communities and schools may be experienced as a sensory bombardment.

> **Box 2.23**
>
> Nan appears unusually agitated on the bus ride to day camp on the third day. She is sitting in her usual seat at the front of the bus and there are no changes in the routine. On the fourth day she does not want to get on the bus. Her mother discovers that Nan could smell that a child in the rear row had eaten huevos rancheros for breakfast and she was upset because she does not like the smell or taste of salsa.

The Significance of Understanding the Characteristics of Autism Spectrum Disorder

Lorna Wing (1980), an English psychiatrist who specializes in ASD, provided the insight that "An autistic child can be helped only if a serious attempt is made to see the world from his point of view, so that the adaptive function of much of his peculiar behavior can be understood in the context of his handicaps." Often the behavior of individuals with ASD is misinterpreted. It is now understood that these individuals do not choose to misbe-have. However, recreation providers who are not trained in ASD may feel rejected, unrewarded for efforts or may make negative judgements about a participant with ASD. Therefore, participants with ASD may be denied access to recreation programs, because of a lack of knowledge about their disability and how to support them.

ASD can cause confusion, frustration, and anxiety that is expressed in a variety of unexpected ways, such as withdrawing, engaging in unusual repetitive behaviors, and occasionally in extreme situations by aggression and/or self-injury. Table 2.1 illustrates how the behavior of an individual with ASD can be a manifestation of the disorder, although it resembles behavior that typically receives a negative label. Strategies for preventing these behaviors are described in Chapter 6.

Table 2.1
Examples of Common Misinterpretations of Behavior

Participant Action	Common Interpretation	Autism Perspective
Does not give ball to peer when requested	Uncooperative; selfish; possessive	Does not understand sharing; may not understand he will get another turn with the ball; difficulty with motor planning
Responds to, "Eyes up here" by putting face on female instructor's chest	Wise guy; sexual harassment	Complied with directions to put "Eyes up here" literally.
Repeatedly says, "Go home" first day of activity	Wants to go home; does not like activity	Anxious because does not know routine; does not know when activity will end; attempt to initiate conversation
Hits goalie during soccer game when goalie caught ball	Physically aggressive; poor sport	Rigid understanding of rule that players should not touch ball with hands; does not know who has authority to enforce rules.
Knocks objects off shelf	Destructive; uncooperative; clumsy	Cannot tolerate objects being in certain arrangements; difficulty judging body position in relationship to objects.
Screams when touched in touch football	Poor loser; immature	Experiences uninvited touch as painful
Always poking others	Physically aggressive, trouble maker	Does not know how to initiate interaction; has unclear understanding of own strength; unable to judge where his body is in relationship to others.
Passes ball to member of other team in basketball	Inattentive; poor team player	Does not understand the concept of "us against them"; difficulty tracking movements of team members
Only engages in sedentary activities	Lazy, lacks energy	Movement is unpleasant and unpredictable; motor planning difficulties
Tantrums at door to the gym	Does not like physical activity	Experiences the bright lights and sound reverberation as uncomfortable
Walks to front of line in relay race and pushes others out of the way	Wants his own way; physically aggressive; noncompliant	Does not understand waiting in line for his turn; does not know that pushing can hurt people, does not know where his body is in space
Lines up rubber bands in a tie dye class	Noncompliant; off task; disinterested	Does not understand or cannot sequence steps in directions

Knowing that these behaviors may occur does little to help us provide recreation services unless we understand what is going on under the surface. It is vital to understand that the behavior that we see is caused by a disorder in processing, integrating and understanding information. Figure 2.3 illustrates that what is observed is just the tip of the iceberg.

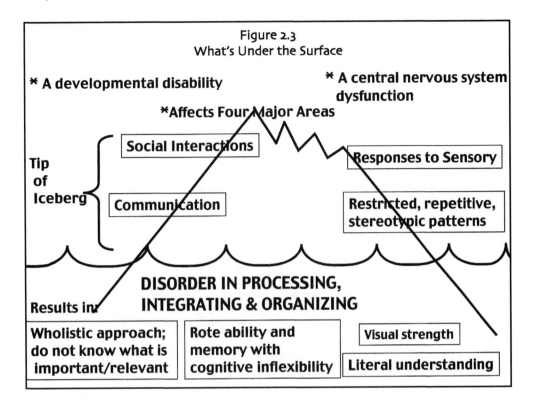

Figure 2.3
What's Under the Surface

* A developmental disability

* A central nervous system dysfunction

*Affects Four Major Areas

Social Interactions

Responses to Sensory

Tip
of
Iceberg

Communication

Restricted, repetitive, stereotypic patterns

DISORDER IN PROCESSING, INTEGRATING & ORGANIZING

Results in

| Wholistic approach; do not know what is important/relevant | Rote ability and memory with cognitive inflexibility | Visual strength |
| | | Literal understanding |

Strengths Associated with Autism Spectrum Disorder

The strengths and abilities associated with ASD are often not recognized or utilized. Understanding the strengths is equally as important as understanding the limitations of individuals with ASD. Some of the characteristics of ASD may be strengths that, with proper motivation, can be used to enhance participation in recreation activities. Incorporating strengths into activities can lead to a decrease and/or elimination of challenging behaviors and more positive interactions. Individuals with ASD may have a wide range of strengths. Table 2.2 illustrates how some common characteristics can be strength.

These strengths can all be used positively to develop interests and skills in recreation. Many individuals with ASD are highly motivated to learn in areas of interest to them. Recreation providers need to capitalize on strengths and preferences of participants with ASD.

Research and Literature Related to Recreation Participation for Individuals with Autism Spectrum Disorder

Currently, there is considerable literature and research on the problems and needs of individuals with ASD. While knowledge about diagnosis, theoretical understanding and intervention possibilities is steadily growing, there is limited literature on ASD and leisure. Fortunately, research into interventions related to play and education can provide guidance for effective approaches.

Table 2.2
Some Characteristics as Strengths

Use visual information meaningfully: *Nina follows the diagram for how to assemble trellises that baffled everyone else in her Girl Scout troop, including the leader.*
Attention to minute details; perfectionism: *Jamil impresses other members of the rock gym with the precise nature of his knot tying.*
Strong visual-spatial intelligence related to how objects and figures relate in three dimensional space: *Patty makes lovely furniture with intricate and precise dovetailing in her woodworking class.*
Take in chunks of information quickly: *While the rest of the weaving class is repeating the lesson on how to work the shuttle, Larry demonstrates, because he learned it right away.*
Basic motor skills and motor activity, such as running, jumping, spinning, bouncing and climbing: *Noels has stamina and well-developed gross motor skills. He enjoys directing his desire to jump, bounce and climb into his gymnastics class.*
Concrete and literal: Understand and use concrete, content free information and rules: *Manny is a valued member of Game Club because he can be relied on to know the complex rules to several games.*
Unusual talents, such as musical or artistic ability: *Zack impressed his music teacher at the School for the Blind with his ability to play tunes on the piano after hearing them once. He has become an anchor in her blues band.* *Georgena has been taking group painting classes with a private instructor for two years. At an exhibit of Georgena's paintings, the critics comment on her amazing ability to combine realism with a superimposed three dimensional aspect.*
Persist in completing tasks with a clear beginning and ending: *Kurt stayed after gardening class to complete planting two trays of tomatoes.*
Long attention span to activities of significant interest: *Dale was known for his short attention span. Therefore, many were surprised when he spent hours repairing small engines. Those who knew him well had seen the same focus when he was younger while building with Lego's and on the computer.*
Exceptional rote memorization skills: *Harvey amazes others by giving a play-by-play description of sports games that he has seen. He says, "Autism serves", when others ask him how he remembers all those details.*
Learn long routines. (Consistent routines and structure helps an activity to become "fun" and personally meaningful for individuals with ASD): *Chase has been taught a specific routine for going to the ice-skating rink. He follows it precisely even when his buddies are being rowdy.*
Generally compliant when expectations and steps are clear: *Val may have looked noncompliant to others, because she did not follow the instructor's directions to line up for a basketball drill. When she was given more information about where to stand and the step in the drill, she was one of the most compliant participants.*

Research Related to Benefits

Most programs developed specifically for individuals with ASD, such as TEACCH (Schopler et. al, 1995), Pivotal Response Training (Koegel et. al, 1999), and the Children's Unit (Romanczyk et. al., 2000), target goals related to play and leisure, because it is a recognized need. Some research on the benefits of recreation for individual with ASD, particularly in reducing challenging behavior and increasing social interaction, was presented in Chapter 1. Ragland et. al. (1978) also noted a reduction in inappropriate behaviors by individuals with ASD as a result of play instruction. According to McGee and Daly (1999), strategies for promoting engagement have become synonymous with methods of preventing challenging behaviors to a growing extent.

Recent research has focused on the benefits of recreation in inclusive settings. Integrated physical education and recreation activities were found to be effective environments for encouraging social play among the younger participants with ASD in the parallel and cooperative/competitive levels of play (Schleien et. al, 1997).

Sustaining Interest

Because the play of individuals with ASD is often restricted, repetitive and stereotyped, early research on play and ASD focused on what objects could elicit interest and sustained interaction. Given the characteristics of ASD, it is not surprising that this research demonstrated that individuals with this disorder tended to interact more with leisure materials that provide sensory feedback, such as lights, sounds, movements, and/or tactile sensations. These reactive leisure materials provided reinforcement from sensory feedback. When acted upon, they provided lights, sounds, movements, tactile sensations, etc., strong enough to promote interest. The results of several studies (Gutierrez-Griep, 1984; Rincover, Newsom, Lovaas, & Koegel, 1977) suggest that preferred sensory feedback may play an important role in sustaining active engagement with leisure materials. In comparison to nonreactive toys, the reactive toys had substantially greater influence on the amount of time each subject engaged in toy manipulation.

The use of reactive leisure materials may provide one solution for overcoming the problem of stimulating interest. Favell et. al. (1982) found that some effective interventions to address sensory aspects of behavior problems were to substitute appropriate sources of kinesthetic, visual, auditory, or olfactory stimulation for aberrant ones.

Variations of this approach are still used. For instance, at Walden, an engineered environment provides high-preference toys, which are dispensed by teachers in a systematic manner to ensure that children's engagement levels are maintained at least 80 percent of the time (McGee & Daly, 1999). Coyne et. al. (2000) advocate for the use of activities with sensory features that provide immediate meaningful occupation of unstructured time as one of three components in leisure development for individuals with ASD. In addition, a number of programs reviewed in Chapters 7 through 11 utilize activities with sensory features, which are sometimes called fidgets, particularly during times without structured activities.

Symbolic Play

Significant research has been done on the symbolic play development and social interaction of children with ASD who are five years of age or younger. This research has indicated that children with ASD are less likely to spontaneously engage in functionally appropriate play and rarely produce pretend play. When children do show these capacities, the play is less diverse, flexible and variable than that of typical children. Effective strategies for developing social and symbolic play have been identified through this research. Since symbolic and social play are beyond the scope of this book, these strategies are not addressed in this work.

Curriculum and Instructional Approaches

Some promising curriculum and instructional approaches have been developed to more effectively prepare individuals with developmental disabilities in the area of leisure (Project SELF, 1977; Coyne, 1980; Wuerch & Voeltz, 1982; Wehman & Schleien, 1981; Leisure Learning System Project, 1989). Nietupski et. al. (1984) provided a review of task analytic leisure skill training implications and future research needs.

Another area in preparing individuals with developmental disabilities for leisure is curriculum for leisure education. For instance, staff from the Center for Recreation and Disabilities Studies at the University of North Carolina, Chapel Hill (1991 & 1993) has developed curriculum for leisure education programs with a school-community link. *School-Community Leisure Link* (1993) includes six units with corresponding modules on leisure awareness, leisure resources, leisure communication skills, making decisions, leisure planning, and activity skill instruction. The developers acknowledge that ASD is "so broad that there are no general recommendations regarding the use of this curriculum" for this population. The Center for Recreation and Disabilities Studies has also demonstrated successful supports for individuals with ASD through Project Autism (2001). However, there remains a relative absence of both systematic leisure curricula and research, as well as the evaluative support for those programs that do exist.

Continuum of Service Delivery

In the past three decades as individuals with ASD have progressively moved from institutional settings to their communities, service delivery to assist these individuals to live, work and recreate in their communities has been dramatically altered and continues to change. Social factors, such as the disabilities rights and self-determination movements, and a better understanding of disabilities have resulted in dramatic changes in service delivery.

Controversy continues over the most appropriate recreation settings for individuals with ASD. Differences in assumptions about what is possible and what is important to give individuals with this disorder during recreation activities are at the root of this controversy. However, individuals with ASD do not fall into neat categories of needs, which results in specific services. The following three stories illustrate some of the diversity within ASD and the need for different settings.

Ned's Story. Ned loves to swim and his mother enrolls him in Special Olympics swimming. The volunteer swim coach does not understand ASD and has not been prepared for Ned's participation. He is frustrated that Ned does not follow his directions and that Ned loudly says repetitious phrases while laughing. The coach decides that Ned cannot participate in Special Olympics swimming, although he has the best swimming skills of the group. Ned's mother calls his teacher to discuss the situation. His teacher says that he is successful in woodshop at school and is making friends. They problem solve where he can go to swim. His mother and Ned have a family membership at an athletic club, but Ned has never gone. His mother and teacher strategize how he can go swimming at the athletic club. His teacher goes to the athletic club to assess what supports Ned will need to participate in swimming and works with his mother to develop the necessary supports. These same supports would work for Special Olympics swimming if they were implemented there. Ned's mother arranges for free participation at the athletic club for a friend that Ned has met in woodshop. The friend and Ned are prepared ahead for swimming at the athletic club. The two of them enjoy swimming at the athletic club together.

Riley's Story. Riley is fully included at school. He looks forward to the monthly Game Night with others who have ASD and their siblings. He feels relieved that he does not have to struggle to try to figure out what is "normal" behavior and try to act accordingly at Game Night. He feels free to be himself and knows that those who choose to come will accept him for who he is. He wished that there were more places in the community where he did not feel that he needed to strive to be "normal."

Brandon's Story. Brandon's mother had enrolled him exclusively in inclusive recreation programs for most of his 20 years. Last year he went to a specialized canoe camp for individuals with developmental disabilities. Although he had gone to summer camps regularly, he had always refused to participate in the skits. He not only successfully participated in the skit at this camp, he enjoyed it so much that he participated in and led younger campers in several skits at a generic 4-H camp later in the summer.

All people have a right to choose what they would like to do for recreation, with whom they would like to do it and where they would like to recreate. Individuals with ASD may choose to be in a specialized program with people who are similar or may choose this option because the smaller size of the group provides a tolerable level of stress. On the other hand, they may prefer to recreate with individuals who are "typical" or a combination of the two.

Neither generic recreation programs nor special programs are inherently good. Individuals with ASD have differing desires, interests and needs. The ability to participate can be just as dependent on the types of instruction and accommodations provided as on the participant.

Photo by Jason Kinch Photographics,
Courtesy of Mt. Hood Kiwanis Camp

Although professionals may have philosophical differences, most believe that each person should be taught with the goal of successful functioning with as few restrictions as possible and that a combination of inclusive and specialized opportunities is necessary. There needs to be a continuum of service delivery options. Special classes should be available as an option for those for whom these settings are the most meaningful and appropriate. Many recreation providers and parents support the view that a structured program with a 1:1 ratio or small group environment may best address the more severe challenges of some individuals with ASD, while many others may be successful in a general recreation environment with appropriate support. Some individuals with ASD may be fully included, some may start in a specialized program and move on to inclusive programs, some may participate in both generic and specialized programs and others may stay in a specialized program.

In general, no matter what the situation, the initial teaching needs to be provided with maximal individual instruction and support. Prompting is gradually faded as the person is able to participate more independently. Whether a program is specialized or inclusive, the likelihood of failure is greater when an individual with ASD is placed in a setting with no backup, no training of staff and no understanding by other participants.

Inclusion

Individuals with ASD and their families are more frequently choosing to participate in generic community activities rather than entering separate programs, and their decisions are supported, as discussed in Chapter 1, by laws such as the Americans with Disabilities Act (ADA) and the Individuals with Disabilities Education Act (IDEA). Inclusion advocates typically support the notion that every person has a right to be included and that necessary support services and accommodations for the participant must be provided in an inclusive setting.

Box 2.24

Position Statement of the
Autism and Asperger's Syndrome Independent Living Association

The Autism and Asperger's Syndrome Independent Living Association strongly supports:

- promoting recognition of the need for inclusive recreation and leisure activities as an essential component of a quality life for people with Autism and Asperger's Syndrome.
- encouraging organizations currently providing segregated recreation and leisure activities to develop inclusive options.
- developing strategies and techniques to help people with Autism and Asperger's Syndrome and their families make the transition to inclusive recreation and leisure activities, including competitive sports.
- identifying and expanding resources which facilitate inclusive recreation and leisure activities.
- promoting participation of people with Autism and Asperger's Syndrome in organized recreation and leisure groups that are appropriate for their chronological age.

Inclusion means different things to different people. Schleien et. al. (1997) described two approaches to inclusion: 1) creation of programs in a school or community that can include anyone regardless of ability and 2) reverse mainstreaming, in which people without disabilities join previously segregated activities for people with disabilities. A variety of programs that provide inclusive services are featured in Chapters 7 through 10. Camp Ky-O-Wa, Camp Awareness, and Camp Determination in Chapter 10 and Game Club in Chapter 11 are examples of programs that use reverse mainstreaming. These programs are interesting enough that children without disabilities want to go there and are willing to adjust to the needs of others.

Inclusion requires careful planning and consideration on the part of recreation providers. It must involve more than physically including the individual. In fact, immersing an individual with ASD in a program without appropriate planning and support may result in unmitigated disasters for the individual as well as other participants. On the other hand, the success stories from around the country described in Chapters 7 through 11 provide testimony that many individuals across the autism spectrum can participate in regular recreation programs, if sufficient support is provided, all are informed, and effective strategies are used.

The issue of whether to include an individual with ASD depends on many factors, such as:

- Is inclusion a desire for the individual?
- Is the activity of interest?
- Can support be added?
- Can staff be trained?
- Can an atmosphere of supportive acceptance be established?
- Is the environment appropriate or can it be changed?

Individuals with ASD can often be successfully included in generic recreation programs, if staff is open and willing to receive some basic training in how to support participants with this disability. Many times a general overview along with some information about strategies can provide the staff with enough confidence to begin to include these individuals.

Position Statement of the National Recreation and Park Association

The National Recreation and Park Association (NRPA) adopted a position statement on inclusion in 1999. It states that NRPA is dedicated to the four inclusion concepts of:
- Right to Leisure (for all individuals)
- Quality of Life (enhancements through leisure experiences)
- Support, assistance and accommodations
- Barrier Removal

Box 2.25

The American Park and Recreation Society and the National Therapeutic Recreation Society, two branches of the NRPA, have assessed the need for inclusion training for parks and recreation agency staff across the country. They, subsequently, developed the NRPA National Institute on Recreation Inclusion, an annual conference, to provide staff with the tools to design, implement, and evaluate their recreation programs to include all patrons, with and without disabilities.

Many agencies are shifting from specialized recreation programs to more inclusive opportunities. For instance, although the Arc of the United States still may offer some specialized programs, nationally they have changed directions from providing specialized recreation services to encouraging inclusive leisure supports. To accomplish this they have decided to increase linkages between agency and community in order to provide more inclusive recreation. This includes providing training and technical assistance to public and private leisure services personnel and other community members involved in the development of inclusive recreation.

The Arc of Multnomah County, Oregon is an advocacy organization that forges linkages between consumers and providers in both the public and private sectors to create new and better options for people with developmental disabilities. The organization has always had a commitment to recreation and has hired a certified Therapeutic Recreation Specialist (CTRS). Individuals with ASD have enjoyed participating in a computer class at a community college, swing dance lessons and kickboxing at a community center, a music camp, an afterschool gym program, and yoga at an athletic club through the Arc of Multnomah County's Inclusive Companion Project. The Arc of Multnomah County also has the Young Adult Recreation Club to assist an underserved group of individuals from 18 to 26 years old, including four with ASD, to gain skills for more independent community recreation.

Society is ever changing. To make recreation opportunities inclusive for all people, the providers of recreation opportunities need to recognize and accept responsibility for serving all people. Individuals wishing to participate need to identify and express their recreation interests, as well as need for support. The largest barriers to inclusion today are not individuals with ASD or other disabilities, but the ignorance and fears of those who are considered "typical." Although new strategies will continue to be developed, the biggest change in the years to come will occur in the rest of us as we learn how to create more inclusive communities.

Summary

- ASD is a developmental disability that typically appears during the first three years of life. Children and adults with ASD typically have deficiencies in verbal and nonverbal communication, social interactions, and *leisure/play skills* (Autism Society of America, 1998).
- This neurological disorder affects the way information is processed, organized and integrated.
- It is now understood that individuals with ASD do not choose to misbehave.
- Terminology may still cause confusion, since there are two distinct systems for identification. There is a medical diagnosis of related disorders under Pervasive Developmental Disorder and eligibility for special education services under only one category, Autism (Spectrum Disorder).
- Individuals with ASD have difficulty with reciprocal social interaction, verbal and nonverbal communication, restricted and repetitive behaviors and interests, and unusual responses to sensory information.
- Every person with ASD is an individual, and like all individuals, has a unique personality and combination of characteristics, strengths and limitations.
- The way individuals with ASD interact with the environment, materials, and others is often different than the way others spend their leisure.
- Behavior is often misinterpreted when recreation service providers do not understand ASD.
- Some of the characteristics of individuals with ASD may be strengths that, with proper motivation, can be used to enhance participation in recreation activities.

- Research and literature related to the benefits of recreation, methods to sustain interests and develop symbolic play, as well as curriculum and instructional approaches provide direction in recreation service delivery.
- Neither regular recreation programs nor special programs are inherently good. A continuum of options that ensures that individuals make informed choices is needed.

Chapter Three

Parent Perspectives on Leisure at Home and in the Community

Jane Rake

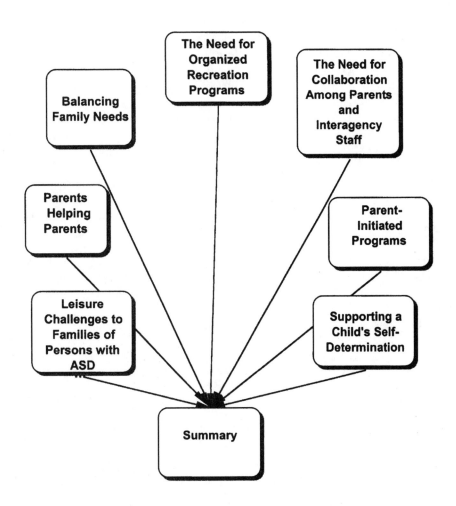

Leisure Challenges to Families of
Persons with Autism Spectrum Disorder

One of the most vivid memories I have of my son Harry's childhood is of a particular soccer practice when he was eight years old. It was autumn, twilight, and as is typical in Oregon at that time of year, it was raining. I stood at the edge of the soccer field with a dozen other intrepid moms and dads huddled under Gortex and umbrellas.

It wasn't hard to pick Harry out even in the gathering gloom. He was the one lying on his back on the sodden grass, happily waving his arms and legs in the air, completely oblivious to the scrimmage raging around him.

To him this was playing soccer; he lay on the field like a drunken turtle as the other players chased the ball from one end of the field to the other, discreetly avoiding this human diversion. The adults on the sidelines on the other hand, weren't nearly as kind; there was snickering and various unpleasant comments regarding my precious son and his admittedly eccentric behavior. I felt angry and embarrassed, but mainly just sad. As a parent, you simply wish for your child to be happy and fit in. As the parent of a child with Autism Spectrum Disorder (ASD), you sometimes feel as though you must make a choice between the two.

There were a number of circumstances that further compounded Harry's sports situation. Unfortunately, at this point in Harry's life we didn't yet know that he had ASD. We knew he was unusual and quirky and wonderful, but no one had yet been able to tell us what exactly was going on with him. Also, having a "non bouncy-ball type" mother and a father that steadfastly refused to have the rules of engagement changed for his son made things even more difficult.

Harry also has a twin brother who for years had to play on the same team because it was "convenient" for us as parents. In retrospect this was perhaps not the best solution for either of them. Alex, Harry's twin, has always been extremely embarrassed by Harry's eccentricities and has occasionally been rather ruthless in his criticism. They also have very different skill levels and although we'd taken great care to separate them at school, for some reason our foresight didn't appear to extend to soccer. Finally, and most importantly, none of us, including his coach, had any idea that soccer could be such a foreign language for Harry.

There is so much that is taken for granted in organized recreation activities, but the truth of the matter is that nothing can be taken for granted with children with ASD. The basic concepts of teamwork, including "sides" and "winning and losing," or even, "which-end-of-the-field-you're-trying-to-kick-the-ball-to" are part of the rules that most kids learn, without much difficulty.

In the game of soccer, typical kids seem to easily understand that:

- All the kids in green shirts are on one team.
- The team's job is to work together to get the ball into the net at the opposite end of the field.
- The "green" team needs to keep the ball away from the players in the red shirts.
- When you kick the ball you try to kick it to someone on your team even if someone on the other team smiles at you or says, "kick it to me."

Then there are all the other rules that *everyone* struggles with when they are first learning soccer, such as who can touch the ball and when, and how you behave if you win or lose the game.

Harry was happy and very proud to be on the Alameda soccer team with his brother and school classmates, but it was on his own terms. The baffled parents, teammates and coach were unprepared to translate the game into a concrete language he could understand. None of us comprehended just how lost he really was; after all he was very verbal and goodnatured.

Full Inclusion was the rallying cry in 1993 and at that point in the evolution of inclusion of children with disabilities, our passion to do the right thing by children was impeded by our lack of knowledge of how to "level the playing field" adequately for a child with ASD. I think one of the hardest problems parents and professionals alike encounter is overcoming the belief that play is a simple universal ability that all children possess, and if you just get them together everything will work itself out.

Years later as I write this, that night at the soccer game is just a distant unpleasant memory. My sons have turned 18 and are now adults. Harry has had his ups and downs like all children, and team sports were never highly successful experiences for him, but we can celebrate some truly marvelous landmarks. When he graduated from eighth grade in general education at his neighborhood Middle School he received the Walter E. Hathaway Award for "Personal Strength and Potential." As he walked to the front of the auditorium he received a raucous standing ovation from the entire student body. This was not because he was "special"; it was because he had won the respect and friendship of almost every one of his peers. These were all students he had gone to school with since kindergarten. Yes, inclusion at school did turn out to be a wonderful thing!

We were always very candid with Harry about his ASD and therefore it's never been a big deal to him. As an adolescent he is generally happy and well adjusted and is glad to be himself: curly hair, ASD and all. Granted, most of his closest friends also have ASD or other quirks, but I think that's because he's most comfortable when he does not have to explain his ASD to others.

He never could quite get the hang of kicking the soccer ball in the right direction, so he's developed other leisure interests. His interests do tend to run along the sedentary line, such as collecting dragon-related items and lore, playing computer and video games, listening to music and going to movies or shopping with friends; but come to think of it, that's fairly consistent with the norm. Left to his own devices he stays pretty inert, but he will go on walks or hikes with others if prodded, and once he's on the trail he does seem to enjoy it.

Our experiences as a family are not unusual. Many parents have stories similar to mine regarding their children with ASD challenges in recreation programs particularly when the nature of the disability is not understood. Another parent shares her experiences in Figure 3.1.

Figure 3.1
One Parent's Experience with Team Sports

"…Of course he still has irritations and confusion typical of ASD. We just finished up basketball season a few weeks ago with a game in which Carl was so eager to get the ball and make a point from his team that he stole the ball from a teammate! When his teammates hollered at him about this, he got very defensive. He had a hard time seeing it from the team or the other kid's point of view.

"Also, at the beginning of the season, he had two games in which he was the "star," making eight points per game by shooting from a certain spot on the floor. Unfortunately, he began to think that was the only spot from which he could make baskets, so he would either stand in that spot and scream at his teammates to pass him the ball, or he'd get the ball somewhere else on the floor and be so eager to run to his magic spot, he would forget to dribble and get called for traveling."

Carl's mom

(Personal communication to Jane Rake, 2002)

Over the years I have spoken to many other parents as we've mutually sought advice and ideas to help our children with ASD fit in with their peers. Many parents have described the challenges as well as the benefits of pursuing recreation and leisure opportunities for their children. Almost without exception, the parents that invested the considerable effort necessary to develop their child's skills indicate that the pay off has been huge. Some parents state that this has been the best avenue for their child to learn social skills; others report decreased hyperactivity and behavioral problems, better concentration and improved sleep. The parents all agree that meaningful leisure activities have greatly improved their child's and their family's quality of life.

Parents Helping Parents

Many parents find that one of their best sources of information is other parents. For instance, the Portland, Oregon area is lucky to have a very large and active on-line parent support group for Asperger's Syndrome, a sub-type of Autism Spectrum Disorder. This group formed in 1998 and has become an amazing source of support for up to 150 families and individuals from around the state. An example of how this works is reflected in someone posting a message about their child's experiences with organized sports and the ensuing lengthy conversation among many families and adults with ASD. A few of their very candid comments appear in Figure 3.2

As you can see by these responses, there is huge variability in the experiences of children with ASD. Some children with ASD have excellent coordination and may adore playing soccer while others have severe problems in this area. Some may have a higher tolerance for sensory stimulation or more social flexibility than others may. This underscores why individualization is so important. There are no hard and fast rules that can be applied across the board.

Leisure and recreation has always been a fundamental dilemma facing parents of children with disabilities. As stated in Chapter 2, the numerous characteristics of ASD often severely affect an individual's ability to play independently and with others, and after all, that's a lot of what leisure is all about.

What is meaningful in terms of recreation to one child may hold no interest to another. As parents one of the most important aspects of our job is to help our child, disabled or not, to find value in and meaningful use of free time. For most this isn't a problem, most typical kids live for free time when they can go off and pursue their interests. For some children with ASD, free time appears to parents and others to be filled with meaningless activities such as arranging objects, or engaging in repetitive actions. The key is to take those driving interests and capitalize on them. By using an individuals skills and preferences you can, if you are creative, help him engage in more traditional leisure activities and also teach new and different skills.

One concern families often voice is just how much to tell a potential recreation provider about their child's disability. They struggle to balance the need to give enough information to assure successful support and participation, while worrying that if they reveal too much the program may be leery of serving their son or daughter. Several parents I've spoken with were initially uncomfortable with even divulging to a recreation provider that their child had ASD for fear of being denied access to the program. By increasing family understanding of the rights afforded individuals under the Americans with Disabilities Act (ADA), this is no longer a great concern for most parents. There do remain times when parents may think of withholding information to avoid stigmatizing their child in the eyes of peers and staff. In actuality, since ASD is invisible, having no outward physical manifestations, providing recreation programs with accurate and detailed information can often

Figure 3.2
Parents' Experiences with Organized Sports

"Has anyone had any experiences with their Asperger Syndrome children and team sports? My eight-year-old wants to play baseball. Last year he played wiffleball and did okay, but there were some problems like personal space, some physical aggressiveness, and lack of attention; he was very wound up afterwards. This year he would have to play Little League baseball…"

In response other families wrote:

"My son's first year in Little League was in the Parkrose Challenger Division which is for kids with physical and mental disabilities. It was a great experience. The kids got to run the bases no matter what, there were no outs, and practices and games were short. Both the parents and the kids were very supportive and were willing to overlook my son's oddities. It was a great introduction to the game. Last year he was able to compete in a "regular" Little League with scoring, outs, and long games and practices. I think if we'd done that right off the bat, it would have been hard for him."

"…For us, team sports was a disaster of unmitigated proportion. My son was miserable, uncoordinated, inattentive, frequent meltdowns, reviled by his team-mates, etc. But he does well in solo sports such as swimming."

"My son has played team sports since he was five. He's 10 now and he still plays soccer. He loves the game and running after the ball. He tried T-ball, but found the game too slow and boring. He also tried basketball, but that takes too much coordination for him. His soccer teammates like him because he's a good defensive player and his coaches have gotten to know him and now understand that he will have some meltdowns. We find that individual sports are hard for him because he's too hard on himself if he doesn't win and he has more meltdowns then."

"…My evaluation is (my son) doesn't do well with team sports. Soccer and basketball did not fit him well because he doesn't like being in the flurry of pursuing the ball; I've learned this is too stimulating and he just doesn't like it and isn't good at going after the ball when he's in a group of kids. In baseball you are both individual and part of the team. That was better. Still better are individual sports like bowling, swimming, and rock-climbing. He would probably be good at track, golf, tennis, and other "solitary" sports. An interesting comment I always hear from people who have no idea what we live with everyday is, 'Why don't you put him in some team sports, that will help him make friends easier.'

"My nine-year-old son is involved in indoor soccer through the Boys and Girls Club…He has Asperger's and has done quite well, they give a lot of encouragement and they don't keep score (they don't tell the kids what the score is). They emphasize good sportsmanship and each child gets fair time to play each game. There is never any 'bad play or bad game'…"

"…(My son) could not even play a game at home without falling apart if someone even slightly bent what he felt the rules should be or how the game should be played. I envisioned a nightmare on any sports team. I feel he could probably handle things better now, unfortunately all the kids his age have been playing for years on teams, and he would have to be put on a beginning team as he is very uncoordinated…"

(Personal communications to Jane Rake, 2002)

prevent misunderstandings about the child. For example, with knowledge of the child's diagnosis a recreation provider would understand any behavior difficulties as disability-related.

Balancing Family Needs

Another issue facing many parents is the challenge of balancing the needs of their child with ASD and the interests and pursuits of the rest of the family. Parents are often spread thin by their attempts to juggle all the facets of regular family life and still have time (and energy!) for the family to have fun. When the needs of the family member with ASD are in conflict with the needs of the rest of the family real problems can result (see example in Figure 3.3).

Figure 3.3
Finding Common or Compatible Leisure Interests

Eight-year-old Lance comes from a family of enthusiastic hobbyists. His parents and siblings look forward to their time together to work on family projects. The problem is that someone has to watch Lance, because no matter how hard they have tried to figure out a way for him to be included, he only seems to want to take apart what they have just completed. It's gotten so frustrating for them that there have been times when they have just put him in his room with his favorite video and let him watch it over and over, just so they can have some peace. They feel it's not right to shut him out like that, but they've run out of other ideas; there isn't much that he likes to do on his own.

Recently Lance's Uncle John suggested teaching him how to take apart computer components to remove the precious metals for resale. This way Lance can take things apart constructively, and work alongside his family when they are doing their projects. Lance's family has decided to give this a try.

Parental guilt at having "failed" one or more of the family is often an issue. One parent I interviewed expressed frustration and regret as she described her family's attempts to recreate together. Everyone except Jack enjoyed skiing and snowboarding and this often led to tension in the family. They rarely got to do these things together as a family because she or her husband usually had to stay at home with Jack or take him on a separate outing.

Sometimes siblings of children with ASD feel that they are less important because of all the effort that their parents put into supporting their brother or sister with the disability. This can lead to serious and long-lasting resentments and alienation or even depression in some siblings.

Although it was never my intent or even my impression, I'm sure that there were times when Harry's brother felt he was getting less attention. I have found that it's been helpful to allow my boys to compete on "their own turf." I've always been careful, with the notable exception of that soccer team, when they were young to avoid having them on the same team or in the same activities, and they've never been in the same classroom at school. In this way they are never compared to each other and they can each shine with their individual qualities.

One wonderful resource available in many communities in North America is the program Sibshops, developed by Donald Meyer at the University of Washington. This is a recreation-based support group specifically for brothers and sisters of children with a disability. More information on this innovative program can be found at the website: www.seattlechildrens.org/sibsupp/

The Need for Organized Recreation Programs

Probably the primary reason why families of children with ASD currently underutilize generic community recreation and leisure resources is their concern that their child's individual needs will not be met. Many families have at one time or another tried enrolling their family member in a program, such as a dance class or arts and crafts group, and had disastrous or at best disappointing results. Maybe the child exhibited a behavior that scared the teacher or other participants or the child had difficulty engaging appropriately in the class. Even with what a family may think is sufficient background about the child and her ASD, staff is often at a loss about how to adequately support the participant for success.

A systematic approach to designing appropriate individualized supports is critical. The following chapters in this book will outline practical approaches to maximize success, from the initial planning steps in Chapter 5 to customizing supports for participation in Chapter 6. Later in the book there are descriptions of exemplary programs providing leisure experiences for individuals with ASD (Chapters 7-11).

The Need for Collaboration among Parents and Interagency Staff

One of the more frustrating problems that parents run into when seeking supports and services for their child is assuring that all the people who best know their child, such as the various therapists, teachers, and support staff, have the opportunity to communicate their knowledge to any new personnel becoming involved. There is truly nothing more disconcerting to a parent than being asked the same questions over and over when you know that other key people already have that information. Having the family sign a release of information so that program staff can directly contact the other key professionals in the child's life can easily circumvent this problem.

Many parents maintain their own comprehensive records about their child and are usually more than willing to let a new recreation provider make a copy of anything that would be helpful. By keeping their own set of records, parents can assure themselves that the interested party will be receiving the most recent and accurate records. In addition, by supplying the records themselves, they can make them available immediately as opposed to the sometimes-lengthy process involved when using a release of information.

Guardians or parents of minors can easily obtain most records. By law, a copy of the IEP or 504 Plan is provided to the parent at the annual meeting. Other records may be available by simply asking for a copy. In some instances parents may be requested to fill out a release in order to receive a medical record. Figure 3.4 contains a suggested list of information that parents can provide to help recreation providers develop supports for their child in a recreation program.

Figure 3.4
Information Parents May Provide to Recreation Providers
for Purposes of Providing Supports and Accommodations

- Medical diagnosis and treatment history, including current medication record if applicable.
- Current IEP or 504 Plan.
- Recent educational and medical reports from speech pathologists, occupational and/or physical therapists, autism specialists, or psychologists.
- Information on social supports and visual/written supports.

Collaboration is particularly important when the leisure participant is non-verbal or has limited expressive skills. It cannot be overstated how important it is to understand that for people with ASD, **behavior is communication**, and the decoding of that behavior is critical to understanding how to support the person. Families are often adept at this interpretation, but sometimes the participant may not have immediate family members available for this information, or perhaps the individual has been living in foster care or another situation where staff are the only ones who really know the individual well. In these instances communication and information sharing among the people knowledgeable about the individual are essential.

Box 3.1

14-year-old Terry had been exposed to many forms of recreation and leisure activities through the years by his family and within the school setting. He always seemed to gravitate to solitary pursuits and when pressed into trying something new, especially if it involved interacting with people, he would become aggressive to the point of striking out against others. When an autism specialist explained to those close to him that his sensory and processing issues made it difficult for him to tolerate the noise and confusion of group activities, his family, teachers, and other staff developed strategies to help him cope, such as limiting the number of people he would need to interact with and carefully developing high-interest activities. He has been able to slowly expand his interests to include some small group activities.

Families are often at a loss about how to best support their children with ASD in pursuit of leisure. This notwithstanding, parents are almost always the best resource available to understanding how their child "ticks." Involving the parents, and often siblings, in the planning of specific activities and supports is crucial not only to the troubleshooting necessary for a good leisure fit for the individual with ASD, but it's critical that the family's values are respected and supported.

A number of parents noted similar strategies that maximize the success of participation for their children with ASD. These are listed in Figure 3.5:

Figure 3.5
Strategies Parents Find Maximize Success

- Building on the child's areas of interest.
- Repeated exposure to an activity. Novelty and change are difficult for most individuals with ASD. Trying things over and over can lead to tolerance and then enjoyment of the routine.
- Trying "small doses" of an activity at first. As the comfort level increases, extend the time.
- To avoid having the child stick out in the group, think of strategies that will work for them all. Making the rules visual is something that will benefit many children, not only the one with ASD. For example this can be done by posting a written list for those who read, or creating drawings or pictures for non-readers. The rules can then be referred to by pointing to them in addition to saying them verbally. As pointed out in Chapter 2, individuals with ASD are often visual learners.
- Rehearsing before an activity is another way to help avoid problems. This can help allay anxieties as it shows the person what will be happening.

When and if a family takes the plunge and approaches a recreation program at school or in the community, their initial experiences with it will often determine whether or not they have the comfort level to entrust their child to the staff's care. It is, therefore, imperative that staff in charge of the intake process have an understanding not only of ASD, but also how to supportively relate to families' concerns about their individual child's needs and be able to demonstrate the adequacy of the program to serve their child. An initial contact with a brusque or confused staff person could be an automatic turn-off for an already stressed and worried parent.

Parent-Initiated Programs

Parents' early perception of the level of their child's impairment often presages whether they will even consider approaching recreation resources. For instance, one family I spoke with never even thought of attempting to utilize existing programs because they assumed their son was too severely impacted by his ASD to be adequately supported in them. They

set about to develop their own recreation resource to specifically serve children with ASD. For a second parent, providing inclusion for her children with neuro-typical peers has evolved into creating a program to explore their cultural roots with other Native American families (see Chapter 11).

In terms of being advocates for change, families often go beyond collaboration with recreation providers on behalf of their own child. They are often the ones who are the catalyst for change within existing recreation programs and the innovators of entirely new recreation experiences. Such parent-initiated programs are described in Chapter 11 and additional examples are found in Chapters 9 and 10.

Supporting a Child's Self-Determination

Parents are typically the glue that holds their sons' and daughters' leisure lives together. This is an almost universal fact of life for families, particularly in a child's early years. We are the ones arranging everything from play dates to the swim class carpool. We become the mediators in childhood disputes and have the usually happy responsibility of teaching our kids how to find the joy in play. Once again, it becomes a bit more complicated when it comes to ASD. Many parents need to continue to advocate for their child's recreational needs into adulthood while others will be able to relinquish this role (see Figure 3.6).

Figure 3.6
Moving from Parental Advocacy to Self-Advocacy

Throughout his early school years, Paul's parents were very involved in all aspects of his educational planning, including paying particular attention to his physical education programming. Physical activity is a high priority for Paul's entire family; however, with Paul's ASD and his seeming dislike of sports, his parents realized that he would need certain accommodations in the school setting to be successful. They went as far as to have him exempted from PE in middle school because they thought that participating in the regular PE program would be very stressful for Paul. During middle school they enrolled him in private swim lessons to earn his PE credits.

When Paul entered high school his parents took a deep breath and decided to let him try to find his own way. Typically high schools offer a wide variety of sports options for students to fulfill their PE credits. The school's wrestling coach also worked in the Educational Resource Room where Paul received support. Paul felt comfortable approaching the coach on his own and finding out about joining the team.

In addition to joining the wrestling team Paul joined the cross-country running team. He became the only student in his large graduating class to take a sport every season all four years and also received "Most Inspirational" member of his wrestling team twice. It turned out that Paul didn't hate sports after all when he could participate on his own terms.

There comes a time in most lives when it's important to experience self-determination. As a parent it is often difficult to balance your child's need for autonomy with your understandable concerns about her potential vulnerability. Some individuals with ASD will always require assistance in self-advocacy but that doesn't mean that we shouldn't support them at every opportunity to make as many life decisions on their own as possible.

Summary

A decade has passed since that miserable night at the soccer practice. My son has grown into a young man with friends and leisure interests of his own choosing. Sure, he never did experience much success or ongoing enjoyment playing organized sports, but as we've seen from many of the comments from other parents in this chapter, that isn't true of all children with ASD.

For parents of children with ASD, every day brings new challenges, experiences and insights. Like all families we spend those days helping our children become the best people they can be, but unlike many other families each of those days can be a struggle as we contend with the "uncharted territory" of ASD. There is little available in terms of an ASD "road map," in particular when it comes to enhancing recreation and leisure skills and opportunities for our children. This is because even though there have been comprehensive lists generated of the characteristics of ASD, the variability of the individual's expression of these characteristics is highly unique. It is that variability that requires such creativity on the part of families and service providers. Although the road is life-long, as children continue to grow, new and different leisure options can become available to them (see Figure 3.7 for an example).

Figure 3.7
New Leisure and Social Opportunities

Rick didn't have any friends until he was in high school when his great interest in computers led him to join the computer club. In computer club he was able to function on his own terms in an activity where he excelled.

Given his previous need for social supports, his mother Diane, up to this point, had always played a pivotal role in his social activities. However, the mutual interests of the members of the computer club made Rick's acceptance easier and he didn't tend to "stick out" as much in this group. His mother, also, discovered that belonging to this group helped him become more accountable for his actions, since the club members applied gentle peer pressure to help him conform. He wanted to be involved with the group so much that he was often willing to do things for and with the group that he had been unwilling to do previously.

His interest in computers continues to provide social and recreational outlets for Rick. Now that he's graduated from high school he often spends the night with his computer friends in the nearby college campus dorm.

The high point in his life so far occurred just this year when he was invited to an all-night computer game party in the garage of someone he met on-line. Diane had to overcome her concerns about letting him go off to the home of someone she'd never met, but since he was 21 she felt he had the right to go. When he returned home at 4 AM he told her, "It was the most wonderful time of my life."

(Jane Rake, personal communication, 2002)

We are blessed to live in a time when there is increasing research and development in the field of ASD, and we know much more today than we did when my son was first identified. Maybe there will never be "road maps" for our children but it is my hope that this book will pave the way for young families living with ASD to have broader and better recreation and leisure experiences in the future.

In summary, important points for recreation providers to remember are:

• Parents want to find recreation programs that will not only be fun for their child but will also be accepting of their differences. It's important to see the person instead of the disability.

• Parents are often worried about revealing the extent of their child's special needs out of fear of rejection or stigmatization. It's important for program staff to be open and supportive while discussing the participant.

- Parents are juggling many aspects of family life such as their jobs, school, and the individual social and emotional needs of each family member, so some families may not be as involved with the recreation planning as others. It's important for staff to respect individual family differences without making judgment.
- Parent to parent support is a wonderful avenue for families to support each other and share information. Some of the most innovative programs for individuals with ASD have been generated through such parent interactions.
- Parents are almost always the best resource about their child. Take advantage of their expertise whenever possible.
- An understanding not only of ASD but also insight into the stresses and concerns of a parent of a child with ASD is important.
- A family's values are extremely important, it's important to be flexible and respectful.

Chapter Four

A Few Perspectives and Experiences of Individuals with Autism Spectrum Disorder Related to Recreation

Jane Rake & Ann Fullerton

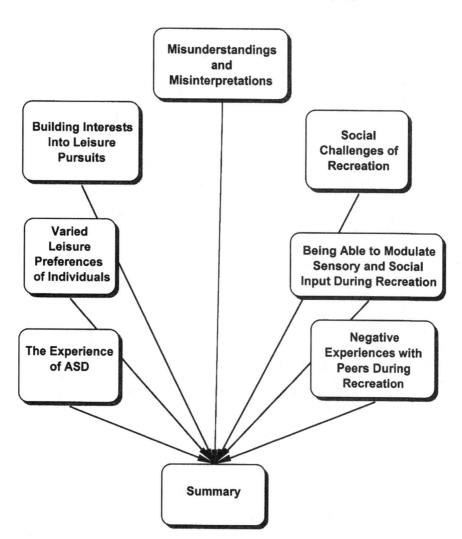

Introduction

The perspectives of individuals with Autism Spectrum Disorder (ASD) can be a source of useful information for recreation providers seeking to better understand how ASD can impact recreation preferences and participation. Individuals with ASD spend their leisure time and participate in recreation in as many varied ways as any other group. At the same time, however, the sensory, cognitive, and social challenges associated with ASD can influence how these individuals come to define and enjoy as leisure.

In this chapter, individuals with ASD, who are verbal and able to express their insights, shared their perspectives on recreation. These accounts were gathered from several sources. A segment of these individuals have been diagnosed with Asperger's Syndrome. First, we invited a group of young adults with ASD that we know to respond to several questions about their leisure experiences in an informal discussion. Second, we informally interviewed other individuals with ASD about the topic. Third, we compiled additional anecdotal data from our cumulative years of experience with individuals with ASD and our readings of first-hand accounts written by individuals with ASD. From this body of qualitative information, a few themes emerged. No presumption is made here that these perspectives are in any way representative of all individuals with ASD. The individuals who contributed to this chapter speak for themselves; they are articulate and insightful in discussing their experiences and what recreation providers could do to support them in recreation.

Several topics are addressed in this chapter related to recreation and individuals with ASD. First, information is shared from a study in which young adults with ASD described their experience of ASD. These first-hand accounts are helpful in understanding how ASD impacts sensory, cognitive, and social functioning. Second, the broad range of leisure activities, from solitary to social, that the individuals who contributed to this chapter enjoy is described. Third, the challenges associated with the social components of recreation faced by individuals with ASD are explored in depth. Fourth, the importance of being able to take a break from sensory and social input for individuals with ASD during social recreation is discussed. Lastly, experiences of disclosing one's ASD to other participants in a recreational activity are discussed.

The Experience of Autism Spectrum Disorder

ASD is a neurological difference that can result in sensory, cognitive, and social consequences for an individual. In recent years a growing number of individuals with ASD have written about their personal experiences with ASD. These accounts have been of tremendous help to family members, friends, and professionals associated with individuals with ASD in better understanding the gifts and the challenges of ASD. It is highly recommended that the reader explore these powerful and insightful accounts. Appendix A provides a list of suggested books and articles.

In order to better understand their own ASD, small groups of young adults with ASD came together in three separate classes designed to develop skills for self-determination and the transition to adulthood (Fullerton & Coyne, 1999). In one portion of the course, the young adults read published accounts of the experience of ASD. The young adults then discussed these accounts and shared their own experiences. The diagram in the upper left-hand side of Figure 4.1 was used to organize the discussion into the sensory, cognitive (thinking), and social realms. A compilation of the young adults' responses is provided in Figure 4.1.

Figure 4.1
Sensory, Cognitive, and Social Experiences of Young Adults with ASD

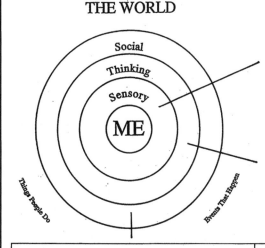

Sensory Experiences

1. If there is too much stimulation, I shut down.
2. My sensitivity to smell affects what I like to eat.
3. I can distinguish the separate smells in someone's breath.
4. I love tight spaces, if I am in control of them.
5. I am sensitive to light and to touch.
6. I have 'bionic' senses.
7. Sound sensitivity is the worst. I have pain or fear with some sounds.
8. I am color sensitive, hyper visual.

Thinking Experiences

1. It's hard when two people tell me to do something at once.
2. I have a strong memory.
3. When too many words are spoken, I get lost, need to write it down!
4. I have to learn by myself, alone.
5. When a lot of information comes in at once it is hard to learn.
6. I am a visual learner.
7. I don't know double meanings, don't understand vague questions.
8. It's hard to make decisions.
9. It's hard to know where to begin.

Social Experiences

1. I have to move when I talk.
2. I can't look at people when I talk. Eye contact is hard.
3. It's hard to understand 'tone of voice.'
4. People [like me] need to know what jobs to avoid [given their own challenges].
5. People don't explain why we need to learn things, why we should study something.
6. It's hard to understand sarcasm.
7. I don't enjoy people coming to the house.
8. I am bored with what others are interested in.
9. Social situations can be distracting.
10. It is hard to know who to talk to about what.

11. How do you know when you are being a good communicator?
12. I need time to form what I want to say but this is not always available in a conversation.
13. I get distracted when people roll their eyes.
14. I have been told I interrupt, but I don't know when exactly I do this and how to diminish interrupting.
15. Sometimes when another person says something it sparks a thought of my own [and it is hard not to say it right then]. Another person's talking can activate my brain to talk.
16. It is difficult to hold information in my head long enough while the other person is talking.
17. It is hard to follow a conversation when people talk too fast, engage in what I call 'machine gun talk.'
18. People don't understand me, they misjudge me.

Sensory, cognitive, and social experiences of young adults with ASD shared in self determination class. From: Fullerton, A. & Coyne, P. (1999). Developing skills and concepts for self-determination in young adults with autism. Focus on autism and other developmental disabilities, 14(1), page 48. Reprinted with permission from PROED.

Taken together, the young adults' comments are consistent with the information provided in Chapter 2 that described the characteristics associated with ASD. The young adults were often highly sensitive to sensory input, which sometimes resulted in what they described as shutting down and not being able to stay focused or respond. Descriptions of their cognitive experiences suggest that in certain situations, when information was given too quickly or amidst distractions, it was difficult to follow instructions and learn. In the social realm, it is evident that these individuals are aware that they do not pick up on social cues and the unwritten social rules that are obvious to others; and that this can often lead to being misunderstood by others. These kinds of sensory, cognitive, and social experiences can impact one's functioning in different situations and settings, including those that arise in recreation activities.

Varied Leisure Preferences of Individuals

Leisure interests and pursuits are highly individual; people with ASD are no different. We are drawn to activities that we personally find relaxing or exciting, simple or complex. What one person may consider to be leisure, another may view as "work." For some of us, most of our discretionary time is spent in social activities; others choose solitary pursuits; and still others thrive on a variety of the two. For some of us, physical activity enlivens and rejuvenates; for others leisure means the absence of activity.

We asked six young adults with ASD about recreation, and how they defined leisure. Their responses span the same spectrum as described above:

- Doing things I enjoy.
- An atmosphere where I can be myself, don't have to put on an act.
- Doing things that use my interests and skills.
- Easygoing, getting away from routine.
- When I do leisure, it's still got to be routine.
- Getting together with people I can associate with and sharing ideas and things I like to do.
- Leisure is exercise and taking care of my emotional health.
- For me it's not the activity, it's getting along with the people, the emotional rapport. The activity is on the side.

Some members of this group like to exercise or play sports; others enjoy watching movies, reading or listening to music. Some write and share poetry or engage in visual arts. Some enjoy computer games. Others said that solitary activities in their areas of interest were a way to relax after socially stressful situations.

Some preferred their leisure to involve social activities that met certain criteria. For some, social situations were enjoyed if they involved being with a group of people who shared a mutual interest, e.g., computer club, poetry group, or Anime Japanese animation. Others enjoyed social situations in which they felt accepted and among friends or family. This was true for a particular group of young adults who had initially come together in order to meet others with ASD. The group met regularly and enjoyed the social aspect of spending time together. The fact that they shared the experience of ASD was one of the reasons why they continued to see each other. They also expressed a comfort in being among friends with whom they did not have to explain themselves.

Building Interests into Leisure Pursuits

In our experience, individuals with ASD may develop very specific interests. Individuals with ASD can be highly self-motivated and self-directed in learning everything they can about their interest. This ability to sustain and develop an area of interest is a real strength that can lead to accomplishment and satisfaction.

> **Box 4.1**
>
> "...I have lots of interests and hobbies. My first major interest when I was three years old was stairways and escalators. I especially liked curved stairways, and I would look for them and climb them wherever I went. Since then, I have intensely studied many other things. I consider myself an expert in gear assemblies, Lego construction toys, Spirograph drawing equipment, and several Nintendo™ games.
>
> I taught myself origami when I was nine. With the help of various origami books, I graduated from cranes to other figures. I can now make many kinds of animals and the most complex geometric models...
>
> My current major interests are fractals, Nintendo™ video games, and hyraxes. Fractals involve the computerized generation of fractal graphics pictures based on mathematical chaos theory... Hyraxes are small mammals from Africa, I am trying to learn everything about them..."
>
> Ward & Alar, 2000, Pages 233-234.

Sometimes these interests can evolve into a leisure pursuit. If the leisure pursuit involves social interaction, the fact that the individual with ASD is highly knowledgeable about the topic can help facilitate their social interactions with others in the group. The mutual interest can make social interaction much easier.

> **Box 4.2**
>
> Rick's interest in computers has served as a bridge to his forming lasting friendships within a computer game group. The fact that he is very competent with computers has helped him blend into the group. Despite the pervasive impact of ASD in other areas of his life, when it comes to computers he's just one of the boys.

Box 4.3 At camp one year, Jon, who had been fascinated with missiles for some time, discovered horses. After camp he learned a great deal about caring for horses and training horses. He got a job helping out at a stable where he deeply enjoyed his relationship with each animal. From Jon's perspective, his social needs are also met at the stable, since he can talk to others who also love talking about horses.

Misunderstandings and Misinterpretations

The young adults who contributed to this chapter had not been diagnosed with ASD until adulthood. As a consequence their families had not understood their condition. Families were disappointed when these individuals with ASD as children had not enjoyed a recreation activity which was loved by the other family members. All these young adults had all had childhood experiences where recreation instructors, or others in a leadership role, had misinterpreted their behavior in a class or activity. These unpleasant childhood experiences some times led the individual with ASD to avoid the activity altogether in the future.

Instructors or leaders had misinterpreted these individuals with ASD in class by assuming that they were not complying with or not listening to instructions and the instructors responded accordingly. In reality, the individual with ASD may have been confused or may have sincerely misunderstood the directions and thought they were doing the right thing. Such stories, although regrettable in their outcome, illustrate how important it is that the instructor understand the needs of the participant with ASD and the instructor is providing information in ways that the participant can access.

When stressed, people can temporarily lose their ability to communicate effectively. This is particularly true for individuals with ASD. When an individual with ASD is concerned about something, s/he may be unable to put the concern into words. Instead s/he may express his or her anxiety by talking about something else or showing frustration physically.

Box 4.4 As a youth, Cameron was a good downhill skier and sometimes skied competitively in Special Olympics. At one competition Cameron was having trouble with his new skis and he was falling down more than usual. He felt he was having a great deal of difficulty skiing at the level he knew that he was capable of. During the trials he did OK but as he advanced to the finals he found himself competing at a higher level than ever before and he felt that the skis were impacting his performance.

When Cameron went to his coach and reported that there was something wrong with the new skis, his coach dismissed his concern and wouldn't examine the skis. Cameron said that he felt discounted and that he was not listened to. Looking back, he said he wished that the coach had at least looked at the skis, even if Cameron's concerns turned out not to be credible.

At that moment, in the middle of the stress and excitement of a competition, Cameron said when his concern about the skis was dismissed by the coach, the situation became a huge problem for him. His own thinking got stuck on the fact that the coach would not look at the skis, and this impacted his subsequent performance in the competition. The experience for-

Continued

Box 4.4 Cont.

ever colored his interest in skiing and he stopped entering competitions he has only been back on skis once since that day.

What can we as recreation instructors learn from this experience? It seems that at least interest in two things were occuring. Cameron was adjusting to new skis and to a more challenging level of skiing at the same time. He may have had trouble sorting this out on his own, and he needed his coach to help him consider and sort out each aspect of the situation.

In instances such as these we need to "read between the lines" to see what may be driving the anxiety. The anxiety is legitimate and sincere, and it cannot be dismissed simply because the individual cannot communicate about it effectively. Even when we may feel that the individual's concern is invalid (there's something wrong with the skis) it's imperative that the individual's interpretation of events not be discounted but instead that we help the individual move through a thinking and problem-solving process about the situation that concerns them.

Sometimes individuals with ASD may know they need assistance. However, they may not be able to adequately describe what they need, or to sufficiently explain the reason for the request in a way that convinces others of its importance.

Box 4.5

In high school, Mary found it to be highly difficult to get through all six periods in the school day while remaining focused and able to learn. The crowds, the noise, and negotiating the lunch line and large cafeteria all served to increase her tension each day. Mary was a member of the track team, and she loved to run. Running relaxed her and helped her regain her composure so that she could learn in class. She knew that if she could run for 30 minutes in the middle of the day, she would be able to make it through the afternoon.

She asked her teachers to enroll her in the third period gym class and let her run the track. When they said they could not make a special arrangement for her, she did not know what else to say. She recalls that she did not know how to explain her reasons, frame her request as a learning accommodation in terms that the teachers would understand, or how to advocate for herself. But, she did know what would help her be a better student. Years later, as an adult, Mary sought help to communicate her insights to others, at work and in recreation settings.

It is critically important that we listen to and respect the opinions and concerns of individuals with ASD and that we utilize their self-knowledge to develop accommodations for them. Because an individual with ASD may not communicate as others do, this does not mean that his or her judgment is faulty. Some communicate to us in words, others with actions. Many teachers and parents of individuals with ASD come to see themselves as interpreters. They learn to interpret the individual with ASD's behavior and words, and at the same time they learn to translate the social world to the individual with ASD.

The young adults who discussed their experiences in recreation activities with us, offered the suggestions in Figure 4.2 to recreation providers:

Figure 4.2
Suggestions from Adults with ASD for Recreation Providers

- Give the person with ASD complete information and all the details in sequence. Make things clear and don't leave steps out.
- Don't leave kids out or force them into things.
- In PE, grade on participation, not ability.
- Don't assume you can read people's minds.
- Consider the person's personality, their individuality, and their interests. Be creative, use their interests.
- Some may need one-on-one time. Don't get mad if they do not "get it" at first.
- When a person with ASD gives you information, try to see the situation through their eyes, whether or not you think the information is credible.

Social Challenges of Recreation

The difficulty individuals with ASD have understanding social situations cannot be underestimated. This is equally true for individuals with ASD who are highly intelligent and verbal (Gray, 1996; Fullerton, 1996). Individuals without ASD find it hard to believe that the capable individual with ASD would not be able to use his or her intelligence to interpret social contexts and to develop social abilities on a par with their capabilities in other areas. Thus, individuals without ASD often have unrealistic expectations for individuals with ASD. For those of us without ASD, our highly complex and sophisticated ability to engage in social behavior comes with relative ease. In trying to illustrate this difference, Jim Sinclair, an author with ASD writes, "I needed an orientation manual for extraterrestrials. Being autistic does not mean being inhuman. But it does mean being alien. It means that what is normal for other people is not normal for me, and what is normal for me is not normal for other people. In some ways I am terribly ill-equipped to survive in this world, like an extraterrestrial stranded without an orientation manual...." (Sinclair, 1992, page 302).

One woman with ASD describes her experiences in social situations:

Box 4.6

"I find the most difficult social situations are those where I have different relationships with different people, where some people know each other and others don't, where there is no formal activity and so I have to respond as best I can to the utterly confusing social cues, where there is some sense of occasion and everyone is in a sense acting up to that occasion. A perfect example is a cocktail party. I can say for a fact that I get more, socially, from a visit to the dentist than from organized social events. But if you spoke to my dentist he'd probably tell you that I'm so at ease while he's drilling away that I must be quite brilliant at a 'real' social occasion!

I've learned a couple of things about social events. One is not to try and do more than I really can. This means that I hang round in the background and chat briefly with one or two people as they go past, and I don't bother trying to be part of a group. I try to ignore the bizarre impression that people give me socially – the facial and vocal contortions, the sudden moves of eye, gesture and head, which they do so easily and which strike me as so sudden and confusing. I try not to get fixated on people's hands, waving so distractingly and strangely. I find the hardest thing is to avoid getting paranoid. I always get the impression that everyone is watching me fumbling away in the background and that everyone is talking about me. They may be, of course..." Horner (1993), page 22.

One observation we have made is that some individuals with ASD seek out and enjoy social interaction that occurs within a routine that they understand, and in which they can experience more social competency.

Box 4.7

Mary is a highly social person who attends a variety of social activities. One form of activity that she consistently enjoys is attending festivals of all kinds, including cultural, harvest, religious, and community celebration festivals. She attends with family members or on her own. When asked what she likes about festivals, she described that festivals are usually organized in a similar way each time. At festivals, many booths are set up and one can visit and chat with the various vendors. There are fun activities set up for children and adults that one can join. A larger area is often set aside for music and other entertainment. Mary takes notes and compares the different kinds of activities, crafts, or food that are available at the different festivals. She also loves that festivals offer fun child-oriented activities for all ages. Mary has found a leisure activity that fits her interests and provides social interaction in a format that she enjoys and feels comfortable with.

Sometimes we can mistakenly conclude that an individual with ASD dislikes social interaction. It is more likely that individuals with ASD, like the rest of us, do not enjoy social situations in which they are not sure what they are supposed to do, what is going to happen, or how to interpret the social behaviors of others.

A couple, both of whom have Asperger's Syndrome and are successful computer programmers, enjoy cycling and have participated in 700-mile cycling events and weekend cycling tours. The two share how they got started in cycling and their experience with cycling as a social activity:

Box 4.8

The husband writes: "...It [bicycling] was 'the' sport I could deal with in the pressure-packed high school years. It also appealed to me on a mechanical level—bikes are devices that have all their complexities exposed. (Plus they don't talk back!)

I've never been a 'competitive' cyclist – I do enjoy getting out and riding for hours. I've found that cyclists can be as clique-ish as the rest of the society, though. I guess I've found the 'odd' corner of the cycling world."

His wife adds: "...Some of our bike rides are with other people we know so it becomes a way of socializing for us...One thing I've noticed is that we haven't developed close relationships with people in our bicycling groups, whereas they have developed close relationships with other members in the group. We don't have friends from our biking group who we see outside bicycling group activities. I guess this is probably due to our poor social skills. This also somewhat lessens my motivation to be as heavily involved with cycling as I have been."

(Personal communications to Jane Rake), 2002.

Taken together, these accounts illustrate the importance of the social component of recreation experiences to individuals with ASD. When helping an individual with ASD to explore different recreation options, it's useful to look at the relative social ambiguity and complexity of the social context separate from the activity itself. It may be that the activity would be enjoyed, and even preferred, under certain social conditions. Or, it may be that by providing sufficient information about the social dimensions of the activity, individuals with ASD will have an entirely different experience than if left to interpret the social aspects of the activity on their own. Methods for providing social information are described in Chapter 6 and resources are listed in Appendix A.

Being Able to Modulate Sensory and Social Input during Recreation

The young adults who contributed to this chapter emphasized the importance of being able to take a break from the activity and interaction with others if they needed to. If individuals can take a break before experiencing sensory or social overload, they can regain their equilibrium and then come back to the activity. If this opportunity is not available, a recreation experience can be miserable:

> **Box 4.9**
>
> Stan's family was committed to assuring that their son had the same opportunities for recreation and leisure as other children his age. One year he was sent to Outdoor School, a weeklong overnight camp provided to all public school students in his school district. He vividly recalls trying to memorize the route the bus was taking in case he needed to get home on his own.
>
> He remembers that during that week at camp he was under "a lot of duress." At home, he would go to school and only "have to put on an act from 8 to 3," but at camp he felt that he needed to be "on" 24 hours a day, and that his peers didn't accept him. He felt trapped, with no escape and no place he could go to be alone, to "be himself."

A procedure for how an individual can take a break can be arranged before an activity:

> **Box 4.10**
>
> Ann wanted to hold a party for the young adults with ASD who had participated in her class. Tom and Joe both said they did not do well at parties and that they thought it best that they did not attend. Ann wrote them each a note with the invitation and included a little map of the layout of her home. She identified two spare bedrooms, one that would be Tom's safe haven and another that would be Joe's room to go to if he wanted to during the party. The two men decided to give the party a try. When they arrived, Ann showed each of them their "party break rooms." A sign that said "Tom" and a sign the said "Joe" marked the doors to the rooms. During the party, each man went to their party break rooms to relax on a few occasions, and then rejoined the group.

Individuals with ASD often have a great deal of difficulty with sustained social interactions, and they may need a place where they can get away from others to take a break. Affording someone the opportunity to be alone when s/he wishes can turn an experience like camp or a party from a nightmare into a manageable and even fun experience. Allowing a person with ASD as much control as possible during activities will often alleviate some of the anxiety they feel as they experience something new, and while they cope with social behaviors or expectations that they find confusing.

Negative Experiences with Peers during Recreation

Sadly, all children can be subject to teasing, bullying, and other forms of inappropriate behavior from peers. Children and youth with ASD can be especially vulnerable to these situations for several reasons. First, individuals with ASD may not read the social cues and contexts involved, and they may not realize at first that peers are making fun of them. Second, individuals with ASD tend to understand language literally, and their social naivete can result in their being duped by peers into doing things that they don't realize are inappropriate. Third, once individuals with ASD realize that they are being targeted by peers, they don't know how to ignore it, deflect it, or enlist the support of adult allies. Left with no appropriate defenses, individuals with ASD can go to extremes of avoidance or reaction, feeling that these are the only alternatives available to them.

> **Box 4.11**
>
> "...A lot of kids in my classes thought I was retarded because I looked and acted kind of weird. I got picked on a lot in junior high because I was so different. I didn't know the social rules and sometimes did strange things or made strange noises. For example, I really liked *Bugs Bunny* and *Road Runner* cartoons when I was younger. I can call up memories of things like cartoons so clearly that it is almost like playing a videocassette in my head. I used to do that and make the sound effects along with the story in my head. Other kids heard me making those noises and thought I was nuts, but I didn't know they thought that. I didn't know other kids were able to think about me, because I couldn't think about them.
>
> The thing I hated most in junior high was being teased. That was even worse than the homework. Mean kids used to try to upset me by imitating me or trying to get me in trouble. They thought it was funny that I was so 'weird.' They wanted me to act even stranger so they could laugh at me. I knew they were being mean to me, but I never could understand exactly what was happening. Sometimes, I got so frustrated that I just lost it and threw a fit. I didn't know that was what the mean kids wanted me to do.
>
> Sometimes, nice kids would try to help me when I got confused. I could usually tell who was really trying to help me, but I'm not sure how. I almost never can remember other people's names, but sometimes I could remember the names of the nice kids..."
>
> Ward & Alar, 2000, pages 232-233

Gray (2001) observes, "When children with ASD are involved, bullying frequently assumes one of two unique profiles. First, *Backhanded Bullying* involves the use of kind gestures or statements with the intent to mislead. Another type of bullying, *Absurd Information and Requests* involves the use of directives to engage in out-of-context, silly, or inappropriate activities, gestures or tasks. Both forms seem to capitalize on factors directly related to ASD; for example, their limited friendships and tendency to interpret information literally...." (Page iii). Examples of these types of bullying are in Figure 4.3.

Figure 4.3
Examples of Bullying

Example of Backhanded Bullying:

Seth, a 13 year old with ASD, loved the city's basketball team and knew the team's statistics in great detail. A few boys in the school would engage him in talking about the team and then intentionally say something outlandish and incorrect about the team. Seth would correct them, they would disagree, and Seth would become upset. Seth did not understand that the boys were pretending to disagree with the facts in order to get him to react. The boys did this repeatedly in order to upset Seth.

Example of Absurd Information and Requests:

On the playground a group of 11 year old girls were telling an off-color joke. Linda, a girl with ASD, memorized the joke quickly. The girls told Linda the boys would like it if she told them the joke. Later in class, Linda told the joke to classmates and the teacher overheard. The teacher criticized Linda for telling an inappropriate joke.

The adults with ASD who contributed to this chapter could recount negative experiences with peers in and out of school. It's critical that recreation providers are aware of the potential vulnerability of individuals with ASD to peer manipulation. At the same time, recreation providers can take steps to prevent and minimize these occurrences, using a three-pronged approach.

First and foremost, it is important to establish clear guidelines on acceptable behavior in a recreation setting. Developing ground rules as a group for how to treat each other and interact with each other is the first activity that should occur in a new class or program. The instructor and participants can construct a list of ground rules or guidelines together. These should be posted in the area and referred to as needed. In the guidelines it should be clear what an individual does if they experience or witness behavior that is not in accordance with the guidelines.

The second strategy to reduce the impact of teasing is to provide the individual with ASD skills for coping with it. Gray (2000, 2001) has developed an excellent set of strategies to help an individual with ASD know what to do when teased or bullied and to help adults know how to be problem solvers and allies. The materials include a curriculum that uses visual teaching methods to present social information about teasing, such as how to recognize teasing, clear steps for responding to it, and role-play scenarios for practicing appropriate responses. In addition, the guide for parents and professionals offers many solutions and ways to approach the issue as a team effectively.

Third, the individual with ASD may choose to share information about the challenges he may experience in the class with the other participants. The choice to disclose this information to other participants depends on the nature of the activity, the composition of the group, and the wishes of the participant with ASD and their family. An individual with ASD can also choose to be present and talk, with supportive allies present, or to let someone else provide information to peers.

> "…In both grade school and junior high, my mom came to school at the beginning of the year and talked to both the students and the teachers about autism and about me. I think that helped everyone understand me better. I especially liked it when she talked about all the things I am good at. I noticed the teasing was less once the other kids better understood autism and its effect on me…"
>
> Ward & Alar, 2000, pages 232-233

Box 4.12

It's important for parents, friends, and recreation providers to help the individual with ASD consider the advantages and disadvantages of disclosure so that he or she can make as informed a choice as possible.

> Mary, an adult with Asperger's Syndrome, has been employed as a special education assistant in public schools for five years. In her work setting, she has learned to request workplace accommodations (that allow her to use her abilities and function more effectively on the job) such as written instructions, social information, and diagrams that show the relationship between each person's role in the workplace.
>
> For recreation, she enjoys volunteering as an adult assistant in organized youth activities. She has volunteered in general and specialized camps as well as evening and weekend youth recreation programs. Deciding what to disclose to the leaders of these programs with regard to her ASD and the accommodations that she may need, has been the challenging aspect of her volunteer work.
>
> At first, she chose not to disclose her Asperger's Syndrome because she knew that she risked being viewed as "different." But this choice led to misunderstandings and unsuccessful experiences.
>
> At other times, Mary has chosen to meet with the leader of a youth program where she wants to volunteer. She informed the leaders about Asperger's Syndrome, explained her particular challenges, and described her skills as an educational assistant in the schools and the accommodations that make her effective at work.
>
> Mary loves volunteering in youth recreation programs and her dedication helps her face and overcome challenges. Once when she was leading a group of children in an activity, some of the children began to make fun of her. Rather than quitting her volunteer work, she consulted with adult friends to determine what kinds of recreation programs would support her strengths and allow her to contribute and succeed. For example, Mary is skillful in facilitating the inclusion of children with disabilities into activities with their peers.
>
> Disclosure is usually anxiety-producing for Mary. She has had the painful experience of having her confidential information shared with others without her permission. Mary knows that disclosure is a risk, but, then again, so is nondisclosure. At this point, as she finds her way through the adult social world, Mary has decided that she will live with the risk of disclosure and find the recreation leaders and programs where she will be valued as a volunteer so that she can do what she loves.

Box 4.13

If information about ASD is delivered skillfully, most participants will interact with the individual with ASD with better understanding, and they will become allies and supports. Others may be curious or uncomfortable until they have time to observe the participant with ASD. "Circle of Friends" (Perske; 1998, Whitaker, et. al. 1998) is an approach often used to share information on a child's disabilities with peers to develop peer empathy, and to gather peers' own insights and ideas about how to support an individual with a disability. Children and youth can be more insightful and creative than adults about inclusive strategies (Staub & Peck, 1995; Brannan, et al in press). In chapter 10, methods that inclusive camp programs used to explain ASD and Asperger's Syndrome to peers are described.

Summary

Several topics are addressed in this chapter related to recreation and individuals with ASD. Descriptions of the experience of ASD from young adults with ASD were shared. These first-hand accounts help recreation providers understand how ASD impacts sensory, cognitive, and social functioning. Like the general population, individuals with ASD choose a broad range of leisure activities. A strength of individuals with ASD is their ability to focus on and sustain an interest. These interests can evolve into highly satisfying leisure pursuits that may also provide a shared context for social interaction with others.

Some of the particular challenges associated with the sensory and social components of recreation for individuals with ASD were explored. In order to cope with too much sensory or social input, individuals with ASD sometimes need to take a break from an activity to regain their equilibrium.

Some of the experiences individuals with ASD have had in organized recreation activities were discussed. Without sufficient information, recreation instructors/leaders can misinterpret the actions of an individual with ASD and respond in ways that hinder participation.

Although the individuals with ASD may have difficulty communicating their needs, their self-knowledge of what will assist them to learn or participate is highly valuable in developing effective accommodations. Thus, it is vital that recreation providers persist in finding ways to interpret the underlying meaning of an individual's words or behaviors and that they respect and use an individual's self-knowledge.

Also addressed were the possibility of individuals with ASD having negative experiences with peers in a recreation setting and the strategies that will prevent or minimize such experiences. Lastly, the issues involved in disclosing to other participants that one has ASD were discussed.

These are a few of the issues that our group of young adults with ASD raised as they considered their recreation experiences and their search for leisure pursuits that add meaning to their lives. In many ways, the current generation of adults with ASD are pathfinders and pioneers. As they pursue a life of joy and meaning of their own making, they open doors and invite others to understand the challenges and strengths associated with ASD.

Once those without ASD step beyond their initial impressions, they find that individuals with ASD are refreshingly authentic, true to themselves and that they lack pretense. Willey (1999), a woman diagnosed with Asperger's Syndrome, a form of ASD, wrote a personal account of her experiences. She referred to herself as an Aspie, in order to create a self-reference without the negative connotations associated with a syndrome. Attwood and Gray (1999), two professionals in the area of ASD, described the positive qualities of the social interaction of Aspies found in Figure 4.4.

Figure 4.4
Qualities of Social Interaction with "Aspies" Described by Attwood & Gray

[*Aspies* are characterized by...] ...a qualitative *advantage* in social interaction, as manifested by a majority of the following:

(1)   Peer relationships characterized by absolute loyalty and impeccable dependability
(2)   Free of sexist, "age-ist," or cultural biases; ability to regard others at "face value"
(3)   Speaking one's mind irrespective of social context or adherence to personal beliefs
(4)   Ability to pursue personal theory or perspective despite conflicting evidence
(5)   Seeking an audience or friends capable of enthusiasm for unique interests and topics
(6)   Listening without continual judgement or assumption
(7)   Interested primarily in significant contributions to conversations; preferring to avoid "ritualistic small talk" or socially trivial statements and superficial conversation
(8)   Seeking sincere, positive, genuine friends with an unassuming sense of humor

Attwood & Gray, 1999, page 3.

Chapter Five

Planning Participation in Recreation for Persons with Autism Spectrum Disorder

Phyllis Coyne

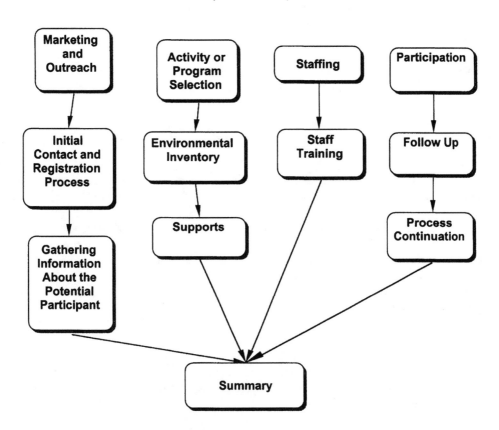

Although many professionals and volunteers want to facilitate recreation participation for individuals with Autism Spectrum Disorder (ASD), they may have limited ideas or not know how to adequately prepare for and provide effective recreation opportunities. In addition, families or caregivers may be emotionally stretched to the limit, because of the many challenges that result from supporting an individual with ASD. To ensure success, the approach to participation must be systematic and planful. The following steps for planning participation in recreation for persons with ASD can greatly enhance successful participation. The size, staffing pattern, and purpose of the program that provides recreation services will determine the particular process for each of these steps.

- Marketing and Outreach
- Initial contact and registration process. The application is reviewed and the individual is registered.
- Gathering information about the potential participant. The individual with ASD and/or the parents/caregivers are contacted to discuss interests, questions, concerns, and requests for specific accommodations.
- Activity or program selection. A suitable program and recreation activity is identified.
- Environmental inventory. The recreation environment is surveyed to determine any factors that may require modifications and/or accommodations, as well as preparation needed by staff and participant.
- Supports. The need for accommodations and/or companions is determined and provided.
- Training. Staff and companions are given information and training on individuals with ASD, as well as any relevant information on the participant.
- Participation. After program staff and the companion have received training and information, the individual is prepared for participation and begins to join in the activity or program.
- Follow up. The Leisure Coordinator or companion appraises the degree of success of the accommodations and participation on an ongoing basis.
- Process continuation. Staff and companions stay in touch with the individual and/or parents/caregivers to encourage involvement in other programs.

Marketing and Outreach

Many individuals with ASD and their parents/caregivers have had unpleasant experiences in community settings, because these participants with ASD were misunderstood and supports for participation were lacking. They may be very apprehensive about the risk of yet another failure in the community and may, additionally, have ambivalence about the importance of community recreation involvement. Overcoming the fear of the unknown may be a major challenge. Some may appear to want a guarantee of success. Others may withhold information about their situation because of a fear of rejection by a program. Program staff may need to help individuals with ASD and their families to develop confidence in the program.

Box 5.1

Three of Catherine's four sons have ASD. Because her oldest son, who is now 20 years old, has experienced various forms of discrimination over the years, she is uncomfortable telling programs about her sons' disability before they are enrolled in a program. She still believes that programs will tell her that they are full, if she reveals hers sons' special needs before they are enrolled. After they are enrolled, she always provides a leisure companion who is familiar with their individual needs to ensure that her sons are successful.

Flyers and brochures that are posted at schools, libraries, neighborhood stores or other community locations can increase awareness of recreation opportunities. However, many potential participants with ASD, as well as parents/caregivers, may not believe that these opportunities apply to them, particularly if they are generic programs. They may only pay attention to flyers that say AUTISM in big letters. They may not know that effective approaches to recreation participation can occur in a variety of settings. However, a growing number of potential participants and parents/caregivers are inquiring about participation. Even flyers and brochures for generic programs should provide a general statement regarding ADA compliance, such as "Please call in advance of programs if you require an accommodation" to inform the public that they will address special needs.

Outreach to such organizations as schools, special education departments, parent groups, membership organizations, such as the local chapter of the Autism Society of America, churches, group homes, and other human service agencies can increase participation. Press releases may be an effective means to inform potential participants.

Specialized or membership programs often have a participant or membership list that is the basis for mailings. These generally alert those with ASD, who are already involved in the program, about upcoming events. A number of agencies have developed a consistent design that helps participants in their groups to recognize the mailing. For instance, The Arc of Multnomah County, Oregon mails out a monthly activity list on the same colored paper with a tie dye design to make their mailing distinct from others. This type of mailing is particularly appealing to those with ASD, because of its predictability and familiarity. Many programs list the instructor, because participants with ASD might come to a new activity if they know the instructor.

In the end, the best advertisement is perhaps through "word of mouth" and positive experiences.

Initial Contact and Registration Process

Requests to participate in activities are made in a variety of ways. Although the majority of contacts are either self-initiated or initiated by a family member or advocate, outside-agency referrals also occur and offer an opportunity for collaboration that will help create the most success and enjoyment.

Most programs have a general application or registration form. A statement is often added to the brochures and application forms to alert the program if they will have a participant who has special needs. These are usually general statements that will require follow up. Although someone else may answer for the person with ASD, some agencies are committed to facilitating self-determination and may word the statement in a manner that respects the person's participation in all stages of participation, such as "Do you need special assistance? Please call the director and discuss how the program can best help you to have a positive experience. We'll probably ask you to help us further by providing information about you and your needs" (Portland Bureau of Parks and Recreation, 2002).

Sometimes adequate information is available to proceed with registration at that time. However, more information is usually needed to plan for the participation of an individual with ASD.

Gathering Information about the Potential Participant

Assessment or gathering information about the potential participant may be done through a more informal or more systematic process depending on the program's size, staffing, and time constraints. However, gathering information about the potential participant is critical to the selection of recreation activities that match the unique needs and interests of the individual with ASD. In addition, it provides the foundation for making decisions about programs, activities and accommodations. Gathering information will save time and frustration for both individuals with ASD and people who want to facilitate their recreation participation.

Programs cannot just assume that the behaviors of an individual with ASD are too severe to be included successfully into the program. The ADA specifies that an individualized assessment must be done to determine if the particular needs of the individual can be met without fundamentally altering the program. Program providers must be careful not to base decisions on preconceptions or stereotypes about what individuals with ASD can or cannot do, or how much assistance these participants may require.

Leisure assessment does not need to be complicated. Parents/caregivers and others who know the potential participants well, in addition to the individual, have important information to help determine appropriate programs, activities and accommodations.

Many recreation agencies have guidelines regarding information to be gathered when they will have a participant with special needs. Often these do not cover critical areas for individuals with ASD. Given the characteristics of ASD and how it can affect participation, it is recommended that information be gathered regarding preferences and talents, how the person understands and uses communication, social skills, group skills, community skills, reactions to change, reactions to sensory input, behavior challenges, and needed accommodations. Behavioral difficulties must be considered since they affect both the participant's functioning and considerations for accommodations. In some situations, not all these areas may be relevant, and in other situations there may not be time to gather complete information. While the focus is on recreation, it is also crucial to consider anything that will impinge upon the ability of the individual with ASD to carry out a leisure activity. However, many of these are a necessary part of leisure participation and can be taught or enhanced through recreation participation.

Figure 5.1 provides a list of questions in critical areas of assessment for participants with ASD. Recreation providers can chose key questions for their setting from those listed to determine appropriate accommodations.

Methods of Gathering Information

There are a variety of ways to attain the necessary information on preferences, communication, social skills, groups skills, community skills, reactions to change, reactions to sensory input, behavior challenges, and needed accommodations. These include participant information forms, interviews with the participant, interviews with parents/caregivers, and direct observation. The size of the facility and amount of staff available will determine whether or not to use one or more of these methods. The reader is encouraged to select the methods that are most useful in individual situations.

Figure 5.1
Questions for Planning Supports

Preferences. It is important to know what the participant likes to assist them to have fun and to motivate them to participate.

What are the participant's:

❑ Sensory preferences?
❑ Favorite activities?
❑ Interests?
❑ Special talents?
❑ Skills that will enhance the learning of a new activity?
❑ Favorite objects and food?
❑ Favorite people?

Communication skills. Understanding how the participant understands and uses communication is vital to successful participation.

❑ Can the participant follow one or two step verbal directions with gestures in a novel activity?
❑ How long does it take for the participant to process auditory information and to shift attention?
❑ Does the participant need visual cues through writing, pictures or models?
❑ How does the participant request objects, activities, more or help?
❑ How does the participant refuse and protest?
❑ How does the participant express emotions?

Social skills. The social skill difficulties of individuals with ASD must be supported in recreation settings.

❑ How does the participant respond to those of the same age? Older? Younger?
❑ Can the participant share close proximity with other participants?
❑ Can the participant share materials or does s/he need own?
❑ Can the participant take turns?
❑ How does the participant respond to losing a game?

Group skills. Since most community recreation participation involves others, it is vital to know how the participant is in a group situation.

❑ How long is the participant generally able to attend in a group situation?
❑ How long is the participant generally able to participate in a group situation?
❑ Does the participant imitate the actions of others after a demonstration?
❑ Does the participant know how to wait and walk in a line?
❑ Does the participant stay with the group?
❑ What size group is the participant most comfortable in?

Continued

Figure 5.1 Continued
Questions for Planning Supports

Community skills. Other community skills may be required for participation in recreation activities and may require accommodations.

❑ Does the participant know how to cross streets safely?
❑ Does the participant have a general sense of danger?
❑ Does the participant know how to use money?
❑ Can the participant tell time?
❑ Do family members or support staff always set up or start activities?

Reactions to change. Many individuals with ASD react strongly to change; therefore, it is important to anticipate and prepare for areas of change that may be intolerable to the participant with ASD.

How does the participant react to:
❑ Wearing different clothes?
❑ Small schedule changes?
❑ Change in activity?
❑ Change in locations of activity?
❑ Staff being absent?
❑ Friend or companion being absent?
❑ Family member or friend being late or not coming?
❑ Anticipating an event or activity?
❑ Cancellation of an event or activity?

Sensory reactions. Individuals with ASD may seek out or avoid sensory information in unusual ways that are important to understand.

Does the participant seek out any sensory input, such as movement, scents, textures, etc?
How does the participant react to:
❑ Crowds?
❑ Noise?
❑ Unexpected sounds?
❑ Being surrounded by too much movement?
❑ Being surrounded by competing visual stimuli?
❑ Not having enough space?
❑ Being touched?
❑ Various textures?
❑ Aromas?
❑ Other distracters?

Behavioral challenges. Behavioral difficulties must be considered since they affect both the participant's functioning and considerations for accommodations.

❑ How are emotions such as frustration or confusion shown?
❑ Are there any stressors and triggers for the participant?
❑ Are there any trigger words?

Continued

Figure 5.1 Continued
Questions for Planning Supports

❏ Does the participant have any unusual fears?
❏ Does the participant have any strong dislikes?
❏ Does the participant touch others inappropriately?
❏ Does the participant aggress toward him/herself or others? Under what conditions has this occurred?

How does the participant react to:
❏ Not being understood?
❏ Not understanding?
❏ Not having choices?
❏ Making a mistake?
❏ Having to wait too long?
❏ Losing things of value?
❏ Being corrected?
❏ Being denied?
❏ Being interrupted?
❏ Being teased?

Needed accommodations. In many cases, structure and systems that are used in other parts of the participant's life that will be appropriate in recreation settings.

❏ What are effective strategies for calming the participant?
❏ What amount of staff support is required, e.g., adult or more natural support from a peer?
❏ What visual supports, such as schedules, checklists, templates, etc., have been effective?
❏ What communication approaches are most effective?
❏ What is the best way to teach something new?

Participant Information Form

Parks and recreation departments, specialized camps and other organizations that frequently have participants with disabilities often develop a participant information form to gather specific information about an individual and his or her needs. These forms usually include:

• participant information, such as name and address
• emergency information, such as contact person for emergencies and physician
• disability(s) and medical information
• mobility information
• personal care information
• dietary information
• safety information
• communication information
• behavior/personality information
• swimming information, and
• release of information for medical treatment, prescription medication, and photos.

These forms may be part of the initial registration process for specialized programs or be used in the next phase of registration in generic programs.

Questions that are short, concise, easy to read, and require only a simple checkmark or circle to answer usually are completed the most thoroughly by registrants. These forms usually gather excellent information, but the participant and/or parent/caregiver will usually need to be contacted to clarify information, as well as to discuss questions, concerns, accommodation requests and any other necessary information regarding the participant.

Since most programs do not serve individuals with ASD exclusively, participant information forms seldom gather information regarding all the areas in Figure 5.1. However, much useful information is provided related to individual participants with ASD on most of these participant information forms. Figure 5.2 highlights questions particularly relevant to participants with ASD from the Participant Information and Medical Form from the City of Eugene (Oregon) Recreation Services. More details about this program can be found in Chapter 8.

Figure 5.2
Sample Questions from Participant Information and Medical Form

***Please answer the questions in the remaining sections only if they are applicable to you and/or could be helpful to our staff. Otherwise, please skip to the Release of Information Section. ***

PERSONAL CARE INFORMATION

Yes   No Needs assistance in the bathroom
Yes   No Needs help locating personal clothing
Yes   No Needs assistance in eating
Yes   No Needs assistance in dressing

DIETARY INFORMATION

Do you have a special diet, dietary restrictions, or any food that may cause behavioral change?
Yes   No   If yes, please explain:

Do you have any issues around food that we need to be aware of?   Yes   No
If yes, please explain:

SAFETY INFORMATION

Yes	No	Stays with the group	Yes	No	Wanders or leaves a group
Yes	No	Responsible for your belongings	Yes	No	Will take others' belongings
Yes	No	Independent in the community	Yes	No	Cannot be left alone
Yes	No	Will ask for assistance	Yes	No	Unable to express needs
Yes	No	Can recognize danger	Yes	No	Puts self at risk

Please use the following space to explain any of the above or provide us any additional information that may be helpful:

_____

Continued

Figure 5.2 Continued
Sample Questions from Participant Information and Medical Form

COMMUNICATION INFORMATION
Is English your primary language?   Yes   No
If no, what is your primary language?

Do you use verbal language? If yes, please skip to the next section. Yes   No
What is your primary form of language?
Communication board   Sign language   Pictures   Other
Please explain:_____

Please use the following space to provide any information that would be helpful in communicating with you: _____

BEHAVIOR/PERSONALITY INFORMATION
Explain methods or ways that encourage or motivate you to fully participate:_____

Describe any fears or issues that might explain your unwillingness to engage in certain activities:

_____

_____

Are there any settings or activities that might cause distress or unease for you such as noise, machines, lights, smells, animals, etc.?

_____

Please indicate anything else that we need to be aware of concerning stimuli or conditions that could adversely affect your well being or ability to enjoy activities:
_____

_____

_____

SWIMMING INFORMATION
Yes No Needs 1:1 assistance in the water Yes No Independent and safe in the water
Yes No Needs flotation vest for safety   Yes No Comfortable in the water
Yes No Able to swim/move in the water   Yes No Can swim 25 yards unassisted

(From Participant Information and Medical Form (2002) Eugene, OR: City of Eugene Recreation Services. Used with permission.)

Organizations may need to ask additional questions that are specific to individuals with ASD to determine the types of supports that will be needed for an individual. Figure 5.3 provides sample questions from the Autism Society of North Carolina (ASNC) Summer Camp Information Forms that may be critical for participants with ASD. Because the organization specializes in ASD, the forms they have developed are customized to gather information related to ASD and recreation participation.

Some organizations, particularly specialized camps, get a release of information to talk with special education teachers or residential providers of individuals with ASD to get additional information. The Autism Society of North Carolina gathers information from

---

Figure 5.3
Selected Sections from ASNC Summer Camp
PROGRAM INFORMATION FORMS

_____ will be attending a week of residential camp at the Autism Society of North Carolina Summer Camp. It would be very helpful to the camp staff if you would take the time to complete this form. Please respond with detailed, specific answers. The more we know about your camper, the better we can prepare to make his/her stay at camp as enjoyable as possible. <u>Please attach a copy of your camper's most current behavior program, daily schedule, etc.</u> Any information you can give us regarding him/her would be greatly appreciated. THANK YOU!

INSTRUCTIONS: Please check the appropriate description(s) for each item. You may check more than one. Feel free to use additional sheets of paper.

SCHEDULES

Which types of schedules work best with your camper?

A. _____ Written Schedule   B. _____ Full Day
   _____ Line Drawing Schedule   _____ Day
   _____ Photo Schedule   _____ 2-3 Events at a Time
   _____ Object Schedule   _____ 1 Event at a Time

Additional Information: _____

_____

COMMUNICATION

Receptive   Expressive
_____ Sentences   _____ Sentences
_____ Short phrases   _____ Short phrases
_____ One word   _____ One word
_____ Signs   _____ Signs
_____ Gestures   _____ Gestures
_____ Reads sentences   _____ Writing
_____ Reads 2-3 word phrases   _____ Pictures
_____ Reads single words
_____ Pictures

Additional Information: _____

_____

Continued

Figure 5.3 Continued
Selected Sections from ASNC Summer Camp Forms

REINFORCEMENT

Reinforcers:

_____ Edibles (food or drink)
_____ Music
_____ Tokens
_____ Particular object
_____ Preferred activity

Schedule of Reinforcement:

_____ Fixed time interval (i.e., every 2 min)
_____ Completion of task or activity
_____ End of day
_____ End of time period

Please describe manner of reinforcement: _____
_____

BEHAVIORS

This section is very important and we ask for as much information as you can provide. Please specify the consequences for the behavior (for example, tightening the structure, redirection, withholding reinforcement, time out, etc.). We ask that a copy of the behavior program be attached to this form, underlined: particularly if an aversive procedure is being used. If the behavior program should change after you have returned this form, please send an addendum to the camp program (your local TEACCH Center can help with this). If the behavior program is dependent on any specific materials (data sheets, tokens, favorite object, visual system, etc.), please send the materials to camp.

Behavior	Consequence
Throwing materials	_____
Running away	_____
Hitting others	_____
Spitting	_____
Kicking others	_____
Biting others	_____
Self-Injury	_____
Screaming	_____
Refusing activity	_____
Other:	_____

What warning signal(s) indicate that the behavior will occur?_____
_____
_____
_____
_____

ADDITIONAL INFORMATION

Please check either "yes" or "no" to the following questions and explain as needed.

___yes ___no   Can the camper ask for help?**
___yes ___no   Is the camper upset by changes in the routine?
___yes ___no   Is the camper upset by changes in the environment?
___yes ___no   Does changing the staff working with him/her upset the camper?
___yes ___no   Does a warning of change help the camper deal with the change?
___yes ___no   Is a transitional cue or signal used?**
___yes ___no   Does the camper communicate a dislike?**

Continued

Figure 5.3 Continued
Selected Sections from ASNC Summer Camp Forms

___yes ___no Does the camper communicate an illness?**
___yes ___no Does working closely to other people bother the camper?
___yes ___no Is the camper bothered by excessive noises?
___yes ___no Does the camper have a particular fear?**
**Please explain: _____

_____

_____

_____

INDOOR AND OUTDOOR / GYM ACTIVITIES PREFERRED BY CAMPER

Please fill out the two attached forms. These forms will be given to the camp Activity Directors who are responsible for planning events. As much information as you can provide them will be greatly appreciated.

1.   Bathing

_____ camper willingly takes showers
_____ camper resists showering
_____ camper takes only baths
_____ camper resists bathing
_____ camper needs assistance showering/bathing
_____ camper needs assistance washing hair
_____ camper needs assistance drying hair
_____ camper is completely independent bathing

How long does your camper's bathing routine typically take?_____

_____

Please describe your camper's usual bathing routine or any special assistance he/she may need: _____

_____

2.   Bedtime

_____ camper goes to sleep with no problems
_____ camper sleeps soundly until morning
_____ camper sleeps little, wakes up easily during the night
_____ camper gets out of bed frequently during the night
_____ camper makes lots of noise at night
_____ camper needs private room in order to sleep well
_____ camper should sleep fine in a large room with up to 8-11 other campers
_____ camper sleeps with light on

Continued

Figure 5.3 Continued
Selected Sections from ASNC Summer Camp Forms

Does your camper need to be taken to the restroom during the night? _____ Yes _____ No
If yes, how often?
_____

What do you do if your camper wets the bed?
_____

What is your camper's normal bedtime routine?—————————————————————
_____

BEHAVIORS

Please indicate how often, if ever, your camper does the following behaviors and the consequences. We must have accurate information about your camper's behaviors and how to respond to them.

Behavior	Never	Seldom	Often	What you do when this occurs?
Camper scratches, pinches, bites, or hits self				
Camper bangs own head				
Camper scratches, pinches, bites, or hits others				
Camper grabs other people				
Camper touches others inappropriately				
Camper throws things				
Camper gets into personal belongings				
Camper runs away				
Camper climbs on furniture				
Camper uses inappropriate language				
Camper spits on others				
Camper dumps liquids				
Camper strips own clothing				
Camper exposes self in public				
Camper masturbates inappropriately				

Continued

Figure 5.3 Continued
Selected Sections from ASNC Summer Camp Forms

Please describe in more detail these behaviors or any other behaviors that you do not want your camper to do and explain how you want the camp staff to deal with them:

Behavior   Consequences
Example: Camper throws objects   Must pick up object and return to proper place

_____   _____

_____   _____

_____   _____

EMOTIONAL RESPONSES

___camper prefers to be by self   ___camper clings to other people
___camper does not like to be touched   ___camper gets upset if the routine changes
___camper cries for no apparent reasons ___camper laughs for no apparent reason
___camper is bothered by excessive noise

Please list things that scare or upset your camper: _____

_____

Please describe what helps to calm your camper when he/she is sad, hurt, afraid, or otherwise upset:_____

_____

SENSORY RESPONSES

Please indicate your camper's reaction to the following sensory input if the response is unusual:

	Over reacts	Under reacts	Comments
Visual stimulation Lights			
Sunlight			
Heat			
Touch			
Thunderstorms			
Pain			
Animals			
Sounds			
Voices			

Continued

Figure 5.3 Continued
Selected Sections from ASNC Summer Camp Forms

Please note other sensitivities or provide additional information: _____

_____

ACTIVITY LEVELS

_____ camper has typical attention span and level of activity for his/her age
_____ camper has a very short attention span
_____ camper is less active/needs motivation to participate
_____ camper is overactive
_____ camper is easily distracted by sights, sounds, people, etc.

Please describe how you manage your camper's activity level; motivate him/her to participate, etc: _____

_____ Camper will do fine working at a table with several others.

_____ Camper needs to have his/her own personal work area separate from others to be
successful.

What else should we know about your camper to make his/her camping experience a great
one? Please use as much additional paper as you need. The more we know about your
camper's likes, dislikes, skills and needs, the better we can serve them.

(Selected items from Autism Society of North Carolina (2000) Summer Camp Program
Information Form and Summer Camp Current Information Form. Moncure, NC: Camp
Royall. Used with permission.)

---

the camper's teacher or day program supervisor, as well as from parents or caregivers.
Many organizations have developed an additional participant information form for completion by staff who work with the individual in educational and/or residential settings. Figure 5.3 includes items from this type of form. More details on the Autism Society of North
Carolina's Summer Camp are provided in Chapter 10.

Gathering Information from the Potential Participant

Recreation participation should have a strong element of self-determination, with
opportunity to make informed choices, set personal goals, and take initiative to achieve
them. Sometimes individuals with ASD already have a specific activity in mind, but their
choices may be restricted by limited experience with leisure activities and choice making.
These individuals may have difficulty identifying or choosing recreation and leisure activities.

Gathering information from verbal participants with ASD. The potential participant is the ultimate source of information regarding his or her preferences and non-
preferences. When possible, the individual should be interviewed by a person whom the
individual knows well during a time that s/he is used to responding to questions and/or
making choices. It should begin with an explanation at the potential participant's level of
comprehension of the purpose of the interview, what will happen and how long it will take.

Since the semantic and pragmatic challenges of ASD cause difficulties in answering questions for even the most verbal person with ASD, the interview needs to be carefully structured. Providing information about the interview and the questions before the interview can help prepare the participant with ASD. A written or pictorial mini-schedule, such as those described in Chapter 6, a timer, and/or a written list of questions that are checked off as questions are answered may help the individual to answer the questions. Changing the questions to a request form can make the type of response desired clearer. For instance, rather than asking, "What do you like to do?" which may appear amorphous to an individual with ASD, the interviewer might delimit and clarify the information desired by saying, "Tell me three things that you like to do for fun." Figure 5.4 provides sample request statements that may be useful when interviewing a potential participant with ASD.

Figure 5.4
Sample Request Statements for Interviews

- Tell me three things that you like to do.
- Tell me one thing that you do really well.
- Tell me one thing that you like to do with your mother, father, sister, or brother.
- Tell me two things that you do at home for fun.
- Tell me one thing that you like to do in physical education.
- Tell me one thing that you would like to learn.

(Coyne, P., Nyberg, C., Vandenburg, M. L. (1999). *Developing Leisure Time Skills for Persons with Autism. Arlington, TX: Future Horizons.* Used with permission.)

The anxiety of being "put on the spot" may make it difficult for some individuals with ASD to respond to these requests. Those who write may respond better by giving written answers or preparing their answers ahead. For some, the responses may be the most complete, if they are written during a time when they are used to writing new information, such as language arts time at school. For others language arts time may be associated with demands and, thus, they will respond better during free time.

The nature of the requests in Figure 5.4 may still be too open for some verbal individuals with ASD. Because of the difficulty in answering questions and the limited recreation experiences of many individuals with ASD, many programs use a written list of recreation activities for individuals who can read. The person indicates with an X if it is an activity that s/he 1) Presently does, and/or 2) is interested in doing. An example of this type of Leisure Interest Survey can be found in Schleien et. al (1997).

Box 5.2 The Arc of Multnomah County, Oregon developed a written checklist, "Checklist for Customer Interests," to assess the interest of members and for program development. The results from this checklist are put in a database of all participants and can be used to help members to find companions who are interested in the same activity(s).

Gathering information from nonverbal potential participants. It can be difficult to determine the preferences of nonverbal and minimally responsive individuals with ASD. Pictures of activities may help to generate responses. Some individuals with ASD who are nonverbal can choose and point to pictures when asked about interests or certain aspects of the picture. For others, interest is indicated subtly, such as leaning forward in the chair to get a better look at a picture, pausing to look longer at another picture, or a positive facial expression.

In general, it is important that the pictures used for indicating recreation choices only show the activity with limited background, so that these individuals are not confused or distracted by irrelevant details in the picture. This can easily be controlled through the use of uncolored line drawings.

> **Box 5.3**
>
> Eli eagerly looked at the photos of activities and handed the interviewer a picture of a boy at a swimming pool. He was subsequently enrolled in a swimming class. At the first class, he started screaming and tore up his swimming trunks in the locker room at the swimming pool. In the photo, the boy's swim trunks were red and his were blue. Red is Eli's favorite color and he had chosen the picture because of the red trunks the boy was wearing.

Many recreation providers develop their own series of pictures to represent activities that they can provide. A number of companies have developed line drawings of activities to aid in identifying activities of interest. Sources for these are presented in the Appendix. However, not everyone with ASD will understand the symbolic meaning of a picture of an activity. The ability to respond may also be hampered by limited knowledge of the activities presented.

> **Box 5.4**
>
> To assess interests in recreation activities, The Arc of Multnomah County, Oregon uses a book with pictures of a variety of recreation activities. Individuals are asked, "What have you done?" and "What would you like to do?" As activities are identified from the book, a small personalized book of activities of interest is developed for the individual. This personalized book with pictures of desired leisure activities can be used as a choice book, as well as to provide the individual with ASD with a means to tell others about their interests.

The next area of inquiry is to determine more specifically what the person is interested in doing related to that activity. For instance, does pointing to a picture of a drum mean that the person wants to play the drum, or likes to listen to drums, or both? Or does it mean the person likes to roll round objects?

Gathering Information from the Parent/Caregiver

Talking with people who know the person well, such as a family member, friends, teachers, residence staff, and others to gather information about favorite activities, strengths, interests and needs is important to ensure the needed information is attained. These individuals usually have invaluable information. This is also a time to start building rapport for future collaboration and teaming on behalf of the individual with ASD.

Interview with parent/caregiver. A structured interview with parent(s) and/or others who know the individual well can gather valuable information efficiently in an hour or less. Sometimes when a parent or other caregiver is not available for a face-to-face interview, an alternative method, such as a telephone interview, may be necessary.

Coyne (1980) found that information reported by parents/caregivers in a structured interview was 90 percent in agreement with those from behavior observations of performance and a reliable indicator of interests, behaviors and skills. In addition to being a reliable source of information, parents/caregivers usually are the people who know the most about the individual with ASD.

Parents/caregivers may be hesitant to share information that can be misunderstood and used to reject their dependents. Since it is important to dialogue honestly about the potential participant, taking time to provide reassurance and develop trust may be necessary. The key questions presented in Figure 5.1 can be used as a guide to questions to interview a parent.

Two types of questions can be asked in an interview: closed-ended and open-ended questions. A mixture of both types of questions, such as those in Figure 5.1, is good. Closed-ended questions, such as "Does he like physical activity or more sedentary activities?" give little flexibility and are best used to get an initial response. The interviewer should ask open-ended questions to gather additional information.

Open-ended questions, e.g., "What does s/he like to do?" do not presuppose an answer. It is good for individual interviews, but may be time consuming. Figure 5.5 provides some additional examples of open-ended questions that may be asked during an interview with parents or caregivers to get a general idea about the potential participant's functioning during leisure.

Figure 5.5
Sample Open-Ended Questions to Introduce Areas of Inquiry

What does your son/daughter do during unstructured time at home? school? community settings?
What special interests does your son/daughter have?
How does s/he express interest?
Describe what s/he does in that activity.
How often does s/he do that activity? How long?
Where does s/he do that activity?
Who does s/he do the activity with?
How does s/he get involved in the activity?
What activities does your son/daughter resist or avoid?
What new activities would you like your son/daughter to participate in?
What has kept your son/daughter from being involved in this in the past?
What questions or concerns do you have?

The information generated from these questions helps guide decision making. Knowing what an individual actually does in an activity is important because it indicates skill level and type of interest. For instance, if basketball is listed as a special interest, it could mean throwing a basketball in the air and catching it, bouncing it, throwing it into a basketball hoop, playing Hoop with one or more peers, or playing regular basketball. Each of these represents different skill levels in a variety of areas.

Direct Observation

At times, no one who knows the individual with ASD well may be available to answer questions about the person, or those involved may have limited information. Because the individual with ASD may express likes and dislikes in ways that are not readily understood, even those who know him or her well may not know what recreation activities might be of interest. In this case, direct observation of the individual with ASD, during exposure to current and/or new activities, can be used to gather information. It is important to know what materials the potential participant shows interest in now and what is done with the materials even if s/he does not know how to use the materials. Leisure preferences may be demonstrated by an attraction to certain types of materials (e.g., prefers round objects, toys that move, realistic replicas), types of interactions with materials (e.g., prefers to spin toys, line up toys, conventional object use), choice of activities (e.g., prefers rough-housing, quiet play, constructive play), and choice of leisure companions (prefers no one in particular, one or more peers). Identifying the types of materials, interactions with the materials, choice of activities and choice of companions provides vital information to creatively identify potential activities for enjoyable participation.

Assessment through direct observation may include going to the potential participant's school, work place or home during unstructured times such as lunch, recess, or break. It may involve observing a participant visiting a pet shop or gym, trying a line dancing class, or coming to the desired activity/program. Also, observing an individual in structured times at school, home or work, in which they function well, can provide additional information regarding the accommodations that enable them to have optimal participation.

There are a number of assessment instruments that can be used for structuring direct observations and recording results. Systems for coding observable reactions to leisure materials and activities by individuals with severe disabilities in order to assess leisure preferences and behaviors have been developed by Coyne (1980), Wehman & Schleien (1981), Voeltz & Wuerch (1982) and Dattilo (1986). In their book on assessment tools for therapeutic recreation, burlingame & Blaschko (2002) provide over 30 assessment instruments that are commonly used by Certified Therapeutic Recreation Specialists. Some of those designed for use with individuals with developmental disabilities under the areas of functional skills, participant patterns and community integration programs can be useful with individuals with ASD.

The Leisure Lifestyle Profile (Coyne et. al., 1999), shown in Figure 5.6, is one of the only instruments designed specifically to record information about the interests and skills of individuals with ASD. It is also an effective summary profile for planning individualized programs and to monitor progress. Information from the interviews and observation, along with ongoing assessment can be consolidated on this form.

Questions from Parents/Caregivers and the Potential Participant

The parent/caregiver and the person need to know how the program is structured, about the key components, and about the facilities. Parents/caregivers and the person often have questions for the staff. They may be anxious about participation and ask very detailed questions. It is important to take the time to answer questions in order to develop trust and more comfort. Figure 5.7 lists some questions that staff should be prepared to answer.

The information gleaned through assessment provides the foundation for making decisions about programs, activities and accommodations. Gathering this information will save time and frustration for all involved. This section has provided suggestions on gathering information about the potential participant, which will lead to the selection of recreation activities and accommodations within those activities to match the unique needs and interests of the individual with ASD.

Figure 5.6
Leisure Lifestyle Profile

Student:	Dan	Date:	April 24, 2002

	ACTIVITY	Id Time	Resources	Choice	Initiate	Skills	Interact	Problem Solve	COMMENTS
HOME (Activity within property boundaries of home or personal space)									
Alone	Exercise Bike	I	I	I	I	I	NA	NA	
	Mini Tramp	I	I	I	I	I	NA	NA	
	Stereo Cassette	I	E	E	I	I	NA	TA	
	Hoop (Basketball)	I	E	I	I	E	NA	NA	
With Others	Stereo Cassette with mom	E	I	E	I	I	E	TA	
COMMUNITY (Activity beyond property boundaries of home)									
Alone									
With Others	Walking	PA	I	E	I	I	E	TA	
	Bowling	PA	TA	TA	E	PA	E	TA	
	Swimming	TA	E	TA	PA	E	E	TA	
SCHOOL/WORK (Activity during recess, breaks, lunch, elective classes and extracurricular activities)									
Alone	Talking Books	E	TA	E	E	E	NA	TA	
With Others	Jogging (PE)	PA	E	E	E	E	E	PA	
	Hoop/Catch	PA	E	I	E	E	E	I	
	Woodworking	PA	E	E	E	PA	E	PA	
	Assemblies	PA	E	E	E	E	E	E	

Record enjoyed activities engaged in for at least 15 minutes, 12 times a year.
Enter the appropriate code using the following:

I=Independently completes without cue or prompt.
E=Emerging; knows what the activity is about, or can partially complete it without adaptations.
PA=Participates with adaptations at predetermined level.
TA=Total assistance needed to complete.
NA=Not applicable; not required in activity, or unconventional activity in which skill is not defined.

(Coyne, P., Nyberg, C., Vandenburg, M. L. (1999). Developing Leisure Time Skills in Persons with Autism. Arlington, TX: Future Horizons. Used with permission.)

Figure 5.7
Questions Family Members or Caregivers May Ask

- Have you and the other staff worked with individuals with disabilities before? With ASD?
- How many participants are there in the activity?
- What is the age range of participants?
- What is the ratio of staff to participants?
- Do you have resources to provide 1:1 assistance?
- What information or strategies do you use to prepare the participant for the activity?
- Is there a consistent routine for the activity or are things different each day? What is the routine?
- How is instruction usually provided?
- Are you willing to use visual supports, social stories or other accommodations with the participant?
- How will the staff be trained to use the adaptations or modifications?
- Are you interested in training opportunities?
- How do you deal with behavior problems/discipline?
- What procedure do you follow if things are not working out with the participant?

(Adapted from Hammel, M. & Vandenburg, M. L. (1998). Portland, OR: Columbia Regional Program, Autism Services.)

Activity or Program Selection

Often parents/caregivers and/or the individual with ASD already have a specific activity in mind. In this case, they often go to an agency or organization that provides that activity. However, individuals with ASD, parents/caregivers and professionals sometimes have difficulty identifying or choosing recreation and leisure activities. Sometimes they will need assistance in selecting an activity or program.

When potential activities have been identified and information about the preferences, strengths and needs of the individual with ASD is gathered, the appropriateness of potential activities can to be determined. Taking time for the selection of appropriate leisure activities ensures a more effective and meaningful program and reduces the time spent trying new activities and accommodations.

Recreation providers have the opportunity to be creative, since there are no recreation activities that will suit every person with ASD. Individuals with ASD can learn to do almost any leisure activity, but if it is not a preference, it is unlikely to be pursued in the future. By definition, leisure is a time to participate in things that one likes to do. Some specific features in favored recreation activities may have been identified for the individual with ASD during the information-gathering phase. Incorporating strong and unusual interests often keeps motivation to participate high. Although these unusual interests are sometimes considered to be inappropriate, these interests can frequently be directed and broadened into more conventional leisure activities.

Box 5.5 Paul broke light bulbs, broke the glass on fire alarms, and enjoyed playing music on his cassette recorder. He also flapped his arms when he was excited. Although only one of these activities was a conventional leisure activity, his behavior indicated that he liked to manipulate objects to make noise. His educational team, including his mother, brainstormed how Paul's preferences might be expanded. One of the members of the team was a percussionist and agreed to see if Paul would like the bass drum. Paul enjoyed learning to play the bass drum and now marches with the school band. His favorite song has become "The Little Drummer Boy," which he calls "Rum-pa-pa." He likes the experience of being known, being liked, interacting, participating, and belonging with others as he plays the drums.

Box 5.6 Tamara repeatedly threw objects in the air and was fixated on silky textures. Her school happens to have a group that juggles and her teacher also taught juggling. Tamara was delighted to be taught to juggle with silky scarves in adapted physical education. Her slow, flowing juggling is a wonderful addition to the variety of juggling that the group demonstrates.

Paul would not have developed interest in drumming and Tamara would not have developed interest in juggling if they had not had the opportunity to experience these activities. A person can only have interests in activities to which s/he has been exposed. Interests will be limited by past experience. Therefore, new activities and experiences will often need to be offered to the individual with ASD to develop interests.

If a person demonstrates a particular interest and strength in a specific area, i.e., music, drama, art, graphics, or computer, then s/he should be given opportunities to develop further expertise in the area. This may not only provide enjoyment and success, but may also lead to the development of skills for future employment.

Box 5.7 Mark Rimland had natural talent in painting that was encouraged. He has become a well-known artist with ASD. His work is shown and sold around the country.

Despite personal differences in individuals with ASD, some features of recreation activities may make those activities more meaningful, motivating and successful. The results from information gathering will reveal the features that are most important for a particular individual. Table 5.1 lists some features of successful recreation activities for individuals with ASD. Although each activity is listed with only one feature, activities were chosen that meet the criteria for most of the features. The examples are a sampling of the possibilities.

Table 5.1
Some Features of Successful Recreation Activities

Feature	Example
Highly organized and structured	Aerobics class, yoga class
Regularly scheduled	Swim team practice 6:00 - 7:00 M,W
Concrete; clear, static rules	Tae Kwon Do class, playing checkers
Rote, predictable or repetitive quality	Line dancing, making gimp keychains
Close ended; clear beginning and end	Plant 10 bulbs in area, crochet coaster
Visual clarity of what to do	Make mini trellis following jig
Active/ limited waiting	Cross-country skiing, hiking
Sensory feedback, such as lights, sounds, movements, and textures	Play instrument, model car racing
Visual spatial	Painting, computer games
Putting things in order or into spaces	Auto mechanics, make silk screen cards
Low demands for complex social interaction	Bicycling, photography
Limited sharing or random turn taking	Latch hook, swimming
Limited communication required	Swimming, woodworking
Minimal verbal direction	Jogging, collecting
Choices within the activity	Possible in most activities

Combining the above features and knowledge of the individual with ASD will guide the selection of recreation activities. For instance, at first glance golf may seem like an unlikely pursuit for a person with ASD, but it has many of the features in Table 5.1. When looked at more closely, golf can be seen to have many components that may appeal to some individuals with ASD. It is a quiet activity with clear rules, a single focus, and a clear beginning and ending. It involves walking, repeatedly taking clubs in and out of a bag, repeatedly swinging a club at the ball, and repeatedly looking for the ball. When the ball is hit, something happens. Golf has a routine and concrete static rules. Although many play golf competitively and for social interaction, the game itself does not require competition or social interaction.

> **Box 5.8**
>
> Don enjoys playing golf. He learned the basics of the game in an adapted physical education class in middle school. He continued to develop skills through taking classes at a local golf course operated by the Parks and Recreation Department. Don plays along with his golfing friends and occasionally makes a comment. His friends appreciate that he does not interrupt their concentration with chitchat. His mother believes it is "the activity" for individuals with ASD.

If features of the activity are not considered, an individual with ASD may become involved in an activity that is very uncomfortable and heightens anxiety in him or her. This can lead to behaviors that are difficult for others.

Box 5.9 Byron's family and friends decided that it would be "good for him" to be on the bowling team that his coworkers had organized. They knew that Byron had learned to bowl when he was in school. Byron, who used only a few phrases, endured bowling for several weeks and amazed everyone by using a new phrase. He said loudly and emphatically, "No more bowling." The lights, movement of others and noise were very uncomfortable for him. Although he liked rolling the ball down the alley, he disliked having to wait his turn to roll it. He also did not like sitting in close proximity to others while waiting for his turn and did not have the ability to chitchat like the others did when it was not their turn. Others with ASD might like this activity with the appropriate supports, but it was not an enjoyable experience for Byron.

There are additional considerations in selecting leisure activities for individuals with ASD or anyone with a significant disability. Several authors have proposed general criteria for activity selection for individuals with severe disabilities (Coyne, 1980; Wehman & Schleien, 1981; Wuerch and Voeltz; 1982, Leisure Learning System, 1989) that may also be used for individuals with ASD. A combination of these criteria is found in Figure 5.8.

Figure 5.8
General Criteria for Selection of Recreation Programs and Activities

- Enjoyed by same age peers in that community
- Readily available in their community
- Can be done in a variety of environments and situations
- Economically feasible
- Are of interest to family members and friends
- Have a potential to be done at least 12 times a year
- Have potential as lifelong leisure
- Socially flexible
- Can be engaged in alone or with others

Both participants and those who provide recreation activities put a great deal of effort into recreation activities. The knowledge of the individual with ASD and general criteria for the selection of activities will help recreation providers chose activities that are enjoyable and successful for all involved.

Environmental Inventory

The environment can have a major impact on the ability of a person with ASD to participate in recreation activities. The behavior of a participant with ASD will vary depending on aspects of the setting, such as novelty, degree of structure provided, and complexity of the environment, so observation of the environment is vital. Surveying the recreation environment for factors that may lower a participant's ability to function in activities can help determine the match of the participant with the activity and the activity demands, along with needed accommodations and modifications. Figure 5.9 provides a list of key questions to ask about the environment and structure of the activity.

Figure 5.9
Environmental Inventory

Novelty
- Are elements of the activity predictable and consistent?
- Is the location of the activity always the same?
- Is staff prompt and consistent?
- What is the likelihood of the activity being postponed or cancelled?
- Will there be any fire drills?
- Is the number of participants consistent?
- Are the participants the same every time?

Degree of Structure
- Is the schedule consistent?
- Is there a predictable and consistent routine?
- What are the stated and unstated expectations?
- Do activities have a clear beginning and ending?
- Are visual supports used with any of the participants?
- Does staff always set up and start activities?
- How much do participants need to wait to listen or take a turn?
- How is instruction given?

Complexity of the Environment
- Are there competing visual stimuli, such as light, movement, reflection, or background patterns, particularly between the participant and the instructor or leader?
- Are there fans, loud speakers, fire alarms, several people talking at once, air conditioners, bells, dogs barking, or unexpected sounds?
- Are there textures that could be aversive?
- Are temperatures appropriate?
- Are there aromas that could be aversive?
- Do participants share close proximity with others?
- Do participants need to share materials?
- What is the size of the group?
- Are there other stressors or triggers for this particular individual present?

To determine needed supports for a participant, it is also necessary to identify the steps, procedures and specific skills involved in an activity. Many behavior problems are the result of misunderstood procedures, so the procedures need to be identified and taught. Figure 5.10 provides a sample format for gathering information about procedures that can be completed by an observer or the activity instructor.

Gathering information about the potential participant and the activity itself is critical to the selection of recreation activities that match the unique needs and interests of the individual with ASD. In addition, it provides the foundation for making decisions about supports. Gathering information will save time and frustration for both individuals with ASD and people who want to facilitate their recreation participation.

Figure 5.10
Activity Procedures

Within activity. What do you expect the participants to do when:

They don't have needed supplies? _____

They have a questions during instruction? _____

They need to go to the restroom? _____

They need a drink of water? _____

They arrive when the activity has already begun? _____

They prepare to leave? _____

They need to get into smaller groups or partners? _____

Transitions. What are your procedures for:

Entering the area? _____

End of the activity? _____

Movement into or changing groups? _____

Signaling and quieting the group? _____

Supports

To profit from any recreation setting or program, participants with ASD need assistance to organize information and their environment for basic meanings and relationships. Thoughtful preparation must go into creating safe, familiar, predictable and highly motivating recreation environments. The information gathered during assessment on preferences, communication skills, social skills, group skills, community skills, reactions to change, reactions to sensory input, and behavior challenges will guide the specific manner in which supports will be developed and implemented.

Although individuals with ASD share major difficulties in the normal acquisition of social, imaginative and communicative skills, all of them have significant individual differences, which have to be taken into account. They vary in the degree of their symptoms and the amount that their characteristics can be modified by the supports available to them. Therefore, generic supports will not suit all with this disorder. Participation must be individualized for each person with ASD by using appropriate accommodations. Specific types of support, such as those listed in Table 5.2 and described in Chapter 6, have proven to be effective, but must be individualized to the needs of the particular participant.

The leisure coordinator must determine what kind of support the participant might need and convey it to staff who will be working directly with the participant. Figure 5.11 shows information that may be provided to the instructor and leisure companion.

Recreation providers may be part of a team that develops an individualized plan that encompasses more than leisure and recreation. An individualized program plan is required in some settings, such as schools, post-secondary programs, and group homes. Each of these settings has a slightly different name for these plans. These plans help direct and guide participation and highlight areas in which the individuals need accommodations. Some sample goals that may be worked on during recreation activities are:

- Given preparation and a visual cue, participant will transition from one activity to the next independently within one minute.
- At the beginning of an activity that is new, participant will use relaxation cue.
- Participant will throw and catch a nine-inch ball four out of five times.
- When given a mini schedule of showering, participant will take a shower at the swimming pool.
- Participant will wait his turn to bowl four out of five times.
- Given the cue, "Arm's length away," participant will remain at an appropriate distance from other participants during the activity 80 percent of opportunities.

Table 5.2
Supports for Maximizing Success for Participants with ASD

Name: Date:
Activity: Instructor:

Visual supports to help minimize the participant's difficulties in auditory processing, attention and organization, as well as to maximize independence in participation.

Comments

✓ Tangible, pictorial or written daily schedule
✓ Visual directions, e.g., templates, finished examples, mini-schedules
✓ Work system
✓ Checklists or reminder cards for rules and expectations

Structuring for a predictable environment: Organization and modification of the environment to assist the participant with problems in organization. So student knows where to be, what to do, how much to do, with whom and for how long.

✓ Consistent routines and schedules with clear structure
✓ Clear physical boundaries in the environment, e.g., lines on floor, carpet squares
✓ Labeling or color-coding objects
✓ Provision of clear beginning and ending to activities/tasks
✓ Clear ending, e.g., timer and finished box or folder

Sensory Support: Sensitivity to the intense sensory needs and comfort requirements of the participant with ASD.

✓ Reduce environmental distractions or add something to help
✓ Decrease distractions, e.g., headphones
✓ Sensory diet incorporating exercise, carrying heavy objects, swinging, climbing
✓ Relaxation protocol
✓ Breaks in and out of the classroom
✓ Fidget toys for waiting times
✓ Personal space for breaks

Table 5.2 Continued
Supports for Maximizing Success for Participants with ASD

Preparation for change to assist with the difficulty with new or different environments, activities or expectations.

- ✓ Prepare ahead with schedules
- ✓ Gradually introduce to new situations
- ✓ Describe what to expect with visual supports, such as mini-schedule or social story

Communication supports to help the participant to communicate and understand communication.

- ✓ Augmentative or backup communication systems
- ✓ Allowance for delayed processing time
- ✓ Staff use of gestures, models, visual supports and demonstration with verbalizations
- ✓ Concrete, specific language used by staff

Social supports to help the participant relate well with others.

- ✓ Provision of situation specific expectations of behavior with social stories or other visual supports
- ✓ Trained leisure companion
- ✓ Circle of friends

Behavioral supports.

- ✓ Remove from stressful situations
- ✓ Functional Behavior Assessment
- ✓ Avoidance of disciplinary action for behaviors that are part of the disorder

---

Staffing

Agencies vary in their staffing. However, there are three major roles that are needed to assist individuals with ASD to participate in recreation activities. These are:

1) someone to coordinate and develop accommodations,
2) someone to accompany and assist the participant, and
3) someone to instruct the group.

In some cases, particularly in smaller programs, staff in one or two positions fills these roles. In larger organizations or agencies, these may be specific positions that have varying titles. For the purpose of the following discussion, these roles will be called the leisure coordinator, the leisure companion and the activity instructor/leader.

Figure 5.11
Recreation Inclusion Form

Participant: Jody   Age: 10
Instructor: Companion:
Program: Swimming   Session: Summer 2002

Pertinent Information

Fully included at school.

Communication: *Does not ask for help. May just run to activity to demonstrate what he wants to do. Has difficulty expressing his needs. Difficulty with abstract concepts; concrete, literal thinker. Follows rules he understands.*

Social: *Socially 2 -3 years behind peers. Wants to fit in. Does best with female peers. Very sensitive to being teased. He does not understand sarcasm or some other types of humor.*

Change: *Difficulty with change in rules and transitions.*

Behavioral concerns: *When pressured or stressed, he will scream, giggle, or develop tics. When this happens, reduce pressure and redirect or give him a task as a helper.*
He may try to run out of the room, so define physical boundaries, e.g., shut doors, and put up gates in pool.

Accommodations

- *Develop a consistent schedule/routine.*
- *Prepare him for class ahead with pictures of steps in the class.*
- *Define physical boundaries, e.g., shut doors, and put up gates in pool.*
- *Prepare him ahead for transitions with five, three, and one-minute transition cues. Use pictures with words to help with transition.*
- *Provide a safe area away from others and stimuli to take a break.*
- *During instruction, have him near the instructor. Leisure companion can highlight the key points and write it down for him.*
- *Be precise, clear and calm.*
- *Provide scheduled quiet breaks.*
- *Reduce pressure and redirect or give him a task as a helper, if he appears stressed.*
- *When waiting, have his stand at the front or the end of the line and carry equipment or otherwise help.*

(Adapted from City of Eugene Recreation Services. Used with permission.)

The Role of Leisure Coordinator

The role of the leisure coordinator should be filled by someone with experience working with individuals with disabilities in recreation and in facilitating inclusion. This may be a paid professional or volunteer with considerable expertise. Many professionals, including therapeutic recreation specialists (CTRS), special educators, residential staff, service coordinators, and adaptive physical educators may serve as a leisure coordinator, in addition to fulfilling their other job duties. For instance, a smaller parks and recreation department may hire a Certified Therapeutic Recreation Specialist to run specialized programs and coordinate inclusion.

The leisure coordinator role has many vital functions. These are listed in Figure 5.12.

Figure 5.12
Functions of the Leisure Coordinator

- Communication and planning with participants with ASD and/or parents, caregivers or guardians
- Assess needs of participant through observation or conversations with the participant, and/or parents, caregivers, or guardian
- Determine needed support and accommodations
- Recruit support staff
- Organize and maintain a cadre of leisure companions
- Assign and supervise staff to facilitate participation
- Contact activity instructor/leader
- Identify activity prerequisites, routines and environment
- Coordinate training of staff related to ASD and effective strategies for recreation participation
- Consult and problem solve with leaders and leisure companion
- Outreach to such organizations as schools, churches, group homes, and other human service agencies

---

Recruitment of the leisure coordinator. There are different ways to recruit a leisure coordinator. Many agencies advertise for individuals with experience in inclusive recreation and education programs to fill the role of the leisure coordinator. Certified Therapeutic Recreation Specialists, adapted physical education teachers, and Registered Occupational Therapists with experience in inclusive recreation programs for persons with disabilities, as well as teachers who have taught in inclusive classrooms or schools are good potential candidates.

Volunteers with formal education or experience who are already familiar with the program may be able to serve in a volunteer capacity with a minimum of problems in volunteer organizations. For instance, a volunteer Girl Scout leader, who is also a Registered Occupational Therapist, has done an exemplary job in the Totem Council in Seattle, Washington. Two autism specialists have transformed a Challenger Sports League soccer team through volunteering in this capacity. These examples are described in detail in Chapter 9.

Family members, friends, and neighbors may fill the role of leisure coordinator for specific activities or events. For instance, parents started and coordinate a monthly Game Club for individuals with ASD in West Linn, Oregon. This example is described in detail in Chapter 11.

Sometimes recreation programs co-create and co-staff with an organization or agency that serves persons with ASD and other disabilities to meet staffing needs. Often this is an organization with expertise in the needs of these individuals. In this case, staff from the specialized organization and staff from the recreation program work together to develop supports that will facilitate the individual's participation.

The Role of Leisure Companion

One of the most significant supports that can be made to ensure the success of participation is the provision of a person in the role of a leisure companion who can accompany an individual with ASD to programs or classes. A leisure companion may be needed during at least part of the activity to be sure that the participant gets the input s/he needs to make sense of the activity, prevent behavior problems and reinforce his/her efforts to participate. Leisure companions support participation and implement the accommodations that have been developed by the leisure coordinator. They may help develop additional supports as they find out more about what the participant wants, needs, and responds to in the new situation. They usually continue in this role until natural supports emerge or they are no longer needed.

The leisure companion role has many vital functions. These are listed in Figure 5.13.

Figure 5.13
Functions of the Leisure Companion

- Acts as an advocate for highlighting the individual's abilities and developing a climate of acceptance
- Provides one-to-one assistance so that the instructor or leader does not need to spend an inordinate amount of time with one individual
- Predicts potential problems and intervenes to prevent problems
- Identifies the cause of frustration and confusion
- Makes activity procedures visually clear through schedules and other visual supports
- Produces practical aids to assist with organizational difficulties, e.g., checklists
- Facilitates developing relationships with others
- Interprets social cues and situations to the participant
- Provides alternative stress-reducing activities

The leisure companion helps alleviate the dependence of many individuals with ASD on family members or service providers for the opportunities to learn and engage in leisure activities. Leisure companions may be paid staff, volunteers, or friends. An agency cannot require a participant who exhibits unusual behavior to bring a personal care attendant, but it is allowed.

As much as possible, the leisure companion is behind the scenes supporting the participant to be as independent and involved as possible. They generally will need to spend more time with participants who cannot speak or have bad reputations. There is no set time that a leisure companion should remain in a setting with a participant with ASD. This can vary from several days or a few weeks to as long as the participant is involved. The best leisure companions are calm, positive, consistent and have a good sense of humor.

Recruitment of the leisure companion. Many leisure companions are volunteers or friends. In recent years, there has been a major focus on strategies to develop natural community supports for this purpose and to build a circle of friends for each individual through person-centered planning. To expand leisure options for individuals who may always need some level of support for participation, it is important to identify potential leisure partners and possible common interests among the individual's family and friends. This will expand the number of opportunities that the individual has to practice and continue to enjoy activities that s/he has learned.

In optimal cases, friends become the volunteer leisure companions. Coyne et. al. (1999) proposed the use of the Leisure Interest Inventory as one way of matching peers' interests to that of the individual with ASD. An example of matching a young man with ASD with a friend he had made in woodshop for swimming at an athletic club was presented in Chapter 2.

Photo by Jason Kinch Photographics,
Courtesy of Mt. Hood Kiwanis Camp

Box 5.10

Buddy Ball Sports League in Landing, NJ

Buddy Ball provides organized sports activities for children with ASD and other disabilities ages 6 to 16. Children with disabilities are matched with "buddies" who assist the children to play sports such as baseball and bowling. The league also offers basketball and soccer clinics during the year. "Buddies" can be individuals or members of community organizations such as Cub Scouts, Girl Scouts, cheerleaders, 4-H Club, and Brownies.

Peers are a natural and readily available source for supporting individuals with ASD. Often someone of the same age can serve as a role model in a way that is more motivating and effective than when adults are directing the individual with ASD how to behave. Research on peer-mediated instruction for children with ASD have been promising in identifying effective strategies that teach peers how to initiate and persist in physical engagement (Odom & Strain, 1986). At Camp Awareness, which is featured in Chapter 10, peers are trained to be companions. It is, however, important to establish limits to how much is expected from a peer. For instance, peers should not be expected to deal with challenging behaviors.

Some agencies have an active volunteer program. Interagency cooperation often leads to additional sources of volunteer leisure companions. Members of school sponsored Friendship Clubs, Scouts, church groups, Big Brother, Foster Grandparent Programs, or The Arc Friend to Friend Program may be companions for after-school athletics and clubs, as well as support during organized community recreation activities.

Box 5.11

Inclusive Recreation Companion Project, AmeriCorps and the Arc of Multnomah County, OR

The Inclusive Recreation Companion Project is an AmeriCorps sponsored program serving the greater Portland, Oregon community. This unique AmeriCorps project is a partnership of the Arc of Multnomah County with local community recreation providers, such as Portland Parks and Recreation, YMCA/YWCA, Boys and Girls Clubs and after-school programs. These agencies, along with six inclusive recreation companions, are addressing the recreational needs of children, youth and adults with developmental disabilities, including ASD, in inclusive recreation settings. The main objectives of the Inclusive Recreation Companion Project are:

1) Assess the support needs of individuals with disabilities through person-centered planning and assisting them in experiencing a more healthy leisure lifestyle,

2) Improve the leisure lifestyle of individuals with disabilities through participation in inclusive recreation activities, and

3) Increase community awareness and inclusion of people with disabilities in community recreation programs.

At the end of each year, the AmeriCorps volunteer companions will train six more AmeriCorps volunteer companions. By the end of the three-year project, 18 volunteer companions will be trained.

College students from local universities who volunteer may be able to get college credit. A number of camps that utilize volunteer leisure companions for college credit are presented in Chapter 10. One of the many benefits to individuals who volunteer is an increased awareness of the capabilities of individuals with disabilities.

Box 5.12

One volunteer companion who did a six-credit practicum at Mt. Hood Kiwanis Camp in Oregon said, "It taught me that anyone can do anything. It just takes having enough people behind them."

Volunteers with adequate expertise for a particular situation are not always available or appropriate. A qualified leisure companion may need to be hired to work on an hourly basis. The provision of a leisure companion may be an area of agency collaboration. For instance, one young man with ASD has a mentor, provided by a county community mental health consortium, who accompanied him to swimming at a community center. Another young man has a skill trainer hired through county developmental disabilities self-directed support who accompanies him to archery lessons. An educational assistant from the participant's school program might be an excellent leisure companion and may be provided by a local education agency as part of an Extended School Year (ESY) program.

Box 5.13

In Oregon, anyone with a developmental disability has universal access to self-directed support. Brandon and his family decided that recreation was a critical area for him during his essential lifestyle planning. They are using some of the money available through the universal access to self directed support to pay the fee for Adventures without Limits, an outdoor adventure program, and to pay an hourly rate for a 1 : 1 leisure companion during his participation in this program.

The role of leisure companion may be particularly attractive to teenagers and college students, who regularly participate in the program of interest. College students in therapeutic recreation, special education or other fields are often interested in paid positions. Older teens, with prior experience in working with individuals with disabilities are often ideal, particularly if they have taken a special needs childcare course.

Whether the leisure companion role is filled by paid staff or volunteers, this person will typically need initial training, as well as ongoing direct supervision or support for areas such as dealing with challenging behavior. Problems can occur as companions inadvertently become involved in ineffective interactions without feedback from the leisure coordinator.

Activity Instructor/Leader

The activity instructor or leader usually is someone who is skilled in teaching or leading a group in a particular activity or program. They may be paid staff or volunteers. Although the instructor or leader has responsibility for the whole group, s/he has many vital functions with the participant with ASD. These are listed in Figure 5.14.

Figure 5.14
Functions of the Activity Instructor/Leader

- Creates a calm, stable environment
- Creates a positive, accepting atmosphere
- Ensures that the structure of the activity and expectations are clear
- Establishes routines
- Breaks instruction into small steps
- Teaches new steps by providing examples or modeling
- Presents instructions visually
- Assigns specific models for the participant to observe and imitate in group activities
- Gradually increases demands on the participant with ASD
- Provides some individual assistance
- Develops adaptations with the leisure coordinator and leisure companion

---

Staff Training

One of the most critical issues in organized recreation for individuals with ASD is the preparation of community programs to include this disorder. Staff members, like participants, are unique. They come to programs from diverse backgrounds. Many leisure companions and activity instructors/leaders do not have previous experience with participants with ASD. Some staff members may have different views on ASD and how to deal with behavior. Some may not have the most current information and erroneously believe that they know what to do. Information is important since individuals with ASD can seem a paradox of strengths and weaknesses. The increasing use of inclusion makes some form of instruction on ASD important for all recreation providers, as well as support staff, such as receptionists and bus drivers. For staff to feel competent and to prevent burnout, they need training in understanding ASD and positive behavior support.

Recreation providers, such as leisure companions and activity instructors/leaders need basic information about characteristics of ASD, behavioral support and other supports useful for participants with ASD. They need to know specifically how ASD impacts the participant with whom they will be working. A general overview along with some information about accommodations can often provide the staff with enough confidence to begin to include these individuals. Ongoing training or mentorship through a leisure coordinator is the second level of training.

Trainers

Organizations vary in their capacity to provide training on recreation and ASD. Those responsible for training should know about ASD not only from books, but also from their work with children, adolescents and adults with this disorder. Book learning is important, but tells only half the story.

Sometimes the leisure coordinator or other program staff has this expertise. However, generally the leisure coordinator will need to participate in a training program focused specifically on ASD. Outside specialists may be needed to help provide staff training. Organizations may contract with autism specialists to provide ongoing training and consultation or train designated staff who will eventually take over the responsibilities for training and consultation.

Autism specialists may come from a variety of sources. Sometimes faculty from universities or consultants are available to assist in training. Given clear guidelines regarding what information is needed, specialists are able to select practical advice and strategies that are applicable in that environment. A staff member with expertise in adapted physical education and recreation from the Indiana Resource Center on Autism has been involved in training staff from some local recreation programs. A Therapeutic Recreation Specialist from the Arc of Multnomah County, Oregon, who also has knowledge of ASD, has trained staff from local community recreation programs and after school programs. During the duration of the project, staff from Project Autism at the Center for Recreation and Disability Studies at the University of North Carolina provided extensive training to local community recreation programs. In addition, numerous state and federal agencies provide technical assistance to existing programs. The Indiana Resource Center for Autism publishes an annual directory of autism training and technical assistance.

Basic Training in ASD

To develop basic training in ASD, the program needs to identify the purpose of the training. The length of training may range from hours to weeks in length, depending on the type of organization and purpose of training. It is strongly suggested that the main purpose is to help trainees understand ASD well enough to be able to look at the world from the point of view of a person with ASD and come up with practical solutions. If trainees truly understand the profound problem of processing, integrating and organizing information, they are most likely to have the capacity to support and problem solve creative ideas for these participants. In order to facilitate recreation participation, the staff needs to have a basic knowledge of ASD and knowledge of effective strategies.

First, trainees must have basic facts about ASD, such as a definition, causes, and incidence. This information is provided in Figure 2.1 in Chapter 2 and can be conveyed in a mini lecture format.

Second, trainees need to understand about the primary behaviors or characteristics that they might see, as well as reasons for these behaviors. Staff who do not understand these characteristics may overreact to the initial behaviors demonstrated by a participant with ASD and feel unable to cope with the behavior. Some examples of common misinterpretations of behavior are provided in Table 2.1 in Chapter 2, but this is an area in which active learning is important and will be further discussed under training methods.

Third, trainees need to understand basic strategies for supporting participants with ASD. A checklist of these strategies is provided in Table 5.2 earlier in this chapter and strategies are described in Chapter 6.

Training methods

Staff members, like participants, learn best through multiple exposures, opportunities to practice, and active involvement in learning. Training is most effective when provided in units over time and when there are opportunities to practice new skills with feedback. The most effective training has a strong hands-on component along with lecture.

Five particularly effective training methods will be discussed in the following section. They include:

1) Directed group discussion,
2) First-person accounts,
3) Simulations,
4) Role-plays, and
5) Positive staff experiences.

Directed group discussion. Trainers can engage participants by generating group input about characteristics and then elaborating on their responses. For example, if at least half the trainees have known someone with ASD, the trainer can ask what behaviors trainees have seen individuals with ASD exhibit. A knowledgeable recorder or the trainer can record what trainees say on a paper that is divided into quadrants. Each quadrant is unlabeled, but coincides to one of the four areas of impairment in ASD: communication (verbal and nonverbal); social interactions; restricted, repetitive and stereotypic interests; and responses to sensory information. The trainer can then label each quadrant and give a mini-lecture on how and why behaviors manifest in each area. This exercise allows people to feel good about what they already know, while clarifying misconceptions.

First-person accounts. It is next to impossible to truly understand the experience of having ASD. However, infusing personal accounts of individuals with ASD through a live talk, videotape or writings by them regarding their experiences can have a profound impact. Perhaps you look at ASD differently after reading the accounts of the individuals with ASD in Chapter 4. More and more individuals are writing about their experience, since the seminal work of Temple Grandin (1985). Books, articles in magazines, and stories on the Internet are no longer difficult to find.

Simulations. Another means of learning more about the experience of having ASD is through simulations. Simulations increase the trainee's ability to see situations from the perspective of the person ASD. An excellent example of such a simulation is the one used by Camp Determination described in Chapter 10.

The Picnic: Simulation for Groups of 6 - 12 Trainees.

A prerequisite is that the group members know each others' names.

The group sits in a circle. The leader tells the group that s/he is going on a picnic at a location the group would enjoy. The leader says the s/he is going to bring something to the picnic and does not tell the group that it begins with the first letter of his or her first name. Sometimes it helps to have another person who knows the game to speed up the process.

The trainer asks trainees what they will bring going counterclockwise. If a trainee says something that begins with the first letter of his or her name, they are told that they can come. If they say an item with a different first letter than their name, they are told that they cannot come. However, they need to figure this out.

The trainer keeps going around the circle until everyone has guessed the game. Then the trainer asks questions, such as "How did you feel when you could not come because you did not know the unspoken rule?" "What emotions or behaviors did you need to control?" "What would it have been like if you had to do another activity at the same time?" "What would it be like if you experienced this type of situation on a daily basis?"

The trainer relates the trainees' answers to the experience of having ASD and elaborates on some of the reasons for behaviors.

These simulations make the experience of ASD more real and give trainees a deeper understanding of the pervasive nature of the impact of the disorder.

Role-play. Another effective training approach is to have two trainers role-play different situations that may occur and then let trainees discuss and decide what they would do in each situation. The scenarios in Figure 5.15 are designed for trainees to identify why the participant with ASD reacted, what went wrong and what would have made the situation better. Two trainers can camp it up with these scenarios. Some of what went wrong is highlighted in these scenarios to help trainers with key points.

Some key issues for discussion and teaching points related to the role-play scenarios in Figure 5.15 are:

- Effective interaction style—calm, predictable, compassionate, and patient, kind, flexible and orderly
- Provide assistance only when needed
- Behavior is communication
- Avoid power struggles
- Communication tips/ language; avoid questions and "You need to"
- Communication systems
- How to foster independence
- Use of visual supports and modification of the environment to help compensate for the individual's problems with organization
- Visual Supports: schedules, mini schedules, visual clarity for beginnings and endings
- How much to put out

- How to prepare participant for change
- Providing choices
- Most stressful times are unstructured and wait times
- Quickly overwhelmed and react more severely to failure
- How to redirect behaviors

Figure 5.15
Role-Play Scenarios to Illustrate Problems

The following scenarios can be used to train staff about ASD. The words in bold type indicate the aspects to emphasize in the discussion after the trainers role-play the scenario.

Lotto (open-ended activity). The participant is sitting at a table. The instructor puts the Lotto materials on the desk with **no preparation**. There are **so many Lotto materials** that it would take an hour or more to match them all. The **instructor is talking a lot**, but not giving instruction on how to do the game. The participant is passive and becomes more and more withdrawn. The instructor's response is to **move too close and talk more**. Finally the participant goes under the desk. The instructor **tries to pull the participant out while continuing to talk.** The participant is like a dead weight.

Puzzle (closed activity). The participant is sitting at a table doing a puzzle. There are two more pieces to put in before the puzzle will be finished. The instructor **says it is time to go home while removing the puzzle** from the table. **(No preparation for change. Did not allow to finish.)** The participant falls to the floor kicking and screaming. The instructor tells the participant to sit down and the participant screams louder.

Sponge paint (open-ended). The participant is sitting at a table. The instructor places a piece of paper, a sponge, and a puddle of green tempera paint in front of the participant. The instructor shows a completed sponge painting in blue and says; "Do this." **(No sequence of steps. No clear beginning or ending. Finished example is different color.)** The participant knocks everything off the table and bolts for the door.

Basketball. The instructor puts out a wastepaper basket, hands the participant a large ball and says, "Throw it in the basket." The participant walks up and drops the ball in the basket. The instructor says, "No, like this. Throw it" while throwing the ball into the basket. The instructor hands the ball to the participant and says, "I know you can do it. Throw it." The participant just stands there. The instructor then comes behind the participant to help him throw. The participant head butts him and drops the ball. **(No clear boundary of where to stand. No clear beginning and ending. Unclear steps. Too close with participant's touch issues.)**

Trainees can practice strategies through role-plays. Two or more trainees are given a scenario to role-play before the group where they demonstrate what they would do in the situation. The discussion concludes with a summation by the trainer(s) of basic guidelines to use in each situation. A variety of role-plays related to facilitating participation are used as part of the training of one-on-one volunteer counselors at Mt. Hood Kiwanis Camp. Figure 5.16 provides an example of one of these role-play scenarios.

Figure 5.16
Facilitating Participation Role Play: Life Vest

Strategy to use: feedback
Materials needed: life vest
Situation: You are both at the canoes. This is the second time that you have been to this activity. You have been working on showing the camper how to put on his life vest. The person is still not able to do this independently.
Camper role: You remember a little bit about how to put the vest on, but are not able to remember all the steps yet. You respond very well to positive feedback. Remember to do each of the steps after the counselor has shown you. Simulate not doing a step or two the correct way.
Counselor role: Remember to reinforce any approximations. If they bang the vest on their head, tell them, "Yes, you remembered that the vest goes over your head!" Make your feedback very specific and descriptive. Tell them exactly what they are doing well. Avoid "good job." Remember to model the task step by step.

Staff experiences. Another method of training is to describe the accommodations and support strategies that have been used in the past for participants with ASD. Stories and experiences of staff in finding ways to accommodate different participants with ASD are shared. The message conveyed is that flexibility, collaboration and creative problem solving are the keys to successful participation.

Ultimately, the goal of the staff training must be to leave staff feeling more, not less, confident in their ability to assist participants with ASD. In these practical training sessions, staff members learn to come up with practical solutions.

Training Specific to the Future Participant

Photo by Jason Kinch Photographics,
Courtesy of Mt. Hood Kiwanis Camp

Staff needs to know about any areas of difficulty, special talents, and other important information. Sharing information with staff about the strengths, preferences, and interests of the individual allows the staff to focus on abilities, rather than the challenges. All too often only the challenges are shared; the hard issues are highlighted so that the individual is preceded by a reputation that may not be the whole picture.

Providing staff with participant specific information when available allows for planning, developing and implementing supports for use in the program. An example of a written means of providing information was provided in Figure 5.11. In addition, videotape of the participant using accommodations or a demonstration of the use of any supports will help the staff implement these supports more effectively. Once staff is working with the participant, ongoing training, mentorship, technical assistance and/or supervision may be necessary.

Information for Other Participants

Other participants may also need information. In some cases providing other participants with simple information about ASD is likely to make interactions more successful because they will know more about why s/he does the things that seem odd to them. This should be provided in a respectful manner and without stigmatizing the participant with ASD.

Participation

Since individuals with ASD may be reluctant to engage in new activities or have difficulty understanding them, it is important to provide multiple opportunities to experience an activity before trying to determine if it would be meaningful and enjoyable for the individual. It may take several experiences with the activity for the participant with ASD to feel comfortable with it. This exposure needs to be structured and carefully directed so that the individual can experience what it is like to appropriately engage in the activity. This exposure process is a major part of training in leisure skills for individuals with ASD at Jay Nolan Centers in California and Gateway in British Columbia. Their process is described in detail in Chapter 7.

Generally, interest is assumed when an individual moves toward, grabs or hugs or otherwise manipulates an object. Similarly, disinterest is assumed when an individual wanders away from leisure materials. However, the individual with autism may show interest in subtler ways, such as several sidelong glances. It is, therefore, important to consult with people who are familiar with how the individual expresses interest and enjoyment, such as parents, siblings, caregivers, and friends.

Follow up

Recreation providers have learned that even with adequate planning, neither the staff nor the parents/caregivers can anticipate all possibilities. Some needs are only evident after the participant is involved in the program. The leisure coordinator should contact the participant and/or parents/caregivers, as well as the instructor of the program or activity after the first session to appraise the success of the accommodations. Direct observation is an additional effective method for evaluating the success of the supports and participation. This is important because problems can grow if they are not recognized.

Process Continuation

The leisure coordinator and leisure companion stay in touch with the individual to encourage participation in other activities or programs. It is important to remember that interests change over time and that an individual may like something better later on in life. Participants and companions assess their experience.

Summary

- Although many professionals and volunteers want to facilitate recreation participation for individuals with ASD, they may not know how to adequately prepare for effective participation.
- Assessment is critical to the selection of recreation activities that relate to the unique needs of the individual with ASD.
- There are many ways that an individual's leisure competencies and interests can be assessed, such as through interviews, questionnaires and direct observation.
- Assessment methods need to be chosen based on what is already known about the individual with ASD.
- Individuals with ASD need to be exposed in a structured manner to a wide variety of experiences and activities to develop broader interests.
- Leisure materials and activities that make materials and activities are more meaningful and more successful if they are understandable, reactive, comfortable, active and spatial manipulation.
- The systematic selection of recreation activities based upon this assessment will ensure more effective and meaningful participation.
- Taking time for the selection of appropriate leisure activities ensures a more effective and meaningful program and reduces the time spent trying new activities and accommodations.
- Despite personal differences in individuals with ASD, some features of recreation activities may make them more meaningful, motivating and more successful.
- Participation must be individualized for the participant with ASD by using appropriate accommodations.
- One of the most critical issues for persons with ASD is the preparation of community programs to understand and accept the behaviors commonly associated with this disorder.
- Since individuals with ASD may be reluctant with new activities or have difficulty understanding them, it is important to provide multiple opportunities to experience an activity before trying to determine if it would be meaningful and enjoyable for the individual.
- Staff has learned that despite these preparations, neither the staff or the parents/caregivers can anticipate all possibilities and some needs are only evident after the participant is involved in the program.

Chapter Six

Supports for Maximizing Success in Recreation Activities

Phyllis Coyne

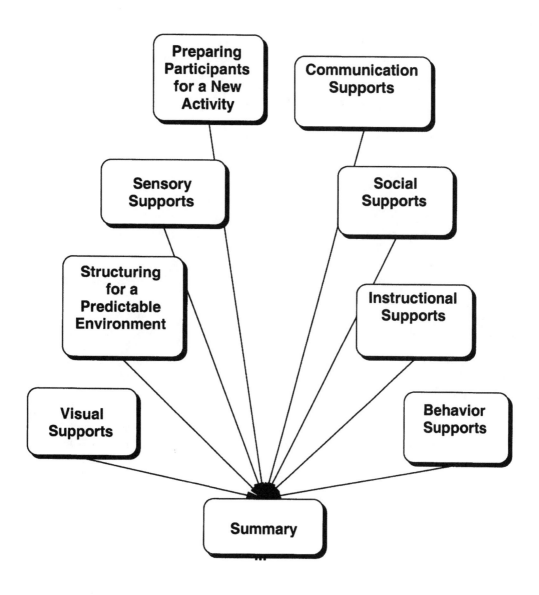

Participants with ASD can successfully participate in a variety of recreation activities, if they receive appropriate preparation and support for their impairments in communication and social skill development, unusual responses to sensory information and challenging behaviors. Careful planning, systematic programming and sustained efforts are needed to ensure success for the person with ASD, as well as other community members. Due to the considerable variability in how individuals manifest characteristics of ASD, programs must accommodate the unique needs and abilities of each participant. The ultimate goal is to promote a successful experience for both the participant and the rest of the group. The consistent use of techniques that support the unique needs of individuals with ASD in recreation settings creates effective environments that prevent behavior problems while enhancing skill development and enjoyment for all.

Knowledge of how to help participants with ASD in community recreation settings is expanding. In the future, new and innovative methods may be found and developed to help participants with ASD in community recreation settings. However, a number of interventions have consistently been found to be effective with individuals with ASD. The intervention strategies for persons with ASD reviewed in this chapter are from both the professional literature and professional experience. They are drawn from a variety of sources and reflect many effective strategies. These strategies are outlined in Table 5.2 in Chapter 5 and will be addressed in detail in this chapter. They include the following broad areas:

- **Visual supports**, e.g., schedules, checklists, etc., to help minimize the participant's difficulties in auditory processing, attention and organization, as well as to maximize independence in participation.
- **Environmental supports**. Organization and modification of the environment to assist participants with problems in organization.
- **Sensory supports**. Sensitivity to the intense sensory needs and comfort requirements of the participant with ASD.
- **Preparing for novelty**. Preparation for change to assist with the difficulty with new or different environments, activities or expectations.
- **Communication supports** to help the participant to communicate and understand communication.
- **Social supports** to help the participant relate well with others.
- **Instructional supports** to help the participant understand the meaning of a skill and how to use it independently.
- **Behavioral supports**. A team approach to solve behavior problems with intervention that is positive and free of punishment.

Combining the above approaches for individuals with ASD that are user friendly for all is the key to the successful participation of individuals with ASD. Most participants with ASD will need many of the above strategies. The level of support needed by an individual can change. For some, maximal individual support may be needed at first and may be faded, as the participant becomes more independent. Sometimes an individual needs more assistance than was initially anticipated or as the complexity of the activity increases. The supports will depend on the needs of the individual participant.

The approaches discussed in this chapter make recreation programs accessible to a wider range of individuals. Many other participants will benefit from the same approaches. When they are regularly used as part of a program, there is less need for individual accommodations.

Visual Supports

As evidenced in Chapters 7 – 10, as well as throughout this chapter, the most universally used strategies for participants with ASD are visual supports, including schedules and social stories. Visual supports are those things we see that enhance understanding. Visual supports utilize the visual learning strength of individuals with ASD and help compensate for their auditory and attention differences. Brief auditory information and the rapid rate of normal speech present a severe challenge to many of these participants. Visual supports can provide concrete information that remains available to help the participant better understand the activity.

One of the advantages of using visual supports is that they can be examined for as long as needed to process the information. In contrast, oral information is transient. Once it is said, the message is no longer available. In addition, it may be difficult for the participant with ASD to attend to the relevant information and to block out the background noises. The use of visual supports enables the individual to focus on the message. In general, visual supports are used to organize the activity for the participant, as well as give it meaning. Therefore, visual tools provide the supports necessary to increase levels of independence in participation and are useful for most participants with ASD, even if they appear to understand directions.

> **Box 6.1** The power of visual supports is in their permanency and utilization of a learning strength of individuals with ASD.

We all use visual strategies to help us move through our day, but individuals with ASD often need to have these supports developed for them. What we see in the environment gives us many clues about what is happening and what we should be doing.

A variety of professionals have developed key components and strategies for the use of visual supports for individuals with ASD. Some of the key professionals who have influenced the content of this section are: Mesibov (1985), Schopler et. al. (1995), Project Autism (2001), Hodgdon (1997), Quill (1995), Dalrymple (1987), Gray (1996) and Janzen (1996).

Many of these visual supports can be used in recreation settings to assist individuals with ASD. A variety of visual strategies that may be used to help the participant in recreation activities are described in this chapter. Table 6.1 illustrates how visual strategies may assist a participant with ASD. The key to ask when planning an activity or giving an instruction is "How can this information be presented in a simple visual format?" Most programs featured in the following chapters utilize visual supports.

Levels of Representation

Visual supports may be in the form of objects, exact outline drawings, photographs, line drawings or written words depending upon what the participant understands even when stressed. The type of visual aids and symbols vary in complexity. The selection of visual supports is guided by an understanding of the participant and his/her abilities and responses. The ability to understand different levels of abstraction varies from participant to participant. Objects, such as a cup representing drink, are the most concrete form. Exact outline drawings and photographs represent the next level of representation. Black and white line drawings and graphic symbols, such as written words, are the most abstract. Figure 6.1 illustrates these increasingly complex levels of representation.

Table 6.1
Visual Supports that Provide Important Information

Information → / Type of Visual ↓	Provides environmental supports	Clarifies past, current, future events	Clarifies expectations	Clarifies instructions	Provides social understanding	Provides alternative prompts & cues
Visual schedule		X	X	X		X
Checklist		X	X	X		X
Choice board		X				X
Object & furniture arrange	X	X	X	X		X
Label or color-code	X			X		X
Signs	X				X	X
Charts	X	X	X	X	X	X
Maps	X	X				
Diagram	X	X	X	X	X	X
Posted rules			X		X	X
Posted routines		X	X	X	X	X
Social stories					X	X
Pictorial instructions			X	X		X
Templates			X	X		X
Completed samples			X	X		X

A word of caution needs to be added about the use of photographs. Photographs should be as simple as possible and include only one object in the picture with no distractions in the background. Some participants with ASD will focus on irrelevant details of the picture, such as the color of the kickboard in the back of a photograph of a swimming pool or a sign in the background of a picture of waiting for the bus. These participants can become upset when the object is not there, because they have the whole picture in their mind and did not know what was most relevant.

Line drawings provide a simple and effective way to represent objects and actions for many participants with ASD. Because line drawings have been widely used, and have been successful with many individuals with ASD, a variety of examples of the use of line drawings is provided throughout this book and resources for line drawings and their use are provided under Resources in Appendix A.

Examples of line drawings from computer software programs are primarily provided in this book. However, this type of line drawing does not have to be used. Hand drawn pictures can be more practical, because they can be drawn on the spot for individual situations and understood by many participants with ASD. A sample hand-drawn picture sequence for an art activity can be seen in Chapter 11 (Figure 11.6). Instructors and leisure companions should always keep writing materials, such as pencils, pads of sticky notes or index cards available to draw picture sequences.

Figure 6.1
Levels of Representation

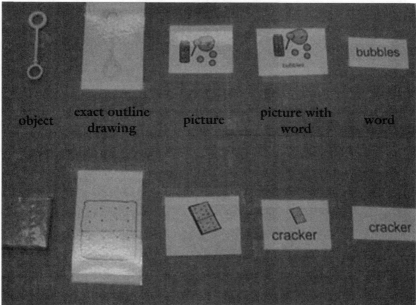

http://www.Do2learn.com. Used with permission

Because visual supports are often very effective accommodations in all areas of life for the individual with ASD, many participants will have been taught to use specific structure and visual supports that were designed to suit their individual needs. It is generally more successful to use the type of visuals that the individual has experience using. A speech and language pathologist or other professional with expertise in determining level of representation and effective visual supports often has developed these supports, so that they are appropriate for the individual. Getting copies of the visual supports that the participant uses in other settings can save a great deal of time and effort.

In some cases, the use of visual supports may be new to a participant. Many will understand visual supports that are at their level of representation automatically because it matches their learning strengths; however, most new users will require some instruction on how to use the visual supports. In addition, the expertise of a speech and language pathologist or other professional with knowledge in this area can help to ensure that the level of representation and format of the visual supports are appropriate. However, not all participants with ASD will automatically understand line drawings.

Visual Schedules

For most of us, written schedules, in the form of time management systems or day planners, are vital to help us get through the day and to organize what needs to get done. Visual schedules, using written words, photos, line drawings, or actual objects to represent activities of the day or steps within an activity, are even more important for individuals with ASD, because these visual supports facilitate the participant's ability to predict events and activities, anticipate change and understand expectations. The daily schedule visually tells the participant what activities will occur and in what sequence. Visual schedules take an abstract concept, time, and present it in a more concrete and manageable form. Another advantage of visual schedules is that they help the individual to anticipate change.

Figure 6.2 presents an example of a daily schedule, which uses a combination of written words and line drawings. This particular schedule is set up using a top to bottom or vertical format. The pictures are attached with paper clips for ease of setting up and removal of pictures. In this example, activities are checked off as completed, because the participant was able to independently track and check off activities.

In addition to providing cues for completing tasks, visual schedules inform the participant about: 1) what s/he is suppose to do and 2) what order to do the activities or task.

For those activities in which the participant moves from area to area, it is important to make a portable visual schedule of the bigger activity with a mini schedule in each area. A mini schedule outlines the sequence of steps that will occur during an activity. Both a schedule and mini schedule are often needed for recreation activities. For instance, a visual schedule for swimming may include—enter pool building, pay the attendant, put on swimsuit, take a shower, swim, play ball with peer, get out of pool, and change clothes as depicted in Figure 6.3. In addition, a participant with ASD may need mini schedules for changing clothes, the routine in the pool, and taking a shower. This type of mini schedule for the after swimming locker room routine used by ACAP is presented in Chapter 11 (Figure 11.3).

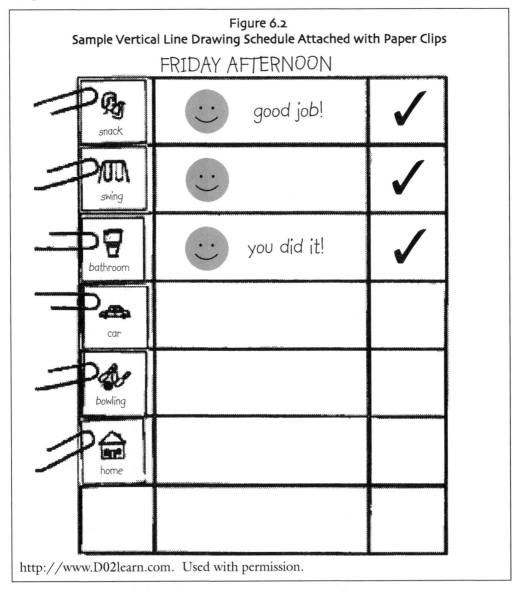

Figure 6.2
Sample Vertical Line Drawing Schedule Attached with Paper Clips

http://www.DO2learn.com. Used with permission.

Figure 6.3
Sample Line Drawing Mini Schedule for Swimming

(P. Coyne, C. Nyberg, & M. L. Vandenburg, 1999. *Developing Leisure Time Skills in Persons with Autism.* Arlington, TX: Future Horizons. Used with permission.)

When teaching an individual with ASD to participate in a recreation activity, it is important to break it down into steps, so that the individual understands what is expected. A sample of a mini schedule for an art activity can be seen in Figure 6.4.

Figure 6.4
Sample Mini Schedule for Art Activity

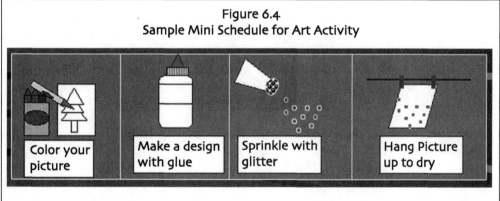

Color your picture | Make a design with glue | Sprinkle with glitter | Hang Picture up to dry

D. Green (Personal Communication, September 8, 2002). Created with The Picture Communication Symbols © 1981-2202 Mayer-Johnson, Inc. Used with permission.

For those who read with comprehension consistently even when stressed, written information may be enough. Figure 6.5 provides an example of a written mini schedule for a gardening class for a participant who comprehends what he reads well. His leisure companion wrote it as the instructor gave directions. This mini schedule is in a checklist format, which highlights the steps of the activity from initiation to termination. The participant checks off each step as he completes it. When a checklist is used when introducing a new activity, it provides a structure to allow the participants to ultimately perform independently without verbal assistance. However, unless a participant is familiar with the process, someone should be available to assist the participant, at least initially.

Figure 6.5
Sample Written Mini Schedule for Gardening Class

❏ Put pencil and seeds in my pocket at collection area
❏ In potting area, fill bucket with soil to red line
❏ Put water from hose on soil until one drop of water can be squeezed from it
❏ Place tray in bucket marked disinfectant and count to 10
❏ Fill tray with wet soil
❏ Press down soil with fingers
❏ Press pencil point in center of each cell starting with top left
❏ Put one seed in each hole made by pencil starting with top left
❏ Cover each seed with a pinch of soil
❏ Put seeded tray on red bench in greenhouse
❏ Put away everything in my area
❏ Get a gardening magazine to read

Additional examples of mini schedules are presented in Chapters 7–11. Different organizations may call them different names. For instance, ACAP in Chapter 11 has developed schedules for their community outings that they call "trip books." They help the participant understand expectations whatever they are called.

Box 6.2

Paula is excited about her tie-dying class. However, her instructor's verbal instructions are too long and fast for her. As a result, she repeatedly dips her T-shirt into all the colors. She does not like the result and is so upset that she knocks over one of the buckets of dye. Her instructor realizes that they need to make the steps of the activity clearer to her. Paula becomes successful when she is given a pictorial list of the steps (mini schedule) using a format similar to what she uses at work. This mini schedule includes choosing two colors then matching the colors to the buckets with the corresponding color dye in them. It also shows a picture of a timer set at the appropriate length of time to put the T-shirt in each color. The pictorial list indicates that the last steps are to hang up the T-shirt and clean up. Paula loves her T-shirt and signs up for another class at the recreation center.

Developing a visual schedule. Not all schedules look the same or are used in the same manner. Visual schedules may be developed in a variety of forms and should be developed using the level of representation understood by the individual participant. The following provides some options in formats for visual schedules.

- Visual schedules can be either horizontal left to right, as in reading, and in Figures 6.3 and 6.4, or vertical top to bottom, as in lists and in Figures 6.2 and 6.5.
- Visual schedules can be displayed in a variety of ways. As evidenced in Chapters 7 – 11, staff often design a variety of creative options. The schedules are often on poster board, clipboards, photo albums, three ring binders, manila folders, key rings or walls. Photos, line drawings or written representations of the activity can be attached to the schedule with paper clips, library pockets, clothespins or Velcro. Real objects or partial objects for those who need a more concrete representation can be attached with Velcro or set up in boxes. Many participants with or without a disability will benefit from having a set of 8 1/2 x 11 pictures posted for the group, while the participant with ASD may need to refer to a smaller personal schedule at his/her level of representation.

- Visual schedules get handled frequently and must be durable. Covering the representations of the activities and the display background with clear contact paper or laminate makes them last longer.
- Participants with ASD need a means to track where they are on a schedule. This can be achieved by crossing or checking off the activity represented, moving the picture to a "finished" envelope or container, or turning the picture over, when it is completed.

Schedules do not need to be fancy. Sometimes if staff has spent an inordinate amount of time developing a schedule, they are hesitant to modify it, if needed. If it is not possible to prepare a visual schedule ahead of time, a pad of paper or yellow sticky Post-it Note can be used to draw out the steps of an activity as it is happening.

Social Stories

Social stories, a strategy developed by Carol Gray (1993), is one of the most common strategies for providing social information and clarifying expectations used with individuals with ASD. It is an example of a visual support that assists with social understanding. A social story is a short story written following a specific format and guidelines that objectively describes a person, skill, event, concept or social situation (Gray, 1996). It includes the social cues and appropriate responses, and is written for a specific situation and individual. Every social story provides accurate information, which is stated positively and matter of factly.

A social story can be used for a variety of purposes, including facilitating the inclusion of participants in regular recreation settings, to introduce changes and new routines, to explain reasons for the behavior of others, to teach specific social skills, and to assist in teaching new skills. A story may help increase appropriate behavior, although the purpose is not to get compliance.

According to Gray (1996), the process of writing a social story begins with the identification of participant needs through observation and assessment of a difficult situation while considering the perspective of the participant in terms of what will be seen, heard and felt. A story is written at an appropriate comprehension level for the participant. Depending on the participant's level of comprehension, a social story may be presented through pictures with words or words alone.

Three types of sentences are most commonly used in social stories: 1) descriptive, 2) directive and 3) perspective statements (Gray, 1996). The descriptive sentences provide information on the setting, activity, and people involved. The directive statements are positive statements of the desired response for a given situation. The perspective statements provide a description of the possible reactions of others. It is important that there is only one, if any, directive sentence for every four to six other types of sentences. The purpose of social stories is to provide information, not to get compliance. A control sentence, which is developed with the participant, can be added to help the participant remember the story. A cooperative sentence can be added to say what others will do to assist the participant in the targeted situation.

Figure 6.6 provides a sample social story for Caleb, a participant in an after-school program who would not go to the playground because he was afraid that he would blow away. The social story was written by his Autism Specialist in a format similar to the types of books that he read. After one week of reading the story with his leisure companion at the beginning of the after-school playground program, he willingly went out on the playground even when it was windy. This social story gave him the accurate information that he needed to assuage his fear. It does not discount his fear, although he lives in a part of the country that does not have tornadoes.

Sometimes people believe they are writing social stories, but do not know about or utilize Gray's guidelines. Complete information on how to write social stories is beyond the scope to this book. However, resources related to how to write good social stories are provided in Appendix A.

Figure 6.6
Social Story: The Wind

D. Greene J. Miyake, illustrator. (2001). Columbia Regional Program Autism Services. CD ROM. Portland, OR: Columbia Regional Program and The Art Institute of Portland. Used with permission.

Other pictorial and/or written material that provides information or scripting can also provide effective visual information. They are described in this chapter and additional examples are presented in Chapters 7-11.

Structuring for a Predictable Environment

Thoughtful preparation needs to go into creating safe, familiar, predictable and highly motivating recreation environments for participants with ASD. The environment should be structured so that it provides consistency and clarity. Structure helps an activity to become "fun" and personally meaningful for individuals with ASD, because structure helps them understand what they need to do and what others are doing. When the activity lacks structure, it may set the participant with ASD up for failure and frustration.

Division TEACCH (Treatment and Education of Autistic and Related Communication Handicapped Children), one of the early leaders in the use of structure and visual strategies for individuals with ASD, has identified key components and strategies for structure that have been used extensively in recreation settings. According to TEACCH (Schopler et. al., 1995), participants need to know:

✔ Where things belong,
✔ What is expected of them in a specific situation, and
✔ What comes next

By knowing the answers to these questions before the activity, the participant will be more successful in participating. Having a clear understanding of what is happening and what they are supposed to do will also decrease the anxiety participants with ASD may feel when they are confused.

The information gathered on interests, strengths and the supports needed to maximize success should all be taken into account when setting up the areas and activities for recreation. Organizing the environment, making expectations clear and explicit, and using visual materials are particularly effective accommodations for individuals with ASD to participate in recreation activities as independently as possible. Structuring recreation instruction and activities in these ways helps to compensate for their difficulties in imitation and learning in informal ways, as well as their difficulty in initiation.

Although the systematic process for organizing and structuring the environment, events, space and time developed by TEACCH, Structured Teaching, is not entirely adopted in this section, it has extensively influenced the content. The elements of structuring for a predictable environment addressed in this section are:

- Routines
- Physical organization
- Expectations
- Visual structure
- Clear endings

Routines

A routine is repeating the same sequence of steps in doing an activity. Developing routines for activities can provide consistency and help the participant understand what is expected of him or her. Consistent schedules and routines provide a sense of familiarity and predictability. In a world that may appear to be confusing and filled with change, predictability is extremely comforting for individuals with ASD. Routines may serve to comfort the individual and lessen anxiety. The following provides some guidelines for creating routines for participants with ASD.

- Have a consistent beginning and ending routine for the activity, e.g., five-minute walk at beginning of aerobics class to warm up and the same four stretching exercises at the end of aerobics class.
- Have a consistent place/spot where the participant stands/sits at the beginning of the activity, e.g., on chalk line at edge of basketball court.
- Have a consistent sequence of steps or components.
- Present the sequence of steps in visual mini schedules for routines the participant seems unable to remember. As the participant moves through the activity the steps can be removed from the board so they know what has been done and what is next.

Each routine is learned by doing tasks in sequential order. Some participants may need written and/or pictorial sequences for routines only temporarily to learn certain sequences. Other routines will always need to be presented in a visual format. The goal is to create an environment where each participant can understand.

Physical Organization

Physical organization refers to how the physical environment is organized through using clear boundaries to decrease distractions, increase the ability to focus, understand what is required and understand where to be. Objects need to be organized in space to clarify:

✔ Where things are done
✔ Where things are located
✔ How to move from one place to another

Physical organization can define a variety of aspects of activities. The organization and arrangement of furniture and materials define the social and task context of activities. Individuals with ASD benefit from recreation environments that have defined areas that provide clear visual boundaries for specific activities. Boundaries help the participant understand where each area begins and ends. Physical organization can inform the participant about where s/he is supposed to be.

Materials and furniture can be arranged in a variety of ways to establish spatial boundaries and a context for the activity. These include, but are not limited to:

- String, yarn or plastic tape, chalk line or furniture, such as a table or bookcase, across an opening can serve as a cue to stay in or out of an area.
- Stakes, traffic cones, string or natural objects, such as sticks, can define an area where an activity will take place.
- A piece of paper, a small piece of tape, chalk line or natural object, such as a stick or leaf, placed on the ground can indicate where to stand or line up during an activity or while waiting.
- Carpet squares, hoops, or chairs, including rocking chairs or cube chairs, can define where to sit.
- Strategically placed labels or signs on objects, such as a name on a carpet square for where to sit, facilitate understanding.

These visual markers provide information about one's own space, the activity area and boundaries. The section on Mt. Hood Kiwanis Camp in Chapter 10 provides pictures of the defined spatial boundaries for the stream crossing area.

Staff may not always anticipate the physical organization that a participant will need. In this case, spatial boundaries can often be added quickly by thinking "on your feet."

Box 6.3

> When Davante arrives for his first day of horseback riding, the participants are asked to line up along the wall of the riding arena. Davante is confused and excited, so he runs around the arena while making a hooting sound. His leisure companion realizes that there are no spatial boundaries for Davante. She quickly takes out a piece of paper and draws two footprints about the size of Davane's feet. She places it on the ground near the wall and brings Davante over to show him where to stand. Davante stands on the footprints and waits his turn to ride.

Expectations

In order for participation to take place, a person with ASD needs to know what is expected of him or her. Participants with ASD need to have limits, boundaries and rules stated to provide clear and consistent expectations. In fact, the performance of an individual with ASD often improves dramatically when expectations are clearly defined and the world makes sense. Knowing the expectations avoids later confusion, anxiety, or anger. A format for determining expectations that should be communicated to participants is provided in Figure 5.10: Activity Procedures in Chapter 5. Clearly articulating expectations also decreases the possibility of the participant engaging in inappropriate behaviors, which result in correction from others that, in turn, can upset the participant.

According to Schopler et.al. (1995), information regarding expectations should indicate:

✔ How much will be done
✔ How many times an action will be repeated
✔ How long the activity will last

Expectations for instruction and interaction need to be clearly presented to individuals in a visual manner as much as possible. Expectations, rules or limits can be made clear by using visual supports, such as

- checklists
- reminder cards
- social stories
- charts
- posted rules
- completed sample
- templates

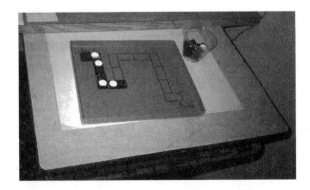

Template—for expectations

Examples of the use of a variety of visual supports are provided in Chapters 7 – 11.

Often expectations need to be stated more explicitly for individuals with ASD. Also, when an individual is stressed, she or he may need information at a more concrete level of representation.

Box 6.4

Sean enjoys swimming. He reads with comprehension and usually does well with a written list of rules for the pool, which includes:

- Walk in the pool area
- Walk directly to the pool
- Use legs and arms for swimming only
- Get out of the pool when the teacher says it is time
- Exit quietly and calmly

Lately Sean has begun to violate the rule related to using his legs and arms for swimming only. He is kicking other participants. Although Sean can read, a picture of "kicking" with the universal sign for "not allowed" is added. It appears that he is not as able to follow written directions when he feels anxious.

This additional visual cue helps Sean. He is following all the rules again.

When thinking through how to visually represent the rules for an activity or site, one also needs to think through any variations or exceptions to the rules. Without this analysis, participants, who are very concrete and literal with rules, may become too rigid about the rules.

Box 6.5

Jose enjoys playing soccer, but his coach is concerned about his participation because Jose has hit the goalie for his team a number of times. Jose believes the rule that players cannot touch the ball with their hands. He tries to enforce the rule when the goalie picks the ball up. Jose plays soccer without hitting anyone after he is provided with a pictorial list of who can purposefully hold the ball in their hands and who is not allowed to touch the ball with their hands. The following provides the list without the pictures.

People Who Can Touch the Ball with Hands during Game	People Who Cannot Touch the Ball with Hands during Game
Goalie Referee Coach Players who are asked	Players, except those listed

Visual Structure

Visual structure is used to organize the activity for the participant, as well as give it meaning (Scholper et. al., 1995). Materials should be organized so the participant can see:

✔ Where to be
✔ What to do
✔ With whom
✔ For how long

Feed Animals—for visual structure

The visual structure sets up what is required for the individual to do in a visual concrete manner following a left-to-right sequence. A concrete ending point and place, such as a basket, helps the individual understand when the task is completed and where to put the completed materials.

A variety of visual strategies may be used to help the participant to complete the activity:

- Labeling or color coding objects and containers can clarify and organize.
- Signs, written or pictorial lists, written and/or pictorial charts, templates, and samples of the completed project can all define the activity for the participant.
- Written or pictorial directions can establish a concrete means to highlight the approach to the activity.
- Templates can help the person with ASD understand what is expected and stay organized.

Templates set up from left to right may be particularly helpful for participants with ASD to clarify expectations. Templates are physical guides or models that are made of various substances, such as Styrofoam and cardboard that will help the individual with ASD know what to do, how much to do and when the activity is finished.

One effective approach that may be used for arts and crafts activities is an activity box that contains all the items needed to complete the activity. Smaller containers can be used to hold small, loose items. For instance, an activity box for completing a beaded necklace might contain the beads, needle, clasp and fishing line in smaller containers and the pliers and scissors in a larger container in the activity box. For other recreation activities, materials and equipment may be organized in duffel bags or other containers that are naturally part of the activity or added.

Box 6.6

John is wandering around the gym and playing with other equipment when he has been asked to throw balls in a lowered basketball hoop. The leader adds a line on the floor at a reasonable distance from the hoop and places a basket of balls to the left of the line. He takes John to the area and lets him know that he will be finished when the basket is empty. John throws the balls into the hoop until the basket is empty.

Box 6.7

Ken is upset at the end of his turn bowling and tries to continue bowling. He does not know that his turn is over after he uses two balls. He wants to keep rolling balls down the alley until there are no more pins standing. The leader arranges it so there are only two balls available on the rack when it is Ken's turn. Ken learns to stop when there were no more balls. Over time, it becomes cumbersome to limit the number of balls to two. Ken is given an index card with a picture of two bowling balls in two separate library pockets. He is taught to turn over one of the pictures of a bowling ball every time he rolls a ball. When both pictures of balls are turned over, he knows that his turn is over.

Finished box—for clear endings

Some activities, such as doing a puzzle, have a clear ending, while others, such as painting a picture may not. While other participants may keep track of the end of an activity by the time, many participants with ASD will need the end made more concrete. A concrete ending may need to be superimposed on the activity.

Box 6.8

Tabor enjoys painting, but he does not know when to stop. During art class, he copies paintings of birds meticulously, then continues to paint over his painting until the whole canvas is black. He does not stop painting until he is asked to stop. Although he copies the painting of birds quickly, he appears to think that he needs to keep painting until the class is over. Tabor responds well to having small red dots placed on each color of paint he will need to copy the bird. He removes each dot when he has used the color. When there are no more dots, he knows he is finished with the painting and can choose a different activity from his choice board. Over time, he begins to understand when a painting is complete on his own and the red dots are faded. He can now use his artistic talent without destroying his painting.

Indicating a concrete ending can be difficult for some activities. Sometimes it is easiest to add something that will mark time rather than concretely represent the ending. Stopping music that is playing or a visual cue can indicate the end of the activity. However, some participants with ASD may react to what still may appear to them to be a sudden change. For these individuals, the leader or leisure companion may need to prewarn the individual of the upcoming end to the activity in a visual manner. For instance, for a participant who can read, his leader or leisure companion can begin to write the name of the activity five minutes before the end of the activity and subsequently time writing the other letters so the name of the activity is complete when the activity ends. For an individual who does not read, a black and white drawing of an object of interest, such as a rocket, can be divided into five sections and one section a minute can be colored, beginning five minutes before the end of the activity. When the sections are all colored the activity is over. A variation of this is to have staff put puzzle pieces into a puzzle. When all the pieces are in the puzzle, the activity is over.

Staff may not always anticipate that a time marking system will be needed. Uncomplicated, easily assembled systems can often be made on the spot.

Box 6.9

Matt is gathering wood to build a campfire. Any amount of wood will do. He is so worried about missing an upcoming hike that he is perseverating on the hike and has only picked up one piece of wood. His leisure companion picks up some pebbles and tells Matt that gathering wood will be finished when there are no more pebbles in her hand. She puts a pebble in her pocket every minute or so and times it so that they will be done when it is time for the hike. Matt happily gathers wood and enjoys his hike later.

In summary, the physical structure and daily schedule help the participant with ASD to understand the environment and the relationship between events. It helps the participant understand what to do and how to approach the activity.

Sensory Supports

Participants with ASD may have an inability to process and respond to incoming sensory information efficiently or effectively. This can result in a variety of sensory sensitivities or needs that interfere with participation in recreation activities. Recreation staff must be sensitive to the intense sensory needs and comfort requirements of the participant with ASD. The sensory disturbances of individuals with ASD are described in detail in Chapter 2.

When these sensory issues are understood, the environment can be examined for items, sounds and activities that may result in sensory overload for the individual. The environmental inventory in Figure 5.9 in Chapter 5 provides one way to gather this information. After the environment is assessed for potential sources of sensory difficulties, a plan can be made to minimize its impact on participation. These may include strategies, such as:

- Change difficult aspects of the environment.
- Screen out some of the difficult sensations.
- Desensitize the person to the sensation.
- Provide a sensory diet.
- Teach to use relaxation and calming strategies to help calm down when the input level is high.
- Teach to self-regulate sensory system.

The use of these strategies in relationship to sounds, touch, and vestibular/proprioceptive input will be described later in this chapter.

Occupational therapists and some other professionals may be available to analyze and devise strategies specifically for the participant. In some cases, occupational therapists may have made recommendations in other settings, such as the school, that can also be used in the recreation setting.

Noise

It may be difficult for the participant with ASD to attend to the relevant information and to block out background noises. Noise from fans, loudspeakers, fire alarms, several people talking at once, air conditioners, bells, dogs barking or scraping may upset the participant. A variety of strategies can be used to ameliorate reactions to sound. Some of these include:
- Note sounds that might cause overload for the participant.
- Provide earplugs, blue tack in the ears, soft foam earplugs, or listening to music on a Walkman to screen out noise.
- When feasible, reduce noise that confuses, disorients or upsets the participant, e.g., lower volumes, turn off fans, and close doors.
- Provide sensory experiences that may be calming for the participant, e.g., soft music.
- Provide personal space for relaxation.
- Provide information about the upsetting sound and how long it will last.

Some individuals will tolerate an upsetting sound when they know when it will occur and how long it will last. Sometimes they will need to cope with the distractions and disruptions that are an inevitable part of daily life.

> **Box 6.10**
>
> Wally has screamed when he heard a vacuum cleaner since he was an infant. The janitor sometimes runs the vacuum while Wally is still in his evening woodworking class. Everyone is disturbed by Wally's reaction to the vacuuming, which is to scream and hit his head. His instructor is particularly concerned about his being around electrical equipment when he is in this state. The team decides that it is vital to address his reaction to vacuums if he is going to continue in class. After all, vacuums will exist in many areas of his life. The leisure facilitator writes a social story about vacuums, which includes about how long the vacuum will be on. Wally tolerates the vacuum since he has had a visual timer that shows when the vacuuming will start and when it will end. Like many of us, he can tolerate difficult moments when he knows how long they will last. The same situation can be intolerable when one does not know if they will ever stop.

Sight

Participants with ASD may have increased sensitivity to light. This sensitivity may be neurologically based. Some of these participants may try to avoid outdoor activities, bright lights, certain types of lights, reflections or background patterns. These participants may prefer shaded areas outdoors or may keep their head down. Staff may think the participants are "being difficult" or stubborn when they actually are experiencing discomfort from the light.

- Avoid excessive wall displays.
- Display only what is necessary.
- Provide an area with dividers for less visual distraction.
- Sunglasses or a visor can to help the individual filter stimuli.
- Lamps with low wattage bulbs or soft, natural light rather than overhead lights may be easier on their eyes.

Touch

Some participants with ASD may not like to be touched with certain textures or on certain parts of their bodies or react to temperature. Tactile sensitivity frequently involves the hands and/or face. A tickling, light touch may cause the participant to become very excited or even cause discomfort. In some cases, the participant may demonstrate a need to explore through touch yet avoid being touched. This is called "tactile defensiveness."

- Avoid very light touch because it will increase distraction.
- Approach the individual from the front rather than behind so that he can see you coming.
- Provide space for the individual, e.g., end of the line or carpet square.
- Provide desensitization to surroundings.
- Encourage the participant to explore new textures gradually, in a step-by-step fashion, such as holding, putting on and using equipment for various amounts of time.
- Allow to wear alternative clothing.

Nathan usually takes his shoes and socks off whenever he has the opportunity. At home, this is accepted as his way of communicating that he does not like the feeling of constricting objects on his feet. He would like to take a class at the community arts center, but they require that everyone wear shoes for safety reasons, because there could be sharp objects on the floor. After experimentation, the leisure coordinator discovers that Nathan will tolerate wearing Birkenstock sandals. Nathan is allowed to wear his sandals in class. He completes the class and takes several others later with this slight accommodation.

One successful method to desensitize participants with ASD to textures is to begin with textures that are dry, move to moist, then to wet, and eventually to sticky textures. Present the textures to parts of the body, which are less sensitive, e.g., bony areas and areas not covered by hair, such as elbows, shoulders, knees and back of the hands. These areas of the body may tolerate the textures first. Exposure to potentially aversive textures, such as immersing hand in gooey liquids, has been used successfully. In some cases, a barrier, such as gloves, can be added to decrease the effect of the texture on the participant.

Logan wants to take a papier mache class, but he has difficulty tolerating wet, sticky objects on his hands. His instructor agrees to let him wear surgical gloves and to warm the water for the papier mache. His family helps him practice holding mushy things with gloved hands before he goes to class. Logan is proud of the whale's tail that he makes in class.

Some participants seek deep pressure, such as crawling under a gym mat. This may have a grounding or calming effect on some participants. Occupational therapists can give strategies of how to best meet this need for an individual.

Vestibular/Proprioceptive

Some participants with ASD need to move and exercise frequently. Others may appear anxious when they need to move their body through space. A variety of recreation activities incorporate heavy work patterns that are beneficial to individuals with ASD. According to Kashman & Mora (2002), these activities include, but are not limited to walking, running, hiking, swimming, horseback riding, weight training, bowling, gardening and woodworking. Ceramics and pottery also provides proprioceptive input to the hands.

When not engaged in these active recreation activities, participants with ASD may need regularly scheduled vestibular and/or proprioceptive input, such as:

- Movement with a heavy work pattern
- Movement breaks, e.g., jumping on the mini tramp every 20 minutes or simply walking to the water fountain 50 yards away once during an activity
- For participants who jump around during a seated activity, a cube chair turned upside down with a pillow in it, a rocking chair, a three-legged stool, a therapy ball or a beanbag chair
- Weighted items, such as weighted vest, lap pillow, and weighted blanket
- Pressure items, such as a lycra body sock or neoprene vest
- A small fanny pack with "fidgets," such as a koosh ball or squish ball.

Successful programs must recognize and accommodate the sensory disturbances experienced by individuals with ASD. Waiting times may be particularly difficult. Many participants will do best when they have something in their hands or mouth when they are not otherwise occupied, e.g., waiting for a turn. Although they may appear to be preoccupied with these items, they may often listen and process information better when they are getting preferred sensory input.

Sensory Diet

A sensory diet consists of regularly scheduled activities for specific sensory input to help individuals modulate their sensory system. It is designed to enhance performance through calming and regulating sensory techniques. Occupational therapists can provide ideas for grounding and a sensory diet. Sometimes participants have a "sensory diet" that has been developed by an occupational therapist and has been used effectively in other settings. Many of the techniques from a sensory diet can be easily incorporated into the recreation setting or adapted for that setting.

Tali usually stays focused on an activity for a brief period. Her occupational therapist at school has developed a sensory diet for classroom staff to implement three times during the school day for five to 10 minutes each time. Tali's mother shares the written plan listed below with camp staff and requests that the sensory diet be used at camp also. Her sensory diet includes the following.

Sensory Diet for Tali
Follow each vestibular (movement activity) task with a proprioceptive (deep pressure, heavy work) activity.

Vestibular activities:
- Jump on a trampoline or similar surface
- Sit and bounce on a therapy ball

Proprioceptive activities:
- Lie with her back down on the floor and bring her knees to her chest. Hold for five minutes
- Lie on her stomach and roll the therapy ball firmly over her legs and torso
- Lie on one beanbag chair and use another to apply pressure on top of her
- Carry a heavy bin to an area, e.g., recycle bin with two phone books inside
- Ride a bike for five minutes
- Carry the heavy bin back to the area

After reviewing the sensory diet, the camp staff talks with the occupational therapist to clarify the approaches, as well as which are the vestibular and proprioceptive activities. They also discuss the activities that Tali will be doing as a camper, such as hiking, horseback riding, swimming and so on. They decide to have Tali use the hammock swing, carry a box with wood to the campfire, use the therapy ball in the pool and apply firm pressure with hands on her shoulders. Thanks to the sensory diet, Tali's attention is longer than the staff anticipated and everyone is happy.

Box 6.13

Relaxation

Many individuals with ASD need times to relax during the day or during an activity. At times, it may be necessary to have a calm, quiet, designated area where the participant can go to relax. This type of relaxation is often referred to as "taking a break." Individuals may be taught to respond to a break card on their schedule for regularly scheduled breaks. Since staff cannot always anticipate when a break will be needed, the participant can also be taught to respond to a break card, red light or stop sign presented by the instructor or leisure companion to signal the need to go to the quiet area. This must be done before the participant has lost control. Since a break is a self-regulation calm down time, the participant may be given a designated number of break cards and taught to present a card when s/he needs a break. Even those who are verbal may benefit from having break cards, because they need a back-up system to use when they are under stress.

Various strategies, such as deep breathing and progressive muscle relaxation, can help an individual with ASD learn to relax his/her body. When relaxed, s/he is better able to position his/her body, to use his/her senses, and generally feels better. Cautela & Groden (1978) pioneered specific techniques to teach relaxation to individuals with special needs. Participants who have had this training can be encouraged to use it before potentially stressful situations, such as a change in routine. Visual supports are often useful to cue relaxation. Figure 6.7 illustrates a sequence for progressive muscle relaxation that can be used in teaching the routine.

Participants who become overstimulated easily may benefit from massage throughout the day to help them calm down and relax. The individual may relax through deep, firm touch on the shoulders. Waiting until the individual is rigid or in a tantrum to work on relaxing is usually too late.

Self-regulation

Recognizing signs of stress is an important self-monitoring strategy for participants with ASD. Individuals with ASD may learn to regulate their sensory system. Williams and Shellenberger (1996) developed a sensory integration program entitled, *How Does Your Engine Run: A Leader's Guide to the Alert Program for Self-Regulation.* This ingenious program teaches individuals to recognize their level of alertness or arousal and to change that level as necessary to meet social demands. Another approach, a calming down theme board, is used to help the participant recognize and self-monitor their sensory issues by POPARD in Chapter 7.

Preparing the Participant for a New Program or Activity

Although the objective is for the recreation activity itself to be enjoyable and reinforce the participant, a new activity may be difficult for the participant with ASD. Anticipation of the unknown can be frightening for participants with ASD. Thoughtful preparation to assist with the difficulty with new or different environments, activities or expectations is vital. Before beginning a new program, try to alleviate any anxieties the participant with ASD may have in the new situation. By systematically preparing the participants for the new activity and environment, they will be able to anticipate what will happen in the activity.

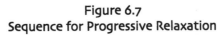

Figure 6.7
Sequence for Progressive Relaxation

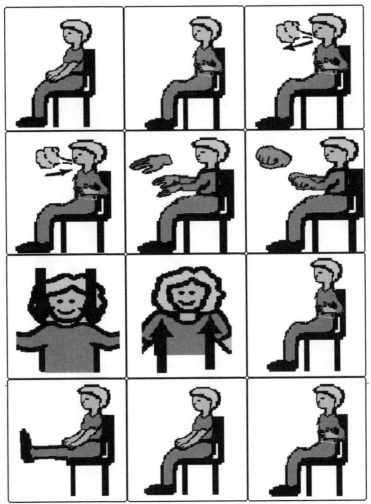

(Personal communication from M. Hammel, November 18, 2002. Created with The Picture Communication Symbols 1981-2002 Mayer-Johnson, Inc. Used with permission.)

When preparing participants with ASD for an activity, they will be most successful if they are provided with the following information through the use of visual supports, such as pictures, videotapes, and/or social stories:

✔ What am I expected to do?
✔ How much am I expected to do?
✔ How will I know when I am finished?
✔ What will I do next?

By knowing the answers to these questions before the activity, the participant will be more successful in the recreation activity. Having a clear understanding of what is happening and what they are supposed to do will also decrease the anxiety they feel when they are unsure and unable to ask for clarification.

Perhaps the advanced organizers at the beginning of each of the chapters in this book have helped you anticipate what will happen in each chapter. This type of mapping or flow chart can also help participants with ASD to understand how information or events fit together.

Participants with ASD also benefit from knowing what the roles are in a group and what other people will be doing. Figure 6.8 provides a written chart about the game of baseball, which was developed to prepare a participant to watch and understand a baseball game at his school. Since some of the vocabulary in this chart was new to him, such as inning, foul, and outs, these baseball terms were shown to him in a video of a baseball game.

Figure 6.8
Written Chart for Baseball Game

BASEBALL

Events	Teams	Players
Ball	1.	Batter
Strike	2.	Catcher
Hit		Pitcher
Out		Base players
Foul		Field players
Homerun		

Bases	Length	Snack
First	1 Inning = 3	1.
Second	outs for each team	2.
Third	9 Innings = 1 game	(Participant
Home	(unless both scores	chooses ahead)
	are the same)	

Different participants may require various combinations of supports to prepare them for new activities. Below are suggested supports to prepare a participant with ASD for a new activity.

- Someone familiar with the participant "scouts" the situation ahead of time to anticipate possible problems.
- Introduce exactly what will happen ahead of time in a visual manner.
- Provide an outline of the class or program, including content, times, and dates, to the participant.
- Use social stories to describe situation.
- Give the parents/caregivers a copy of the activity plan ahead of time, so they can go over it with the participant before coming to the activity. It is helpful to provide pictures.
- Prepare a small scrapbook of the setting and/or activity.
- Develop videotape about the new program and provide visual information about specific situations so that the participant can learn and rehearse for the new situation.
- If the activity will take place in a new setting, visit it on a number of occasions.

- Introduce new leaders, instructors and companions to the participant.
- Reduce expectations/demands at the beginning of participation.
- If using new materials, look at or try things out ahead of time.
- Provide access to comfort materials, such as a familiar object from home, and other sensory supports to decrease anxiety.
- If the participant is particularly resistant to change, introduce new aspects slowly with rehearsal and/or desensitization. For example, the initial visit may be devoted to simply going to the facility and going in the front door. On another visit, the participant might visit the room in which the activity will take place.
- Have participant observe several sessions before s/he is asked to participate.

Box 6.14

Cedric enjoys movement and water, so his family believes that he will enjoy canoe rides. However, he has never worn a life vest, been in water outside of a bath or been in a boat of any kind. He is very hesitant to try new experiences and canoeing is full of new experiences.

His parents help him prepare for canoeing. They start by showing him pictures and talking about canoeing. They drive by the canoe area. Then they drive to the canoe area and get out of the car. They watch people canoe and meet the instructor.

The next time, the instructor begins to introduce Cedric to some of the components of canoeing. First, the instructor helps Cedric get used to putting his feet in the lake, then wearing a life vest, then sitting in a canoe on dry land before all of these things are put together. After several classes, he loves riding in a canoe and putting his hands in the water.

Despite their best efforts, sometimes staff members do not prepare participants as well as they thought they had. They cannot always anticipate how a participant with ASD will interpret information. Usually, more information can be added to remedy misinterpretations.

Box 6.15

Mei Mei is enrolled in a swimming class for the first time. The staff has carefully prepared a pictorial activity schedule with all the steps of the activity and written a social story regarding the expectations for participation in the swimming class.

Mei Mei happily goes to the pool and prepares for her swim class. However, she initially stands at the edge of the water flapping her hands and refuses to get in. One of the staff realizes that no one had told Me Mei that, "You will get wet when you swim." It was assumed that she knew that swimming meant getting wet. Fortunately, Mei Mei likes water and is amenable to going into the water when she is given the additional information that getting wet is part of swimming. She loves swimming and signs up for more classes.

Coyne et. al. (1999) have developed a series of activity cards as a means of providing visual supports when introducing a new activity. The activity cards provide a mini schedule of line drawings for the activity to help the participant understand the sequence, a written activity story to help the participant understand the activity, a list of materials and suggestions for the leader. For each community and social activity presented, there is a "Get Ready" activity card to prepare the participant with ASD for the activity and a "The Real Thing" activity card to help the participant both before and during the activity. Figure 6.9 provides a sample from one side of the "Get Ready" activity card for swimming. The picture sequence from "The Real Thing" activity card for swimming, which complements Figure 6.9, can be seen in Figure 6.3. The suggestions to leaders from these cards and the activity story for "The Real Thing" for swimming are not depicted.

Just because a person with ASD does not respond positively the first time an activity is presented does not necessarily mean that you should give up on that activity. It may be the novelty itself that is the problem. Because one characteristic of ASD is resistance to change in routine, an activity may need to be introduced multiple times before it is accepted. If an activity has been presented five or more times and the person has strong negative reactions toward the activity, it may be time to try something else. However, just because an activity does not seem to be of interest at that particular time, does not mean that it will not be of interest in the future. Like all of us, interests can change over time. The main objective is to give each person with ASD the chance to try a number of options and then choose the activities that s/he finds most enjoyable.

Figure 6.9
One Side of "Get Ready" Activity Card for Swimming

Activity Story

I will look at my calendar to see when I will go swimming.

I will go swimming on (after)_____.

I will look at my calendar to see what I need to take to the swimming pool. When it is

time, I will get my bag. I will put my swimsuit and towel in my bag.

I will take my (swim card, money) with me to get into the pool area.

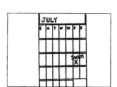   

(P. Coyne, C. Nyberg, & M. L. Vandenburg, 1999. Developing Leisure Time Skills in Persons with Autism. Arlington, TX: Future Horizons. Used with permission.)

Transitions and Changes during Activities

Transitions during recreation activities can also be difficult for the participant with ASD. They frequently resist changes in their routines. They may be frightened, angry, or refuse to participate in the next activity. New materials and activities may be initially rejected. Even moving from one area of a room to another can represent a major change for a participant with ASD. Therefore, participants with this disorder need to be prepared for any transition or change.

Participants can be assisted to accept and understand what will happen next in a number of ways. The suggestions for preparing participants for new activities in the previous section are also applicable to planning for transitions between and within activities.

Some additional suggestions for preparing individuals for transition between and within activities include:

• Avoid surprises and prepare ahead thoroughly in advance of changes regardless of how minimal.

- Give the participant ample warning prior to any transition.
- Use visual schedules to prepare the participant for changes in activities.

> **Box 6.16**
>
> Nick regularly uses a mini tramp for a motor break during ceramics class. The mini tramp is broken today. His instructor and leisure companion discuss how to help him accept this without a tantrum. They decide to show him a picture of his trike as the motor break in ceramics class that day. At the beginning of class, his leisure companion uses the visual schedule to point out the line drawing of a trike for motor break. Nick slaps at the picture. The schedule is shown to him again when it is time for his motor break. This time he accepts the picture of the trike without protest. He was allowed time to process the information as well as to prepare for the transition to the trike. Everyone is glad that they have avoided a meltdown.

- Describe what to expect, e.g., first _____, then _____ in a visual manner.
- When a visual schedule is unavailable, provide an object that will be used in the next activity to help the participant understand what is coming up next.
- Use social stories to prepare the participant for change.
- Allow some choice when possible to provide the participant with some sense of control.
- Help explain changes by providing visual supports.

> **Box 6.17**
>
> Jasmine loves her ballet class. One day the power goes off in the dance studio during class. Jasmine is frightened and runs from the studio. The next scheduled day for ballet class, she screams and drops to the ground at the entrance to the building. Her leisure companion backs off, allows time for her to calm down, and then gives her a card with a picture of ballet on it. Jasmine screams when she sees the picture and bites her foot. The leisure companion backs off for about 30 seconds and then points to the picture of ballet again without saying anything. After several minutes, which seems like an eternity to the leisure companion, Jasmine gets up and starts walking towards the studio. When Jasmine gets to the door to the studio, she screams and drops to the floor again. The leisure companion calmly repeats the procedure that she used outside by pointing to the picture of ballet. The ballet class has begun and the instructor says, "Jasmine, the lights and music are on. You can come in." Jasmine watches the class for about five minutes, then joins the class. Her mother, also, writes a social story entitled, "What It Means when the Power Goes Off," which her father illustrates, to help prevent another fearful reaction to the loss of power.

- If an activity does not have a clear ending, give several notices that the activity is almost over and that a transition is coming up.
- Introduce skill sequences, such as sports skills, before the class to reduce confusion and frustration.
- To keep anxiety low, reduce expectations/demands following change.

> **Box 6.18**
>
> Julia is in a step aerobics class. The instructor says step up and before Julia has responded, goes on to step left. Julia steps up while the class is stepping to the left. Julia becomes increasingly frustrated and begins to make loud vocalizations. The instructor realizes that she or Julia's leisure companion will have to practice the routine with her before class for her to be successful. This is a way of preparing her for the class.

Communication Supports

Communication is important for everyone and encompasses more than speech. Professionals who study communication estimate that 75 percent of communication is through body language. Staff need to understand how the participant with ASD communicates (expressive communication), as well as how to help the participant with ASD understand directions and expectations (receptive communication).

Expressive Communication

Even the most verbal person with Autism Spectrum Disorder who appears to have a superior vocabulary has difficulties in verbal and nonverbal communication. Everyone should be sensitive to the participant's attempts to communicate and try to assign meaning to even subtle communicative behaviors. Watch and look for a participant's behavior to indicate what s/he is saying.

A means to communicate should always be readily available for the participant with ASD. If participants come with any form of communication, such as leading someone by the hand, pointing, picture boards, signing, written language or other means, the recreation staff should learn how to understand and use that system.

Some participants may come with a communication system. Real objects, pictures, or written words can be displayed in a variety of ways for communication. Because the communication system may not have been developed with recreation activities in mind, additional symbols for the recreation activity may need to be added to the system. In recreation settings, it is important that these displays be sturdy, portable, easy to manage and always available. Communication systems need to be available and used rather than put on a shelf somewhere. Compact communication systems can be attached to a backpack or belt or carried in a fanny pack, pocket or purse.

> **Box 6.19**
>
> The counselors at camp know that Ivan points at line drawings in his communication book at school. They get a copy of his communication book from school and add pictures of objects and activities he may want to request during activities at camp, such as horses and marshmallows. They waterproof it and he carries it in his fanny pack. Ivan can communicate his needs and desires at camp.

Some key strategies to assist individuals in communicating are:

- Pause, listen and wait.
- Watch and listen for attempts to communicate.
- Respond positively to attempts to communicate.
- Encourage choice when possible.

Receptive Communication

Because of difficulties in auditory processing, participants with ASD may experience differences in the way they hear what is said, have difficulty sorting out what is important, or have delays in processing and responding to what s/he hears. The following list suggests some effective strategies for assisting the participant with ASD to understand directions.

Photo by Jason Kinch Photographics,
Courtesy of Mt. Hood Kiwanis Camp

- Simplify your language. Omit needless words. Keep it short and simple without patronizing. Do not speak to a participant who is 15 years old like s/he is five.
- Keep facial expressions and gestures simple and clear.
- Use gestures, modeling, visual supports and demonstrations with verbalizations.
- Use concrete, literal language. Observe and check for understanding.
- Break down instructions and use visual supports. Use "what to do" statements rather than "what not to do" statements, e.g., "Sit in the canoe" instead of "Don't stand in the canoe."
- Use statements rather than questions, e.g., "It's time to get out of the pool" instead of "Can you get out of the pool now?"
- Allow time for responses. Slow down your pace.
- Avoid using vague terms like "later," "maybe," or unfinished.
- Avoid abstract "why" questions, e.g., "Why did you do that?"
- Avoid idioms, double meanings, and sarcasm.
- Use visual supports to aid comprehension of oral speech.
- Check for understanding.

Box 6.20

Bryce is taking a drama class. His instructor asks him to read from the playbook. His immediate response is to loudly exclaim, "This is drama, not reading class!" The idea that drama class includes reading is new to him and he needs time to process this request. His instructor says she will come back to him after another participant, Jody, reads one page. The instructor asks Jody to read. Bryce takes out his book to read in about a minute. He has had time to process the information, as well as a model for reading.

The use of pictorial and written cues can often aid in helping the participant to understand directions and expectations. Visual supports for giving directions, such as program rules, file cards with directions for specific activities, and pictorial or written instructions facilitate participation in recreation activities. The sample mini schedules in Figure 6.4 and 6.5 provide directions for their respective activities. Figure 6.10 provides a sample written list of rules for swimming to prepare the participant for expectations. Pictures could be added to this list to increase comprehension.

Figure 6.10
Rules for Swimming

Walk in swimming area.
Wear swimsuit in pool.
Shower before going to pool.
Wait to get in pool until lifeguard says it is okay to get in.
Stay in green area of pool (shallow end).
Get out of pool when asked.

One of the advantages of using visual supports is that they can be examined for as long as needed to process the information. In contrast, oral information is transient. Once it is said, the message is no longer available. This may pose problems for participants who have difficulties processing language, and who require additional time (Hogdon, 1995).

Social Supports

Social skill deficits are characteristic and pervasive in ASD. Social interactions, in general, tend to be difficult. Therefore, support in the social aspects of the activity is frequently necessary.

Box 6.21
Seth loves going to Game Club. When he enters the room he usually hits all the people that he sees. This attempt to greet people is frightening and causes the other participants to avoid him. Parents of the other participants are very concerned that he will hurt their children. Since Seth does not speak, he is shown a non-verbal means to greet people, thumb wrestling. In addition to providing him with an appropriate way to greet people, it provides him with a way to engage for a short time with a peer that does not require a verbal exchange. His peers go from scattering when he approaches to smiling and extending an arm in invitation. Everyone is much happier with this way of interacting. The other participants are glad to see him now.

Developing social skills may not be a focus in every recreation program, but accommodations such as the following can be made:

- Provide the participant with situation-specific social expectations for behavior, including what to talk about and how to get help.
- Encourage watching and physical proximity.
- Allow for extra personal space.
- Allow for solitariness.
- Give the participant time to get to know you.
- When possible, practice social skills in small groups.
- Protect the participant from teasing.
- Maximize opportunities for parallel participation, e.g., ride bikes, roller skate.
- Limit demands for conversation.
- Consider social predictability, language expectations and social rules of the group.
- Limit waiting and turn taking.
- Make guidelines for turn taking and waiting clear through visual support and/or the arrangement of materials.
- Directly present social rules in a very clear, concrete manner through visual support.

Box 6.22 Bill has trouble figuring out when it is his turn in table games even when he is playing with just one other person. His leisure companion helps Bill by giving Bill an index card with "Bill's turn" and a picture of Bill on one side and "Tom's turn" and a picture of Tom on the other side. The card is turned over after a player takes a turn to show whose turn it is. This has made turn taking more concrete and Bill no longer has to be constantly reminded to wait or to take his turn.

- Structure their responses through the use of social scripts. Social scripts provide canned language to use for specific events.
- Provide social supports, such as social stories and cartooning.

Box 6.23 Jeremy always barges into group games and demands to be the center of attention. He always insists on being the key player, such as the pitcher in baseball, the quarterback in football or the goalie in soccer. When peers tell Jeremy to wait his turn, he wrestles the ball away from a peer and makes his peers chase him. On several occasions, fights result from this type of interaction. A directive social script (see below) is developed to assist Jeremy to act appropriately when joining and participating in group games. His leisure companion coaches Jeremy in the use of the script. At first, his leisure companion needs to cue him to use the script, but over time Jeremy uses the script independently.

Social script for Jeremy
When I want to join a game, I will stand at the edge of the field near the children playing the game.
I will say, "Can I join in your game?"
If the players say that I can, I will ask, "What position is open?"
When I am in the game, I will follow the rules.
If my friends tell me not to play because the game has already started or for some other reason, I will say, "OK, but I would like to play next time."

The participant may also approach people very closely in order to use his/her senses of touch and smell or not know appropriate person distance. Sometimes the physical attempts of participants with ASD to begin friendships are seen as frightening by their intended friends if the touch is too rough. It is very important to help him/her touch appropriately before s/he has a chance to scare or hurt anyone. Some situation specific expectations regarding this behavior that may need to be taught are:

- Gently tap others on the shoulder.
- When the person turns toward you, ask or show what you want.
- Stay an arms length from others.

Participants with ASD often get into trouble because they do not understand social expectations that are not directly explained to them, such as:

- "Do not sustain eye contact in a shower room."
- "Don't put your hands in your pants in public."
- "Use facial tissue to blow your nose."

Participants may need additional visual cues or social stories to help them understand these formerly unwritten social rules.

Cartooning is another effective social support. It provides social information in a visual format. Speech and thought bubbles along with color are used to help the individual see and analyze a conversation. One form of cartooning is comic strip conversation. This form was introduced by Gray (1994) to illustrate and interpret social situations through simple line drawing figures and other symbols in a comic strip format.

Assistance from Other Participants

Other participants are often willing to help an individual with ASD with the transition and acclimatization to the new program. By gaining the support of a friend without a disability, the participant with ASD may have greater access to social opportunities during and after the program. Conversely, participants with ASD are often disproportionately a target for teasing and bullying, so it is important for staff to protect them from teasing and bullying.

Participants are naturally curious and may want to ask questions. Recreation providers can encourage them to do so and answer them as simply and honestly as possible. If recreation leaders are uncomfortable answering the questions, parents or others who know the individual with ASD well are often willing to provide information about ASD and the participant. It often helps others to know why the participant with ASD acts in certain ways and what they can do.

The use of a partner system can be very useful, since many participants with ASD relate best one to one. Careful selection of a partner can be a tool to help build social skills and encourage friendships. The effective training and use of buddies at two camps are described in Chapter 10.

Box 6.24

Brian had always been uncomfortable interacting with others. However, his parents persuaded him to go to a drama class at the YMCA. Despite extensive preparation, he did not like the class at first. The class only had 10 participants and most were young women. Most of the drama exercises were done in pairs, so he did not need to interact with the group as a whole in the beginning. His instructor was careful to watch for other participants who seemed to enjoy Brian and utilized these participants as partners with him. Over time, Brian's comfort and interest in drama increased. He then took a drama class with 20 participants. The class size was too large for him and he became very anxious. Everyone, including Brian, learned that he could be successful in drama, but it had to be in a small, supportive group.

Instructional Supports

Staff Assistance

Often participants with ASD continue to need the assistance of at least one staff or family member when they are participating in the community. However, it is important to encourage independent effort and incorporate proactive measures to reduce the likelihood of the individual with ASD becoming dependent on prompts from these support people. The less the participant with ASD needs to rely on others and the more s/he can rely on schedules, structure and him/herself the more independent s/he will be from constant verbal directions.

Some helpful hints for those who provide support are:

- Use visual supports to decrease the reliance on prompts from the instructor or leisure companion.
- Be careful that the support person is not always closely positioned next to the participant.
- Increase awareness of environmental cues, e.g., watching what other participants are doing.
- Provide interaction with the leader, as well as the leisure companion, to facilitate accepting supervision from different people.

Choices/Motivators

Free choice is a key quality of leisure and recreation activities. However, individuals with ASD may not be able to initiate or make choices that indicate self-motivation. By definition, they have restricted repertoires of interests and skills needed for community involvement.

External motivation may be necessary to establish attention and the learning of new skills initially. However, common reinforcers may not motivate the participant with ASD. It is important to know what is reinforcing for each participant, including the amount and type of materials preferred. She or he might prefer some time spent alone, time to talk to a favorite staff member, completion of a task, an exercise routine, such as going for a walk, time to play with a favorite object, music, playing in water, getting to perform a favorite routine, items that provide specific sensory stimulation, or sitting at the window rather than traditional reinforcers.

One approach that has been used successfully to increase participation in activities is the Premack principle. The Premack principle theorizes that less preferred activities followed by preferred activities (First____, then____) become more preferred. Therefore, following a new activity with a preferred activity or object can increase the desirability of the new activity. The structure of short, successful experiences with less preferred activities followed by longer more preferred and easier to tolerate activities works particularly well for hesitant participants with very restricted repertoires of interests.

> **Box 6.25** Reggie does not like to dribble the ball in basketball, but loves to throw it. Through drills in which he dribbles the ball three times and then shoots, he begins to like dribbling the ball.

Another strategy for motivation is providing the chance to make a choice within an activity, e.g., choosing color of beads to use in making a necklace or choosing color of kick board for swimming. A participant might be provided a choice from a board that depicts pictures of possible choices. This is called a choice board. Research has shown that being able to express choice in leisure activities increases participation (Dattillo,

Photo by Jason Kinch Photographics,
Courtesy of Mt. Hood Kiwanis Camp

1988; Realon et. al., 1990). In addition, increasing the opportunities for choice making is directly correlated with increased positive behaviors.

Many individuals with ASD are extremely sensitive to failure. They also often find satisfaction in completing tasks. Therefore, a combination of errorless learning, in which the participant is assisted to do the activity right the first time, and activities, in which successful outcomes can be achieved "here and now" can be motivating in and of themselves.

Extent of Participation

Sometimes the normal length of an activity exceeds what an individual with ASD can do at that point in time. Often the length of participation can be gradually extended over time. For instance, the participant may only be able to participate in skating for 15 minutes and need an alternative for the rest of the time at first. Others may need to sit in a quiet area during more challenging parts of activities.

> **Box 6.26**
>
> Talbot enjoys most of the activities with the parachute. He follows the instructor's directions and giggles happily until participants need to go under the parachute. At that point, he screams and runs across the multipurpose room. His leisure companion joins him in his designated safe area and they watch the other participants going under the parachute. He eagerly rejoins the group in parachute activities after the part that frightens him, going under the parachute, is over. Over time he is desensitized to going under the parachute.

It may be helpful to alternate large group activities or new activities with opportunities for calming activities in a quiet environment or for participation in familiar activities. J. D.'s picture schedule for soccer in Chapter 9 (Figure 9.6) was developed to accommodate J. D.'s need for short periods of play alternated with calming breaks. In contrast, the incorporation of physical activity and exercise at points throughout seated activities may be helpful.

Additional Teaching Considerations

- Plan and present tasks at an appropriate level of difficulty.
- Pay attention to processing and pacing issues that may be linked to cognitive and/or motor difficulties, and give the participant ample time to respond, e.g., provide extra time for dressing. Some need time to process what has been said.
- Wait for a response. Let participants finish.
- Provide preferential seating away from distractions and near instructor.
- Use concrete examples and hand-on activities when teaching abstract ideas and conceptual thinking.
- Alternate familiar, successful experiences with new activities.
- Reduce the number of participants required in an activity or work on a 1: 1 basis as necessary.
- Reduce the speed of moving objects by removing air from a ball, using nerf balls, etc.

When all is said and done, any combination of strategies may be needed for specific situations and the supports needed may vary over time. When a problem arises, even a slight adjustment may make the difference between active, meaningful participation and a failure.

Box 6.27 Andy is excited about playing tetherball and pushes his way to the front of the line. His instructor recognizes that he needs assistance and assigns a buddy to be in front of him in line. Since Andy does not appear to recognize individual participants, a sticker with a ball on it is put on the buddy's back. Andy is also allowed to use objects in his fanny pack while he waits in line. Andy and his buddy practice tetherball and waiting in line together before class. The instructor also creates a rotation of activities so that the line for tetherball is shorter. Andy is successful and all the participants benefit from the changes.

Behavioral Supports

Individuals with ASD may demonstrate behaviors that are frequently viewed as inappropriate. Often behaviors are seen as something to be fixed or eliminated rather than a method of expressing feelings or desires. However, the definition of problem behaviors depends on whether the behaviors are considered from the perspective of an individual with ASD or from the perspective of a recreation provider. From the participant's perspective, problem behaviors include the inability to understand demands of a situation and to communicate needs and wants, severe difficulty in initiating and maintaining social interaction and relationships, confusion about the effects and consequences of many of his or her behaviors, and engagement in restrictive and repetitive behavior and interest that may limit the ability to learn and to fit in. From the recreation provider's perspective, problem behaviors include lack of compliance with or disruption of activities, tantrums, destruction of property, and aggression against self or others.

Box 6.28 "By labeling people's behavior we often feel that we have the right to act on how the behavior affects us rather than on what the person doing it might be trying to communicate" (Lovett, 1996).

The most effective models of behavior intervention for participants with ASD are those that create environments that prevent behavior problems and enhance skill development. This is accomplished by the consistent use of strategies that accommodate the unique needs of individuals with ASD, such as those presented earlier in this chapter. These behavior supports are based on positive strategies that are free of punishment.

Positive behavior supports can be difficult to define given the diversity of strategies and supports that are used under this term. Some hallmarks of positive behavior supports are: a focus on preventing the occurrence of challenging behavior; a focus on teaching socially acceptable alternatives to challenging behavior, while serving the same purpose of the challenging behavior; and a focus on expanding beyond consequence strategies, such as time out.

Box 6.29 There has been a "shift from viewing behavior support as a process by which individuals were changed to fit environments to one in which environments are changed to fit the behavior patterns of people in the environments" (Horner et. al., 2000).

Behavior is functional in that it serves a specific purpose(s). Behavior always happens for a reason that may or may not be obvious to us. Participants with ASD generally are not manipulative and do not intend to disrupt a program. Their challenging behaviors may arise from other needs, such as self-protection in stressful situations.

Effective behavior support is contingent on understanding the participant, the situations in which challenging behaviors occur and the reason(s) for behavior. It is important for staff and parents to work together, since parents often are most familiar with what has worked in the past for a given participant. It can sometimes be helpful to enlist the aid of outside consultants familiar with positive behavior support for individuals with ASD.

Behavior as Communication

Most participants with ASD cannot express some or all of what they want to say through speech, writing, or gestures. When they cannot express themselves in these traditional ways, they often use less conventional means of expression. Participants choose the way that is easiest to get their message across. The participant may communicate through facial expression, body movement, posture, vocalization, crying, tantrums, or other behavior. Outbursts and impulsive behaviors can appear to be manipulative, purposefully rule breaking, or intentionally rude to staff who do not understand ASD. If the communicative function of the behavior is not understood, staff may only want to eliminate the behavior. Merely trying to eliminate behavior results in ever-increasing frustration for all involved. If, instead, the participant's attempt to communicate can be acknowledged and expanded, difficult behaviors may begin to decrease.

Carr & Durand (1988) identified five categories that broadly describe the possible functions of behaviors. The purpose can be:

- Escape/avoidance, if it occurs when you ask the participant to do something or stops after you stop making demands.
- To get something desired, if it occurs when you take a favorite item or activity away; it stops after you give a desired time or activity; or it occurs when the child cannot have a desired item or activity.
- Self-regulation, if it tends to be performed over and over in a rhythmic, cyclical manner; or it tends to occur when there is either a lot going on in the area or very little; or the participant can do other things at the same time as s/he is performing the behavior.
- Attention, if it occurs when you are not paying attention to the participant or occurs when you stop paying attention to the participant.
- Play, if it occurs over and over; it would occur repeatedly when no one else is around; the participant seems to enjoy performing the behavior; or the participant seems to be in his or her "own world" when performing the behavior.

Although these are important areas to keep in mind, it is perhaps even more important to understand the underlying causes of the behavior of an individual participant more specifically. For instance, if behavior is to avoid or escape a person, situation or activity, our response should be "why does s/he want to avoid this activity."

An individual with ASD can become tense, frightened, or angry due to confusion, sensory disturbances, and unexpected change. Reactions to medical issues, the effects of medications needed to manage the medical issues or the effects of disturbed sleep patterns may exacerbate the situation. Conditions, such as asthma, allergies, sinusitis, seizures and other conditions can lead to behavior outbursts.

Gathering Information about the Function of the Behavior

When an individual does challenging behavior, staff needs to ask, "What is being communicated" rather than simply looking at the behavior as something to be corrected.

Sometimes the answer is immediately clear. Sometimes it can only be answered through careful observation and talking with the people who know the participant the best. Sometimes individuals with ASD have only one solution to a variety of problems, so the same behavior could have different functions. When there are persistent challenging behaviors, a functional behavior assessment (FBA) is useful to direct intervention planning.

Hurting others is a behavior of particular concern. It may result from being angry about being bossed about, being sexually frustrated, being insulted, rejected, being teased or a variety of other reasons.

Box 6.30

Jacob likes going to a supervised playground program. Staff and family members are very concerned, because he hits other children who get on the Big Toy at the playground. It appears that Jacob wants to use the Big Toy and does not know how to ask for it or wait his turn, which results in frustration. Since he does not speak, he uses the only way he has to indicate that he wants a turn, which is to hit whoever is on the Big Toy. He does not know that the rule for the playground is, if someone is on a piece of equipment that you want to be on, you count to 100 and then it is your turn. In addition to not speaking, Jacob does not know how to count to 100. The recreation staff problem solve how to help him understand and use the rule. His leisure facilitator writes numbers from 1 to 100 on index cards and puts the numbered cards on a keyring. She adds a "My turn" card at the end of the numbered cards. She also puts a paver on the ground near the Big Toy to help Jacob know where to stand. After she shows Jacob his designated place to wait on the paver and introduces how the card system works, Jacob immediately uses the system. He seems relieved to know how to get a turn and the other children are relieved that they do not get hit. They get off the Big Toy quickly when he shows the "My turn" card. Another advantage of this system is that Jacob also cooperates in getting off the swing when he is shown the "My turn" card by other participants. If the leisure facilitator and others who knew him, had not taken the time to determine why he was hitting, he may have lost the opportunity to participate in this favorite activity during the playground program.

When there are persistent challenging behaviors, a functional behavior assessment (FBA) is useful to direct intervention planning. The FBA identifies both immediate factors, such as request to do something, and more distant factors, such as poor sleeping, which increases the challenging behaviors. It seeks information that increases understanding of the participant, the challenging behavior, and the physical and social setting(s) in which the behavior occurs. Research has shown that the effectiveness of interventions doubled when FBA's were used to determine what reliably predicted and maintained the behavior before undertaking the intervention.

The more formal process of a FBA is less common in community recreation programs. However, recreation providers may be part of a team that does an FBA.

The first step for recreation providers is to begin assigning meaning to behaviors such as proximity, positioning, smiling, crying, or tapping. Certain repetitive behaviors, sometimes referred to as "self-stimulation" e.g., hand flapping or teeth grinding, may also be sensory in nature, but the intensity in which participants with ASD engage in these may be communicative. They may engage in these behaviors, because an individual with ASD can become tense, frightened or angry due to confusion, sensory disturbances, and unexpected change. They may engage in these behaviors more when they are bored, frustrated, stressed, or need to "calm down." Unfortunately, recreation providers may not consider if the individual is bored, frustrated, frightened, does not understand or finds the situation or activity meaningless.

Figure 6.11 provides a list of situations that may trigger behavior for participants with ASD.

Figure 6.11
Situations that May Trigger Challenging Behavior

- Not being understood
- Not understanding/confusion
- Lack of choices
- Lack of structure
- Demands to do non-preferred activities
- Making a mistake
- Being corrected
- Unpredictable schedules and routines
- Small changes in the schedule or routine
- Anticipation of an event or activity
- Cancellation of an event or activity
- Transitions between and changes in activities, locations, or people
- Staff absent
- Friend or buddy absent
- Family member or friend late or not coming
- Having to wait too long
- High stimulation from crowds, noise, too much movement, or competing visual stimuli
- Unexpected sounds
- Not having enough space
- Losing things of value
- Being denied a desired object or action
- Social demands
- Being interrupted
- Being teased or imitated
- Being around others who are very tense or yelling
- Power struggles

Prior to the consideration of any behavior intervention, the nature and extent of the perceived behavior problem and what the person is communicating through this behavior must be determined. This determination takes into consideration perspectives from the individual, his or her family, their social/cultural background and the circumstances in which the behavior occurred. The failure to achieve a full understanding of an individual's difficulties lies at the core of many counterproductive approaches.

Box 6.31

Nate's physical education instructor had not been given information about Nate's resistance to wearing new clothes. The PE teacher demanded that he wear a sweatshirt outside on a 55-degree day. After about three minutes of a power struggle, Nate put his fist through a window.

Often recreation providers need a quick reference regarding the behavior of participants with ASD. Figure 6.12 provides a form for recording information about the participant and his or her behavior. It can be reduced in size, laminated and kept in the leisure companion's pocket as a quick reference.

Figure 6.12 **Quick Reference for Challenging Behaviors**		
Name: Date:	Behavior:	Function of Behavior:
Preferences	Dislikes/Triggers	Warning Signals
Always Needed	Communication System	Reaction Procedures

Preventing Behavior

The best thing an adult can do to reduce behavior problems is to make sure they do not occur in the first place. The leisure coordinator should make sure all the adults who interact with the participant have a clear understanding of the individual's unique difficulties and triggers.

The primary goal of prevention strategies is to prevent or reduce the likelihood of challenging behavior and to set the stage for learning. The importance of prevention strategies should not be underestimated. Participants with ASD often have to manage a great amount of personal stress. There is growing evidence that the most effective form of prevention of problem behaviors is the provision of appropriate supports.

Box 6.32

The leisure coordinator knows that Paige often runs out the door during activities in the multipurpose room. The leisure coordinator works out a prevention plan with the instructor and leisure companion. It includes a variety of supports.

The door is kept closed and a stop sign is put on the door.
Orange cones are set up to make the boundaries more visible.
A pictorial mini-schedule of the activity is developed.
The leisure companion carries a fanny pack with fidgets that Paige needs during the seated instruction time.
The instructor uses a strong voice to gain Paige's attention.
The leisure companion stays close enough to redirect Paige to where she needs to be by pointing to the area.
The leisure companion also is prepared to casually block Paige's path to the door.

Environmental accommodations and adaptations can prevent or minimize the occurrences of the problem behaviors. The strategies presented earlier in this chapter will prevent most challenging behavior.

Providing structure and organization at the participant's level in recreation programs can help alleviate or moderate behavior. Some key strategies for prevention of behavior are:

- Know the participant.
- Anticipate potential problems.
- Be alert to body language that signals anxiety or confusion.
- Read behavior as communication.
- Make a plan, including schedules, instructions, and routines.
- Provide environmental adaptations, such as changing when or how long an activity occurs.
- Provide predictability and routine in approach and activity.
- Rearrange the physical setting.
- Provide schedules, work systems, and task organization that assist in understanding routines.
- Use the participant's existing communication system.
- Help participant understand instruction through visual supports.
- Use "do" statements, e.g., "Hold my hand and walk," rather than "don't" statements, e.g., "Don't run."
- Use statements, e.g., "It's time to clean up" rather than questions, e.g., "Can you clean up now?"
- Back off when a participant is very upset rather than demanding compliance.
- Introduce any change gradually.
- Help explain changes through visual supports.
- Give participant sense of power through choices and options.
- Redirect or use obsessions rather than trying to eliminate them.
- Lower expectations on stressed days.
- Reduce stressors.
- Don't take the behavior personally. (If the participant bites you, it may be because you took the ball away before s/he was finished. S/he does not hate you.)
- Treat all people with dignity and respect.
- Identify key person(s) or a mentor the participant can go to if s/he is having a difficult time adjusting or understanding a certain situation.

- Find a location where the participant can go to relax and to regroup.
- Provide the participant with a visual menu of coping strategies.
- Read the warning signs and take quick action when these signals are present.

There are currently no medications that effectively treat the core symptoms of ASD, but there are medications that can reduce problematic symptoms, and some that play critical roles in severe or life-threatening situations, such as self-injurious behaviors.

Recreation itself is a preventive strategy and its influence should not be forgotten. Both parents and recreation staff have remarked that when participants with ASD are doing things that they like and that make sense to them, challenging behavior often decreases. To a growing extent, strategies for promoting engagement have become synonymous with methods of preventing challenging behaviors (McGee & Daly, 1999).

Alternative Behaviors

The prevention methods will not prevent all behaviors. Behavior change will occur with the greatest success through positive interventions that teach participants how to replace inappropriate behavior with more acceptable behavior. Since behavior often serves a communicative function, increasing communication skills will frequently result in a decrease of undesirable behavior. The participant can be shown a more acceptable way to communicate what s/he has to say, after acknowledging the communicative intent.

Learning a new way of responding usually requires repetition, patience, flexibility, consistency and commitment by all. The participant may not learn the alternative behavior quickly, because the challenging behavior may have a long history and be well ingrained.

Bambara and Knoster (1995) provide a useful framework for guiding efforts toward teaching alternative skills by examining the following three categories of training alternative behaviors: equivalence training, general skills training, and self-regulation training.

Equivalence training requires staff to ask the following sequential questions:

- What is the function of the challenging behavior?
- What alternative skill(s) will be taught which serves the same function as the problem behaviors?
- How will the alternative skill be taught?

Box 6.33

Kevin is taking a woodworking class. His instructor and fellow participants are very concerned, because Kevin sometimes hits the person next to him for no apparent reason. Other participants do not want to sit near him. His instructor asks for help from the leisure coordinator. When the leisure coordinator and instructor look more closely at when Kevin hits other participants, they discover that it occurs when he has made an error and needs help. To try to prevent the behavior they move his seat farther than an arm length from other participants and the instructor walks by his work area more frequently to prevent mistakes. Since mistakes will still occur and Kevin's hitting is almost automatic when he is frustrated, they teach him to use a similar motor action to hitting to signal he needs help. They teach him to wave a red handkerchief that is loosely attached to his belt. This catches the instructor's eye quickly. Over time, Kevin learns to raise his hand in a more customary manner. No one shies away from sitting near him or helping him now.

General skills training requires asking the following sequential questions:

- What skill deficits are contributing to the problem behavior?
- What other social or communication skills will be taught that will prevent the problem behavior from occurring?
- How will these alternative skills be taught?

Box 6.34

Chelsea asks everyone in her drawing class, "Why is the sky blue?" multiple times. Her questions are increasingly annoying other participants. The leisure companion and instructor realize that Chelsea really wants to interact with the other participants, but has limited verbal language. They make a chart with the picture of each participant and a picture of a shared interest that Chelsea may have with that person. For instance, Chelsea loves her dog and Dahlia loves her dog. Chelsea is also given a small photo album with some of her favorite things to show others. She is taught how to use it. Since the "why" questions are an ingrained habit, the leisure companion and instructor decide they also need to find a way to limit how many times she asks her question. Chelsea is given five cards with WHY written on it and taught to stop asking her question when she has no more cards.

Chelsea enjoys sharing her pictures with others and seeing their pictures. Everyone now knows that Chelsea wants to talk when she asks her questions and that they can show their pictures to her. She does not need to ask her question to initiate an interaction any longer. These exchanges have led to Chelsea drawing pictures for the other participants. She loves to see their pleased reaction.

Self-regulation training requires asking the following sequential questions:

- What events appear to be contributing to the participant's anger or frustration in reference to the problem behavior?
- What self-control skills will be taught to help the participant deal with difficult/frustrating situations?
- How will these skills be taught?

Box 6.35

Nicolai is sitting in the lodge with his group coloring his journal. Suddenly, he raises his felt pen like he is going to throw it. He promptly throws the pen as his leisure companion says, "Don't throw it." The companion bends down to pick up the pen and Nicolai grabs her hair. Everyone noisily gathers around to free the leisure companion and Nicolai begins hitting himself.

At first, everyone is convinced that there was no reason for Nicolai's behavior. However, as the group reviews what happened, they realize that several people entered the building talking and laughing loudly about the same time that Nicolai raised his pen. They realize that the quiet environment had suddenly and unexpectedly become very noisy. He dislikes being told, "Don't" so this further aggravated him.

His leisure companion works with the leisure coordinator to get him some earplugs, but they decide he also needs to self-regulate himself. They teach him to use a quiet area to calm down and to use a "break card" to request the quiet area.

If an appropriate alternative behavior that accomplishes the individual's purpose(s) is not taught, the individual may find a replacement behavior that is even less desirable than the initial behavior. Teaching alternative skills will require more effort on the part of all involved, but the benefits will be long lasting.

Reaction

Challenging behavior may continue to occur until the participant is taught alternative behavior and/or the triggers are eliminated. It is always advisable to have a plan of what staff will do when and if the behavior occurs. The emphasis is on positive behavior intervention, so the reaction should not be a consequence. Some of the following reactions may be helpful:

- Talk softly or stop talking
- Redirect participant back to the activity
- Direct participant to calming area
- Remain calm
- Avoid touching or physically restraining participant

Sometimes participants attend programs for a time period that is too short to teach alternative behavior. However, behavior supports can be put in place even if the participant does not learn a new skill.

> **Box 6.36**
>
> Pat has a long history of "running away" from places. Although his initial reason for "running" was to avoid new situations, he also discovered that being chased was fun. The camp director is concerned that Pat might "bolt" into the river at camp. The camp staff and parents discuss what can be done to ensure safety for Pat. They realize that they are unlikely to change this long-standing problem during the five days he will be at camp. Since a reason for "running" is to get away from new situations and the camp will be full of new situations, the camp staff carefully prepare visual supports using the type of line drawings that is familiar to him to help prepare him for the myriad of changes. They also set up a designated quiet area for him to calm down in each activity area. They recognize that this will only minimize his "running," since he still thinks he can have fun being chased. The camp staff continues problem solving with the parents and discover that some visual approaches that have worked with other campers, e.g., presenting a card with a picture of a stop sign or a designated place to run to, will not inhibit Pat's running. Therefore, they develop a reaction plan to help when he runs away. This includes a designated staff member stepping between Pat and his direction of flight, since he will not run into people and is unlikely to run to the side. The staff may need to gradually and quietly walk toward him. Then he is redirected to a familiar activity that he enjoys in the original area.

When behavior is looked at from the point of view of individuals with ASD, recreation providers can determine appropriate supports to change behavior. Any of the supports described in the preceding sections of this chapter may be useful to increase appropriate behavior, depending on the function of the behavior.

Summary

- Careful planning, systematic programming, and sustained efforts are required in order to ensure success for both the person with ASD, as well as other community members.
- Organizing the environment, developing schedules and work systems, making expectations clear and explicit, and using visual materials to develop and participate in recreation activities independently increase meaningful participation.
- Adapt tasks and materials to promote successful participation.
- Whenever possible, give the participant time to prepare for changes to help him/her feel comfortable and to develop trust.
- Make available those sensory experiences that may be calming for the participant.
- When feasible, decrease environmental distracters that interfere with learning or confuse, disorient or upset the participant with ASD.
- Staff needs to create support for participants with ASD by avoiding labels and asking, "What does this behavior communicate and how can I help?"

Chapter Seven

Strategies Used by Special Programs to
Develop Recreation Skills in Individuals with
Autism Spectrum Disorder

Ann Fullerton

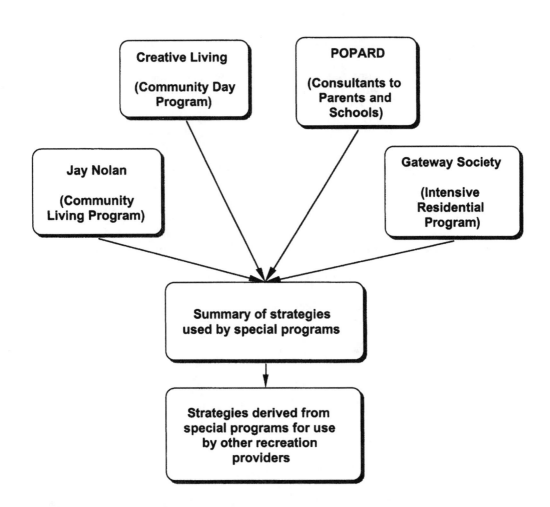

Introduction

Special programs are agencies that specifically serve persons with ASD and/or consult and train others to serve persons with ASD. The specialized programs described in this chapter utilize strategies that recreation providers can apply in more generic recreation programs.

These agencies are involved in or use recreation with persons with ASD in three different ways. Some agencies focus on assisting individuals with ASD to experience more community recreation and find their preferred leisure pursuits. Their goal is to increase community access of their community and improve their quality of life for the individual with ASD. Other agencies provide consultation and training to teachers, families, and service providers on how to facilitate community recreation for individuals with ASD. Still other agencies use recreation activities to achieve other learning goals for persons with ASD. These agencies find that recreation is a rich social and environmental context in which to teach social and self-management skills. They use recreation activities as a milieu in which to achieve these outcomes. Aspects of the four agencies described in this chapter are summarized in Table 7.1 and described in the following pages.

Table 7.1
Characteristics of Four Special Programs

Program/ Who Served	Services Described	Key Practices Described
Jay Nolan Community Services (JNCS), California Adults with ASD	Supported community living. Assisting adults with ASD to explore and develop leisure pursuits in their community.	Use of strategies that allow individual to self-direct their life and to discover what leisure activities they enjoy. Emphasis on quality of life and participation in one's community
Creative Living, North Carolina Adults with ASD	Day program to develop leisure and community living skills.	Use of Division TEACCH (Univ. of North Carolina) Structured Teaching methods in the development of recreation and community living skills.
Provincial Outreach Program for Autism & Related Disorders (POPARD), British Columbia Children with ASD	Training and consultation to teachers, families, and residential service providers in developing community recreation skills.	Use of a 10-step process for assessment, preparation, and teaching of recreation skills in community settings. Emphasis on developing competence, self-management, and ability to cope with setting conditions.
Gateway Society, British Columbia Adolescents with Asperger's Syndrome	Residential program, intensive treatment group home	Use of recreation activities in the community as milieu for developing self-regulation, social skills, and pragmatic communication skills.

Jay Nolan Community Services (JNCS)
San Jose, California

Background and Goals

Jay Nolan Community Services (JNCS) is a statewide nonprofit agency in California serving persons with disabilities. Among the many services they provide, one of their areas of expertise is supported community living for individuals with ASD. In this section, the strategies used at JNCS to support adults with ASD living in the community are described.

In California, recent legislation has established access to supported living services for persons with developmental disabilities who would be able to live in their own home in the community, if they had up to 24 hours of one-on-one support per day from an assistant. This has allowed persons who were formerly living in institutional settings or group homes to live in their own home or apartment.

How supported community living services are provided to an individual, by an agency such as JNCS, will make all the difference in whether an individual is directing their own life activities and choices, or whether others are making those decisions for them. The core philosophy of JNCS in providing supported living is that their role is to empower the individual to live life the way that he/she chooses, within established safety parameters.

Individual participate in selecting assistants and determining living arrangements (e.g., whether they live alone or with a roommate). He or she decides what they will do during the day, where they will go, and what they will eat. The goal is to create a living situation for the individual in which he or she experiences self-determination that is facilitated by an assistant that provides supervision and growth opportunities.

For adults with developmental disabilities who grew up in institutions and have seldom had the opportunity to make life choices, it takes time for them to trust that they can now direct their life, and that staff will listen to and honor their preferences. If the individual is a person with ASD with a limited vocabulary and life experiences, it can be challenging to help him or her discover what they want to pursue in their leisure time and in their community. Moreover, individuals with ASD often prefer routine and predictability because they have difficulty understanding what is going on in new situations. Staff must find a balance between honoring the individual's tendency to do the same things over and over and to have a narrow set of interests with the individual's right to fully explore his or her world and perhaps find new things that bring joy. Unless an individual explores more of the community in which he or she lives, he or she may never discover new interests that, in the long run, turn out to be very important to him or her. So, the challenge for the staff at JNCS is: "How do we help someone, who prefers things to stay the same and to be predictable, to explore new horizons?"

The JNCS office in San Jose provides supported living for 16 individuals, five of whom are adults with ASD. To illustrate how JNCS provides supported living and recreation for adults with ASD, one client's experiences will be shared.

Supported living for Kary

Kary is a woman in her 30s with ASD who uses one to five spoken words on a regular basis. She lived in a group home with five other individuals with ASD for 15 years. For the past seven years she has lived in her own apartment with the help of supported living services. Kary resides in Silicon Valley, in an urban neighborhood. An assistant is with her 24 hours a day. At night she has a roommate stay with her for safety.

At first, it was very difficult for her assistants, given her limited verbal skills, to know what she wanted to do for activities. One thing was clear from her actions, however, she loved food to the point of an obsession. She stole food when she had the opportunity and would grab food off another's plate. This kind of behavior is often learned in residential facilities where individuals do not have control over what food items and how much food is available to them. These patterns of grabbing and hoarding food can be hard to break. In Kary's case, however, as she began to trust that she would have access to food and she developed other interests, the food-oriented behaviors became less of a problem.

Initially, Kary was only interested in doing things associated with food. Going out to eat, buying food, cooking and eating food were all preferred activities. The staff was having a hard time figuring out what else she might want to explore in her community. Because Kary would take food off another person's plate when possible, the staff decided to try introducing her to places in the community where food was not the focus of activity or present. Staff members also wanted to see if she enjoyed listening to music and offered Kary a Walkman. She learned to use the Walkman, loved listening to music, and now is seldom seen without it.

After this discovery, the staff decided to try other music activities. They wondered if she might enjoy a social activity if it involved music. They began to think about where in the community Kary could listen to music and be with other people. Rather than a concert which might be too loud and unpredictable for Kary, they wanted to first try a musical activity with a lot of routine and predictability associated with it.

They decided to try a visit to a senior center during their music period. Kary enjoyed the visits to the senior center, the music, and gradually the seniors as well. Kary and her assistant went to the center at the same time every week. At first, the assistant just let Kary observe and get familiar with the senior center. Kary started to participate and clapped to the music. She got to know some of the seniors, and they got to know her. She made friends, and eventually she began to visit at other times during the week. She baked cookies, took them to the center, and passed them out to the seniors. As Kary got comfortable in the setting, she was able to be more appropriate regarding food, when food was present in the setting. Visiting the senior center continues to be a regular part of her weekly schedule. She has become very fond of the seniors.

The director described several features of their approach to introducing Kary to the senior center, which she feels are important for success. Making a commitment to go to the same place at the same time each week is essential for establishing a situation that can develop into a leisure interest and activity. The event needs to have a routine in place so that the individual sees the same people each time and experiences a sequence of activities that are similar each time. These conditions help the individual become comfortable in a new setting. The likelihood that the individual will connect with people in the setting increases because the individuals are free from the anxiety that arises in an unpredictable situation.

After this initial success, it was clear that music could be an entree into social activities for Kary. The staff wanted to try another social activity involving music. Since Kary had come to enjoy doing things for the seniors, the staff wondered if she might also enjoy being with and helping children. One of her assistants had a friend who was an elementary school teacher. Arrangements were made for Kary and her assistant to visit the class during their music lesson. Kary came and observed the class a few times. She was then given a structured task to do, which was to show the children how to clap to the music. She got acquainted with the students and vice versa. Over time, she was a welcome guest in the classroom during music time and at other times.

Staff then decided to introduce Kary to a third activity, an aerobics class at the health club. This was chosen because Kary is overweight, and she has a family history of health problems related to obesity. The staff felt she might like this form of exercise because of the music. She quickly adjusted to the setting, and followed the instructor's moves as a member of the class. As a result, exercise has now become a part of her weekly routine. Kary does not like to miss her exercise classes. In fact, recently when a staffing meeting was scheduled at the same time as her exercise class, she protested, pointing to her schedule and saying "exercise, exercise" Kary now participates in the class independently while her assistant watches from the side.

Kary has now learned to manage her own weekly visual schedule, which she uses to let others know what she wants and to make sense of her life. Kary uses actual photographs of various locations in the community in her schedule. Velcro is used to attach the pictures. At the beginning of each week, she arranges her schedule. Kary may place a visit to the senior center and the elementary school into her schedule. Usually she does her laundry at the first of the week. Every once in a while though, she might put off laundry until, say, Thursday. When she does this she is watches her assistant for a reaction. It's her way of testing if whether she really does have control of her life, and how she spends her time. In seven years time, Kary has progressed from a lifestyle of narrow leisure interests and a minimal use of community resources to one enriched by varied recreational and social activities in her community.

Strategies Used By JNCS Staff to Support Individuals with ASD

The staff at JNCS uses specific strategies to help adults with ASD to gain greater access to their community and to try new activities. These strategies is highly individualized to the needs of each person. For some individuals, very little preparation is needed, and for others, a great deal is required. It's also true that as individuals become more adjusted to their community, they are more comfortable in new situations. The director described seven steps used by the JNSC staff.

Step 1: Know the individual. An important first step is to thoroughly know an individual's sensory sensitivities and methods of communication. The staff carefully observes the individual in different situations with various mitigating factors including levels of noise and light, degree of routine and predictability, etc. The staff thoroughly reviews whatever information is available about the individual's past (prior trauma, antecedents to behavioral outbursts, etc.). Staff members also need to know the various ways the individual communicates through behavior. They must be able to identify what behaviors are the first indications of anxiety or discomfort so that they can give the individual a break or assist them to leave the situation. All staff are informed of the individual's tolerance levels, sensitivities, and needs.

The staff's goal is to be sufficiently tuned into the individual's behavioral and other communications, so that they can anticipate and respond before the person reaches a level of anxiety at which they will act out or flee a situation. This is not always possible. Community environments always have an element of unpredictability, but the director has found that it is possible to be sufficiently thoughtful and prepared to avoid nearly all outbursts and problems.

Step 2: Know the site and activity. With this information in mind about the individual, staff observe places and activities of potential interest to the individual. Staff members take note of whatever aspects of the setting might be difficult for the person. They develop a plan for how they can gradually introduce the person to the setting and diminish the impact of any problematic environmental aspects. Back-up and contingency plans are also prepared in advance. If only one assistant is accompanying an individual to a community setting, the assistant has a plan how she or he will handle an emergency alone if it should occur. JNCS backup is also a phone call away.

Step 3: Prepare the community teacher/activity leader. Sometimes staff members talk to a teacher or leader of an activity in advance about the person they will be bringing to the class. For example, they might meet the teacher of a class at the community center to describe an individual's needs beforehand. They find that teachers have more success if they have been prepared in advance.

Step 4: Prepare the individual. The next step is to prepare the individual for the experience. Staff develop visual (pictures and written) descriptions about the place, use these to talk about what is at the site as well as what will happen. A picture sequence (mini schedule) of what will occur in the situation might also be used. This is a necessary step for most individuals, but some get too anxious learning about the activity beforehand and thus this step is omitted.

Step 5: Gradually introduce individual to site/activity. The next step is to accompany the individual to observe the activity for a brief period. The first visit may only last five minutes, the second visit will last longer, and so on. Staff members often spend up to a month making weekly visits to a new activity before the individual actually starts participating in the activity. Thus, staff members use a very slow introduction process. The goal is to make the process sufficiently gradual so that the individual has no adverse experiences along the way.

The director has found that nonverbal individuals let you know what they need. An individual might drag you to the car. When they need to say, "I have had enough." Some use a particular vocalization, which is their way of saying, "let's go home." Staff members honor these communications and leave when the individual wants to leave.

Step 6: Evaluate and learn. Staff members have learned that if they don't engage in careful planning and preparations (Step 1-6), consequences can result. If an individual becomes too anxious or afraid, they may refuse to go again. One example is a woman who loved to go to craft shows, but she was very noise sensitive. Staff pushed her to go. She left 30 minutes later, in the midst of a panic attack. She will not go again, and if staff talk about the craft fair she becomes anxious.

Program Philosophy

The philosophy at Jay Nolan is that staff members can know individuals well enough to prevent negative situations from occurring in the community. The director explained, "I teach my staff that in my opinion, if an individual has a major behavioral outburst in the community, then we missed something. We as a staff did something wrong; we can avoid most negative situations. We screwed up, not the person. This approach brings all of us as a staff to a different plane of thinking. It emphasizes for us how vital it is to learn how to listen to the individual and accurately interpret their behavioral communications. When a negative experience occurs in the community, we sit down and analyze it together. We try and go back and reconstruct what was the antecedent, what was the start or the trigger. We support each other to learn from these incidents and revise our strategies for an individual for the next time."

Staff members have told the director that one of the most difficult things for them to learn to do is to let the individual take risks. It is difficult to let go, and not overprotect the person. Assistants are sometimes worried that someone in the community might hurt the individual's feelings or rebuff them, but they know they cannot hover over the individual because that will interfere with the individual's interactions with community members.

Through practice and experience, staff members learn that when they give the process a chance, it will work. When they let the individual and community members meet and interact, often greater inclusion and acceptance is the result. Assistants have to take a risk that it may not work out, but no progress will be made unless they step back and let the person with ASD get involved on their own. The director makes this an important aspect of her staff training.

Another important expectation of staff members is that they will overcome their own discomfort in public situations when the individual is behaving in ways that call attention to them. This is an important point of discussion in the interview with an applicant for a staff position. Assistants need to be resilient in this area and let comments from people in the community "roll off their back." They cannot be uncomfortable with public scrutiny and embarrassment. Otherwise, their discomfort may result in the individual's opportunities being compromised.

The program philosophy and strategies used by Jay Nolan Community Services demonstrate how the quality of life and community participation of adults with ASD can be developed and supported. An important dimension of this work is discovering and developing an individual's leisure and recreation options.

Creative Living
Autism Society of North Carolina
Raleigh, North Carolina

Background and Goals

Creative Living is a program for adults with ASD in Raleigh, North Carolina sponsored by the Autism Society of North Carolina. The program was started in 1997, and currently serves 15 individuals ranging in age from 22 to 58, with most participants in their 30s. Creative Living employs a full-time Certified Therapeutic Recreation Therapist (CTRS), vocational, art, and music therapists, and instructors and assistants. The goals of the program are to create opportunities for:

- Creative expression through art, music, crafts, cooking and other activities.
- Vocations and avocations through training, volunteer activities and supported employment.
- Social skills enhancement through leisure skills, sports, social interaction and community integration.
- Lifelong learning through community college and other learning activities.

In 2002, Creative Living served 15 participants. About half were individuals who were nonverbal, three of who were also hearing impaired. Some participants used some sign-language and/or visual communication systems to indicate their needs and wants. Due to the communication challenges of the participants, Creative Living uses individual and program-based visual communication systems extensively with all participants. Creative Living works with a consultant from Division TEACCH (Treatment and Education of Autistic and Related Communication Handicapped Children) of the University of North Carolina to develop these systems. Division TEACCH is a national leader in the area of interventions for individuals with ASD (Schloper, Meisibov, & Heasey, 1995; see also Appendix C for contact information). A TEACCH therapist consults with the program one day each week.

Program Description. The program consists of a variety of individual and small group activities conducted at the center, or in the community. At the center, individuals or small groups work on a variety of goals with the various therapists and teachers. Structured free time is also scheduled every day before and after lunch. During this time, each individual chooses from an individualized array of pictures of activities, or they practice something they are learning.

Community outings are an important part of the weekly program schedule. Each day of the week various community experiences are scheduled for small groups of participants. These include vocational, recreational, community living, and volunteer activities. Some are routine outings; for example, on Mondays a small group goes grocery shopping and then returns to cook a snack. On Tuesdays a group exercises by walking at the local mall, and on Wednesdays a group bowls. Each week on Friday, however, participants experience a new place and/or activity. This balance of several familiar outings, with one new outing included each week, helps participants expand their experiences and learn to adapt to change, while minimizing their anxiety.

For the novel activities, participants are prepared ahead of time with visual information (pictures, brochures), a verbal description of what will occur, and/or a schedule of what the group will do. Some individuals are very reluctant and anxious about venturing into a new part of the community and, thus, staff members spend time preparing them each day, Monday through Thursday, for the Friday outing. The staff tries to predict areas that may be troublesome using past experiences as a reference. The staff knows what can be a source of anxiety for a particular individual, and these details of the trip are described and previewed. For example, an individual may dislike escalators, so, before the outing, staff members explain that the stairs in the building are available for use instead of the escalator.

Visual schedules. As discussed in Chapter 6, individuals with ASD often have difficulty understanding what they need to do, where they need to go, when an activity is completed, and what activity is next. At Creative Living, every individual has his or her own visual schedule for the day. Schedules vary based on individual needs, but a typical design is a series of removable pictures or line drawings of different activities. At each activity site, a second copy of the picture of the activity is also displayed. Thus, individuals know they are in the right place when they match the picture on their schedule with the picture at the activity. When they arrive at an activity, the steps in the activity are visually represented through a series of pictures. At the end of the activity, the final instruction is: "check your schedule." The individual then looks at his or her own personal schedule, which directs the individual to the next event in their day. The schedules or routines greatly reduce anxiety for the participants because whenever they are not sure what is happening or what is going to happen, staff prompt them to check their schedules where they can find the information they seek.

The participants' individual schedules are coordinated with the program schedule. The staff at Creative Living has found that a consistent program schedule reduces anxiety about what is going to happen which can lead to behavioral problems. Some participants identify each day of the week with the outing that occurs on that day. An activity is a concrete and experiential marker of time as opposed to the abstract name of a day of the week. The program schedule does change from time to time, and staff must prepare participants for a change. One way that staff helps participants learn to adjust to novelty and change is through the use of the novel activity every Friday. Visual schedules are a way to provide information to adults with ASD that they cannot access in the same ways that adults without ASD obtain information. Visual schedules allow individuals with ASD to be free from the constant verbal direction of others.

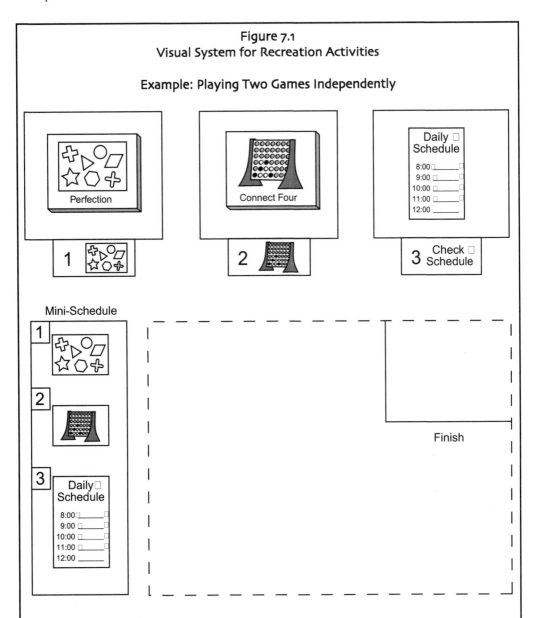

Figure 7.1
Visual System for Recreation Activities

Example: Playing Two Games Independently

This drawing shows how a recreation activity could be visually structured for an individual with ASD. On the tabletop depicted here are three areas. The dash-lines area is the individual's task area. On the bottom left, is a mini schedule of three steps. The pictures in the mini schedule match the games placed in trays 1 and 2 above the task area. The individual looks at #1 in the mini schedule and matches it to the first step. S/he takes the "Perfection" game out of its tray and places it in the task area. After playing with the Perfection game they put it in the "Finish" area. Step #2 in the mini schedule indicates they are to take the "Connect Four" game out of its tray and place it in the task area. After playing with the Connect Four game, they place it in the "Finish" tray and once again refer back to the mini schedule. Step #3 is to check their daily schedule to find out what they need to do next. Practice with simple mini-schedules leads to the ability to follow more complex schedules independent of constant verbal direction from others.

Visual Organization of Recreation Activities. The materials needed for an activity are carefully arranged in the sequence of use, and visual instructions indicate how to start, what to do step-by-step, and how to end the activity and put away the materials (see Figure 7.1 for an example).

Addressing Sensory Needs. The sensory area at the center is set aside as a place where participants can take a break, relax, and use various sensory items to address their sensory needs. A variety of visual and tactile materials are available, such as different sources of light, a variety of objects with different tactile features, a tactile board with different textures made from fabrics and other materials, and large pillows and beanbag chairs. Participants use the area to take a break between activities, and when they need to refocus or calm themselves.

Role of the Certified Therapeutic Recreation Therapist (CTRS)

The CTRS at Creative Living provides a range of individual and group activities involving health and wellness, leisure education, community inclusion, and independent recreation. Recreation or other activities in the community are a vehicle for teaching social and other skills needed to participate in community activities. For example, a critical skill is learning to patiently wait for one's turn in a social situation.

Individual recreation therapy. The CTRS develops goals for each individual incorporating assessment information and participant and parent requests. Each participant works with the CTRS on his individual goals at least once per week. For example, one participant with ASD who is also deaf is working on writing letters to her relatives. This goal helps her develop her writing and reading skills and provides an alternative means of communication with her family members.

The goal for several participants is to try new and different recreation/leisure options and to find more activities that they can enjoy in their free time. Participants are also learning how to access the activities available in the community. The ways in which the CTRS develops these skills are described below.

Learning to make choices and expanding repertoires. As discussed in Chapter 2, individuals with ASD may have a very narrow range of interests. It is often important to parents and therapists to expand an individual's range of experiences so that he or she has more choices as to how to spend his or her discretionary time. During an individual's recreation therapy sessions, the CTRS may expand an individual's interests by offering a range of choices of only new activities. The activities are depicted in a series of pictures on the wall with each picture corresponding to an activity. A second picture of the activity as well as the materials for the activity are arranged on a cart next to the wall. This set-up is used to teach participants to use a visual system for making choices from an array of alternatives. For example, when one participant first came to the program, the only activity he wanted to do during his free time was to watch videos. In order to push him gen-

Leisure Choice Board

tly to try other things, the CTRS removed "watching videos" from his array of choices, and offered a variety of other activities instead. Left with a new set of options, he began to choose, learn, and eventually enjoy a table game.

Community inclusion. Another area of focus for the CTRS is community inclusion in various activities. First, the CTRS uses the individual's assessment information and ideas that the participant and parents may have to select a community activity. Second, the CTRS investigates possible sites for the activity, assessing each site's physical aspects (e.g., sensory, safety issues) and human-social aspects (staff or participants receptive to inclusion and accommodations) with respect to the needs of the individual. Third, the CTRS develops a plan for gradually introducing the individual to the site and activity: this process includes developing their schedule and routine at the site, developing accommodations, and teaching the individual whatever skills are required. To illustrate, the story of how Tom, a man with ASD, learned to use a gym for exercise over the course of five months, will be described.

Tom's Story

Tom's mother wanted the CTRS to try to develop a plan for her son to get some much needed exercise. However, this was challenging because he occasionally engaged in verbal outbursts or touched other people inappropriately. The CTRS found a gym that was part of a hospital's cardiac rehabilitation wellness center. As compared to a fitness center, this gym was smaller, fewer people used the gym at any one time, people were not engaged in bodybuilding, and they were more conservatively attired.

A picture schedule was developed that sequenced the following activity steps: enter the gym, greet staff at the desk, use exercise bike, go to the track, walk three laps, say goodbye to the staff at the desk, and leave.

Tom learned to use the equipment at the gym, including setting the timer on the exercise bike, but he had difficulty greeting the staff appropriately. The CTRS was able to motivate him to practice a routine for greeting the staff appropriately, by adding a final step to his activity schedule of purchasing his favorite drink after leaving the wellness center.

In one month's time Tom progressed from using a picture schedule to a written one and now with minimal supervision, he can use the gym independently. After five months of attending the gym once a week, he now places the exercise activity in his personal schedule twice a week. On occasion he does yell in the setting, but the staff onsite are now comfortable re-directing Tom by calling him by name.

By carefully selecting the site, the CTRS was able to offer Tom more independence than would have been possible at a large, typical fitness center. Another positive outcome of this process has been that the center's staff have learned about individuals with ASD and the CTRS plans to introduce other participants to the gym in the future.

The program structure at the Creative Living program is an excellent example of how schedules and other visual communication systems and other accommodations can be used to facilitate recreation and community inclusion for individuals with ASD. Creative Living demonstrates how TEACCH Structured Teaching methods work to support recreation. Some thoughts from the CTRS at Creative Living about her role in this program are shared in Figure 7.2.

Figure 7.2
Thoughts on the Roles of Therapeutic Recreation Specialists

"… While studying therapeutic recreation at the University of North Carolina at Chapel Hill, I focused on health care and rehabilitation. During my internship at Duke University Medical Center with patients in adult rehabilitation, I viewed the work of a CTRS as one of helping people to get better and regain functioning. But here at Creative Living, working with adults with ASD, I see there are other important tasks for recreation therapists. Here, my goal is not to cure, or rehabilitate. Instead my goal is to support people with ASD as they explore appropriate leisure outlets and learn skills for independence. Thus, being a recreation therapist for persons with ASD has expanded my understanding of what recreation therapy needs to encompass. Here, I help people develop skills they never had before instead of being healed or cured, as in a rehabilitation model…"

Kelly Stone, C.T.R.S. at Creative Living, Raleigh, NC

Provincial Outreach Program for Autism and Related Disorders (POPARD) and Provincial Resource Program (PRP) Delta, British Columbia, Canada

Background and Goals

Provincial Outreach Program for Autism and Related Disorders (POPARD) in Delta, British Columbia, Canada, provides outreach consultation and training to school districts throughout the province of British Columbia for children with ASD attending local public schools. POPARD uses assessment and intervention techniques to serve the goal of teaching parents and staff how to then teach and support the child with ASD. POPARD also provides a variety of training programs for teachers, residential staff, and families. A staff of nine consultants serves the province of British Columbia and includes masters and doctoral level special educators and psychologists. Currently, POPARD serves about 500 children and is funded by the Special Programs branch of the Ministry of Education.

POPARD provides assistance in the development of communication, self-management, domestic, vocational, community access, academic, and recreation skills. The staff at POPARD believes that an individual with ASD should not be excluded from any generic recreation in their community. Their goal is that the individual with ASD will engage in recreation at the same times, and in the same ways, as their peers, and that they may do so in an independent and self-managed manner as possible. This goal has shaped their approach. They ask the question: "What do we need to do so that the individual with ASD can cope with the settings' environmental and social conditions?"

The POPARD consultants work closely with their teaching colleagues assigned to the Provincial Resource Program (PRP). The PRP provides two school locations offering educational services to approximately 25-30 students between the ages of 12 and 19. The students attending the PRP classroom at Delta Secondary, a local public secondary school, may be fully integrated with their same aged peers into both core and elective subjects. The students attending the PRP classrooms in the Off Campus program are provided with extensive community based training including work experience, functional academics and life skills.

In this section, the methods that the POPARD consultants and the PRP staff use to create recreational opportunities for individuals with ASD in their community are described. These methods have been organized into two general guidelines and a 10-step assessment, preparation, and teaching process. The process is individualized for each child and situation. In order to illustrate the process, an example of teaching an individual to ice skate at a community ice-skating rink will be used.

POPARD Guidelines for Teaching Recreation Skills in the Community

Two general guidelines form the basis of the POPARD approach to teaching an individual with ASD how to participate in community recreation.

Guideline I. Teach the individual recreation skills in the setting where the skills will be used. POPARD consultants and staff trained by POPARD teach recreation skills at the site where the individual will continue to recreate in the future. They do not attempt to teach a skill in one setting and then expect the individual to be able to readily transfer the skill to another setting with different social and environmental conditions. This is an approach that reflects an understanding of the learning style of persons with ASD. As discussed in Chapter 2, it can be challenging for individuals with ASD to generalize skills to another setting because they tend to focus on a variety of features of the setting, some skill-relevant and others irrelevant, and mentally file all of these features as required features of the experience.

Box 7.1

Teaching Ice Skating:

When learning to ice skate, the individual with ASD may notice that skaters pay at the blue booth and rent their skates at the black counter. To individuals without ASD, these environmental features are not critical to ice-skating, but for an individual with ASD they may become an integral part of their definition of ice-skating. This learning style, in which irrelevant features of an activity become important to the learner with ASD, can make it difficult to adapt to other skating rinks that have different physical features.

After the individual has mastered the recreation skill in one location, then staff may begin to introduce the individual to other locations and at different times in order to ensure that the individual begins to generalize the recreation skill across settings and under a variety of conditions.

Guideline II. Use recreation sites where site operators and users will support the training process and the individual's continued use of the site. Some individuals with ASD will need accommodations in order to use a recreation site. Unless the site operators and those in attendance are supportive of the individual with ASD's participation, the site is not used. Considerable time and effort will go into training, and thus it is important that the staff at the site understand what will be needed from the site.

Box 7.2

Teaching Ice Skating:

For example, A boy with ASD may want to learn to ice skate, but he can't handle the noise from the loud speakers. If he and his teacher could have access to the rink at a time when the loud speakers are off, he could focus and learn to skate. Later, after he has mastered skating, he can learn to cope with the loudspeaker noise.

Thus, teaching him to ice skate will require the cooperation of the facility operators. So the consultant explores with the site operators whether they will make the rink available for several weeks in the morning when it is quiet, while the boy learns to skate. Once the boy has learned to ice skate, then the consultant and teacher can work with him on ice skating when it is noisy.

In order to provide successful experiences learning recreation activities, POPARD recommends that school staff arrange with the local Leisure Center to initially bring individuals with ASD in at times when the general public is not present, or when the number of people using the facilities is limited. The director's observations of what can occur when appropriate accommodations are *not* used in teaching community recreation skills are shared in Figure 7.3.

Figure 7.3
The Difference Between No Accommodation and Appropriate Accommodations

"… What I see a lot of the time in recreation programs is what I call benevolent tolerance…. The recreation providers at the site are tolerating the behavior of the individual, up to a point. No one is doing the things that would change the behavior and give the individual with ASD the structure and support they need to participate more fully and with greater enjoyment.

The recreation provider says, for example: '…We don't have a problem with this child in this setting…' However, when you look at the child's functioning in the setting they are much more dependent on others and much more stressed than they need to be. They are much more confused and anxious and not participating than they need to be. At this stage, the provider is tolerating behaviors that may get out of hand later if not addressed.

The recreation provider may also put a contingency on the individual's participation, saying, '…But if the child has trouble with the setting, then they will have to go…' This is a way of saying: '…If we at the site cannot handle the child's behavior, they will need to go…'

In this situation, we seek the opportunity to teach the individual and help them cope in the setting so that they can participate fully… But, they can't do that unless they have access to the setting and the cooperation of the setting…"

JoAnne Seip, Director of POPARD

Phases and Steps in the Assessment and Teaching Process

POPARD uses a 10-step process, with three phases: assessment, preparation, and teaching, develop recreation skills in the community for individuals with ASD. These phases and steps are listed in Table 7.2.

Table 7.2
Phases and Steps in the POPARD Process

Phase I: Assessment

Step 1: Assess the general skill level and support needs of the individual with ASD.

Step 2: Assess physical and social aspects of the site.

Step 3: Assess the site's willingness to support the individual's learning process and ongoing participation.

Phase II: Prepare for Teaching

Step 4: Select needed accommodations.

Step 5: Select methods that will be used to prepare the individual for the activity and site.

Phase III: Teach

Step 6: Prepare individual for on-site teaching.

Step 7: Teach on-site under optimal conditions for learning.

Step 8: Teach the individual to cope with the site's typical environmental and social conditions.

Step 9: Transition the individual into engaging in the activity with family or peers.

Step 10: Introduce the individual to other sites and times for engaging in the activity.

Phase I: Assessment

Step 1. Assess the general skill level and support needs of the individual with ASD. All students in the PRP classrooms enter an initial assessment phase, generally lasting two weeks. The student is assessed to determine skill levels in academics, social skills, and communication (both receptive and expressive), community skills, work experience skills, self-help skills, and recreation skills.

To provide as clear a picture as possible, an assessment of students' receptive and expressive communication skills is conducted. Levels of representation are assessed to determine whether or not the child can understand actions and concepts through the use of augmentative aids ranging from actual objects to more abstract supports, such as colored photographs, pictures and symbols, line drawings, signs, or printed words. The assessment also provides a baseline of the student's fine and gross motor skills, academic skills, and community functioning. Through discussion with parents and direct observation of the student a preference profile is created identifying his or her specific likes and dislikes. Problematic behaviors are recorded.

At the end of the two-week assessment phase, staff reviews the data collected and develops an interim program for the student. In the area of recreation activities, staff looks at five main areas before making recommendations: behavior, health, social, and sensory issues, and personal preferences. Then, based on this information, staff determines what kinds of accommodations and supports the individual is likely to need in the community. This information, along with the individual's interests, helps the POPARD consultants decide what kinds of recreation activities will be pursued.

Step 2. Assess physical and social aspects of the site. After a recreation skill is chosen for training, the POPARD consultant and PRP staff seek an appropriate site. They consider the site's environmental features in light of the individual's sensory and other needs.

Step 3. Assess the willingness of staff at the recreation site to support the individual's training and ongoing participation. The PRP staff determines if site managers and site users will support the individual's initial training needs and continued use of the site to engage in the recreation activity.

Phase II: Preparations for Teaching

Step 4. Select needed accommodations. PRP staff uses two types of accommodations. The first type of accommodations involves assisting individuals to understand what they need to do and to help them self-manage their behavior. These accommodations can be generalized across settings and activities in which the individual participates. In Figure 7.4 some examples of such accommodations are described.

Figure 7.4
Examples of POPARD Accommodations Used Across Settings

The Zone Meter

Example 1

Example 2

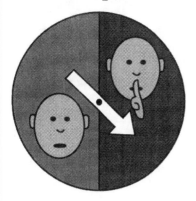

RED - STOP TALKING

GREEN - NORMAL VOICES

The Zone Meter is a way to let individuals know how loud their voices can be in different settings or at different times. Different speaking volumes are associated with different colors. An arrow is turned to the correct speaking volume. On the left, in Example 1 a zone meter poster placed on the wall: Red indicates quite voice and green normal voice. Example 2 is a small portable card. Here, red means quiet, yellow means inside voice, and green means outside voice.

The Theme Board. Example: Bowling

The theme board is a visual schedule, or pictorial task analysis, of every step involved in an activity. Theme boards are constructed in the same format using the same types of line drawings or pictures for every activity in the individual's day. The cards are sequenced on a strip that is laminated. The POPARD staff members have developed pictorial task analysis of many different community recreational activities for use in theme boards. A theme board sequence for bowling is shown above.

The second type of accommodations respond to the individual's specific needs in the context of the site's attributes. Examples of different accommodations for two boys who are learning to ice skate are described in Figure 7.5.

Figure 7.5
Examples of Site-Specific Accommodations for Ice Skating

Two boys with ASD learning to ice skate may have very different needs.

John may develop a pattern of skating around the rink once, and then going to the exit. In order for him to experience and begin to enjoy the rhythm of skating, the trainer holds up a visual array on a board with five strips of paper on it. John is taught that he needs to keep ice-skating until all the strips are removed from the board. Each time John comes around the rink, a strip is removed. Thus, John takes five turns around the rink.

George, on the other hand, has difficulty leaving the rink when it's time to go. George is taught that when he sees the visual array of strips, he has five more trips around the rink, before he has to exit the rink. George checks the board as he passes. When one strip remains he knows he can take one more turn around the rink before he needs to exit.

POPARD consultants and PRP staff members look very carefully at the interaction between (1) the characteristics of the setting and (2) the skills and abilities of the individual. So, for example, one individual may need fewer, or very different, accommodations than another in the same setting.

Step 5. Select methods used to prepare the individual for the activity and site. Different individuals need more or less preparation, and different kinds of preparation, in order to reduce anxiety and be willing and able to learn a new recreation activity in the community. The POPARD consultants and PRP staff find that unless they engage in the necessary preparatory activities first, the likelihood increases that once the individual is in the setting s/he will not want to learn and participate. Some of the methods that POPARD consultants recommend to prepare an individual for training are described in Figure 7.6.

Figure 7.6
Methods Used to Prepare an Individual for a New Community Activity

- The teacher and individual may discuss the recreation activity, read stories about, or watch a video about the activity.
- The individual may rehearse steps involved in the recreation activity using cue cards or pictorial social scripts that will later be used on-site.
- The teacher may provide social information about the activity in the form of a social story.
- The teacher may demonstrate how to interact in a situation and role-play what will happen in a situation. This may be taught in the child's social skills class at school.
- The teacher and individual drive to the activity site and walk around the site or building.
- The teacher and individual may observe others at the site engaged in the activity for a period of time before training begins.

Phase III: Implement Training

Step 6. Prepare individual for on-site teaching. The selected preparation methods are implemented to help the individual with ASD to become comfortable with the site and to be ready for training.

> **Box 7.3**
>
> **Teaching Ice Skating:**
> The teacher and the individual visit the ice skating rink and observe people skating several times before beginning training. A social story that describes the ice skating experience, and addresses the individual's particular fears or concerns, may be written by the teacher and read by the individual for two weeks before beginning training. The individual and the teacher might read stories about ice skating, watch videos, and discuss skating.

Step 7. Teach at the site under optimal conditions for learning. Usually, initial teaching is done at the site when the sensory stimulation and distractions are as minimal as possible. Training under these conditions continues until the individual has mastered the recreation skill involved.

Step 8. Teach individual to cope with the site's typical environmental and social conditions while performing the recreation activity. Once the individual has learned the recreation skill under optimal conditions, they are more equipped to learn to cope with the sensory input and distractions that will usually be present at the site under typical conditions. The POPARD consultants and PRP staff have learned that most individuals with ASD have difficulty learning a new skill *and* learning to cope with sensory input and distractions at the same time.

> **Box 7.4**
>
> **Teaching Ice Skating:**
> After an individual has learned to ice skate in an empty rink, then the individual and one-on-one assistant begin sessions on Saturday afternoons when the rink is in full use.

In Figure 7.7, the POPARD director describes the rationale for this approach.

Figure 7.7
Thoughts from POPARD's Director on the Training Approach Used

"First, I would build the child's skill. Once she has competency and mastery of the skill, then I would gradually introduce the child to the peak times at the setting. I would then work with teaching the child to handle the noise, the changes, transitions, interruptions, etc. If I tried to do all of it at once, it wouldn't work. I can't train, and the child can't learn, under those conditions. In fact, we could end up setting up an aversion to the setting and skill in the child, because they would have such a negative, anxious experience.... The child needs to learn how to manage herself in a recreation setting. The child can't do that by simply being taken there and immersed in it."

— *Joanne Seip, Director of POPARD*

Step 9. Transition the individual into engaging in the recreation activity with family or peers. This step involves gradually fading out the presence of the consultants, and/or the teacher, as the individual participates in the recreation activity with family or peers. The consultant teaches others to use the needed accommodations to support the individual in the setting.

Step 10: After mastery in one location, teach the recreation skill in other locations, and at different times, in order to facilitate generalization of the skill across settings and under a variety of conditions. Generalization of the recreation skill usually involves steps 2-9, with preparations and adjustments for the site's new features. The individual may need visual and social information to adjust to aspects of the site that are different from the first site. Other skills and steps in the routine may transfer with little difficulty.

The POPARD approach to developing community recreation skills for individuals with ASD emphasizes careful planning and site selection, preparation of the site and the individual with ASD, and the use of visual supports and other accommodations. By first teaching the recreation skill itself under optimal sensory and social conditions, the POPARD and PRP consultants and teachers can then help the individual to learn to cope with the sites' typical conditions.

Gateway Society Residential Services
Delta, British Columbia, Canada

Background and Goals

One agency that works closely with POPARD and the PRP in British Columbia is the Gateway Society. The Gateway Society operates several small group homes designed for intensive training and intervention, provides behavioral support and supported employment services, and conducts training for families and staff of other agencies. One of these group homes is designed to help adolescents with ASD aged 12-19 (many with Asperger's Syndrome, a form of ASD), to learn self-management, communication and social skills. This program is of interest here because the staff members use recreation extensively as the medium to teach these other skills.

Up to ten youths at a time from throughout British Columbia come to live at the group home for one to three years. Typically, these are youths who have had difficulties in their local public school and community and may have dropped out and/or have been temporarily suspended from school. They are often physically mature, strong youth who have poor anger-management skills and social awareness and have difficulty understanding the consequences of their actions. For example, they may have become frustrated and angry when trying to communicate at school and were then suspended. Thus, the youths are at a crisis point and need to learn self-management skills before returning to their home community.

Program Description

While living at the home, the youths attend the PRP classroom located in the public high school. The PRP staff members work closely with the group home program. At school, the youths attend academic, work experience and community living classes in the morning and participate in recreation programs in the afternoon. Their after-school time, and evening hours, and weekends are also highly scheduled with a variety of social and community-based recreation. On weeknights, for example, youths might go to the gym twice a week, eat out in a restaurant, and participate in another community event. Because learning to cope in social environments is a core part of the program, the youths' time spent on the computer, playing video games, or watching TV is restricted.

On the weekends the youths might engage in outdoor recreation, such as skiing, hiking, canoeing, and tobogganing. Other community-based recreation activities include jogging, walking, skating, inline skating, bike riding, roller blading, picnics, dances, ferry rides, bowling, swimming, and other social opportunities. For the various community outings, a staff to youth ratio of one to one is often needed. These activities are conducted with small groups of the youths from the home and staff.

Courtesy of Mt. Hood Kiwanis Camp

All of these recreation activities are used to teach and practice self-management and social and communication skills. Because the youths want to engage in these recreation activities, they are motivated to use the self-management skills required by the staff in order to participate. The staff members try to work with each youth's strengths and preferences in planning recreation activities. The recreation activities also keep the youths active and greatly reduce the incidents of challenging behaviors. Moreover, each new recreation activity is used as an opportunity for the youths to generalize and transfer self-management and social/communication skills to new situations.

Specific goals to increase social understanding and regulate behavior are developed and monitored for each youth. When the youths first enter the program, they usually have a high rate of challenging behaviors. This rate is carefully measured and monitored as the staff begins to use various teaching strategies. The staff keeps data on the youths' behavior during every activity in order to assess whether the methods are effective. The staff also gives the youths constant feedback on their progress. The staff bases expectations for a youth on his/her current capabilities, and raises those expectations as the youth learns self-management.

Examples of Self-Management Techniques

The Gateway Society group home staff uses the same accommodations as the PRP school staff and the POPARD consultants. Staff may gradually introduce a youth to a new activity using rehearsal and desensitization techniques. Before an activity, youths are provided social information about the situation and a description of what will happen. The staff may demonstrate, and then the group role-plays how to interact with others during the activity. Theme boards with a sequence of line drawings are used with each individual across all activities of the day. Incidents that occur during a recreation outing also become important learning opportunities. If the group is having difficulty knowing what to do, the activity is stopped, and the group role-plays before proceeding. Two accommodations are used for youths that perseverate on particular topics, or ask questions repeatedly when stressed, in order to learn to self-limit their behavior. "Topic Cards" are used to help a youth focus on the current topic or activity at hand. The topic is written on the card and staff point to the words to redirect a youth when needed. "Question Cards" are used to help youth learn to refrain from asking questions repeatedly. The individual's persistent question is written down on one side and the answer is written on the other side. Each time the youth asks the question again, staff refer them to their card where they can obtain a concrete answer in written form.

A picture and word sequence placed on a theme board is also used to help youths calm down and relax when they get anxious and agitated. The visual sequence leads youths through a series of steps to identify their level of frustration and to use a specific routine to calm down, as described in Figure 7.8.

The program at the Gateway group home illustrates that community-based and social recreation can be a vital milieu for teaching individuals with ASD; through such specialized training and intervention programs critical life skills and behaviors may be learned and practiced.

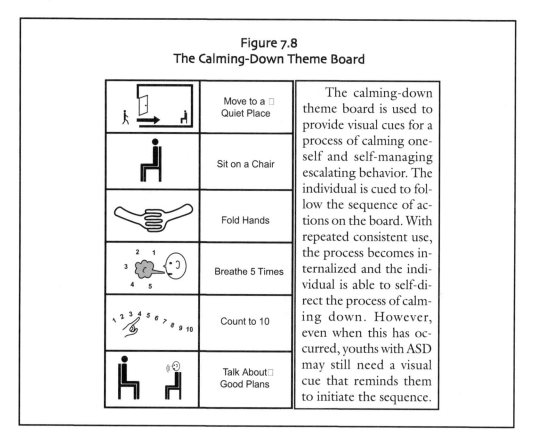

Figure 7.8
The Calming-Down Theme Board

	Move to a □ Quiet Place	The calming-down theme board is used to provide visual cues for a process of calming oneself and self-managing escalating behavior. The individual is cued to follow the sequence of actions on the board. With repeated consistent use, the process becomes internalized and the individual is able to self-direct the process of calming down. However, even when this has occurred, youths with ASD may still need a visual cue that reminds them to initiate the sequence.
	Sit on a Chair	
	Fold Hands	
	Breathe 5 Times	
	Count to 10	
	Talk About□ Good Plans	

Summary

In this chapter, four specialized programs and their strategies to develop recreation opportunities and recreation skills in individuals with ASD were described. Two of the agencies, JNCS and Creative Living, directly teach individuals with ASD to engage in community recreation, and a third, POPARD, provides consultation and training to others to achieve this aim. The fourth agency, Gateway Society, uses recreation as a milieu for development of other important skills, along with learning recreation skills. Although the agencies differ in these ways, the strategies used to develop community recreation skills are similar. These key strategies are summarized here.

First, all of the agencies emphasize the importance of knowing as much as possible about the individual with ASD's history, communication skills, sensory needs, preferences, interests, and stimuli or situations that have triggered anxiety in the past.

Second, staff members in these specialized programs carefully select community sites or activities based on two criteria. They analyze the environmental and social aspects of the location/activity in relation to the individual's sensory sensitivities, need for predictability, and behavioral triggers. They also determine beforehand if the site operators and users are supportive of the individual's training process and ongoing participation. If a site/activity contains features that will be too difficult to mitigate with accommodations or taught coping strategies, or if the people at the site are unwilling to support the needed accommodations, a different site is selected.

Third, considerable effort is devoted to preparing the individual with ASD for the recreation activity. Many of these strategies fall into the rubric of desensitization procedures. These include:

- Providing information about the activity in general. Examples include reading stories, watching videos, and viewing pictures of the activity.
- Providing information about the specific routine and the series of steps or actions that will occur during the recreation activity.
- Based on knowledge of the individual, providing (1) social information that may help the person understand the social expectations involved in the activity, and (2) information about pre-planned alternatives to avoid experiences that are difficult for the individual (e.g., taking stairs instead of the escalator).
- Rehearsing aspects of the activity or social skills needed ahead of time.

These programs use one or more of these desensitization procedures, based on their knowledge of the individual as part of the training process.

A final desensitization strategy, used by all of the programs involves the trainer and individual with ASD visiting the site and observing the activity before beginning to participate. This allows the individual to see what has been verbally and pictorially described to them and to connect this information with the actual routine or event. Pre-visits are gradually introduced, beginning with short visits and progressing to longer visits. The number of pre-visits depends on how quickly the individual becomes comfortable with the situation and ready to participate. The pre-visits are added to the individual's weekly schedule and often occur at the same time each week.

When the individual is ready, then agency staff members begin training. Training is highly individualized, as are the accommodations used. The training methods and accommodations used by these agencies are similar to those described in Chapters 5 and 6. A task analysis of the steps involved is visually represented as a mini schedule or sequence and is used to cue teacher and student. The individual is provided ways to take a break from sensory stimulation or social demands if needed. Motivators may be incorporated into the routine and teacher prompts are faded as the student gains skill. POPARD conducts their training in two phases. First, they teach the recreation skill at the site without the interference of sensory and social challenges. Then, after the individual has learned the skill, they teach them how to cope with the sensory and social conditions that are typically present at the site.

Finally, a common strategy across agencies is the use of visual information to support all aspects of the preparation and training process. A visual representation of the recreation activity is placed in the individual's overall schedule so that they know when it will occur. The activity itself is explained through a visual sequence of steps. Activity choices are visually depicted. If relevant to the activity, the materials needed are visually organized to show where to start, what to do, and how to finish the task. Instructions and reminders for social skills and appropriate behavior are pictured and/or written. And lastly, ways to cope with sensory stimulation or anxiety are cued through picture and/or word sequences of calming routines to guide self-management. It's clear that these agencies have found many different ways to incorporate individuals with ASD's strength as visual learners into their training methods.

Chapter Eight

Serving Individuals with Autism Spectrum Disorder (ASD) in Parks and Recreation Agencies

Ann Fullerton

Northern Suburban Special Recreation Association, Northbrook, Illinois

Disabled Citizens Recreation/ Inclusion Program, Bureau of Portland Parks and Recreation, Portland, Oregon

Specialized Recreation Program, Recreation Division, Eugene, Oregon

Common Strategies and Issues of Recreation Agencies

In this chapter, ways in which three different parks and recreation departments—two public and one private-nonprofit—that offer recreation experiences for participants with ASD are described. Traditionally, parks and recreation agencies are the major providers of public recreation programs in larger communities. Their goal is to create programs and facilities that cater to the various recreation interests of local citizens including nature activities, sports, fitness, and artistic pursuits. Specifically, this chapter examines the ways parks and recreation agencies support individuals with ASD through specialized activities and by facilitating inclusion into generic activities. The chapter ends with a summary of current practices and issues as well as the new directions for expanding and improving services for individuals with ASD within community parks and recreation.

The three parks and recreation programs described vary in size and each has developed a service delivery model that fits the community that they serve. The staff in each agency continues to gain experience in serving individuals with ASD. The staff incorporates new insights into the needs of participants with ASD and develops new ways to address those needs. The three agencies are:

- Portland Bureau of Parks and Recreation, Portland, Oregon
- Northern Suburban Special Recreation Association, Northbrook, Illinois
- City of Eugene Recreation Services, Eugene, Oregon

These programs are not necessarily representative of parks and recreation departments in general. Instead, their experiences are illustrative of some of the issues and strategies evolving in parks and recreation agencies with respect to serving individuals with ASD and their families.

Disabled Citizens Recreation and Special Needs Accommodations/Inclusion Program
Portland Bureau of Parks & Recreation, Portland, Oregon

Introduction

Portland Bureau of Parks and Recreation in Portland, Oregon serves urban and suburban communities through community recreation centers and community schools. The Bureau's Disabled Citizens Recreation and the Inclusion Program offer a range of activities and outings for individuals with developmental disabilities, as well as support services for inclusive recreation. The program includes three full-time masters level and/or certified therapeutic recreation specialists (CTRS); two specialists organize the specialized programs and one coordinates inclusion services. Part-time staff members are hired to assist in specialized programs and inclusion assistants. In the summer, an inclusive day camp is also offered (see Chapter 10 for a description). One of the specialized recreation program specialists and the inclusion specialist were interviewed regarding the participation of individuals with ASD in their respective programs.

More children than adults with ASD register for Portland Parks and Recreation activities and classes. Parents of children with ASD seek classes that provide physical activity and that might address, in an informal way, the sensory needs of their children. Parents request activities that might let their child release tension, have fun, and feel successful without pressure.

Disabled Citizens Recreation

A variety of specialized recreational activities including outings, events, and classes are offered by the Disabled Citizens Recreation Program. The program publishes a seasonal catalog four times a year with a range of activities, such as outdoor and indoor sports, community outings, social events, fitness, and arts. The program specialists teach classes, lead activities, and also hire other recreation instructors.

Usually, community members sign up for activities on their own from the program catalog. If contacted, the program specialist assists participants in selecting classes or activities they might enjoy, and they discuss any accommodations that maybe needed. The program specialist then prepares and coaches the specific recreation instructor regarding any accommodations that might be needed by a participant when attending their class or activity. In order to determine the assistance needed, the program specialist might attend the first few sessions of a class, to observe and assist the instructor and the participant. This can lead to developing other needed adaptations, or forms of assistance, such as a visual schedule or communication board, which the specialist develops for the instructor to use in the class. For example, in Figure 8.1, photos of a participant performing various tumbling routines are shown. These were taken of the participant and used to help her know what activity to do, and in what sequence.

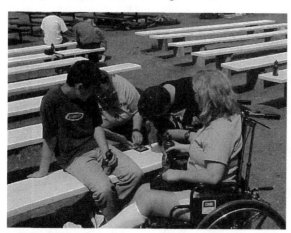

The program specialist also utilizes the parents as a resource for the instructor regarding the participant's needs. The program specialist asks the parents to give the instructor information that will help them make the experience successful for the individual. The program specialist sees his or her role in these situations as one of facilitating a good working partnership between the parent and the instructor.

Specialized Recreation Classes.

In the Disabled Citizens program, the staff has developed several classes for children and youth who are of particular interest to parents of children with ASD. These classes contain features that are beneficial for participants with ASD. For example, the classes have been taught by the same instructors for some time, and they are offered in the same location each time. Familiarity with the instructor and location can reduce anxiety because fewer aspects of the situation change from class to class. The classes include tumbling, trampoline, adapted sports, and martial arts classes in Tae Kwon Do and Aikido. These classes are usually organized for a 5-11 age group or a 12-adult age group. The program specialist finds that a few youths with ASD register for these classes each time they are offered.

The martial arts classes are particularly popular with participants with ASD, in part because they are highly structured. The instructors use a methodical teaching style with precise steps and sequences for movement patterns, as well as a predictable routine throughout the class session. The instructors have clear rules for taking turns and for how dyads interact during practice sessions. Moves are verbally described but also demonstrated repeatedly. In the Aikido class, the instructor's assistant is an educator who works with students with ASD. This team of a martial arts instructor and an educator of children with

**Figure 8.1
Photos Used in Visual Communication System
for a Participant in a Tumbling Class**

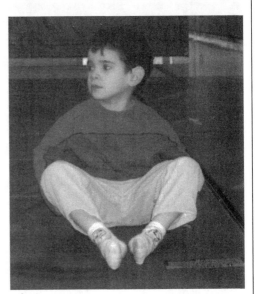

Photos courtesy of Portland Bureau of Parks and Recreation, Portland, OR

ASD allows sufficient time for a participant to cognitively process and respond to instructions. The team has also simplified the social skills needed in class. The instructors find that the structure inherent in martial arts training results in predictable routines that helps children with ASD to master the skills involved. Some of the participants with ASD have attended the classes for several years and have developed considerable skill in Tae Kwon Do and Aikido. One student with ASD has been attending the Aikido class for two years, and he has become the role model for the class. The instructor asks him to demonstrate moves and techniques to the rest of the class. These martial arts classes are an example of how specialized recreation classes have a place in a continuum of program options offered to participants with ASD. In this case, a specialized class has allowed participants with ASD to develop advanced skills.

Special Needs Accommodations/Inclusive Recreation

Providing inclusive services is a priority in the Portland Bureau of Parks and Recreation and a full-time inclusion specialist oversees these services. Inclusion services are sought primarily by parents for their children, especially in the summer. For example, in the summer of 2001, the inclusion program assisted over 227 children in 189 activities with a total of 3,458 hours of 1:1 assistance. Forty-three of the participants were individuals with ASD. Twenty-five part-time assistants were hired to support children in various classes and activities. The majority of the 1:1 inclusion support is provided for children with ASD.

The inclusion specialist makes every effort to be available to any family or individual with disabilities seeking assistance to participate in a class at any of the community recreation centers or community schools in the city. Usually, individuals seeking recreation first contact their local community center about a class or activity that is offered. Most inquiries come from parents on behalf of their children, not from adults seeking recreation for themselves. The staff at the local recreation center informs the parents about the special needs accommodation services available, and refers them to the inclusion specialist.

The inclusion specialist calls or meets with the parent to learn about the child's needs and interests in order to develop whatever accommodations might be needed. The inclusion specialist also calls and/or visits the instructor of the class to find out how the class operates. Ideally, the inclusion specialist can visit and observe how the instructor teaches as this information is invaluable in thinking through needed accommodations for an individual. But time constraints and the distance between centers limits the inclusion specialist's opportunity to do this.

The inclusion specialist then writes a description of the accommodations needed and sends it to the parent and the instructor for review (see Chapter 5, Figure 5.11 for an example). The inclusion specialist also seeks an opportunity to talk with the instructor about the accommodations, but again, this is usually not possible because the part-time recreation instructors at the centers are not always available for a pre-meeting.

Given the limited opportunity to prepare the instructor in advance, the inclusion specialist finds alternatives to work around this. The inclusion specialist usually meets the parent and child at the center before the class starts to talk about the class and prepare the child. Sometimes the inclusion specialist, parent, and child may meet and observe a class session together before the child joins the class. The parent, child, inclusion specialist and instructor meet after the first class session.

When the child joins the class, the inclusion specialist assists the child and the instructor as needed. Usually, for the first few sessions, the specialist teaches the child using the accommodations they have developed alongside the instructor as he or she is teaching the other students in the class. The instructor then has an opportunity to observe what the inclusion specialist is doing to accommodate and teach the child with ASD. This approach also provides the child with some initial one-on-one instruction. By the second to fourth class session, the inclusion specialist works less and less directly with the child and moves into a coaching role as the instructor takes over.

After these initial class sessions, the inclusion specialist may problem-solve with the instructor, answer questions, and give feedback. Both instructor and inclusion specialist also consult with the parent during this process. Depending on the child's and the instructor's needs, at some point the inclusion specialist no longer attends the classes, but remains available to the parent and instructor. At the end of the class, the inclusion specialist asks the parent to complete an evaluation form and give feedback on the effectiveness of the inclusion process, the instructor, and the inclusion specialist.

As noted earlier, part-time inclusion assistants are employed during the busy summer months. The inclusion assistants utilize the accommodations developed by the specialists and provide the in-class teaching with the participant and coaching for the instructor. Depending on the child's needs, an assistant may remain with one child during all of the class sessions, or move on to assist other individuals, if the child is able to participate on their own.

One of the challenges for the inclusion specialist is to teach the 90 full-time center-based recreation instructors, plus the 700 part-time summer recreation instructors, how to provide accommodations and inclusive classes. To address this training need, the inclusion specialist has established a citywide Inclusion Committee with a representative from each community center who is a member of its full-time staff. The Inclusion Committee meets three times a year to discuss inclusion, disability, and accessibility issues. The inclusion specialist uses these meetings to develop in each community center a sense of ownership of the responsibility to learn about and provide appropriate accommodations and inclusion services. The staff representative at each center learns from the inclusion specialist how to facilitate inclusion and will then teach these skill to the other recreation instructors at their center. This approach develops capacity within each community center over time to provide needed accommodations.

Planning and Providing Accommodations: An Example of Swimming Lessons. One activity that parents of young children with ASD often request from the inclusion recreation program is swimming lessons. Parents inquire about lessons both because they want their child to learn to swim and also because of their child's love of the sensory sensations associated with being in the water. The inclusion specialist arranges various supports according to a child's needs. One accommodation that has been successful with several children with ASD is individual swimming lessons taught alongside a group swimming lesson. Families pay the group lesson rate for the individual lesson. A local swimming instructor is taught by the inclusion specialist to provide the individual lesson.

The pool is a very active, noisy, bright environment that can be overstimulating for a child with ASD and, as a result, challenging for the instructor. To alleviate these challenges, the inclusion specialist has developed communication systems to use during swimming lessons for children with ASD. The inclusion specialist studied how instructors teach swimming as well as the needs of several young children with ASD who have taken lessons. She put together a mini-schedule of line drawings for participants with ASD that follows the lesson sequences. The materials used were waterproofed as much as possible for use in the pool. The system allows the instructor to show the sequence of steps, or schedule, for each lesson. The system also has a section where the instructor can show the child the choices for water play after the lesson. Because many of the children love to play in the water, offering specific choices for water play after the lesson is important in order to focus the child on first learning the skills associated with swimming before they engage in water play. This visual system is shown and described in Figure 8.2.

Figure 8.2
Mini-Schedule and Choice System for Swimming Lessons
Sample Swim Lesson

Free Time Choices

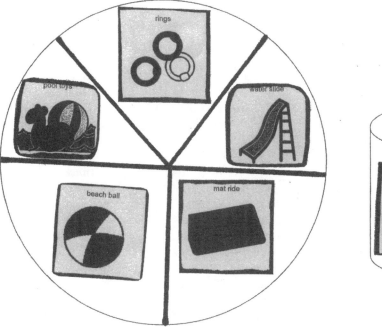

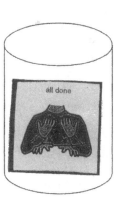

This figure depicts a mini-schedule and choices for a swim lesson. At the top, the sequence of activities for the swim lesson are shown. As each activity is completed the participant and instructor remove the picture and place in the can marked "all done." The last step in the swim lesson is choice time. The bottom half shows the various choices available to the participant for choice time in the pool.

The inclusion specialist teaches the swimming instructors what to do to teach and support a child with ASD and demonstrates how to use the mini-schedule and choice system with a child during swimming lessons. Sometimes an instructor is skeptical that the visual system is really necessary for children with ASD. The inclusion specialist has had the experience that if she is not able to be present for a lesson, the instructor may tell her later: "I didn't use the pictures, we didn't need them." However, when the inclusion specialist returns for the next lesson and uses the system with the child, the instructor is amazed at the child's increased understanding of what to do, compliance with instructions, and progress in learning to swim.

Example of Swimming Lessons for a Child with ASD. To illustrate how the visual system is used with a child with ASD, the story of Gina's swimming lessons will be shared. In Gina's first year of instruction at age five, the swimming instructor did not feel the need for help from the inclusion specialist to provide lessons to Gina. The instructor reported that the two weeks of lessons with Gina had gone fine. But the second year, when Gina's parents registered her for another class, the inclusion specialist was asked to be present at the first lesson. The inclusion specialist could see from the swimming instructor's reaction upon seeing Gina again, that the lessons had not gone well the year before. It was then revealed that during the first year's lessons, Gina had done whatever she wanted to while in the pool. Essentially, Gina had a fun time, but she did not learn swimming skills.

The inclusion specialist was present for the first few lessons and modeled for the instructor how to use the pictorial sequence of steps to support swimming lessons for a child with ASD. The inclusion specialist used a strategy to increase Gina's ability to focus on the visual system. Every time Gina became overstimulated, distracted, and was not attending to the visual system and the instructor, Gina was assisted out of the pool for a 20-second break. One source of distraction for Gina was the presence of her older brother who was also taking a group swim lesson in the pool. Gina wanted to go over to him, give him a big hug and pull him underwater. This was a safety issue for the brother and for other kids in the group. The breaks out of the pool helped Gina relax and re-focus on the visual system and instruction.

During the first lesson the inclusion specialist used the breaks out of the pool at a high frequency. After all, the year before, Gina had done whatever she wanted during the lessons and now it took time to teach her to rely on the pictorial sequence of steps for information. During the second lesson, Gina began to respond increasingly to the visual system. Her favorite water play activity was throwing and fetching the rings. At first, the inclusion specialist let her make this choice over and over from the choice board in order to reduce the number of breaks out of the pool and to start getting Gina to respond to the visual system. By the third lesson, the inclusion specialist was using very few breaks, because Gina increasingly responding to the instructions in the visual system, would do the various skills in the lesson such as blowing bubbles, leg kicks, and arm strokes. When her favorite activity, the rings, was available on the choice board, she always chose it. When it was not present on the board, she followed directions and performed the other swimming skills. Thus as Gina's repertoire expanded and she began to understand that the instructor was using the visual system to tell her what to do, she was less fixated on her favorite activity.

This story illustrates an important lesson for recreation providers. The performance we see in a participant can be just as dependent on the type of instruction and supports provided as on the individual's disabilities. When recreation instructors see a participant with ASD perform using visual supports it broadens their view of the educational possibilities. Otherwise, instructors may think that they have done all they can to teach an individual, and that the individual's performance in a class is a result of their disability, as opposed to the instructional methods used.

In striving to provide inclusive services citywide, the inclusion specialist recognizes the importance of training more and more of the center-based recreation instructors by demonstrating strategies with actual participants, as in the story of Gina's swimming lessons. The inclusion specialist, Jan Book observes: "inclusion is a process. It takes time for people to have exposure and experience working with children with ASD. I have seen so much progress here in the last two years. People are less fearful, more open-minded, and working with the children independent of my help."

Portland Bureau of Parks and Recreation staff members have utilized accommodations for participants with ASD in both specialized and inclusive recreation settings. In addition, they have found that certain specialized classes have filled a niche for some participants with ASD. Finally, they continue to expand the expertise of all the agency's staff regarding the needs of participants with ASD.

Northern Suburban Special Recreation Association
Northbrook, Illinois

Introduction

The Northern Suburban Special Recreation Association (NSSRA) was established in 1970 and was the first "special recreation" association in the country. The extension of 12 suburban park and recreation agencies is funded principally by a local property tax that can be spent only on recreation for people with disabilities. In 2002, there were 26 Special Recreation Associations (SRA's) in Illinois. SRA's are a model for providing recreation for individuals with disabilities, and the governmental partnership is unique to the state of Illinois, as well as in its size, scope, and longevity. School districts and other agencies partner with NSSRA to provide after-school, extended school year, and other programs. The partner parks and recreation departments utilize NSSRA staff to facilitate inclusion of community members with disabilities into community recreation.

In 2001 NSSRA served about 2,500 individuals with disabilities; and about half were children and half were adults. NSSRA serves residents in the ten partner park districts and two municipalities in the northern suburbs of Chicago. In 2001, NSSRA employed 10 full-time Certified Therapeutic Recreation Specialists (CTRS) divided among the areas of special services and inclusion services and programs. The full-time staff plan programs, conduct assessments, and adapt programs to the needs of individual registrants. About 500 part-time recreation assistants are hired annually to assist in carrying out programs. Together, this staff offers more than 700 different programs and events throughout the year.

Specialized recreation provides after school programs, Saturday programs, day camps, trips, indoor and outdoor sports, Special Olympics, community outings, exercise, dance, craft, and other classes; as well as social activities such as dances, parties, and playtimes for different age groups. In 2001, the inclusion services department facilitated the inclusion of 500 participants into public parks and recreation programs.

When a child's family or an adult inquires about NSSRA, they are asked to complete a questionnaire and to meet with one of the CTRS's. At the interview the participant's recreation interests and his needs for accommodations are discussed. After choosing and participating in a few of NSSRA's activities, a participant usually continues to choose and enroll in activities from the NSSRA catalog on his own. The CTRS also describes how NSSRA coordinates and facilitates inclusion into the participant's local parks and recreation programs and if desired, initiates this process.

Participants with ASD. In the early 2000s, NSSRA found that the association was serving an increasing number of participants with ASD. The Superintendant of Recreation at NSSRA estimated that three percent or about 75 of the participants in 2001 were individuals with ASD. Most of the new participants in the specialized programs were children and adults with more severe ASD, who were nonverbal and needed more intensive supports in order to participate. NSSRA also saw an increase in requests for inclusion services by parents of children with ASD. A new generation of parents of children with ASD was seeking opportunities for their children to participate in recreation with children who do not have disabilities in their local community.

Increasing Staff's Knowledge of Individuals with ASD. With the increase in numbers, it has become important that the CTRS staff understands the needs and learning style of participants with ASD along with how to communicate with, teach, and develop accommodations for these participants. Recreation program development is under the guidance of the Superintendent of Recreation. To better program for individuals with ASD, the Superintendent took several steps to increase the staff's knowledge of individuals with ASD.

First, NSSRA sought out ASD specialists, such as CTRS's, teachers, psychologists, speech/language therapists, or occupational therapists with expertise in ASD. These specialists have observed and analyzed situations involving participants with ASD and offered solutions. Teachers have invited NSSRA's CTRS staff to observe children with ASD while in school and see the communication systems and teaching strategies used in the classroom.

Second, NSSRA has formed a partnership with the Elaine Kersten School of Northbrook, IL; a private school for students with ASD. NSSRA provides an after-school program at the school. This relationship has provided CTRS staff opportunities to learn communication and instructional strategies from the teachers.

Third, NSSRA's staff has sought out workshops and seminars on strategies for individuals with ASD. Their school partners have invited the NSSRA staff to attend their own inservice training. The CTRS staff has encouraged their own professional recreation associations to bring in ASD experts as speakers at state conferences. These have all been low-cost avenues for staff development in the area of ASD.

Addressing participant needs with new knowledge about ASD. In recent years, NSSRA has been incorporating new knowledge about ASD into their processes for analyzing and addressing the needs of participants with ASD. One important change has been how the challenging behaviors of participants are viewed. Rather than seeing these behaviors as the participant's attempts to get attention or act out in some way, they are recognized as the participant's way of communicating a need or desire. So the first thing to be done is to determine what it is that the participant is communicating. Through the training seminars and work with their consultants, the CTRS staff is learning that participants with ASD:

- May be expressing frustration because they don't understand the instructions or don't know what they are expected to do.
- May need a slower pace because the usual pace of the activity is too fast for their level of motor coordination.
- May be confused and anxious because the situation is loosely structured and frequently changing instead of being structured and predictable.
- May have sensory sensitivities that are exacerbated by aspects of the environment (noise, light, smells, physical contact, etc.).
- May need the deep pressure of a hug to address sensory needs and calm them. If not provided, the participant may seek deep pressure from objects, and, for example, crawl under the mats in the gym or into a small space.

These are all possible reasons why a participant with ASD may have difficulty in a recreation program. The NSSRA staff is learning how to analyze the participant-environment interactions to find the trigger for a challenging behavior, and then to change the situation accordingly.

NSSRA conducts a large number of programs in many locations with many participants enrolled at any one time. This situation has required NSSRA to develop methods for quickly responding to problems and challenges that occur for instructors and participants. To this end, they have developed a Program Advisory Committee and a problem- solving team. The new information learned about individuals with ASD has changed the ways these two groups function within the organization.

Parent Advisory Committee. In 1998, NSSRA formed a Parent Advisory Committee, consisting mostly of parents of young and old program participants. The committee helps NSSRA work closely with parents to address needs and concerns. For example, to expedite communication between parents and staff when a problem occurred, the parent committee developed what is called the "Behavior Bulletin." This is a one-page, two-copy report form that staff can complete and send to a parent describing a participant's behavior during a program activity. At the bottom of the form, the staff person might indicate that they will call the parent to discuss and problem-solve a situation with the parent. Parents can respond on the form, keep one copy, and return the other. The Bulletin keeps the parent informed and coordinates staff efforts with parental efforts. NSSRA staff use the Behavior Bulletin to communicate back and forth with parents of participants with ASD about sensory, communication, and other issues as related to a participant's behavior. The Program Advisory Committee has been a useful forum for parents of participants with ASD to share their expertise about ASD.

Problem-solving team. When difficulties arise for a participant in a recreation activity, the CTRS staff first observe the situation and work with the program leader. They also seek input from the participant's family. But if more help is needed, then a problem-solving team is convened. The team includes the participant's parents, teacher, and sometimes consultants, along with NSSRA staff. The goal is to gather together what everyone knows about the participant that is important for solving the problem. The meetings are conducted using a modified McGill Action Planning Process (MAPS) to focus knowledge and resources on the problem (Vandercook et. al., 1989).

New information and understanding of the needs of participants with ASD has been incorporated into the work of the problem-solving team. In the past, the problem-solving team usually developed what was viewed as a behavior plan, but this concept has been modified and expanded to include an array of environmental, sensory, motor, and communication issues. Now, the team analyzes the environment and looks for the trigger for a challenging behavior. The participant may be observed in the recreation setting and other settings by staff and others with expertise in ASD. Then the team meets with all the information available and develops a plan of action. After the plan has been implemented for two weeks, the team reconvenes to evaluate progress.

Supporting Participants with ASD in Specialized Recreation

NSSRA has used several strategies to provide information and more structure for participants with ASD in their specialized programs. For example staff members have developed visual and written schedules and social stories (Gray, 2000). They have used the first-then approach (first we do this, then we do this) in which activities are arranged so that a non-preferred activity is followed by a preferred activity (as described in Chapter 6). On occasion, staff members have encouraged parents to have an individual (such as a baby-sitter, nanny, respite provider, or family member), who knows the participant with ASD to accompany the participant.

Figure 8.3
Developing Recreation Interests Over Time: A Case Study

A boy with ASD first came to NSSRA with his mother at age six. The mother wanted NSSRA to help her find leisure activities that he would enjoy. The boy was very active, so they tried a variety of active sports. During these sports activities, he ran around all the time and all over the place without connection to the activity. They tried many different activities, but nothing seemed to capture his sustained interest and motivation.

The CTRS suggested they try an art activity, even though it was much more sedentary. He was enrolled in an art program for young children. In the first class the children were instructed to take a greeting card and re-draw it from scratch. The CTRS set the task before him and he became engaged. The CTRS remembers looking away for a few minutes, and then returning to his side to see what he had done. To her surprise he had copied every detail of the greeting card, including the tiny Hallmark logo on the back perfectly. That day, an artist was born. The boy, now 16, has increasingly developed into an artist, and he greatly enjoys it. When drawing, he stays more focused and sustains his interest and effort more than in a sports activity.

When the boy was younger, the CTRS had also introduced ceramics to the boy, but he made it clear he did not want the wet and gooey clay on his hands. Years later, when he was a teen, he tried a pottery class once again. By that time he had learned to tolerate more textures, and he became an avid potter.

The story illustrates the importance of trying a variety of activities and reintroducing activities of potential interest. Sensory sensitivities and other needs do change over time.

Facilitating Inclusion into Parks and Recreation Programs

The inclusion recreation staff includes three full-time professional staff and 200 or more leisure companions. Additional staff is employed in the summer, when more families are seeking inclusive recreation.

The professional staff works with the parks and recreation agency staff to assess participants and to plan accommodations needed for individual participants. They also train and support parks and recreation instructors and the leisure companions who provide one-on-one assistance to participants. Families can sign up for any recreation activity available to them in their suburb or other suburbs. If a leisure companion is needed for their child, this is arranged by NSSRA. NSSRA then bills the park and recreation agency for the cost of the leisure companion. Each park and recreation agency has set aside an inclusion fund that is used to pay for the leisure companions or other accommodations that might be needed. The park and recreation agencies can serve families with children with disabilities well because they have backup support and expertise from NSSRA, and they have set aside sufficient funds to offer inclusive recreation.

Examples of facilitating inclusion. To illustrate the way that NSSRA staff facilitates inclusion for participants with ASD, several examples are provided. In the first example, NSSRA facilitated the inclusion of a child with ASD into a parks and recreation after-school program. After-school programs usually last for three hours and are loosely structured. Children have lots of free time and many choices. This can be too open-ended for a child with ASD, so the CTRS added structure for the child with ASD and trained a leisure companion to provide the accommodations.

The CTRS first analyzed all aspects of the after-school program's offerings, including the routines that were already in place. She also talked with the parents and with the child about needs and wants. Then she developed a personal schedule for the child that provided information on what was next, arranged nonpreferred and preferred activities, and provided choices. The schedule was calibrated to the length of time that the child could be engaged in one activity successfully. For example, the schedule might start with: use bathroom, wash hands, and then snack. Next the child might engage in a less preferred activity for 15 minutes (e.g. homework) and then be able to choose between two preferred activities, (e.g., pinball or basketball), for 20 minutes. The schedule might continue to alternate between sedentary and active experiences in this fashion.

Each time period spent doing homework or activities was kept short enough that the child did not become frustrated and remained successful. For example, if the after-school program offered a one-hour craft project, the leisure companion engaged the child in the project for 15 minutes, and then took a break for a walk around the gym before resuming work on the project. The goal was to assist the child with ASD to do the same things as her peers, but to do so in time blocks and at a pace that worked for the child. Before new activities were introduced, the CTRS staff sometimes wrote a social story (Gray, 1996, 2000) for the child to read several times before the activity began.

In a second example, NSSRA leisure companions are employed to support children with ASD in parks and recreation preschool programs. These preschoolers have a sensory diet (as defined in Chapter 6) prescribed by an occupational therapist. Different children need a different form or multiple forms of sensory input throughout the day in order to be able to stay focused, reduce anxiety, and address sensory needs. For example, the leisure companion prompts one child to push against the wall, a form of joint compression, when he needs to calm himself down. At other times a little lotion is massaged into his hands, or the child plays with shaving cream, which provide different sensory experiences. Therapy objects and toys are also used, such as the Bumble Ball, which is a small ball that vibrates when turned on and has a variegated surface of indents and soft points. The sensory diet prescribes the activities used to provide calming, organizing, and alerting experiences that help develop sensory integration.

In a final example, the sensory needs of a boy with ASD are being addressed so that he can learn to swim. The CTRS and leisure companion provide a planned routine of joint compression whenever the child begins to escalate behaviors that will disrupt his swimming lesson. Each of his joints (fingers, wrists, shoulder, knees, etc.) is moved back and forth five times in a set sequence. The boy counts the repetitions with his leisure companion and helps monitor the sequence. The companions have found that once this routine was initiated, they were able to use it, instead of having to remove him from the pool, at those times when he became overstimulated. The joint compression helps him to calm down, re-focus, and be able to continue his swimming lessons.

In summary, NSSRA has implemented a number of practices to serve participants with ASD. The agency has used new knowledge about ASD to enhance their problem solving approach and to develop accommodations in both specialized and inclusive recreation.

Specialized Recreation Program
City of Eugene Recreation Services, Eugene, Oregon

Introduction

The city of Eugene's Recreation Services serves a city of 141,000 in Eugene, Oregon. The Specialized Recreation Program provides both special programs and inclusive recreation services as well as supportive services for agencies and groups working with persons with disabilities. The staff includes two full-time CTRS's, 16 part-time instructors, one full-time recreation leader, and two part-time office coordinators.

One instructor in the Specialized Recreation Division in Eugene, Oregon brings particular expertise in the area of ASD, given her own experiences as a woman and artist with ASD. She first became involved with the recreation division by participating in an adult support group for persons with ASD. She interviewed and was hired as an art instructor within the division's Art Careers Program. This instructor has been a role model of a successful artist for the program participants, one-third of who are individuals with ASD. The director has found that at times this instructor has demonstrated a deep understanding of the difficulties facing students and an intuitive sense of effective ways to guide students through difficult times inside and outside of class.

The specialized recreation program offers both specialized and inclusive recreation services. It is housed at the Hilyard Community Center. Built in 1990, this fully accessible facility was designed to serve persons with disabilities in a community setting. The staff offers activities at the Hilyard center, and at all of the other recreation centers in the city, as well as inclusive support at the various centers.

Specialized Recreation

As of 2001, about 1,200 individuals regularly participated in specialized programs; about 450 were individuals with moderate to significant developmental disabilities and of these, about 10 percent (or 40) were individuals with ASD. A variety of specialized recreation events and classes are developed and described in a seasonal leisure guide. For example, outings to various parts of the state for outdoor recreation are offered, such as waterfall tours, whale watching, drives to see the fall colors, and other activities such as: holiday crafts and cooking, attending university sports events, visiting the aquarium, museum, or zoo. In providing specialized recreation, the staff has learned about some of the needs of participants with ASD and has developed particular approaches and program offerings.

The staff finds that participants with ASD are more likely to sign up for an activity if they are aquainted with the leader/instructor. The full-time staff in specialized recreation has been with the department for 12 to 20 years. This stability means that participants with ASD have been able to get to know the instructors/leaders over time. Familiarity with the instructor appears to make the participant with ASD more comfortable trying something new or being with a group of new individuals. Two factors are involved. First, the participant knows that the instructor is familiar with their communication or other needs and has provided accommodations successfully in the past. Second, the participant is familiar with the instructor's teaching and leadership style, so they are free to focus on the new activity, instead of on learning how to interact with a new instructor.

Thus, for some individuals with ASD, the particulars of the activity itself may be less important than familiarity with the instructor. As a result, the seasonal leisure guide always lists the name of the instructor for each activity or class. This increases the likelihood that certain participants will sign up for activities. In fact, some families have suggested that the program offer an activity called: "A Fun Day with Molly" because that would attract a number of individuals with ASD who have known this staff member for many years. This is an interesting suggestion for other agencies that have long-term staff as a way to encourage greater participation among individuals with ASD in their community.

Even with a familiar instructor, some individuals with ASD do not attend many of the recreation activities because they are offered in a group class format with other students who do not know each other. This is a social situation that can be challenging for an individual with ASD. The individuals with ASD who do not sign up may indeed want to try the recreation activity, and if given the opportunity, they might discover that they would enjoy it a great deal. In this case, it is the format of a group class composed of new people, not the activity per se, that is a barrier limiting participation.

Staff members have discussed various alternatives to address this issue that could be offered, if resources become available. These include a computer game class, family events, cooperative programs with agencies and organizations working primarily with persons with ASD and their families, and hiking trips designed only for youth with ASD. There appears to be a need for recreation providers to be creative and try out different activities and formats that might help individuals with ASD access more community recreation.

One way that the specialized recreation program introduces youth with disabilities to community recreation is to connect with their high school teachers before the students leave school. Recreation can be an important source of social connection and maintenance of physical and emotional well being for young adults with disabilities after graduation that helps prevent isolation after graduation. Each year, the CTRS contacts special educators in secondary schools to arrange a visit to the recreation center so that students can become acquainted with the staff and activities before they leave public school. Several activities are designed specifically for young adults aged 18-24 to encourage socialization and recreation.

The Arts Careers Program. Specialized recreation has developed an Arts Careers program designed to meet the needs of adults with more severe ASD and other cognitive differences such as chronic mental disorders and traumatic head injury. These young adults have found it challenging to successfully locate and keep employment. The city of Eugene Recreation's services "Arts Careers Program" established in 2000 is a cooperative program with the local Amazon Art Center. The program provides individuals with ASD an opportunity to practice and create marketable art. While participants gain knowledge of various artistic skills, the program promotes creative expression, personal identity and pride, self-esteem, and it fosters socialization and inclusion. The program provides income earning opportunities for the participants through gallery shows and sales.

The Arts Careers program meets two days a week for four hours. In 2002, 14 young adults participated, and two instructors, one assistant, and two volunteers conducted the program. The participants are young adults who wish to explore their artistic interests and talents as an avenue toward developing a saleable art or craft product. Eugene is a community of artisans and craftspersons, and thus the program fits well with local resources and opportunities.

The staff's goal is to adapt environments and provide accommodations that will help individuals to utilize their artistic interests and skills. The goal is not to "change" the individual to fit the setting but instead to discover what accommodations will let an individual utilize his artistic ability. Changing the environment can involve accommodations such as finding the optimal place for a participant to sit when working on their art projects, setting up the project materials in a certain format, or scheduling needed breaks to reduce anxiety and resume focus on a project.

Other accommodations allow for an individual's fixations and perseverative behaviors to be incorporated into a meaningful activity. For example, one young man with ASD has drawing and design talent, which he hopes to develop. He prefers to work on two applications—designing jacket covers for jazz musicians and designing bus schedules. However, if he is going to develop a more generalized drawing talent, he needs to branch out and draw and design other visual images and media. So, he is encouraged and supported to draw for other purposes, for periods of time, and then to work on jacket covers and bus schedules for a limited time period during his breaks.

Some individuals with ASD in the class perseverate in talking about particular topics. When they get fixated on a topic, their own behavior interferes with their art/craft project. So, project work is structured for a period of time, and then followed by a break period when individuals may talk about their preferred topic. These strategies help individuals with ASD to stretch and develop their capacity to engage in new, desired activities. Participants in the Arts Careers Program have created jewelry, paintings, and other artwork that they sell at shows and sales. The director has also dreamed of creating a low-income housing/art studio community in which local artists with and without disabilities could live in the same complex and support each other's artistic pursuits.

Inclusive Recreation

The city of Eugene Recreation services also provides inclusive recreation services. One staff member works full-time during summers and part-time the rest of the year as the inclusion specialist to support primarily youth with disabilities who want to participate in the 200 or more activities and camps offered. The inclusion specialist employs part-time inclusion assistants, especially in the summer months, to support requests for summer sports, swimming and other lessons, and summer day camp. For example, in the summer of 2001, the inclusion specialist and six support staff served 28 youths.

Parents of children with ASD often request inclusive recreation experiences for their child. The process is usually initiated when a parent calls their local recreation center to inquire about a class and indicates that his or her child may need some extra assistance. Depending on the needs of the child, the parent may be referred to the inclusion specialist by the staff at the community rec-

Photo by Jason Kinch Photographics, Courtesy of Mt. Hood Kiwanis Camp

reation center, or the staff contacts the inclusion specialist directly. The inclusion specialist then calls and talks with the parent and asks them to complete and return an intake questionnaire. The questionnaire is designed to gain information about the interests and needs of the participant. The inclusion specialist has taken care to word the questions in general, functional, informative terms and to avoid clinical and/or labeling terms (see Chapter 5).

The inclusion specialist discusses and plans out supports with the parent in person or by phone and writes a plan for the accommodations is then sent to the parent and the recreation instructor of the class. Whenever possible, the inclusion specialist also meets with the instructor before the class to discuss the accommodations. The specialist is also present at the first few class sessions to train and coach the instructor, model how to teach the participant, and facilitate a working partnership between the parent and instructor. In time, the inclusion specialist decreases his or her direct involvement and eventually will no longer attend the class sessions. At this point in the process, the inclusion specialist either asks the parent to call them or initiates a call to find out how the class is going for the child. The inclusion specialist remains available for problem-solving as needed. The inclusion specialist estimates that from three to 40 hours may be needed to facilitate the inclusion of a participant with ASD into a recreation class or activity.

If warranted, and the staff resources are available, the inclusion specialist may assign an inclusion assistant to provide one-on-one assistance to the child in the class. When initially serving a child with ASD, the inclusion specialist has asked the parent and child to meet with prospective assistants and to choose the assistant they feel is a good match for the child.

The inclusion specialist weighs the needs of the child with the staff's ability to adapt the physical aspects of a recreation situation when recommending a recreation activity for the child. For example, sometimes sensory aspects of the activity and environment, or the size of the group, is not tolerable for a child with ASD. Sometimes the setting has too much sensory stimulation that cannot be modified. Sometimes it's not possible to make a setting safe for a child who wants to explore everything and is having difficulty following directions. Exploring recreation opportunities is a process through which much is learned that can lead to a good match for the participant.

The city of Eugene Recreation Services has found ways to encourage adults with ASD to participate in community recreation, developed specialized programs, and also provides inclusive recreation services for children with ASD.

Common Strategies and Issues of Recreation Agencies

In this chapter staff from two public and one private, nonprofit recreation agencies described how they serve individuals with ASD. Useful strategies, trends, and issues that emerged are summarized below.

Recreation agencies have obtained consultation and staff development in order to serve participants with ASD. These agencies have recognized that the needs of participants with ASD can be complex, as a result, staff need specific training and at times consultation with ASD specialists. Pre-established relationships with schools have been a source of low-cost consultation and staff training opportunities. Staff members can develop their skills in assessing needs and developing accommodations by being able to consult with ASD specialists who are brought in to help solve specific challenges occurring with individual participants. Larger agencies may also establish a problem-solving team that serves the dual function of addressing immediate concerns and developing staff's skills.

One of the most important outcomes of increasing the expertise of CTRS staff members in the area of ASD is that they are then able to assess and anticipate the needs of a participant with ASD, develop accommodations, and teach and prepare recreation instructors and inclusion assistants before a participant with ASD starts a new class or activity. Administrators and CTRS staff are increasingly aware that when accommodations are in place, and recreation instructors are prepared in advance, participants with ASD are able to learn how to participate in a recreation setting.

Recreation agencies need to provide staff with training in ASD. Due to the complexity of ASD and the sensory, cognitive, and communication challenges involved, staff at all levels within the recreation agency need training. CTRS staff needs training in assessing participants' needs, analyzing recreation environments, and developing needed accommodations. In addition, CTRS staff needs to know how to work with parents of children with ASD and utilize the parents' knowledge of their child. And finally, CTRS staff needs the skills to teach recreation instructors, inclusion assistants/companions, and volunteers about strategies and accommodations for individuals with ASD.

Recreation instructors, assistants, and volunteers often provide the direct instruction and support to participants with ASD. These staff members need training so that they understand the sensory and communication challenges and the learning style of individuals with ASD. This knowledge is necessary in order to understand what underlies the behavior of participants with ASD. Staff members need to know why certain environmental situations can be difficult for participants, and why particular instructional and support accommodations are used.

Without such knowledge, staff may not understand the importance of the consistent and precise use of accommodations. Recreation instructors can be understandably skeptical that the accommodations (e.g., visual communication systems, breaks to reduce anxiety, providing basic social information) are really necessary. The inclusion assistant, or a volunteer, without sufficient training and supervision, can drift into doing things for the participant, instead of using appropriate methods to teach the participant how to do things for him- or herself. The way in which the recreation staff instructs and supports the individual with ASD is the most important factor in the quality of his recreation experience.

Training inclusion assistants, volunteers, and recreation instructors is challenging for CTRS staff due to limited personnel and time resources. Part-time inclusion assistants may receive only an hour or two of introductory information about individuals with ASD. Most of their remaining training may be on the spot just before or during the first session of the activity. Most of the agencies relied on parents or other family members of participants with ASD to help teach inclusion assistants, volunteers, and recreation instructors. Although parental input about an individual participant is critical, it cannot substitute for staff training that builds a deeper understanding of ASD and competency in implementing accommodations.

In Chapter 7 we learned how the staff in special programs for individuals with ASD prepare recreation settings, instructors, assistants and participants. These special programs have found that thorough preparation is the key to minimizing or avoiding situations that impede participation and to helping individuals with ASD attain greater independence in recreation activities. Special programs are one source of useful ideas for community recreation agencies as to how to adequately prepare before an individual with ASD begins a new activity. Additional resources for CTRS staff to use in training recreation instructors, inclusion assistants, and volunteers are listed in Appendix A.

Recreation activities and sports vary in the degree of structure and routine involved. These are important factors in helping most participants with ASD choose activities that they will enjoy. Most participants with ASD are more successful and will find greater enjoyment in recreation activities that are structured and use a similar routine in each session or class. For example, martial arts classes are highly structured and follow a similar sequence of activities each time. In contrast, an open-ended art class, where participants choose their subject matter and art medium independently, is an example of a less structured activity. Although it's true that staff can create structure and predictability for a participant with ASD through the use of visual schedules and visually organized tasks, the degree of structure inherent in an activity or sport is still an important consideration when choosing activities that could become life-long leisure pursuits.

Some individuals with ASD are more likely to try new activities if they are familiar with the instructor. Recreation staff members have observed that some individuals with ASD are more likely to sign up for new activities if they know the instructor/ leader. A familiar instructor can be beneficial because he or she knows the individuals' sensory, communication, and learning needs and has provided accommodations successfully in the past. Furthermore, the participant with ASD is already familiar with the instructors' teaching and leadership style which lends a measure of predictability to the new activity. This can reduce stress for the participant who can now focus more on learning the new activity.

There exists a need to develop more specialized and inclusive recreation programs that appeal to adults with ASD. The agencies indicated that fewer adults than children with ASD participate in the recreation programs they offer; especially inclusive recreation. Some of the agencies have developed specialized classes or activities to address the needs of adults with ASD. One example is the Arts Career Program in Eugene, Oregon. There appears to be a need for greater creativity in designing new programs or activities for adults with ASD. Both specialized and inclusive activities are needed, perhaps centered on interests or hobbies.

As parents increasingly seek inclusive programming for their children, social change is underway. Increasingly, parents want inclusive recreation experiences for their children with ASD. These recreation agencies have all developed procedures for providing inclusive services in which they have incorporated specific techniques and accommodations for individuals with ASD. They utilize parental expertise. They train and support recreation instructors and demonstrate the methods in class. And they employ inclusion assistants to provide one-to-one support in classes.

Inclusion specialists acknowledged that at times, it can be personally challenging to facilitate the inclusion of a participant with ASD amidst all the other participants at a public recreation facility. The general public varies in its awareness of why individuals with ASD may act in certain ways, and why certain situations can be difficult for them. For example, when a child with ASD in a recreation class communicates with behaviors instead of words, other parents and children in the class are likely to misinterpret the behavior. They look to the instructor, the inclusion specialist, and the child's parents as if to say: "…why aren't you telling that child to be quiet?"

Inclusion specialists and their assistants are social change agents, and at the forefront of societal shifts that are occurring today as we become an increasingly inclusive society. The range of experiences encountered when facilitating inclusion need to be discussed during the hiring and training of assistants. Inclusion staff members can't allow their own discomfort to interfere with what they need to do to facilitate inclusion of an individual. Administrators need to create opportunities for inclusion staff to discuss situations and support one another in order to move beyond discomfort, celebrate successes, and recognize the significance of their work.

At the same time, the inclusion staff interviewed said that with each passing year more and more members of the community understand that among all who partake in recreation opportunities there is a wide range of learning and other differences, as well as alot in common. Inclusion staff members seldom provide information about individuals with ASD to others in a class in a formal way. Instead, staff members find opportunities to educate others and change misperceptions and attitudes in informal ways (e.g., talking with parents in the class on the sidelines). They report that powerful learning occurs when community members observe the recreation instructor and the inclusion staff use methods that enable the participants with ASD to demonstrate their capabilities. Each time this occurs, the circle of community members widens with a greater understanding of individuals with ASD.

Chapter Nine

Participants with Autism Spectrum Disorder in Youth Service Organizations

Mary Lou Vandenburg and Phyllis Coyne

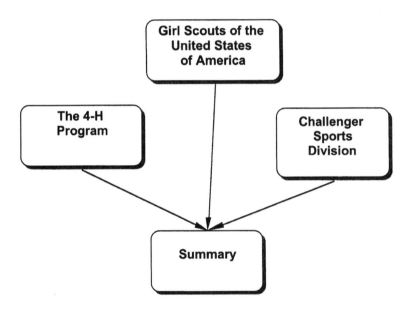

During the early 1900s, the needs of young people and how to prepare them to become good members of society became a focus. As a result, many nonprofit youth service organizations were developed to meet specific needs. Most were organized around specific activities, including recreation activities. In fact, some of these organizations are considered to be amongst the first organized community recreation programs in this country.

To this day, youth service organizations are a primary provider of organized community recreation services. Tens of millions of youth around the country benefit from participation in youth service organizations, such as 4-H, Scouts, and Boys and Girls Clubs, on an annual basis. A growing number of these are youth with Autism Spectrum Disorder (ASD).

Some of these organizations, such as Girl Scouts of the United States of America, have had members with disabilities from their inception. In the past 20 years, individuals with disabilities have experienced dramatic changes in how society has viewed their place in the community. During these years, there has been a substantial increase in the numbers of individuals with disabilities, including those with ASD, who participate in youth service organizations. Many organizations initially responded by having special groups for those with disabilities. However, as knowledge and awareness about the needs and interests of people with disabilities have grown, these organizations have done more to increase inclusion. As a result, these organizations have seen benefits for both individuals with and without disabilities.

One of the unique aspects of many youth service organizations is the extensive use of volunteers. Leaders, instructors and coaches within these organizations are often volunteers. These volunteers come from diverse backgrounds and have differing knowledge, skills and talents. They give freely of their time, because they believe in the mission and philosophy of the organization they chose. Frequently volunteers are parents who have a special interest in the members of the group.

Youth service organizations are able to harness the knowledge, skill and talents of these volunteers through organizational structure and training. In some cases, the organizations have embraced diversity and provide some level of training or resources related to disabilities for their volunteers. In many cases, the successful participation of individuals with ASD is based on the resourcefulness of the volunteers.

The participation of youth with ASD in three youth organizations with different structures is described in this chapter. These organizations are:

- 4-H Program
- Girl Scouts of the United States of America
- Challenger Sports League

These youth service organizations have all made an effort to serve youth with disabilities. They represent a continuum of services. The 4-H Program and Girls Scouts of the United States of America serve youth primarily through inclusive groups and Challenger Sports League is for youth with special needs. Each of these organizations provides experiences for youth with ASD that they might not have otherwise.

4-H Program

4-H, now a hundred years old, is one of the largest youth organizations in the United States. It is the Cooperative Extension System's nonformal, educational program for youth 5-19. 4-H is a program of the United States Department of Agriculture. Each state and county has access to 4-H through a County Extension Office.

Since its early roots to give rural youth a better agricultural education and to advance agricultural technology, 4-H has expanded to include over 110 program areas. These programs include recreation related areas, such as arts, plants and animals, home improvement, and technology and science. 4-H now serves youth through a variety of methods, including organized clubs, school-enrichment groups, special interest groups, individual study programs, camps, school-age child care programs, and instructional television programs.

In recent years, 4-H has shifted its programming to an emphasis on the personal growth of the individual youth member. 4-H projects are used to build life skills that youth can use the rest of their lives. Life skills are built into projects and activities to help participants become contributing, productive, self-directed members of society. 4-H accomplishes this in the context of small groups run by volunteers who usually have expertise in a particular area.

> **Box 9.2**
>
> **Mission of the 4-H Program**: to create supportive environments for culturally diverse youth and adults to reach their fullest potential.
> http://www.n4h.org/aboutus

4-H has recognized the potential value of its organization for youth with disabilities for some time. In the late 1970s, the program began to facilitate the participation of young people with disabilities in their activities. 4-H began to offer separate programs for people with disabilities, as well as inclusive programs. The inclusive programs proved to benefit the young people without disabilities, as well as those with disabilities.

> **Box 9.3**
>
> "4-H enables youth to have fun, meet new people, learn new life skills, build self-confidence, learn responsibility, and set and achieve goals. Youth learn by doing."
> http://www.4-H.org

Pennsylvania State University in conjunction with the Department of Health, Education, and Welfare created two guides for 4-H leaders, ***Recreation and Handicapped Youth*** (1978) and ***Let's Look at 4-H and Handicapped Youth*** *(1978)*, to provide leaders with practical information on how to accommodate youth with disabilities in 4-H activities. The information in ***Let's Look at 4-H and Handicapped Youth*** is presented in the unique form of recipes with "ingredients" for successful clubs. ASD is not specifically mentioned in this guide, but much of the information is applicable to participants with ASD.

> **Box 9.4**
>
> "Be more concerned about people than programs."
> From ***Let's Look at 4-H and Handicapped Youth: A Leader's Guide***

4-H has developed guidelines for the selection of projects based on capabilities, interests, limitations and situations. This is designed to meet the needs of all group members. 4-H has suggested the following questions to identify the appropriateness of projects.

- Is this an interest of the person?
- Would this project allow an immediate accomplishment?
- Does it include tasks which become increasingly more challenging?
- Does this project include activities, which can be practiced in other settings?
- Does it include attainable and/or flexible completion requirements?

The numbers of participants with ASD in 4-H is unknown, since these individuals are just other members and are not reported to the state or national office. However, there are many success stories from creative leaders. Three success stories from around the state of Oregon are shared in the following section.

—Spencer, a Dog Lover

Spencer enjoyed and benefited from being part of 4-H with his dog for about three years. He showed his dog in showmanship, obedience and agility classes at local county fairs and smaller dog shows in the coastal area of Oregon.

Before this involvement, Spencer's parents had become very concerned by his lack of socialization. Like many individuals with ASD, Spencer had become increasingly anxious at school as the curriculum and social demands became more abstract and demanding. By middle school, he responded to the stress at school by isolating himself and spending all his time at home on the computer.

Spencer, who had previously been disinterested in dogs, was drawn to a very friendly Labrador retriever mix who needed a home. His parents decided to combine this interest with an area of weakness, social skills. Spencer was told he could have this dog if he would learn to take care of and train her by joining a local 4-H Club. When Spencer agreed, his parents found a 4-H Club for him.

> **Box 9.5**
>
> "The 4-H model uses approaches that are important for individuals with ASD. It goes to interests. It goes to strengths. It takes kids from where they are with no expectations. No pressure. It is a flexible program."
> *—Spencer's father*

Spencer's parents informed the two leaders, who had no previous experience with a member with ASD, about Spencer and his needs before he joined their group, so that they would be able to accommodate him. These 4-H leaders knew how to patiently coach and refocus all the members. They supported the older members in helping the younger members, so much of the learning was peer to peer. His leaders also understood that Spencer needed extra repeated practice and that he could be successful with support. Because he needed to be reminded of meetings and what to bring, his leaders usually called him the night before with the necessary information. They also picked him up for meetings, as needed. Spencer was successful with assistance from his 4-H leaders.

In the structure and dog training activities of 4-H, Spencer was able to follow directions. The specific steps in dog training and concrete facts were understandable to him. The precise methods of dog training helped him understand cause and effect in interactions with another being. The predictable routine helped to minimize his anxiety.

Spencer's sensitivity to loud noise caused discomfort in many environments. Previous to being involved in 4-H, he was too anxious to go to stores. Through 4-H participation he learned to tolerate the clapping, hooting and hollering that occurs during dog shows. Even under these conditions, he practiced communication skills through answering questions and making some eye contact when he showed his dog before a judge. He also learned to tolerate the noise, crowding and activity of a crowd of thousands through participation in the June Dairy Month Parade.

> **Box 9.6**
>
> "Often kids with ASD want to be with people, but find it too confusing. It helps to be with others who share a common interest. Doing a parallel activity like training dogs is not socially demanding. 4-H provided my son with the structure he needed to relate and associate with other people. It opened up the world to him."
> *—Spencer's father*

In the 4-H club, Spencer learned how to interact with other children and to cooperate with others in a manner that had previously eluded him. In addition to learning about training dogs, Spencer enjoyed the social aspect of a club that had members from 9-18 years. The wide range of ages allowed him to interact with the younger members, with whom he was most comfortable, and to talk about subjects of interest to him, such as video games and dogs. He developed friendships that expanded beyond 4-H. He visited friends, played video games with them, slept over at their houses, and went camping with them.

—Brandon, a Horseman

Brandon and his three brothers go to the 4-H Native American Cultural Camp on the Warm Springs Indian Reservation every summer. Brandon and two of his brothers have ASD. Brandon is impacted the most by ASD in his family. His parents always provide a leisure companion to help facilitate their involvement, although the leaders know the boys well at this point.

Brandon has developed a strong interest in horses through his experiences at 4-H camp, which has lead to positive developments in the leisure, work and social areas of his life. His post-secondary education program has arranged for him to have a work placement at a local therapeutic riding program. Brandon's teacher remarked with amazement after his job interview that, "He was amazingly focused and stayed on topic for the better part of an hour." He now has a more down-to-earth topic to talk about than his previous obsessions with space ships. In the environment of the riding program, people want to talk about horses extensively. He also thoroughly enjoys his work at the stable, especially grooming the horses and walking beside the horse to assist unsteady riders.

—William, a 4-H Champion

The majority of youth between 9 and 14 years of age in Morrow County, a rural county in eastern Oregon, participate in 4-H. Thirteen-year-old William, who has ASD, has been in 4-H for four years. During this time he has been a champion and grand champion in giving a speech, as well as with his pigeons and dog. At the Morrow County Fair, he got Grand Champion in Obedience with his dog twice and all around Obedience Champion twice as well. He has gotten Grand Champion Showman in pigeons twice and overall Champion Pigeon Showman once. He was also the Grand Champion in Speech at the Morrow County Fair twice and at the Oregon State Fair once. William shares his skills as a respected teen leader who assists younger members with training their dogs in his 4-H Club.

Those who see William now find it hard to imagine that he did not talk until he was six years old and that he continues to require significant support behind the scenes. His mother, Patty, has provided this support by assisting him at all the 4-H meetings first as an involved parent and then as the 4-H leader. The county extension agent for Morrow County has also encouraged William's participation in all the activities at times when others may have questioned if William could do them.

William's mother, Patty, tries to anticipate what will happen in events and carefully prepares him before the event. She knows how to present information so that her very literal son will understand. However, she cannot always anticipate how he will use the information.

William's mother had told him that a horse could not kick him, if he was holding on. One year he showed a seven month old colt in Showmanship. While he was picking up the colt's foot, the colt began to buck. William held on tenaciously. When the judge asked William, "Weren't you afraid of getting kicked?", William demonstrated his concrete nature and difficulty in problem solving by saying that he could not be kicked when he held on.

The members of the 4-H Club have not been given any specific information on the best ways to interact with William. However, they imitate the effective techniques that his mother, Patty, uses. For instance, Patty knows that she needs to get William's attention and provide him with time to shift his attention before she says anything to him. She says, "Look at me" before she tells or asks him anything, so now the members of the club automatically say, "Look at me" before they ask William for help.

William has some strengths shared by many with ASD and his mother provides him with the structure he needs to use these abilities to his advantage in 4-H. For instance, William has an excellent memory for facts, is consistent with routines and is perfectionistic. To be successful in giving speeches, his mother helps him select topics that are factual, e.g., "How to Clean Your Dog's Teeth," helps him write notes in his speech regarding when to pause and look at the audience into his speeches, generates practice questions that the judge or audience might ask at the end of the presentation, and helps him rehearse.

William particularly enjoys training his Shetland sheepdog, Teddy, in obedience. The clear step-by-step process of obedience training fits the style of trainer and dog. Many of the other 4-H members do not train their dogs consistently. However, because of his desire for routine, William trains Teddy at the same time daily. William's perfectionism is effective in obedience training for Teddy. William is showing Teddy in increasingly higher levels of obedience classes.

"Participation in 4-H has helped William with his self-esteem and gives him the opportunity to be like any other kid."
Patty McNary, William's mother and 4-H leader

Some of the social aspects of 4-H are still challenging for William, but he and his mother have found ways to ameliorate many of these. Being a teen leader allows him to interact more with the group with whom he interacts best, the younger 4-H members. He often independently notices when these members need help and is sometimes prompted by his mother to offer assistance. The younger members hold him in high regard for his excellent skills in training dogs.

Because part of showmanship is to answer questions about your animal, William generally shines in this area. However, he continues to lose points for eye contact. He also does better in showmanship with his pigeons rather than his dog. He only needs to hold out his pigeon and answer predictable factual questions about body parts, gestation, care, etc. When he is in showmanship with his dog, he needs to follow directions from a judge regarding what patterns to do. The comprehension of what pattern to do is more difficult and uncomfortable for him.

William is not comfortable with competition, so he sets his own goals and standards for what he does. He thinks of himself as competing against himself rather than other people in showmanship. He views obedience classes as the dogs competing against each other rather than trainers against trainers.

William is looking forward to many more years of 4-H. He has a personal goal to be an ambassador for Morrow County to 4-H. He knows that only the top 4-H members in the county can become ambassadors. He intends to work hard for his goal, as he has to achieve all his other 4-H goals.

Box 9.9

"If I was a parent of a child that was lower functioning than William, I would still feel as if 4-H would be an excellent match for him… I am sure larger counties have agents that will let a parent create a club or simply an activity to fit the need of their child… They have clubs and activities that are animal related and non-animal related from story telling, to photography, to cooking, sewing, stamping, creative memory making. Really, the sky is the limit. I can't imagine that a parent cannot take a hobby and design an activity that a child can "present" at the fair. I would encourage all parents not to allow their child's spectrum disorder to deny them a positive place in 4-H."

Patty McNary, William's mother and 4-H leader

In summary, 4-H has provided opportunities for individuals with ASD that these individuals probably would not have had otherwise. 4-H has developed guidelines for the selection of projects based on capabilities, interests, limitations and situations. The volunteer 4-H leaders have made an effort to accommodate all youth who have wanted to participate.

Girl Scouts of the United States of America (GSUSA)

For over 90 years, the Girl Scout program has delivered quality experiences for girls 5-17 years of age locally, nationally, and internationally (GSUSA, 2002). The Girl Scout program includes a myriad of enriching experiences, including field trips, sports skill-building clinics, community service projects, cultural exchanges, environmental stewardship and activities in the outdoors and the arts. According to GSUSA (2002), more than 50 million girls have been members of Girl Scouts over the years. Because the Girl Scouts is an inclusive organization, the number of members with ASD or other disabilities are not counted; however, girls with ASD have enjoyed and benefited from their experiences in Girl Scouts for many years.

Girls with disabilities have been a part of Girl Scouts from the beginning (GSUSA, *1998*). In fact, Juliette Gordon Low, the founder of Girl Scouting, had a severe hearing impairment. The first troop of girls with physical disabilities in the United States was formed in 1917. Girl Scouts developed troops in the institutions where many girls with developmental disabilities, including ASD, resided until the 1970s.

In the past 20 years, individuals with disabilities have become an increasing part of their communities and Girl Scouts. However, this is not an incidental increase. According to GSUSA (2002), "Today, Girl Scouting is designed to be inclusive and flexible to provide an opportunity for every girl to participate in activities." Girl Scouts also promotes an understanding and appreciation of diversity and emphasizes adaptation of the regular program rather than a separate program for girls with disabilities.

> **Box 9.10** Inclusion in Girl Scouts means "that all girls plan and participate in all Girl Scout activities."
> www.girlscouts.org

GSUSA emphasizes the central importance that youth learn to be competent in diverse communities.

> **Box 9.11** "Girl Scouts is an organization that recognizes the strength in diversity and the value of learning to live in a pluralistic society.... A girl who can work and play with people different from herself, who can celebrate differences and be adaptive to change, will have the strength of character or the understanding and leadership ability needed to succeed beyond her own small community."
> www.girlscouts.org

Girl Scouts is an excellent setting for inclusion, since the flexibility of the program allows each girl to progress at her own pace in a variety of activities (http//www.girlscouts.org). This organization gives all girls the opportunity to develop talents and skills.

Several additional factors have lead to the success of Girl Scouts in the area of inclusion. The organization promotes noncompetitive activities to enable a girl to have a high degree of confidence when participating with her age level peers. Many vital skills such as social skills, communication skills, future employment skills, and life skills are learned in a natural environment. Inclusion also provides girls with and without disabilities the opportunity to work together and to get to know each other.

> **Box 9.12** "We believe all girls deserve a chance to overcome barriers that limit their achievement, to learn new skills, and to grow up as self-reliant, self-confident young women who will succeed in today's world."
> —From "Where is the next generation of women leaders? Girl Scouts...Where girls grow strong" (2002), Girl Scouts—Totem Council.

Rather than looking at differences, Girl Scouts emphasizes the similarities in needs and interests of all girls. By training leaders to make adaptations in program activities when needed, Girl Scouts facilitate the inclusion of all girls, both those with and without disabilities (www.girlscouts.org). Adaptations of the original activity to meet the individualized needs of the girls are what are commonly practiced.

According to GSUSA (2002), the organization depends on its more than 900,000 volunteers to be leaders, mentors, etc. Volunteers are the backbone of Girl Scouting and the organization has always had a commitment to training and providing resources for its volunteer leaders. For instance, in the 1920s, Girl Scouts established a system of national training schools for leaders. New GSUSA provides basic training to leaders on how to include girls with disabilities (www.girlscouts.org). GSUSA works closely with local councils to provide support, information and training to volunteers and staff regarding the inclusion of individuals with disabilities. In addition, local councils offer additional trainings, workshops and conferences for staff and volunteers at least annually to share ideas and success stories, learn from each other and learn to create an inclusive environment for girls. Mini-trainings on topics of interest are often provided at leader meetings. Volunteer leaders with experience and skills in working with girls with disabilities often help each other establish inclusive troops and help train each other during these mini-trainings.

In addition to training, the GSUSA has offered resources for learning about Girl Scouts and girls with disabilities for many years. ***Handicapped Girls and Girl Scouting*** was published in 1968 to continue the tradition of the Girl Scouts' concern for girls with disabilities. Since then, the organization has published, ***Focus on Ability: Serving Girls with Special Needs,*** **(1998).** This book offers practical suggestions on how to include girls with disabilities in Girl Scouts successfully. It has information on specific disabilities, suggestions for inclusion and adaptations, and a resource list. GSUSA's web site, www.girlscouts.org, is unique among youth service organizations, in that it provides specific information on "What is a disability," "Inclusion," "A leader should…" and other resources. Links to other sites including the Autism Society of America are also provided on their web site.

The number of Girl Scouts with ASD is unknown. However, the approach encouraged by GSUSA facilitates many successes. An example of a Girl Scout leader who has creatively supported girls with ASD and a Girl Scout with ASD who received the prestigious Young Woman of Distinction Award in 2002 are used to illustrate the successes that can evolve. Both these examples are from the Girl Scouts—Totem Council in Seattle, Washington.

—*Ruth, a Creative Girl Scout Leader*

Ruth Bacha and her co-leaders, Leanne Cloud, and Brenda Nesse, creatively support girls with disabilities, including ASD. Ruth and Leanne have come to Girl Scouting with significant skills and experiences with youth with ASD. Ruth is an occupational therapist who has a daughter with ASD. Leanne is a paraprofessional in the classroom that Ruth's daughter attends. Brenda brings her experience as the mother of four. All three have received the Girl Scouts—Totem Council Vivian Caver Diversity Award for their parts in promoting diversity in Girl Scouting.

Ruth, like a lot of mothers, wanted her daughter to be in Girl Scouts. She had the same hopes and dreams for her daughter as other mothers. She was pleased to discover that the Girl Scouts has the philosophy that every girl deserves to be a part of Girl Scouts. Therefore, Ruth began an inclusive troop in her hometown.

When Ruth and her family moved to Seattle, she did not know many people and began a new troop. This time it was a special troop of girls from her daughter's class at school. By this time her daughter was older and, since older girls interested in Girl Scouting are often already in a troop, it was difficult to find typical older girls interested in joining her troop.

Ruth's troop participated as a group in typical Girl Scouting activities and in various larger activities with generic troops. Over time, Ruth and her troop have done many activities, such as field trips and badge workshops, with two sister troops. The troop leaders planned carefully beforehand to make sure that the activities would match the needs and the interests of all the girls.

> Box 9.13
>
> "One of the things I've appreciated most about Girl Scouts is the opportunity for the girls in our troop to shine among their typical peers in ways they wouldn't have otherwise been able to, and grow personally in ways they might not have otherwise. We've had girls in our troop overcome their fears of boating, spiders, and sleeping away from home. We've had girls, who wouldn't talk to peers in class, gain enough breath volume and increased self-esteem to sell Girl Scout cookies with the troop at stores and banks."
>
> —*Ruth Bacha, Girl Scout Leader, Totem Council, Seattle, Washington*

The leaders of the sister troops also believed in diversity and helped the girls in their troops understand and support the girls from Ruth's troop in their joint activities. Ruth's troop and another troop recently merged. They presently have an equal mix of girls with and without disabilities.

> **Box 9.14**
>
> Personal growth in the Girl Scouts (with and without disabilities [sic]) I've seen has included learning that:
> - They're not the only ones with problems.
> - To work well in a group sometimes they must follow even when they're capable of leading.
> - Life isn't always a race. Sometimes life involves moving at the pace of the slowest member of the group.
> - Everyone has different abilities.
> - Not everyone sees the world the same way or values the same things as you do (and that's okay).
>   —*Ruth Bacha, Girl Scout Leader, Totem Council, Seattle, Washington*

Service projects are equally important to the girls in this troop as any troop. For some of the girls in Ruth's troop it may be the first time that they can see that they can make a difference in the lives of other people and help others. Her troop has done many service projects, such as making scarves for people who are homeless and planting trees. The girls have learned many things from these service projects.

> **Box 9.15**
>
> "We've had girls in our troop personally raise enough money from a bake sale to purchase adapted riding equipment, which they used several times during troop horseback riding events. After the troop members no longer needed the adapted equipment, they donated the equipment to a therapeutic horseback riding organization. Thus, others have continued to benefit from their efforts."
>   —*Ruth Bacha, Girl Scout Leader, Totem Council, Seattle, Washington*

Supports. The girls with ASD in Ruth's troop can do many Girl Scout activities with support. Ruth and her co-leader, Leanne, have developed many supports that have enabled the girls in their troop to succeed. Ruth's philosophy is to change how you do the activity, not the activity itself. For instance, the girls can add to the troop banner in a variety of ways. Those with ASD who can tolerate paint on their hands may add a handprint rather than paint with a brush.

Ruth prepares all the girls in her troop for new activities before they participate. She looks at the activity that is coming up and decides what preparation the girls will need before the activity. Sometimes it is just describing what they will be doing; sometimes it is developing a story about the activity to read before doing the activity; sometimes it is actually practicing what they will be doing. Ruth and her co-leaders also use visual supports, such as developing a picture sequence, a list of rules and social stories, to prepare the girls for what will happen, how long it will last and what they will do when they are finished. They often make more abstract concepts, such as how to live the Girl Scout Law, more concrete by presenting pictures that represent the concepts. The pictures they develop with Storybook Weaver Delux (2000) make the written and spoken information more understandable for all the girls.

The steps of activities are reviewed before the activity to prepare the girls for the activities. A sample page from Our Troop's Flag Ceremony is presented in Figure 9.1 to depict the type of information that is provided.

Figure 9.1
Sample Page from Our Troop's Flag Ceremony

When the caller says, "Color Guard, retreat," we return to the back of the room in a special way. First, the flag bearer gets back to the front of the line. She does this by walking between me and my buddy, and the other buddy pair.

Helping the girls understand the rules or expectations before the activity and ahead of time facilitates their involvement. The rules for an activity may be presented simply, such as:

When I ride a horse I need to:
✔ Wear a helmet and boots
✔ Use my inside voice so I don't scare the horse
✔ Always hold onto the reins
✔ Follow my teacher's directions.

At other times the rules are presented with explanation, as in the five sample pages from Rules for Boating in Figure 9.2.

Sometimes the girls need information before the activity to understand the activity. Figure 9.3 depicts a page from the Veteran's Day Parade to help the girls anticipate and understand what they will see.

The manner in which Ruth prepares her troop for camping illustrates preteaching of necessary skills. Camping is an integral part of the activities of many Girl Scout troops. However, camping can be a challenging experience for anyone who is not prepared for the experience, particularly girls with ASD. Before the actual camp-out, Ruth's troop practices some necessary skills needed for their camping trip during one or more sleep-overs. The girls practice rolling up their sleeping bags on the sleep-overs. They practice cooking on a Coleman stove. They practice washing the dishes using the three-tub method that they will use while camping. The girls in the troop talk about and practice safety skills for the woods, such as fire safety and what to do if you get lost. Written and pictorial information to help the girls understand safety skills are also provided. The girls learn skills related to camping in a safe environment first and are better able to cope with the real life situation of camping.

Figure 9.2
Five Sample Pages from Rules for Boating

There are some rules I must follow when I am in a boat. The rules are there to keep me safe. If I do not follow the rules, it can be very dangerous for me and the other friends. I will be with in the boat.

The first boating rule is that I must wait on the land until the boating teacher invites me onto the dock. I must keep out of the water while I am waiting. My troop leaders will show me a place where I can wait safely. Following this rule will help me stay safe around the water.

Continued

Figure 9.2 Continued
Five Sample Pages from Rules for Boating

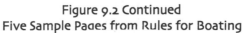

The second rule of boating is that before I get into the boat, I must wear a special vest called a "PFD." The PFD will keep me safe in the boat, because it has special padding in it that helps with floating. My boating teacher will show me how to put one on. I must keep my PFD on until the boating teacher says that I can take it off.

My boating teacher will also show me how to get in and out of a boat safely. When I get into a boat, I must enter at the part of the boat that is the widest. This part does not "wiggle" as much as the skinny part of the boat, so it is the safest place for me to get in.

To get in the boat, I must either crawl in, or else walk while crouched down. We will practice this several times before I get in the boat, to make sure I know how to do this safely.

Figure 9.3
Sample Page from Veteran's Day Parade

People usually march in a parade to celebrate something. It is like a big party. Sometimes they dress up and sometimes they wear regular clothes. There are often people who bring musical instruments and play songs while they are marching. They are called a marching band.

Box 9.16

Ruth's daughter sold 800 boxes of cookies this year and was rewarded for this accomplishment by receiving a scholarship to a residential horse camp. Ruth used a similar process to what she uses in her troop to help her daughter participate in horse camp. Before camp, Ruth helped her daughter plan and prepare for situations that might arise. Although her daughter had a passion for horses, a week of residential camp probably would have overwhelmed her daughter. Therefore, Ruth camped at a nearby campground, so her daughter could participate in the activities during the day and stay with her mom at night.

One of the goals for Girl Scouts is to have girls take responsibility for decision making. Since making choices between options and the concept of voting for one choice can be difficult for individuals with ASD, Ruth utilizes visual supports and structure for the decision-making portions of each meeting. One example is the use of visual supports and structure in determining the activities the troop will do that year. Ruth has developed a large yearly calendar with slots, which can hold index cards for every month. The group brainstorms a list of big events they want to do during the year, then writes the name of each big event on individual cards with assistance, as needed. Before the next meeting, a visual representation of each big event is put on the back of the corresponding card by Ruth and Leanne, so those unable to read or in need of more visual cues can use the picture symbols to make choices. In addition, the leaders make up cards for each possible service activity with the words on one side and the visual representation on the other side. A sample card is depicted in Figure 9.4. Ruth and Leanne print out enough cards for each girl to have a set. The girls choose one big event or service unit activity at a time by voting with their cards. As each choice is made, the card representing that choice is put into a slot on the calendar. As it turns out, most of the girls use the picture side of the card even though they are in sixth grade and can read. It helps them all.

Another example of the use of visual supports is illustrated by how Ruth structures making decisions on what the troop will purchase with money they have raised. Group discussion is minimized. To help the girls make choices and vote, Ruth makes separate posters with written words and pictures for each object or activity with its cost. To vote, each girl stands by the poster that represents her choice. This makes the process of choice

Side 1

Figure 9.4
Sample Service Unit Activity Card

Holiday Ornament Workshop & Service Unit Activity

Rotate around to stations to make holiday ornaments to give to other families.

Side 2

making very concrete and visual. Without this visual support, many of the girls would vote for every choice. It also makes the group decision clear to all the girls and helps them accept the group's choice even if it was not their own choice. The girls learn how to make group decisions, work together to make these decisions and how to compromise, if needed, through this process. The process of group decision making also fosters the growth of social understanding and skills.

> **Box 9.17**
> "Personal growth that the girls with ASD in particular have gained or are in the process of gaining have included knowing that they can make their own choice about what to say, who to sit with, what game to play, etc. They've also learned that even if you don't like another peer, or are mad at her, you can still be nice to that peer... They're starting to learn that it's okay for a special friend to have other friends, and you don't have to take it personally...."
> *Ruth Bacha, Girl Scout Leader, Totem Council, Seattle, Washington*

One of the goals for this troop of sixth graders this year is to foster leadership skills in the girls. Every girl in Ruth's troop gets support in developing leadership skills. Each girl signs up to lead two to three troop meetings over the course of the year by choosing from the index cards of written and pictorial activities on the annual calendar. A mark of & for easy to prepare and # for hard to prepare is also on each card to help the girls in making their selections. (An & can be seen on the card in Figure 9.4.) One to two weeks before the meeting Ruth provides the leader for the next meeting with a written and/or pictorial checklist of what she needs to do to prepare for the meeting. Before the meeting, the girl may need to call or email everyone to determine how many are coming and remind people what to bring to the event. A girl may need to go with her parent to purchase the craft supplies or tickets for the event.

The requirements on the checklist are adapted to focus on each girl's strengths and abilities. For example, those who have difficulty communicating verbally, but can write might help participate in the typing of an email with important information about the activity. For more complicated meetings, such as those for earning a badge, Ruth or the girl's parent will meet with the girl ahead of time to review the Girl Scout Manual together and develop a list of what needs to be done. The process is adapted to accommodate the needs of each girl.

Ruth carefully structures each meeting with the member-leader for the meeting to ensure that the activities will be understood and enjoyed by all members. She ensures that the agenda with timelines is posted and reviewed at the beginning of each meeting, so that all the girls will know what will happen and how long each activity will take place. She and her co-leaders, Leanne and Brenda, develop any visual supports that may be needed before the meeting.

One way Ruth has taught group problem solving is through the use of cooperative games. For instance, the girls must figure out how to get an imaginary fox, a chicken and a bag of grain safely across a river. This game teaches problem solving and working cooperatively. Ruth has related these lessons to real-life situations, such as how she decides sleeping arrangements at camp, to help the girls understand why decisions are made a certain way.

The use of these supports has lead to many accomplishments for all the girls in Ruth's troop, but particularly those with ASD. Figure 9.5 lists some of the accomplishments of the girls with ASD.

Figure 9.5
Some Accomplishments of Individual Girl Scouts with ASD

- Led a flag ceremony for over 100 Girl Scouts
- Played musical selections on the cello for almost 100 Girl Scouts
- Led and taught songs around the campfire and dining hall for over 300 people
- Sold over 800 boxes of Girl Scout cookies to meet a personal goal of earning a camp scholarship and to be named in the Council's newsletter for her efforts

---

Adult involvement. Like all Girl Scout leaders, Ruth encourages each parent/guardian to be involved. Parents/guardians provide guidance regarding appropriate activities and goals for their daughters through an initial meeting. The girls make decisions about the type of activities, service projects, and badges the troop will work on, but parents/guardians also provide input. Parents/guardians do not have to plan an activity, but they are encouraged to be there for support and assistance. Many of the parent volunteers are knowledgeable about how to support girls with disabilities from their own experiences.

Girl Scout leaders usually need to spend extra time to develop supports for their girls with ASD. Ruth relies on a cadre of reliable adult volunteers, who she has cultivated, for most of the activities. This is particularly helpful for camping trips. The adults facilitate and teach the girls how to resolve conflict or solve their problem during the sustained social contact involved in camping. In addition, adult volunteers facilitate more than one activity occurring at a time to meet diverse interests and needs. For instance, some troop members may want to take a three-hour hike up the trail, while others may need a quiet break from all the stimulation of an unfamiliar setting. At times, a girl with ASD may need individual assistance from a volunteer to participate in an activity.

Ruth continues to assess how activities can be made more successful for the girls in her troop. She, along with the other volunteers, observe the girls and note how they participated, what their general mood was, and how much the girls could do on their own. They also ask the girls specific questions, while it is still fresh in the girls' minds. In addition, Ruth asks for feedback from the adults.

Ruth's story provides one example of how one Girl Scout leader is accommodating her members with ASD. The following section presents an individual success story.

Katie, a Young Woman of Distinction

Box 9.18

Katie, 22, has been in Girl Scouts since second grade and received the Girl Scout Young Woman of Distinction Award in 2002. This highest honor is awarded to less than a dozen of all Girl Scouts annually. Girl Scouts who demonstrate exceptional commitment to their communities and an outstanding dedication to achievement demonstrated through their Gold Award project earn this award. Katie founded the Federal Way Autism Support Group, the first support group in her community, that gives parents of children with ASD an opportunity to discuss the challenges they face. Katie organized and facilitated monthly meetings, engaged guest speakers, designed and distributed an information booklet on ASD, and created a web site offering information on the support group with links to other autism related sites. Through this project, Katie overcame her feelings of self-consciousness, discovered her leadership skills, and became more confident.
Katie is now studying Biology and German at Washington State University.
www.girlscouts.org

Photo Courtesy of GSUSA

Those who evaluated Katie when she was young might be stunned by Katie's accomplishments. As a young child, she had delays in language and social development. The professionals told Katie's parents that she would probably never read, amongst other dire predictions. After a series of evaluations, Katie received a diagnosis of ASD.

Katie and her family have been tenacious in working toward her meeting her highest potential and have received vital support along the way. Katie got an excellent start in a special education classroom in first grade. However, she was determined to be in regular education after first grade and worked exceedingly hard to be able to be a student in regular classes.

In second grade, Katie brought home information about Brownies and announced that she wanted to join with the other girls in her class. Although Katie's mother, Lisa, was anxious about how Katie would fit in, she allowed Katie to join. Lisa was hesitant to tell the leaders too much about Katie and her disability, because she did not want to give the leaders a preconceived idea of what Katie could or could not do. Lisa had noticed that Katie seemed to be able to "hold it together" in public, but might then be explosive when she got home. She hoped that Katie would be able to be at her best in Brownies and would be successful. Katie's first experience with Brownies was successful, because the troop leader accepted Katie and the different learning styles of all the girls.

In the mid-1980s, much less was known about ASD than is currently understood. Not everyone has understood Katie as well as her first Brownie leader over the years. For instance, some volunteer leaders at a day camp did not understand why Katie sometimes "did her own thing" during crafts activities and they misinterpreted Katie's behavior as being deliberately defiant. However, even with misunderstandings, Katie enjoyed herself enough to continue going to camp.

Lisa, Katie's mother, hoped that Girl Scouts would allow Katie to develop lasting friendships. Girl Scouts provided Katie with opportunities to practice social skills that she was being taught in school, such as to say "Hi" to someone when they say "Hi" to you. Lisa frequently discussed how to behave in the social milieu of Girl Scouts and that there were times that Katie needed to go along even if she did not agree. Although Katie did well socially within Girl Scouts, these skills did not carry over to other situations.

The complexity of social situations during adolescence is difficult for most individuals with ASD. Katie's social challenges made it more difficult to find a troop to join for her "Senior" level of Girl Scouts when she was in tenth grade. Lisa had been hesitant to be Katie's leader, but Katie needed someone present who could help Katie understand the social world. Lisa was a leader for her other daughter's seventh grade "Cadettes" troop. Although GSUSA policy is to have girls placed according to chronological age, Lisa invited Katie to join her troop.

The girls in the troop knew and liked Katie. Katie was in a leadership role and helped the girls in various capacities. She felt safe enough that she shared with the girls about ASD and what it felt like to her. This was a growing experience for all.

> **Box 9.19** Although Katie is now in college, the girls in her previous Girl Scout troop invited her to go with them on the trip to San Francisco that they were taking with their money from the sale of cookies.

When it came time for Katie's senior project, Lisa suggested that Katie start a support group. At first, Katie said no, because she felt she would have to reveal too much about herself. She, finally, decided that ASD was what she knew the most about and that there was a need for a support group.

> **Box 9.20** Katie wished that she had known at least one other person with ASD who she could have talked with when she was younger. She wanted to talk with someone else who knew the experience of ASD firsthand.

Because of her personal experiences, Katie decided to develop a support group for adolescents with ASD. She developed flyers and passed them out. However, only parents, and mostly parents of young, newly diagnosed children with ASD came, during the first two months. At that point, she changed her focus to a parent support group. Her first grade teacher, Lee Saffrey, mentored her in this project although Katie had not been her student for over a decade.

Katie said that she was inspired to develop the Federal Way Autism Support Group as a Senior Girl Scout by her first grade teacher who never gave up on her.

Katie continued the group through her senior year in high school. The Federal Way Autism Support Group has continued under new volunteer leadership since Katie went to college and now supports over 90 families in the area. Because of this project, Katie was recognized as one of ten girls nationwide to receive the Girl Scout Young Women of Distinction Award in 2002. Katie continues to be an inspiration of what might be for many parents of children with ASD.

"If your daughter could get up in front of all of us, I won't give up on my son."
     —*Parent member of the Federal Way Autism Support Group*

In summary, Girl Scouts is committed to inclusion. The program is designed to be flexible to provide an opportunity for every girl to participate in activities. By training leaders to make adaptations in program activities when needed, Girl Scouts facilitate the inclusion of all girls, both those with and without disabilities (www.girlscouts.org). Creative approaches by Girl Scout leaders and Girl Scouts with ASD have lead to many successes.

Challenger Sports League

The Challenger Division of Little League was established to promote, advance and sponsor sports for children with special needs. The Challenger Division started as a tee-ball division of Little League more than 10 years ago and has expanded to include soccer, basketball and Tae Kwon Do. It enables every child to participate in structured athletic programs regardless of their ability level. The need for this type of recreation program is evidenced in its being the fastest growing division in Little League, as well as the increase of athletes with ASD.

What a rewarding experience it is to see the thrill and pride in the athletes' eyes when they hit the ball, score a goal or make a basket!
     http//www.challenger-sports.org.

One goal of the Challenger Division is to assist individuals with disabilities to learn sports skills and the opportunity to play on sports teams. Another goal is to help establish bonds of friendship and understanding between Little Leaguers from other programs and Challenger Division children amidst an atmosphere of sharing and caring. Challenger Division teams play teams of typically developing children. All the children benefit from this experience. They get the thrill of participating in the game and get to meet members of their community that they may not have had the opportunity to know in the past.

Challenger Division relies on volunteers to be coaches. The parents recruit most of the coaches. Coaches attend a mandatory coaches meeting regarding the structure and schedule for Challenger Division, but do not necessarily receive training in coaching or in disability awareness.

As in many youth organizations, many of the volunteers are parents. These parents often have unique sensibilities and experience related to youth with disabilities that help them be supportive coaches. Parents may, also, volunteer in other capacities, such as developing supports.

Each Challenger Division has its own personality. The Challenger Division in Lake Oswego, Oregon is presented in this section to illustrate a program that has met the challenge of serving youth with ASD well.

Challenger Sports Division of Lake Oswego, Oregon

Through the dedicated efforts of parents, the Challenger Sports Division of Lake Oswego has grown from a baseball program to include soccer and basketball for 5-18 year olds. Challenger Sports has gone from occurring 10 weeks a year to an almost year-round series of sports programs. A different organization in Lake Oswego partners with the parents for each of the three sports.

A number of athletes with ASD have enjoyed playing sports with the Challenger Division in Lake Oswego. Since there are several support groups for parents of children with ASD in the area, many parents heard about the fun other children with ASD were having in these Challenger Division sports programs. As a result of the word-of-mouth parent network, parents from several towns have enrolled their child with ASD in the Challenger Division activities in Lake Oswego. Now this division has many players with a wide range of ASD.

> **Box 9.24**
>
> "My kids have been involved in a lot of regular activities. My son with ASD takes Tae Kwon Do classes in a private Do Jing. He takes group piano lessons at a private school. He practices skateboarding for hours. But he would never have been able to fit into one of the school's recreational sports teams. He would not even have been willing to try. Challenger Division provides him with the opportunity to do the same sports others are doing in an unstressful and accepting environment. He can feel good about his own skills in this program that emphasizes fun rather than competition. He gets a chance to be a star. And he has said that he likes playing on a team that 'gives me cover' and where he does not feel as different."
> —*Joy Lee, parent and a volunteer coordinator of Lake Oswego Challenger Division*

The District #4 Challenger Little League began in 1990 in the largest metropolitan area of Oregon. Since then, the Lake Oswego part of this group has grown to an average of over 50 players on four teams, including a number of players with ASD, who enjoy baseball from April until mid-June.

In 1996, a parent worked with the Lake Oswego School District to include a Challenger Division in the Lake Oswego Soccer League. This parent was interested in an opportunity for her six year old that was not available through other programs in her community.

Soccer has been a particularly popular program and the numbers of athletes with ASD in the Challenger Division of Lake Oswego has grown considerably. For instance, in the younger division for soccer, seven of the 12 athletes have ASD. The older division for soccer has a similar ratio of athletes with ASD. The younger and older divisions practice together, but play separate games.

The Challenger Division for basketball is part of the Lake Oswego Community Schools' Youth Basketball Association. This sport has had mixed success for individuals with ASD. Given the appropriate supports, many players with ASD enjoy playing basketball. However, for some individuals with ASD, particularly those who are younger, the number of players in a confined area and reverberating noise is too uncomfortable at first. Some may be better able to cope with the sensory bombardment in basketball when they are older.

Parent and adult involvement. A major factor in the success of this particular Challenger Division is that parents of children with ASD are involved in a leadership and support capacity. For instance, the coach for the older soccer division is the father of a young man with ASD. The son of the coach is the assistant coach for the older soccer division.

Parents with knowledge and experience organize and provide visual supports and other accommodations. For instance, two parents, who are also Autism Specialists, have helped develop supports for successful participation for their son, as well as others. Other parents provide 1:1 assistance during practice and games.

For many parents, the benefits of Challenger Division exceed those experienced by their children. The time spent at practice and games of Challenger Division have become a valued social outlet and support for the parents as well as the children.

Supports. Providing appropriate supports has been critical to the success of most of the Challenger Division athletes with ASD. These enable the players to develop increasing skills over time. Adaptations, such as using a tee when necessary to hit in baseball, lowering the net in basketball, playing half-court basketball, and slowing the play so that a soccer ball can be put right in front of a player, can help players be successful while they develop skills. The motor difficulties of some of the players with ASD may cause difficulties during the fast play of soccer, so sometimes the ball is stopped to enable an athlete to kick it.

Parents provide one-on-one assistance for athletes with ASD when needed and fade the assistance as the athlete gains skills. This may include running with a player down the field until the player understands following the ball in soccer or physically moving a youth's leg to kick a ball until the concept is understood. Verbal directions and gestures may also be provided that resemble those of any enthusiastic parents during a youth sports game.

Flexibility and adaptability are key elements. For instance, many of the players with ASD could not tolerate wearing a uniform. They looked and felt different than the clothing that they were accustomed to and found comfortable. However, it was important that the team look enough alike so that they could identify each other during play. Since all the players could tolerate wearing a T-shirt, the "uniform" became wearing a red T-shirt.

A variety of strategies, such as written or picture sequences of the activity, social stories, role plays, cue cards and other visual supports, have significantly increased the athletes' understanding and enjoyment of the activity. Figure 9.6 shows a picture sequence developed to help JD, who needed breaks in his playing, understand when he would play in a soccer game.

Figure 9.6
J.D.'s Soccer Schedule

(Personal communication from M. Hammel & S. Peters, November 18, 2002. Created with The Picture Communication Symbols © 1981-2002 Mayer-Johnson, Inc. Used with permission).

Box 9.25

JD hurt several people by hitting them when he was first engaged in Challenger Division soccer. He did not understand what to do or for how long he would need to do it. People were becoming afraid of him.

One of the parents with expertise in ASD decided to introduce him more gradually to the game by having him play in five-minute increments. She set a large visual timer where he could see it from the field and let him know that he could take a break after playing soccer on the field for five minutes. The use of a visual timer and a break area was familiar to him from school. Shortening the amount of time he was expected to play at first, making the length of time visually clear and providing a break enabled him to increase the length of enjoyable participation over time and to interact with others in a more pleasurable manner for all. JD no longer needs the timer, but he still likes to know the scheduled time that he will play.

Understanding the rules of the game can be difficult for the athletes with ASD. Parents have developed lists of rules, social stories, T-charts of what to do and what not to do, and other visuals to help the athletes understand the game. The availability of "fidget" toys during times without active involvement has dramatically decreased problem behaviors.

Figure 9.7 provides a social story that was written for a boy who was having difficulty understanding how to play soccer. He often got upset when the other team got the ball, when his team lost or when he did not get a turn to kick the ball. He always hit the goalie, because the goalie violated his literal understanding of the rule, "Don't touch the ball with your hands." This social story was originally in a book format with one to three sentences and a picture on each page. Each box represents what would be on a page.

Some youth with ASD may not enjoy any or all the sports offered through Challenger League, even with supports. Some youth have no interest in playing sports. However, sometimes parents must get a child with ASD to try sports, before the child can make an informed choice about the activity. Some youth with ASD may like a sport at some time in the future even if it is initially rejected.

In summary, the Challenger Division promotes, advances and sponsors sports for children with special needs. A growing number of players in Challenger Division have ASD. Providing appropriate supports has been critical to the success of most of the Challenger Division athletes with ASD. Parents have been critical to developing and implementing these supports.

Summary

Youth service organizations are one of the largest providers of leisure experiences to all youth, including those with ASD. The most effective youth service organizations hold a core belief that all children are welcome in their organization. They consider individuals, not just their disabilities and recognize that all their members are unique. They get to know each individual involved and the supports needed to meet that member's strengths and weaknesses. It is important to look at the strengths, weaknesses, hopes, dreams, likes and dislikes of each individual, whether she or he has a disability or not, so that youth have a successful experience.

Each of the youth service organizations included in this chapter has a policy of providing supports, if an individual needs them. They encourage considering the needs of individual members and asking questions, such as:

- What will the individual need to participate and understand instruction?
- Will they need extra time?
- Will they need modified expectations?
- Will they need visual representations of what is expected?
- Will they need an extra support person?
- What other resources are in the community to get volunteers?

Youth service organizations provide a philosophy, training, resources and an overarching structure. However, the quality of the experience with youth with ASD is largely dependent on the knowledge, flexibility and leader's willingness to provide accommodations. If the leader is knowledgeable and sensitive to each member's needs, then all the youth within the group will be included and will grow and learn from their experience. The leader needs to be aware of the needs of all the children, including those with ASD, to make all the children feel accepted and a part of the program. Volunteers want to do the

Figure 9.7
How to Play Soccer with My Team

1

Soccer is a team sport.
My team is the Lake Oswego World Cup Team.
My team wears the red shirts.

2

In soccer there are two teams that play each other. Each team works together as a group to try to score a goal.

3

Usually the player closest to the ball kicks the ball. Not every player gets a turn to kick the ball during every game. A player who does not get a turn to kick a ball in one game usually gets a turn in another game.

4

The other teams try to take the ball away. That is how the game is played. They are not being mean.

Soccer has rules. One rule is the only object that is okay to kick is the ball. Kicking or biting other players hurts them and is against the rules. Players who break the rules may have to sit on the sidelines.

5

6

After a goal is scored, the goalie takes the ball out with their hands and throws it to someone on their team. It is okay for the goalie to touch the ball with his hands.

7

The team is playing soccer for fun. Sometimes my team wins and sometimes another team wins.

8

When I play soccer, I will try to follow the rules. I will try to ask for help when I feel upset.

(Adapted from M. Hammel, November 18, 2002. Used with permission.)

"right thing" for the youth in their group, but they usually need some level of training, resources, and support to meet this goal for their members with ASD.

Parents of children with ASD often need to help educate volunteer leaders and provide supports. Their involvement can add to the success of members. In fact, parent involvement is an important component of most youth service organizations. However, parents of children with ASD may not always have the reserves to be as involved in youth service organizations, as they would like to be.

Many of the recreation opportunities in youth service organizations are inclusive and offer experiences for all youth to learn about and from each other. These experiences prepare the adults of tomorrow to live in diverse communities.

Chapter Ten

Camp Programs for Individuals with Autism Spectrum Disorder

Ann Fullerton

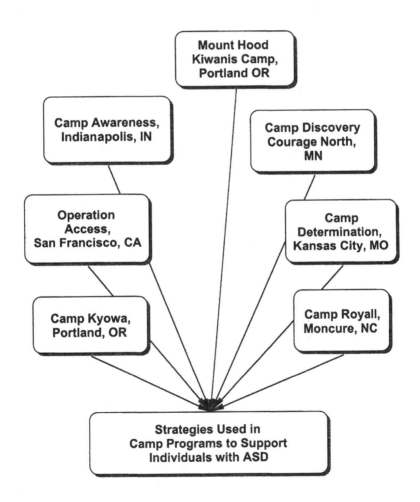

Introduction

Attending a camp program is a rich growth experience for many children and youth. A camp program is an opportunity to learn many social skills and to develop a greater understanding of how groups live and play together. Children and youth with and without disabilities, including ASD, develop increased self-confidence and independence in camp programs that can help to improve a child's functioning at home and school (Fullerton, Brannan, & Arick, 2001; Brannan, Arick, & Fullerton, (2003); Fullerton, Brannan, & Arick (2003). Sometimes, attending camp is the first opportunity child has to stay overnight away from home. Because a child must communicate, problem solve, and negotiate with their counselor and peers regarding needs and wants, camps offer children rich social growth opportunities. One father of a youth with severe communication disabilities commented:

> "Each year at camp, my son must communicate his needs to people who don't know him like his family does, and can't anticipate his every need. He has to communicate with others, and this experience makes him more mature," Fullerton, personal communication, August 9, 1995.

Although a camp experience can be fun and promote social and self-help development for a child or youth with ASD, it is vital that the individual's sensory and communication needs are appropriately addressed while at camp. Otherwise, the experience can be anxiety producing and difficult for the individual.

Organized camping is a major recreation activity for many youth in the U.S. The American Camping Association has over 6,000 member camps (American Camping Association, 2002). Both residential and day camps are available in a wide range of theme- or skill-based programs, and both inclusive or specialized programs are available. Among the specialized camps there are camps for individuals with disabilities. Slowly, more generic camps are becoming inclusive (Brannan, Arick, Fullerton, & Harris, 1997). These inclusive camps provide a rich learning experience for both children with and without disabilities (Arick, & Fullerton, 2003; Fullerton, Brannan, & Arick, 2003.) See Appendix B and C for directories and information about camp programs.

In this chapter, four inclusive camps and three specialized camps for individuals with disabilities are described. Among the specialized camps described there are programs in which a variety of children with different disabilities attend together and programs that are specifically designed for individuals with ASD. Features of the seven camps are summarized in Table 10.1. Contact information for each of these programs is provided in Appendix C.

Camp Kyowa, Disabled Citizens Recreation
Bureau of Portland Parks and Recreation, Portland, OR
Inclusive Day Camp in a Forest Setting

Camp Kyowa is an inclusive summer day camp for children ages five to 11, developed by the Disabled Citizens Division of Portland Parks and Recreation in Portland, Oregon. The camp program has been in operation for 30 years and currently offers three, one-week sessions each summer for 32 children per session. It is a long-standing example of successful reverse mainstreaming; specialized supports for individuals with disabilities are provided within a program that is attractive and beneficial to individuals with and without

Table 10.1
Summary of Camp Programs Described in Chapter 10

Camp	Type of Program	Key Features and Accommodations
Camp Kyowa, Portland Parks & Recreation, Portland, OR	Inclusive day program that serves children ages 5 to 11; 60% with disabilities and 21% with ASD. Forest location with outdoor recreation activities.	• Use of visual systems with all campers to explain schedule. • Use of reverse mainstreaming for inclusion.
Operation Access Project, San Francisco Parks & Recreation, San Francisco, CA.	Inclusive day program that serves children ages 7 to 18. Multiple urban locations with craft, drama, field game activities.	• Multi-agency partnership. • Extended school year site. • Set up alternative activities that invite reverse mainstreaming.
Camp Awareness, Indianapolis, IN.	Inclusive day and residential programs for individuals with Asperger's Syndrome. Young children, school-age, and adult sessions. Science-based curriculum plus recreation activities.	• Parent developed and operated. • Trains nondisabled peers to facilitate peer interaction. • Uses reverse mainstreaming.
Mt. Hood Kiwanis Camp, Portland, OR, Kiwanis sponsored.	Specialized residential program for individuals with a range of disabilities, ages 13 – 35; 40% with ASD. Forest location and outdoor and indoor recreation activities.	• Kiwanis-University partnership. • Doubles as a training/ awareness course for college students. • Use of visual strategies for schedules, activities, and general communication.
Camp Discovery, Courage North, MN	Specialized residential camp serving individuals with Asperger's Syndrome.	• Employs adults with Asperger's Syndrome as camp staff. • Use of visuals and social information for problem solving.
Camp Determination, Kansas City, MO. Autism Asperger Resource Center	Inclusive residential camp serving individuals with Asperger's Syndrome and ASD. Forest location and outdoor and indoor recreation activities.	• Associated with university-based center. • Offers training for graduate students. • Trains peers as social models. • Use of visuals and social information for problem solving.
Camp Royall, Moncure, NC. Autism Society of North Carolina	Specialized residential program for individuals with ASD, ages 4 – adulthood. Forest location and outdoor and indoor recreation activities.	• Uses TEACCH Structured Teaching methods to design and implement activities. • Site built to accommodate sensory and social needs of individuals with ASD.

disabilities. During each session, approximately 60 percent of the participants are children with disabilities and 40 percent are children without disabilities. Of the 96 children who participated in 2001, 20 were children with ASD.

To recruit campers, the program is advertised in the parks and recreation department's catalogs and in the local newspaper. A 30-year word-of-mouth network among parents of children who have attended the camp also assists with recruiting new nondisabled applicants. The director also meets with parent groups to tell them about the camp.

The camp program is staffed by a director, 10 senior counselors (paid, college-aged), and 15 junior counselors (volunteer, high school-aged). Two senior counselors and three junior counselors lead each group of six to eight campers. Thus, the ratio of adults to children is one to two. If needed, campers are provided with individual assistance.

Accommodations

The camp is located outside the city at a forested site near a lake. Campers and staff take a one-hour bus trip back and forth from the city each day. The director found that some of the children with ASD have difficulty with the noise and commotion on the large bus, so a small bus is also used to transport campers and staff. The busses are equipped with "bus bags" full of toys, games, koosh balls, etc. At camp, the groups participate in a variety of activities such as swimming, fishing, paddle boats, arts and crafts, singing camp songs, nature walks, and field games.

Because a number of the campers are children with ASD who need information to be presented visually, visual systems are used throughout the camp. The staff, in developing these systems over several years, has discovered that the visual systems benefit all of the campers, regardless of disabilities in the 5-11 age group. Thus, these accommodations for campers with ASD have actually enhanced the program for everyone.

Each group has its own schedule of activities for the day. When the group arrives in the morning, each group reviews the schedule for the day. The schedule is later reviewed two other times during the day. In addition to the recreation activities, breaks, going to the bathroom, meals, and a surprise "special activity" are also part of the schedule. Some campers with ASD carry the schedule with them via a key ring attached to their belt loop. The keyring holds the activity cards in the sequence of the schedule, and the camper and counselor can use it for constant reference. Before the end of each activity, counselors use the schedules to prepare campers for the transition to the next activity. To help with transitions, counselors also may use a kitchen timer which they set to tick-tock during the last five minutes of an activity and then to ring when the activity is finished. The camper uses the timer as a cue to run out and prepare for the next transition.

Although the schedule is highly structured, the staff meets individual needs flexibly. For example, if a camper does not want to do an activity, such as fishing, he or she is gently encouraged to watch awhile and try fishing after observing other campers. But if after 10 minutes they remain uninterested or afraid, the camper and a counselor find an alternate activity for that time period, such as taking a walk.

Answering campers' questions about their peers. On infrequent occasions, campers without disabilities are curious about how a camper with disabilities will do an activity. The staff addresses these questions as they arise and uses them as an opportunity to talk about differences. Staff members might point out that there is more than one way to do some things, and that everyone needs help sometimes. They explain what they might do to help one camper, and how that is different from how they help another camper.

Camp Kyowa illustrates how an inclusive day camp for young children can incorporate strategies that support children with ASD while enhancing the experience for all participants.

Operation Access Project
A Collaboration between San Francisco State University and San Francisco Department of Parks and Recreation Inclusive Day Camp in an Urban Setting

Through pooling resources and obtaining grant funds from the U.S. Office of Education Rehabilitation Services Administration, a group of agencies in San Francisco, have developed a program in which children with ASD and other disabilities are included in the city parks' day camps. The city's school districts, regional developmental disabilities centers, and the San Francisco Parks and Recreation Department each contribute resources to the camp program. Faculty from San Francisco State University's Department of Recreation and Leisure have teamed with these agencies to create Operation Access, a process for including children with disabilities into the day camps in the city.

The program was started in 1998 by a parent of a child with ASD, who had been underserved by the city's day camps. Although children with a variety of challenges participate, the program has a special focus on the needs of children with moderate to severe ASD. These children often need an inclusion aide in order to participate in the day camps. In its first year, three children were served. In 2002, 35 children were included in four different day camps and 20 of those were individuals with ASD.

Each agency partner contributes different resources. The school districts contribute salary support for inclusion aides in operation access for their students needing extended school year services. The regional developmental disabilities agency also provides funds to hire inclusion aides. The city parks and recreation department operates the day camps and sets aside in advance slots for children with disabilities to attend for six weeks, as opposed to the usual three weeks. Lastly, university faculty provides assistance in developing inclusive strategies and accommodations. Funds from the Parks and Recreation Department and the grant were combined to fund an Inclusion Coordinator position to oversee the program.

Preparing for a Child's Inclusion into the Day Camp

In the spring prior to summer day camp, the inclusion coordinator conducts a school visit and observes the children who will attend summer day camp in their classroom —the inclusion coordinator meets with the child and their teacher and parents and discusses the child's likes and dislikes, accommodation needs, and the goals they have for the child's day camp experience.

The coordinator also gives the parent an opportunity to suggest whom to hire as an inclusion aide. Often the child's school-year aide is a preferred choice, but if this is not the case then a different inclusion aide is interviewed and employed. Generally, with participants with ASD, the inclusion coordinator finds that if the aide and the child know one another, the child is more likely to adjust quickly and participate more fully.

For a child with ASD new to the program, several visits to observe the program before they start attending are arranged. This is possible because the child is still in school at the time the summer day camp begins.

Day Camp Accommodations for Children with ASD

The San Francisco City Parks and Recreation Department have operated summer camp programs for 50 years. In this urban setting, the major goal is for children to have an opportunity to play outdoors safely. Large numbers of children are involved in these activities. For most children with ASD, activities conducted outdoors work well because the child can join in or move away from the noise and activity, thereby modulating the amount of sensory stimulation he or she experiences.

The activities in the day camp programs are often loosely structured. Typically, large groups of children are in one of two modes, both of which can be difficult for some participants with ASD. Usually the day campers are either frenetically engaged in a large group activity or they are in transition between activities and waiting for the next one to begin. During the frenetic periods, participants with ASD have difficulty understanding what they are supposed to do, or what role they should take. During the waiting periods, it's not clear to campers with ASD what is coming up next and when it will start.

To accommodate participants with ASD, the inclusion coordinator and the aides set up a structure within the overall day camp program. The inclusion staff provides a visual schedule so that the children with ASD can see what is coming next, and when transitions will occur. Staff members also provide alternative activities that have a strong sensory motor component during some of the popular camp activities, which may not work well with some children with ASD. For example, they may extend a participant with ASD time swinging in the playground with a few other friends, while the large group engages in a field game.

During the loosely structured free-time periods, the inclusion staff sets up extra small group and individual activities. These activities are selected because of their high interest to both the children with ASD and children without disabilities. Thus children are drawn to the activity to participate and interact with their peers with ASD. As a result, reverse mainstreaming occurs in which children without disabilities participate in a specialized activity, thereby integrating the activity.

Some of the Park and Recreation Department's day camp programs are organized around a theme, such as the arts. The coordinator has found that it's important to review the program director's philosophy and goals in order to determine if the program is a good match for a child. Some directors have product-oriented goals and, for example, want to stage a drama production in six weeks. Other directors' goals are more process oriented, and he or she wants participants to express themselves in a variety of ways. The coordinator finds that children with ASD are more easily included in and enjoy a process-oriented program than a product-oriented program. For example, an expressive arts program held at one of the city's parks has proved ideal for inclusion because the program's goal is to let each child explore personal expression through drama, art, and dance.

Operation Access has developed various strategies for including individuals with ASD into an urban multi-site day camp program. It also has found creative ways to pool resources from several agencies to make the program possible.

Camp Awareness
Indianapolis, IN
An Inclusive Residential Camp

Camp Awareness was created by Sue Hansen, the parent of a young man with Asperger's Syndrome. As described in Chapter 2, Asperger's Syndrome is one of the disorders within the autism spectrum. Sue Hansen started Camp Awareness because she could not find a camp program that could accommodate the needs of her son (see Figure 10.1).

Figure 10.1
Miscommunications in Camps: An Example

In 1998, Sue Hansen's son was in fourth grade, and Sue was trying to find a camp that he would enjoy and could attend. She could not find anything that seemed like a good match. When her son was younger, Sue had been a Cub Scout leader for his troop. One time she had taken her troop of 20 boys and their fathers to a Boy Scout camp. She was, of course, aware of her son's needs and she was trying to be on the look out for possible difficulties he might encounter. Since they were one of many troops at the camp, she could not anticipate everything. Moreover, the camp staff and the other adults present were not aware of her son's needs.

One of her son's sensory difficulties was strong reaction to certain smells, such as tuna. When the hungry troop walked into the dining hall; her son was especially ravenous, and they all smelled tuna casserole. Her son ran into the kitchen area, grabbed some cupcakes, and ran outside as far away as he could from the smell of the tuna. The other boys were upset, saying, "See what he did, he stole our cupcakes!," and Sue quickly explained what was going on.

But the incident made her think about what would have happened if she had not been there. Her son might have been punished, lectured, and possibly sent home. Moreover, he may not have had the social awareness and skills, or words to explain his actions adequately to the adults or to his peers.

The experience made Sue realize that, in many situations, people need to be educated about individuals with Asperger's Syndrome: how they are different, and why they do the things that they do *before* they meet someone with Asperger's Syndrome. The experience at the Boy Scout camp prompted Sue to start Camp Awareness.

Camp Awareness was started in 1998 as a one-week, science-based day camp at a local park. Since that time, through obtaining grants and community support, the camp has evolved into a residential camp for different age groups and families. In 2002, Camp Awareness served 180 school-aged children with Asperger's Syndrome in the science camp. A weekend retreat was conducted for 120 family members with preschool-aged children (38 preschoolers). A retreat for 10 adults with Asperger's Syndrome was also held.

Box 10.1

When starting the camp, the director was offered a school site to hold the program. But she realized given the literal understanding of individuals with Asperger's Syndrome that for them school was school. She knew they would have difficulty with a camp culture and activities being conducted in a school setting. Camp needed to be camp.

Program Overview.   The goal of Camp Awareness is "...to bring social opportunity to a population of children that otherwise have no camp..." (www.campawareness.com). Weeklong sessions are conducted for the 6-11 and 12+ age groups. The 6 to 11-year-olds spend one overnight and the 12+ age group four overnights. The camp sessions for school-age children center on a science theme and also involve a creative array of fun activities. Various community groups or organizations provide many of the activities.

Volunteer Staff. Volunteers, including its director Sue Hansen, operate Camp Awareness. The director has recruited volunteers from different sectors to help with specific aspects of the program. Parents of the participants supervise and assist the campers. The parents involved find that they learn a great deal by observing their own child and other participants and by talking with other parents. High school- and college-aged students are recruited to assist campers and to serve as peer buddies. The director recruits these volunteers from Boy Scouts, a personal network of family and friends, the local high school, and the siblings of the participants. Sue has found that the peers are the most important part of the camp because they make the children with Asperger's Syndrome feel included and appreciated within a peer group. In essence, Camp Awareness uses elected inclusion to invite typical peers to participate in a program for individuals with Asperger's Syndrome.

Training. The peer buddies and adult volunteers received eight hours of pre-camp training on individuals with Asperger's Syndrome. The training focuses on understanding Asperger's Syndrome, and on learning to provide empathic peer support consistent with the goals of the camp program. Simulation learning is used to help peers understand what it might be like to experience ASD (See Figure 10.2 for a description of training methods).

Figure 10.2
Simulation Learning Used to Develop Understanding of
Peers' Experiences with Asperger's Syndrome

The Camp Awareness trainers have created simulation learning experiences for the peer training. While the peers are trying to accomplish a task, they are bombarded with sensory input: a radio is playing loudly, and the fluorescent buzzing lights are flashing on and off. Someone is spraying perfumed hairspray nearby, brushing their arms with a ticklish feather duster, and making distracting scraping and scratching sounds. The peers share what it is like to try to do a task under these conditions. The trainers describe the variety of hyper- and hypo-sensory sensitivities that individuals with Asperger's Syndrome experience 24 hours a day.

Next, the challenge individuals with Asperger's Syndrome face understanding social situations and unwritten social rules are discussed. The TV show "3rd Rock from the Sun" is used to illustrate people who don't understand social rules, and that, even when explained, these rules don't make a bit of sense to them. The social consequences of sensory differences, such as avoiding eye contact or being "mono-channel" (only able to take in either auditory or visual information, but not both at the same time), are described. Parents share the experiences of their children as examples.

Continued

Figure 10.2 continued
Simulation Learning Used to Develop Understanding of
Peers' Experiences with Asperger's Syndrome

The tendency of individuals with Asperger's Syndrome to perseverate on their own preferred topics and interests is explained. Peers are taught conversation strategies, and how to give praise to a peer with Asperger's Syndrome as a way to re-direct the conversation before he or she reaches a point of disengagement from the interaction. Typical peers review 100 ways to praise others and choose styles of praise that they feel are appropriate for them to use to praise a peer. Circles of Friends (Perske, 1988) activities are also used in the training.

The training results in peers developing considerable empathy for their peers with Asperger's Syndrome, especially as they realize the social confusion and vulnerability to teasing and bullying they have experienced. As a final training topic, the goal for each camper at Camp Awareness is discussed: that for this one week of their lives, no one will judge them. It's stressed to peers that this goal is before all else, and if they can't adhere to it, then this is not a good volunteer opportunity for them. In her experience using peer volunteers, Sue has had only one occasion when a peer was not able to support this goal.

Box 10.2

Sue Hanson, Director of Camp Awareness, gives the peer buddies a tip that helps reframe their view of the campers with Asperger's Syndrome fixation on one topic. She tells them to find a camper who knows about something they would like to write a paper about next year at school, and to then interview that camper at length and gather information for their paper!

Program Description. The science camp includes life, earth, and physical sciences. Each day is organized around a theme. For example, Monday might be Science Day. Science teachers and individuals from science centers bring portable, hands-on lab experiments, teach campers how to make aquariums, or conduct nature studies. In addition, visiting artists might lead the campers in making pottery on pottery wheels. Tuesday might be Sports Day with five stations for Tae Kwon Do, gymnastics, obstacle course, tennis, and cross-country running. Later in the day, a final activity might return the group to the science theme with a visit from a zoologist who brings live animals. Wednesday might be Sibling Day when the campers' siblings are invited to join in the fun. A comic strip artist

might be a guest who shows the campers and peers how to draw Spiderman. On a hot afternoon, slides made of bubble wrap with a layer of shaving cream are laid out on the lawn. Campers and adults put on swimsuits and enjoy this great sensory activity together. Thursday might be Music Day with a live DJ providing music and a pizza party, folk dancing, and a petting zoo thrown into the mix. Outdoor recreation activities are held such as a ropes course, nature study and exploration, lunar and constellation study, and creek walks. At the end of

Photo by Jason Kinch Photographics,
Courtesy of Mt. Hood Kiwanis Camp

hot summer days, all may swim in the pool, which provides a relaxing sensory activity and a chance to cool down.

> **Box 10.3**
>
> Campers with Asperger's Syndrome often interpret instructions literally. Once the staff member supervising swimming said, "no non-swimmers in the deep end" This created an uproar among the campers until it was realized that they interpreted "non-swimmers" as meaning they could not go into the pool at all. The instructions were revised to "deep water swimmers in the deep end of the pool, and shallow water swimmers in the shallow end," and all went well.

Preparing Campers for Camp. Parents are given specific instructions on how to prepare their child for camp. They are asked to teach their child the rules of camp and to describe the various activities that occur at camp. Written and pictorial schedules are sent to them, and parents review these with their child. Parents explain that the camp staff care about them and will help them calm down when they need to, and that at camp there is a room specially designed to help them wind down. In addition, parents are asked to drive their child to the campsite and look around before the camp session. Before the session, parents also mail a card that their child will receive while at camp. And lastly, each day of the session, parents place some familiar item in their child's pocket which is calming for the child, such as a favorite stress ball. These preparations reduce the child's anxiety about the new camp experience.

> **Box 10.4**
>
> One recent camper with ASD at Camp Awareness was also blind. As he headed for camp he told his Mom, "...I am going to make some friends!" Among many activities, he completed the entire ropes course. He wowed his peers by playing video games using only the game's noise for feedback.

Accommodations

A variety of strategies are used to visually organize the program and to accommodate the sensory and communication needs of the participants. For example, campers and peers wear different colored T-shirts so that the adults can quickly identify campers and more easily monitor and re-direct situations and anticipate individual needs. The 6 to 11 year-olds have an adhesive sticker placed on the back of their shirts with their parents' names and any important medical information. This allows everyone to respond quickly to a problem. Every camper and peer buddy is given a schedule for each day's activities. The adults and peer volunteers are instructed to honor a camper's choice to decline partaking in an activity, and not to push or cajole campers into participation. The director roams and scans all the campers during the day, anticipating campers' needs for redirection or a break.

> **Box 10.5**
>
> One camper at Camp Awareness needs redirection when he is overloaded from all the activity. In order to give him a meaningful alternative activity, he has the role of helping to stock and set up the camp store. He helps purchase items for the store before camp and whenever he needs a break during camp, he is asked to take inventory. This task helps him to regain his composure and to feel ready to join in again with his peers.

The Calm Room. The calm room is where participants can get away from the action, take a break, or calm down. An experienced parent, who can help interpret a camper's needs and help them regain their equilibrium before returning to the action, always staffs the calm room. The room is quiet, and it has low-level lighting, a variety of sensory materials, computer games, and lots of books. The calm room has become a critical part of the program and is enhanced each year. A local college sorority has made a variety of sensory and tactile objects and activities for the calm room.

The director has found that these accommodations and practices have helped the campers with Asperger's Syndrome to participate, without getting frustrated or upset. The camp program has experienced a low frequency of outbursts that result from misunderstandings and frustration.

Camp Awareness is a well established organization in its community and is supported by a team of committed volunteers. The science-based curriculum, the use of visiting artists and teachers to widen the variety of activities, the attention to sensory and communication needs, and careful training of peer buddies are great features of the program.

Mt. Hood Kiwanis Camp for Children and Adults with Disabilities Portland, Oregon

The Mt. Hood Kiwanis Camp is located in the forests near Mt. Hood in Oregon. The camp has been supported by Kiwanians in Oregon and Southwest Washington for 60 years. The Special Education and Speech and Hearing Sciences Programs at Portland State University PSU offer training and consultation and recruit students to be counselors at the camp. The mission of the camp is to provide recreation for persons with disabilities. As more youth with disabilities are increasingly included in mainstream camps, this specialized program has focused on serving individuals with more severe and complex needs. Participants include individuals with multiple disabilities, moderate to profound cognitive disabilities, physical disabilities, and ASD. About 40 percent of the participants are individuals with ASD, and most are nonverbal and/or minimally verbal with severe communication challenges.

In order to accomplish its mission, the camp formed a partnership with the Special Education Department at Portland State University 25 years ago. The university recruits undergraduate and graduate students to be counselors at the camp for two-week periods. These students are enrolled in a community-based learning course at PSU. The Special Education faculty helps train and supervise the students. In addition, most of the camp's paid staff are graduates of the Special Education program. Graduate students in special education complete projects at the camp to develop and field test strategies for use at the camp.

This partnership has been a win-win arrangement for both organizations. The large number of college student volunteers (200 per year) needed to provide a strong ratio of counselors to campers is possible because these undergraduate students can fulfill a degree requirement by enrolling in this course. The volunteer student-counselors make it possible to provide staffing at a fraction of the cost of a paid counseling staff. These savings can then be passed on to families. The university benefits by offering a unique learning experience for its students.

The summer camp program operates for eight weeks, and campers attend for a one-week session. The student counselors attend for a two-week session. A total of 400-500 campers attend each year, with 55 per weekly session. A main camp program and two offsite programs (canoeing, camping and backpacking), are offered. Because the student counselors have widely varying prior experience working with individuals with disabilities, they receive training and on-going supervision by special educators and recreation professionals. The staff also includes a behavior communication specialist who assesses campers' communication needs, develops and implements communication strategies, and then trains counselors to use these methods.

Since many campers return for more than one year, counselors also complete an Experience Skill Checklist developed by the camp program. The current counselor rates the camper's skill level in all of the various program areas as well as in self-help and social skills. This completed checklist is then available to the camper's counselor the following year. The information makes it possible to encourage the camper's independence in all areas at the most recent level of performance.

Campers, counselors, and staff are organized into living groups that consist of a Counselor Supervisor, Assistant Counselor Supervisor, eight campers and eight counselors. As a group they participate in the program activities including fishing, hiking, canoeing, arts and crafts, overnight campout, swimming, campfire performances, and the activities of daily living.

Accommodations

A number of accommodations are used to support campers with ASD. These include visual schedules, visual communication systems, mini-schedules with visual systems for activities, and options for campers to express and meet the need for a break.

Visual Schedules. Each living group has its own daily and weekly schedule of activities. For ease of use, schedules are available in several formats including a large poster in the group's living area and picture/word cards on keyrings that can be attached to a belt loop. A library of picture/word cards (Mayer-Johnson, 2000), photos, and objects are available to construct schedules as needed. Counselors present the schedule to campers with ASD when they arrive at camp, counselors and refer to it throughout each day and before transitions in between activities. Staff finds that after a full day of using the schedule, campers with ASD begin to rely on it as a constant source of information about what is next, when they will eat, etc. At this point, the use of the schedule can decrease anxiety and facilitate the participation of campers with ASD.

Visual Communication Systems. Along with the schedule, campers with ASD may use a visual communication system. Through the communication system campers with ASD can express their needs and wants and counselors can provide visual information about the activities to the campers with ASD. Some campers bring the communication system they use at home and school to camp. Camp picture/word cards are added to their communication system as needed. Systems can be constructed in different formats using the camp library of cards, which is organized into the following categories:

- Feelings and needs (e.g., hungry, thirsty, tired, happy, stomach hurts)
- Actions (e.g., run, walk, drink, eat, take a break, use bathroom)
- Locations at the camp (e.g., sleeping area, bathroom, fishing pond)
- Activities at camp (e.g., self-help, hiking, fishing, etc.)
- Dining hall options (e.g., food items and feelings/actions).

Examples of notebook and keyring formats for communication systems are shown in Figure 10.3.

Figure 10.3
Note book and Keyring Formats for Communication Systems at the Mt. Hood Kiwanis Camp

In Figure 10.3 the notebook format and the more mobile keyring format are shown for visual communication systems. The pages are all laminated for durability. The keyring format can be attached to a backpack or a belt loop.

One of the daily camp activities is to write and draw in a camper journal, which the camper takes home at the end of the week. For campers with ASD, the communication system is used to share the day's experiences and to reflect on those experiences in the journal.

Activity descriptions and social stories. Some campers with ASD benefit from the use of illustrated, written descriptions of camp activities that explain what will happen and what they and others will do during the activity. For example, there are descriptions of the flag ceremony, going to bed at night, the overnight campout, etc., and each is illustrated with stick-figure drawings (Wilkerson, 2002). The activity description is read to the camper two or more times before the activity occurs. In addition, when needed, a social story (as defined in Chapter 2, Gray, 1994) is written and used when a camper has difficulties with a particular situation.

Mini-Schedules and Visual Systems for Activities
Example: The Adventure Course Stream Crossing

In recent years, the camp staff has developed ways to provide visual information about the outdoor recreation activities that help campers with ASD better understand and participate in activities. The routine and steps involved in an activity are analyzed as well as the roles different individuals take during the activity. Then the sequence and the roles are made visually clear by constructing posters that depict each step, visual boundaries that clarify activity areas, and picture/word cards (Mayers-Johnson, 2002) that symbolize the various roles in the activity. To illustrate, the system developed for the Stream Crossing Activity is described.

The Stream Crossing at the Mt. Hood Kiwanis Camp, Rhododendron, Oregon.

One of the culminating activities in the camp's adventure program area involves crossing a rushing stream on a cable 20 feet in the air. Participants wear a harness and helmet and are hooked onto a safety cable. Although the activity is safe, it is a perceived risk, and campers experience a great sense of accomplishment. A photo of the camper crossing the stream is placed in his or her journal to later share with family. Campers can choose to do this activity by themselves, with their counselors by their side, or to decline and simply watch and cheer others in their group as they go across. Staff finds that over several summers returning campers choose to gradually do more of the activity, until they too cross the stream on their own.

The stream-crossing activity involves several elements that can be confusing and challenging for a camper with ASD. First, some areas at the stream-crossing are off-limits, and these boundaries can be unclear in this forested area. Second, because only one camper can cross at a time, others must wait their turn. It can be difficult for an individual with ASD to understand what to do while waiting and when it will be his turn. Third, campers have choices with respect to how they can complete the activity. To facilitate the participation of campers with ASD, visual boundaries, posters visually depicting the steps and areas, and picture/word cards on necklaces were developed (Ayers, Marquardt, Tingstad, & Fullerton, 2001). These are shown in Figure 10.4.

To establish visual boundaries, colored duct tape was used to mark different areas. White tape marks the area where the campers can watch and cheer on other campers that are crossing the stream. Yellow tape marks the area where a camper puts on the harness and helmet and waits for a turn to cross the stream. Red tape is used to mark the stream-crossing platform where only the camper about to cross the stream, her counselor, and the instructor can be present.

Mounted on a tree is a diagram (see Figure 10.4) that shows the different white, yellow and red sections in the stream crossing area. The adventure course instructor uses the diagram to explain the purpose and the boundaries of each section.

Figure 10.4
Mini-Schedule and Visual System for
Stream-Crossing Activity at Mt. Hood Kiwanis Camp

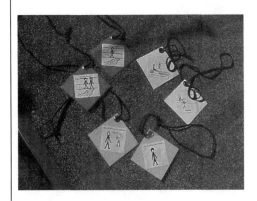 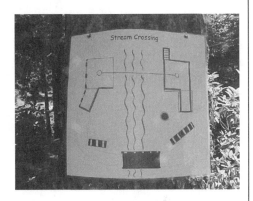

In the photo on the left, cards placed on a necklace are shown. Each card has a line drawing of a different phase of the activity. Participants wear the cards around their neck during different phases of the activity. In the photo on the right, the stream crossing activity areas are color-coded in a diagram. The diagram matches the color-coded boundaries found in the area. The diagram is used to instruct the participants.

At any one time, each camper assumes one of three different roles while engaged in the stream-crossing activity. Several campers are in the watching role, while two campers are getting ready by putting on the helmet and harness, and one camper is crossing the stream. Picture/word cards on necklaces are available for each role (see Figure 10.4). The white "Watch & Cheer" cards depict a figure who is watching and cheering others on. On one side of the yellow "Get Ready" cards depict a figure is putting on the harness and helmet; these are worn by the campers who are waiting their turn to go next. A single red card on a necklace is worn by the camper crossing the stream. On one side of the red card is a picture of a camper going alone, and on the other side is a picture of a camper and counselor crossing the stream together. Campers point to their choice. After the camper has crossed the stream, he or she removes the red card and receives the yellow card again. The yellow card is turned over, and a figure taking off the harness and helmet is shown. After the helmet and harness is removed, the yellow card is exchanged for a white "Watch and Cheer" card.

Photo by Jason Kinch Photographics,
Courtesy of Mt. Hood Kiwanis Camp

A similar system has been designed for the equestrian program. At the equestrian site, campers ride a horse, and while waiting for their turn they can choose from a variety of activities such as cowboy-cowgirl dress-up, a bronco ride (saddle on a hay bale), horse puzzles, and grooming a horse. The visual system for the equestrian site clarifies these choices and represents the various areas in the corral and arena. The stream crossing and equestrian visual systems have helped campers with ASD and other campers participate more independently, and with less verbal direction from counselors.

Addressing the Need for a Break and for Sensory Activity

Campers with ASD may need to take a break from the action and noise at camp to relax in a quiet place with less activity. Campers need a way to tell staff that they want a break, and they need to understand where they can go with their counselor to meet this need. One important question posed to parents is how their child communicates the need for a break at home or school, and what behavioral signs indicate this need. This information is used to determine how the individual will take breaks at camp. In the camp symbol library, cards for "take a break" are available. Campers keep a card in their pocket or on their key ring to show their counselor when a break is needed.

There are several locations around camp that are used for taking a break. Brightly-painted, sturdy, wooden rocking chairs and swinging hammocks are located on the porches of all the buildings. A camper and his or her counselor can retreat to a pair of rocking chairs or hammocks. A teepee is located away from the campfire circle, and a camper can go there to watch the noisy campfire show from a distance. Campers can also return to their bunk or other quiet places around camp.

Another way to reduce anxiety and address sensory needs for some campers is to give these individuals objects to carry and fiddle with. Some campers bring favorite objects from home. Each group has a bag of tactile materials with their supplies. For example, a camper may carry a koosh ball with them all week.

Since forty percent of its campers are individuals with ASD, the Mt. Hood Kiwanis Camp continues to develop new ways to visually interpret the camp program for individuals with ASD and to respect their sensory needs.

Camp Discovery, Autism Society of Minnesota
Courage North, Minnesota
A Specialized Residential Camp

With thanks to Kari Dunn Buron, Director of Camp Discovery, who wrote portions of the following description.

Camp Discovery is a residential summer camp for children with Asperger's Syndrome founded in 1995. The director, Kari Dunn Buron had interviewed adults with Asperger's

Syndrome at the Autism Society of America Conference the year before. When she asked them what kind of support would have been helpful to them when they were growing up, they all agreed that they would have liked to have met other people like themselves. The goal of Camp Discovery is to provide a place for youth with Asperger's Syndrome to meet each other and create meaningful and lasting friendships in an environment that provides encouragement, acceptance and support. The camp is held at Courage North, a beautiful pine filled peninsula on Lake George in northern Minnesota.

Camper Groups and Facilities

The camp conducts two one-week sessions each summer with 36 campers each week. To accommodate campers' needs for personal space, six campers share a large cabin that is designed for 16. An additional private sleeping area is available in the nurse's office in case a camper is unable to sleep in the cabin.

Staffing

Six educators who work with students with ASD are hired as an "ASD Consultant" for each of the six cabins. Several months before the camp sessions, the director and the educators meet and review the camper applications and information forms, contact parents and campers to answer questions about the camp schedule and activities, and design sensory/relaxation lessons for each day at camp. During the camp session, the ASD Consultants supervise the campers in a cabin, post visual information in their cabin daily, and act as an "social interpreter" for the campers. Adults with Asperger's Syndrome are also employed as camp staff. They work as role models for campers and assist in the staff training and the camp program.

Staff Training

All staff receives training in the basics of Asperger's Syndrome. Staff talks about the disorder as "a difference" and how it is "a different way of thinking." Staff is told not to expect to change behavior in a week; rather the goal is to exhibit unconditional acceptance while still maintaining a safe environment. Staff is told to expect some negative interactions due to social misunderstandings, high levels of anxiety and rigid thinking. Staff is instructed to overlook minor behaviors that would typically create confrontation (swearing, noncompliance). Based on an understanding of Asperger's Syndrome, they are also coached not to personalize rude comments. The director leads role-plays to help staff work through some possible difficult moments. The adult staff members with Asperger's Syndrome assist in the training by telling staff about their own anxieties, fears and social issues. Each cabin staff team reviews and discusses each camper's history and plans proactively for any foreseeable problems. After the first full day of camp, the staff and director meet to address specific issues observed the first day and apply relevant concepts from the training. The director reports that in eight years of camp she has never had to send a camper home due to behavior.

Program Description

In addition to typical camp activities (swimming, boating, skiing, tubing, kayaking, fishing, hiking, arts and crafts, campouts, bike rides, etc.) the program also includes other activities that the staff have found to be enjoyable for these campers with Asperger's Syndrome such as orienteering, astronomy, photography, and study of water plant and animal life. The dining hall lounge is open 24 hours a day and is supplied with Jigsaw puzzles, books about facts, science and history, and chess and other board games.

Another component of the program is activities that help the campers learn more about Asperger's Syndrome. One night the adult staff with Asperger's Syndrome participates in a panel discussion. The other staff and campers ask them questions about their experience of ASD and their adult lives (e.g., Do they date? Do they have a driver's license? Do they live on their own?). Each day during rest period in their cabin, the campers learn something about Asperger's Syndrome. The staff might read and lead a discussion of a story (e.g., The Blue Bottle Mystery). Campers and staff may review a checklist of the characteristics of Asperger's Syndrome (e.g., the Asperger's Syndrome Diagnostic Scale) to see if they agree or disagree with the "experts." Both Asperger Syndrome and ASD are discussed and clarified. Along with the "differences," the strengths and positive aspects of Asperger's Syndrome and ASD are discussed.

Program-wide accommodations to support social understanding and social behavior are integral to the program. Visual instructions and schedules are used throughout the camp. Staff and campers wear nametags to help them learn and remember names. Campers are assigned bunks near another camper who has similar interests. Signs are placed on the bed that say "Ask me about _____." Campers attend a class where they learn about Comic Strip Conversations (Carol Gray, 1994) and how this method is used to solve interpersonal problems at camp. The director talks about the camp philosophy, "Every camper has the right to feel safe and accepted at camp," and about community living. A chart that illustrates words that can cause chaos and words that bring peace is also posted and discussed.

Each cabin makes up a list of "*Guidelines for a Successful Week.*" The director finds that this works well to avoid power struggles surrounding "rules." Campers are often fixated on rules and want to know what will happen if they break a rule. Staff tells them that these are guidelines, not rules, and that the guidelines are posted to help campers remember how to have a successful week. The director finds that this seems to take the pressure off for those campers who are overly focused on rules.

All campers receive a copy of *A Guide to Social Success* (see Figure 10.5) which visually illustrates some good ideas to try at camp.

Individual Accommodations. When two campers are having difficulty with each other, social cartooning, as shown in Figure 10.5 is used for problem solving. To deflect camper concerns, the director has installed a "Suggestions, Complaints and General Worries" box outside of her office. The director finds that campers with Asperger's Syndrome have a strong sense of right and wrong and may complain about or insult another camper who they feel has violated a protocol. To deflect these situations, campers are encouraged to write down their concern and let the director know if they are upset about something. The director then finds the camper and chats a bit about the issue. Sometimes it is just an obsessional worry such as, "What if someone coughs on my food?"

An effective strategy for helping campers adjust to and accept needed changes is the use of memos written by the director to campers. The memo describes the situation, acknowledges that change can be difficult, and points out some positive aspects of the change. In Figure 10.6, an example of a memo written to Joey (a camper) by the director (Kari) is shown.

Figure 10.5
Samples from Booklet of Social Skills and
Social Problem-Solving Strategies

Camp Determination's Guide
to Social Success
(A pictorial look at the really important
things to remember while you are at camp.)

(Adapted for Camp Determination with permission of Kari Dunn Buron, Coordinator of Camp Discovery)

The camp motto is: Everyone has the right to feel safe and accepted at Camp Determination. This means there should be no teasing.

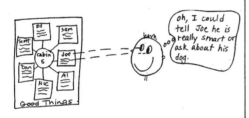

If you have difficulty thinking of nice things to say, ask your counselor to help by using a compliment map. This map could list some good things about other people in your cabin. You can give someone a compliment by commenting on one of those positive things.

If there is a problem, someone will help you to think about the problem by using cartooning. Sometimes drawing things out actually helps to understand it.

The Camp Determination Guide to Social Success is sent out to campers and their parents before camp to read and discuss prior to attendance. The concept of the guide was developed by Kari Dunn Buron, Director of Camp Discovery in St. Paul, MN (see Resources for contact information).

Figure 10.6
Example of a Memo Used at Camp Discovery
To Help a Camper Adjust to Change

To: Joey
From: Kari

You are in cabin 3 with Ed. I know you like Ed, but he seems to make you nervous. When you get nervous, you get into other people's personal space. When you get into Ed's personal space he gets very angry. Sometimes you and Ed fight when this happens. The counselors in cabin 3 have to keep everybody safe. It may seem like it is Ed's fault because when you see Ed you get nervous. A good solution is to get away from Ed.

You can work on relaxing at camp by getting away from Ed. Cabin 5 is a very relaxing cabin. Nick is the Cabin Head in cabin 5. Nick is a very cool guy. Nick can help you to stay relaxed.

You will probably miss Brent and you might be a little nervous about moving to a new cabin. Changes can be hard even when they are for the best. Remember that in cabin 5 you will be able to relax. In cabin 5 you will be able to have a successful week at camp.

Brent and Nick will help you make the change. They will help you move your stuff. Kari will be around to take a walk with you if you get anxious. Jen is in cabin 5. You remember Jen from last year. Jen is cool.

This is a done deal.

Camp Discovery's mission is to bring youth with Asperger's Syndrome together to establish positive relationships and learn from others with the same challenges. Each year an e-mail directory of the campers is established and many campers keep in contact throughout the year.

Camp Determination
Autism Asperger Resource Center (AARC), Kansas City, MO

Camp Determination is a residential summer camp for children with Asperger's Syndrome and other types of ASD. The program currently serves about 80 children (ages eight to 17) conducting two four-day sessions each year. Most of the campers are between the ages of 10 and 15 and are diagnosed with Asperger's Syndrome.

Camp Determination was established in 1997 to address the need for a camp experience for individuals with ASD and to serve as a practicum experience for graduate students at the University of Kansas. A federal grant project at the time helped with the initial startup budget. Thereafter, professionals and parents sought other resources to continue the program. A camp facility is rented for the program.

Currently, the Autism Asperger Resource Center (AARC) operates Camp Determination. AARC is a private, nonprofit organization that provides a variety of services to individuals with ASD, their families, and teachers as well as consultation and training to school districts. The center is funded by fees for services and charitable contributions. AARC is located at the University of Kansas Medical School. The camp program is funded through a combination of charitable donations, camper fees, grants, and fund raising by families and professionals.

Camper groups. Five to eight campers are placed in a camper group according to ages and needs. Three to ten counselors supervise each group, depending on the level of supervision needed by individuals in the group. Groups also include one to three typical peers without disabilities of the same age. Each group of campers, peers, and counselors stay in the cabins together and participate in activities together.

Camper selection criteria. The camp has certain criteria for campers based on the staffing levels available and the program offered. Campers need to be independent in toileting, dressing, feeding, and sleeping. Campers need to be able to function in a group of five students supervised by one adult. It is best if the camper has had prior experience being away from home. An important criteria for inclusion in the program is that the camper has an effective individual communication system to communicate his or her needs and wants. Without such a system in place, the camp staff will not be able to address the individuals' anxieties and potential behavioral challenges that are likely to occur in this unfamiliar setting. Families are required to bring the communication system to camp for use at camp.

Preparing to serve campers. Families complete a detailed Camper Application Form that provides the camp staff with the information necessary to meet the needs of the camper while at camp. Parents are asked to describe all behaviors that staff need to be aware of and the techniques parents use to support and calm their child and manage challenging behaviors. Parents also answer questions about the child's interests, allergies, dietary issues, bedtime routines, sleep patterns, and idiosyncratic behaviors. The camp director reviews all applications and if needed, calls parents and discusses any questions that arise.

Staffing

Paid staff. The program utilizes a combination of paid staff and volunteers. The paid positions at the camp vary from year to year and may include the director, cabin team leaders, activity coordinators and facilitators, medical staff, and peer models. The cabin team leaders coordinate the volunteers with their particular camper groups. The activity coordinators organize all the activities.

Typical peers as social role models. An important aspect of Camp Determination's program is the inclusion of peers as positive, social interaction role models and facilitators of social behaviors. Peers between the ages of 11 and 17 are recruited and complete an application process.

Volunteer counselors. Volunteer counselors are recruited from graduate programs in special education and speech pathology through advertisements in statewide professional publications, and through AARC's training workshops and website. The four-day counseling experience is an invaluable training opportunity for teachers and other professionals where they can learn and practice strategies to support persons with ASD.

Volunteer and Peer Training

The volunteers and peer models receive two days of training; the first takes place a few weeks prior to camp, and the second just before their session begins. Volunteer counselors and peers also are invited to attend AARC workshops free of charge for additional training. Training includes detailed information regarding what to anticipate at camp and the expectations of counselors, peers, and campers. Possible scenarios are role-played and discussed. The importance of understanding ASD, providing needed accommodations, and addressing sensory needs is emphasized. Strategies to facilitate social skills and social problem solving at camp are taught.

Peers are also given introductory information on ASD. They are encouraged to serve as role models demonstrating appropriate social behaviors and importantly, offer positive support for the efforts of the campers with ASD.

Preparing campers for the camp experience. Prior to camp, two booklets are sent to campers. The first is a description of the camp program with photos of the activities and locations. The second is "The Camp Determination Guide to Social Success" (see Figure 10.5) that introduces campers to some of the social problem-solving methods and types of positive social skills that are encouraged at the camp. These were developed by Kari Dunn Buron at Camp Discovery. Parents are encouraged to read the documents on several occasions with their child before camp begins.

Program Description

Each morning, counselors encourage independence by referring campers to visual supports to assist in the completion of morning routines. Counselors review the daily schedule, and each camper receives his or her own copy to keep throughout the day. During the day, campers engage in various activities with their camper groups. These activities may include horseback riding, swimming, canoeing, fishing, archery, art, and field and sports games. Structured sensory activities are used to increase sensory self awareness. Campers create "fidgets" and other sensory items to use throughout the week. Music and movement activities are facilitated by a music educator or therapist. Structured social skills lessons and stress management activities are facilitated by a speech and language pathologist or special educator.

Campers and counselors participate in a rest and relaxation period following lunch. Each camper is encouraged to participate in a relaxing activity. Campers may listen to music on headphones, play a quiet game, read, sleep, etc. Counselors model rest by relaxing themselves.

After dinner, special events are planned. The first night, a scavenger hunt orients campers to various locations across the campsite to preview the week's activities. Other nights might involve a carnival, a magician's performance, a basic yoga class (to demonstrate a form of stress management), a campfire, or a hayride. No camper is forced to participate in any activity that he or she does not choose to participate in or that may cause anxiety for him or her.

Accommodations

Camp Determination uses a number of individualized and camp-wide accommodations to support the campers. Positive reinforcement, structure, and consistency are central to all the activities. Staff encourage confidence and optimism and ensure that Camp Determination is a place where all campers feel like they belong and are accepted for who they are.

Visual supports for activities. Visual supports are present throughout the campsite. Visual supports may be in a written or pictorial format that depict the steps of various activities, chores, daily living skills, and various visual reminders. For example, pictures of the sequence of steps for tooth brushing, showering, preparing for the day, preparing for bed, and washing hands are located in the cabin areas. Visual reminders are displayed that prompt campers to: drink plenty of water, apply bug spray, and use sunscreen. In the dining hall the expectations for setting tables and cleaning up are provided in pictorial and written formats.

Visual supports for social behavior. Social skills and stress management techniques are also facilitated visually. For example, around camp one finds visual reminders to encourage and compliment others. Self-management visuals are also used when needed. For example, a visual reminder of how to respond to a stressful situation, known as "Calm Down Strips," (as discussed in Chapter 7, Figure 7.8) are used. Staff finds that the use of visuals to support self-management reduces the campers' anxiety and increases independence.

Social problem solving and social skills. Camp Determination uses the same strategies as Camp Discovery to promote positive social behavior. For example, when two or more campers have a misunderstanding, or one camper is frustrated with another, their counselor draws a series of pictures where the situation that occurred is reviewed through the use of stick figures with speech and thought bubbles. The campers' perspectives on the conflict that has transpired are drawn out through the process, and this helps the campers identify the source of the misunderstanding (Gray, 1994). Another strategy used to promote social skills is the "Compliment Map," (see Figure 10.5) with which a counselor helps a camper remember positive qualities about each of their cabin mates that they then can share as compliments. When a camper offends another camper, he or she is prompted to either verbally apologize or to write a "Sorry Note." "Consequence Maps" are used to visualize and discuss all the various consequences of certain actions. Structured social skills lessons are also provided each day.

Camp Determination is a program focused on serving children with Asperger's Syndrome and on training professionals. In addition to offering a comprehensive array of outdoor activities, useful strategies for supporting campers' social problem solving and for developing social skills among campers are integral to the camp.

Camp Royall
Autism Society of North Carolina (ASNC), Moncure, NC

With thanks to Becky Cable, Assistant Director, Camp Royall who wrote portions of this material.

Introduction

In 1972, the Autism Society of North Carolina (ASNC) began a residential summer camp program for individuals with ASD. In its first year, the program was held for one week and served six campers. In 1997, ASNC built its own camp, called Camp Royall, and in 1998, ASNC added a second location for a more active outdoor program, called Western Camp. In 2002, 400 individuals with ASD attended one-week sessions at one of the two locations. Campers are residents of North Carolina ranging in age from four to adulthood. Ability levels vary widely from individuals who are nonverbal who need one-on-one supervision and have severe cognitive disabilities to individuals who lead independent lives. On average, 32 campers attend each session, but the number can vary from 24 to 36, depending on the supervision needs of the campers. The camp programs are paid for by a combination of state funding, private contributions, and camper fees.

Philosophy and Goals of the Camp

The philosophy of ASNC's summer camp programs is to provide the campers a structured day of typical camping activities, with an emphasis on the campers' enjoyment. The camp experience is designed to encourage appropriate behavioral, social, and recreation development while the camper is away from home. Further, the camp provides a respite for families and training for camp staff who are working toward careers in the field of human services. Lastly, Camp Royall serves as a model recreation program for individuals with ASD and offers information and consultation to organizations interested in beginning similar programs (see Appendix C for contact information).

Partnership with Division TEACCH Program

ASNC has a unique partnership with a consultation and training group known as Division TEACCH (Treatment and Education of Autistic and Related Communication Handicapped Children) to develop activities and accommodations, train the camp staff, and support campers (Schopler, Mesibov, and Heasey, 1995; see also Appendix C for contact information). Division TEAACH is a department of the School of Medicine at University of North Carolina-Chapel Hill, and an international leader in research and interventions for individuals with ASD. One of Division TEAACH's most important contributions to the ASD field is the development of "Structured Teaching," which uses visual cues and organizational structures to help individuals with ASD understand tasks and instructions. A TEACCH–trained consultant is on-site every day during the camp season to facilitate "Structured Teaching" techniques.

Building a Camp Facility for Individuals with ASD

After 25 years of renting other camps, ASNC was able to build their own site in 1997. The camps they had rented previously were not designed to accommodate the sensory needs of individuals with ASD. A committee of parents, TEACCH consultants, and camp staff worked with the architects to design cabins, a dining hall, an activity center, and a gym that contained multiple private rooms where one or a few individuals could get away from activity, people, and noise. Additionally, all buildings and facilities are fully accessible.

Cabins. The cabins consist of a screened porch and two separate wings joined by a common area and two bathrooms. One wing of the cabin accommodates up to nine in a shared sleeping space. The other wing consists of six private rooms. The large number of private rooms allows ASNC to offer up to half of the campers attending a session a private sleeping room if needed.

Dining hall. The dining hall can seat 84 people in the main room, ten people in a small conference room, and up to six more in an even smaller room. A large porch is attached to the front of the dining hall. Campers who have a restricted diet can eat separately and at a distance from foods they are not allowed to eat. Campers with auditory sensitivities can eat in a quiet room or on the porch.

Activity center and recreation complex. These buildings include a main activity room, as well as smaller activity rooms and quiet rooms. Thus, large and small group and individual activities can be held at the same time. The quiet room is also a place where campers can go to get away from sensory stimulation and where they can relax.

Staffing

The staff for both camps consists of directors, activity directors, counselors, and on-call nurses. Staff members are typically students recruited from universities, and they are selected on the basis of skills, experience, and a sincere interest in the welfare of individuals with ASD. All of the staff is paid. Staff can also receive college credit.

The activity directors plan, set up, and run activities. They put visual structures in place for the group as a whole. Each counselor is responsible for one or two campers. The counselors make any adaptations necessary for their individual camper(s). About one-half of the campers require constant one-on-one supervision. The remaining campers are paired with other campers of comparable age and skill levels and these groups are supervised by counselors. Occasionally, a camper may require two staff for part or all of the day.

Camp Royall also provides employment opportunities for individuals with ASD. For the past few years, 15-20 adults with ASD have worked at the camp performing such jobs as setting and clearing the tables, washing dishes, helping with food preparation, cleaning bathrooms and cabins, removing the trash, and assisting with the preparation for the camp activities.

Staff Training

Camp Royall has carefully developed its approach to training using TEAACH approaches. Camp Royall invites nine or ten campers with ASD to attend camp during the counselor training week. Professional trainers from TEAACH and ASNC act as counselors with the training campers modeling the proven TEAACH techniques in the camp environment. The campers who attend camp during the training week represent a diverse range of ages and ability levels. Some participants are verbal; others do not speak at all. It is the intent of this training week to introduce the counselors to the variety of issues and behaviors that they will encounter during the summer.

Trainers present information in a variety of ways and then have counselors apply what they have learned. Mornings are spent in information sessions. Topics such as characteristics of ASD, receptive and expressive communication, structured teaching, behavior management, and development of appropriate programming are discussed. Each afternoon, the counselors first observe the trainer's work with the training campers and then they practice themselves while the trainers provide supervision and feedback. Then the counselors fill out worksheets that focus their attention on the concepts discussed, demonstrated, and practiced that day.

As the trainers are working with the training campers, many learning opportunities unfold. If a trainer finds that they need to change their approach on the spot, they share aloud their thinking process as they do so. This lets counselors know what the trainer changed and why. The trainers demonstrate how to provide information and guidance to the camper using visual structures, positive reinforcement, and sensitivity to ASD. After staff training week, TEACCH consultants are available to staff throughout the summer.

Program Description

Campers participate in a structured program that incorporates a wide variety of indoor and outdoor activities. A consistent schedule is developed for each day during the session. After breakfast, campers sing songs and participate in an outdoor activity, such as boating, hiking, or field games. This is followed by structured recreation in the gym and a juice break. The campers are then divided into two groups. One group goes swimming at the pool, while the other goes to arts and crafts, and then they switch. This is followed by lunch and rest time in the cabins. The afternoon consists of more swimming and indoor activities, as well as group music time. After dinner, special events are held, such as carnivals, dances, and water games. After an evening swim at the pool, it's time for showers and lights out.

The arts and crafts directors lead the craft and indoor activities. The activity center is divided into different areas and each one is separated from the others by physical barriers such as shelves, benches, etc. The largest section in the activity center has worktables and shelves of supplies for individualized craft or visual motor, tabletop activities. Each tabletop activity is numbered with written instructions on a box of materials. This level of organization and visual clarity promotes independence.

The field activities director visually organizes field activities with arrows and lines which help campers understand where to go and what to do. An obstacle course is one example. Campers crawl through a tunnel, walk a balance beam, etc. Another structured activity is comprised of a number of stations, such as ring toss, tee ball, bowling, shooting a ball in a hoop, etc. Group relay races and adapted sports (e.g. soccer) are also structured to provide visual cues and instructions.

> **Box 10.6** While the openness of the "great outdoors" makes it more difficult to visually indicate the boundaries of an activity, for some campers there are advantages to being outside. The acoustics are much better, so campers who are sensitive to noises are not as likely to be overwhelmed by excessive sounds. The outdoors permits more physical activity, which is very important especially for campers with high energy levels.
> — *Becky Cable, Assistant Director, Camp Royall*

Accommodations

Camp Royall uses a wide variety of accommodations for individuals with ASD.

Preparing the individual for the camp experience. The camp staff encourages the parents/care providers to help prepare the individual for their stay at camp. Parents are urged to provide resources and help with this transition process. On the camp's website there are pictures of the camp and the typical daily schedule, which parents can use to explain camp to their children. Parents and campers can visit camp beforehand to see where campers will sleep, eat, etc.

Use of the individual's communication system. On the information forms (see chapter 5, Figure 5.3) families and teachers are asked to describe the receptive and expressive communication system the individual uses, and whether the individual has any specific rigidity about the system, (e.g., it must be in a certain color, etc.) This information is reviewed, and, if needed, the system is brought with the individual for use at camp.

Individual camp schedule. Each camper receives an individual schedule appropriate to his/her level created by his/her counselor . Schedules are available in four different formats that vary in the level of symbolic representation used to depict events. The four formats are (1) written, (2) line drawings, (3) photos, and (4) a backpack of objects representing the activities (e.g., a toy fish and pole for fishing).

Home/camp schedule. Another schedule helps campers understand when they will go home. The home/camp schedule is a weeklong calendar that visually depicts the camper coming to camp on Sunday, being at camp Monday through Thursday, going home on Friday, and being at home on Saturday. Photos of camp and the camper's home are used in the schedule. The camper draws an "X" over each day as it ends. Campers can look at their schedules to see how much longer until they go home.

Visual structure throughout the camp site and facilities. All activities and areas are visually structured to be easier to understand; arrows and footsteps on the floor show where to go, colored tape defines areas, and objects are color-coded. Pictures and line drawings are used everywhere to provide visual instructions.

Using TEAACH Structured Teaching principles to adapt field activities. Camp Royall has taken traditional games and activities and revised them so that they are structured and visually represented. For example, the campers engage in a variation of soccer practice. Carpet squares are laid out in the field, forming a line of alternating squares running down to the goal. Campers stand on each square, and a camper kicks the ball to the person on the square across from them. This continues until the ball reaches the person closest to the goal, who then kicks it into the goal. The campers rotate so that everyone gets an opportunity to make a goal. The activity structures the kicking and receiving involved in soccer in a way that is visually clear.

Music therapy. Every afternoon campers have a session of music therapy. Visual representations of the characters and actions in songs have been prepared for use during singing. For example, if the campers are singing Old MacDonald, pictures of every animal

are available. Campers who are nonverbal can select the correct animal picture or object as the corresponding verse is sung. The group also tells stories through singing. Each person in the group is a different character and each character plays a certain instrument. When their character appears in the story-song, they play their instrument. Thus, the activity is structured with clear sequencing and cues for taking turns.

Photo by Jason Kinch Photographics, Courtesy of Mt. Hood Kiwanis Camp

Activity Stations: Visually Organizing Camp Activities. Many of the small group or individual activities at the camp are set up at stations. These stations are organized according to structured teaching guidelines with visually represented instructions and components of the task displayed in a clear, unambiguous manner. Each activity is organized sequentially with visuals that indicate where to start and when the activity is finished. Color-coding is used to distinguish different aspects of the activity. Tape or other materials are used to mark boundaries (as described in Chapter 6). Activity stations are used for both indoor and outdoor activities.

When an activity is set up as a TEAACH task, campers with ASD can understand more clearly what the activity is, decide whether or not they want to choose it, and then are able to do the task more independently. Without the visual structure and cues, the individual is dependent on others' verbal statements to explain the task. Verbally provided information is often more difficult for the individual with ASD to understand.

A simple example of an activity station is a color-matching game. A camper takes a box of a specific color and then searches an outside area where many balls of different colors have been scattered about. The goal is to find all the balls that match the color of the box and put them into the box. Staff find that many campers enjoy this activity, including those campers who are very low functioning.

Transitions between activities. Moving from one activity or one location to the next is often difficult for persons with ASD. Sometimes it may appear that a camper is obstinate because he or she does not want to stop doing one activity to go to the next. This may occur because he or she does not understand what the counselor is expecting him or her to do. To help clarify what is going to happen next and to turn the transition itself into a more structured activity, a picture or representational object of the next event can be given to the camper. The camper carries it to the next activity as a visual reminder of where he/she is going.

The staff also anticipates which transitions, such as moving from an active to a more sedentary activity, might be difficult for campers. For example, after campers have been engaged in exciting, gross motor activities in the field, it can be hard to transition to a more sit-down, fine motor task, such as arts and crafts. To ease this transition, when campers first go to arts and crafts, they first do an activity that they have done before in school, which is easy and familiar to them, such as drawing. This familiarity helps them to relax and shift into fine motor tasks, then campers transition more easily to a complex or novel craft project.

Changes in schedule and waiting in between activities. Some changes in the routine are unavoidable, such as bad weather or a temporary closing of the pool for cleaning. To minimize the effect that changes may have on the campers, the staff tries as best they can to prepare the campers for it. This may involve telling them or showing them what the change in routine consists of, and giving them reassurance. Waiting is also very difficult for many individuals with ASD, so periods of time between activities are structured as well. This can be accomplished by having a preferred activity on hand (e.g., bubbles, a puzzle, a simple work task, a radio, etc.) or by taking a break in a rocking chair.

Taking a break. Parents fully describe on the information form how the camp staff can determine if an individual is getting upset, when this commonly occurs, and how this is typically handled. Many of the campers have a specific way to communicate that they need a break. For example one man takes a green card out of his pocket. Others have a card with "help" written on it. The camp staff members use whatever system the individual uses at home, school, or work.

Camp Royall is a unique example of a camp built from the ground up to accommodate individuals with ASD. The extensive use of structured teaching principles throughout the program makes Camp Royall a resource for other camps and recreation programs regarding these methods. Advice from the camps' directors are offered in Figure 10.7.

Figure 10.7
Advice from One Camp Program: Camp Royall

The Camp Royall directors offer the following advice to persons operating a specialized camp for individuals with ASD:

- Find well-trained professionals to assist as consultants and staff.
- Train your staff well and create an on-going learning environment for staff.
- Use visual communication and physical structure, such as the TEAACH Structured Teaching throughout your camp locations and activities.
- Provide individualized attention for campers.
- Understand that the motivations of individuals with ASD are different from ours.

Strategies Used in Camp Programs to Support Individuals with ASD

In this chapter the methods that two day camps and five residential camps use to support and accommodate individuals with ASD were described. Four of the camps offered an inclusive program and two offered specialized programs. In all of these camps, similar strategies and accommodations have been developed and implemented to provide a fun camp experience for children and adults with ASD. A summary of these key accommodations across camps, as well as unique and noteworthy features of specific camps, conclude this chapter.

Most of the camps have established a process whereby staff gathers information about the individual with ASD from parents/caregivers and teachers/vocational supervisors before the individual attends the program. This information is used to plan accommodations and the level of staffing support required for the individual.

Individuals with ASD are prepared ahead of time for the camp experience. They may visit the site and meet staff. They may receive a written description with photos of the programs and a visual schedule of the activities. Parents/caregivers are provided instructions on how to use the materials provided to talk about the camp experience, and discuss issues that may be sources of anxiety for their child. Parents may also send familiar and favorite objects or activities with their child to ease the transition between home and camp.

All of the camp programs use visual accommodations extensively to help campers with ASD understand the camp program. An individual's own visual communication systems for expressing needs and wants is sent to camp and augmented with camp vocabulary and symbols for use in the camp environment. Visual schedules are used to explain each day's activities, the transition from home to camp, and later from camp back to home. Physical locations and boundaries of areas are visually identified. Camp activities and tasks are analyzed, and then each step is visually depicted in mini-schedules and diagrams. The role of individuals during camp activities is also clarified with visual cues. Activity descriptions are used to explain camp activities beforehand. Visual and written materials are used to explain social situations and to engage in social problem solving.

Taken together, the visual systems used in these camp programs give recreation providers in camps, and in other recreation programs, an idea of what a totally visually explicit and visually structured environment can look like. Often autism specialists and parents see themselves as interpreters for individuals with autism. They interpret by creating visual information that translates for the individual with ASD how the world is organized and operates. These residential camp programs provide an opportunity to observe how all aspects of daily life and activities can be visually translated.

Moreover, the inclusive camps report that such a visually explicit environment does not interfere with the experience of individuals without ASD. Indeed, the visual structure helps the other campers and staff to share a consistent knowledge of the schedule, how to do activities, and the camp rules.

All of the camp programs have also developed ways to allow individuals with ASD to take a break, when they need to, from social situations and activity demands. A way to visually indicate "I want a break" is provided to each camper that fits his or her communication ability. Locations for taking a break are previously designated and may include a variety of quiet time and various sensory activities. Staff remains available to assist a camper taking a break as needed. This accommodation reflects the awareness that, a new environment, new people, new activities as well as the active and social nature of a camp can be a source of stress for individuals with ASD. Knowing that they can take a break if needed reduces anxiety for campers with ASD, and the break itself allows them to regain the equilibrium they need to rejoin the activity.

Several camps have partnered with university programs. The camps offer training experiences for undergraduate and graduate students. They also utilize consultants from universities and autism centers to train their staff and develop the program and accommodations. Such partnerships have been an opportunity to achieve adequate staffing at a lower cost, and at the same time gain assistance in program development.

The four inclusive camps have developed successful strategies for creating a program equally enjoyed by individuals with and without ASD. By creating a fun and exciting program of activities, the opportunity for reverse mainstreaming in which children without disabilities join in activities, is created. Another approach has been to train peers as camp buddies to help facilitate the participation of the camper with ASD while enjoying the camp activities themselves.

And lastly, throughout the six camps, some unique strategies and features are of note for other camp programs, as well as for the broader recreation community. Camp Awareness is an example of how a parent can create a camp program by creatively bringing together many resources. Camp Kyowa and Operation Access are two viable approaches to an inclusive program sponsored by parks and recreation departments. Camp Royall is unique in that it was architecturally designed to best support individuals with ASD. Moreover, Camp Royall offers itself as a training site for other camps, and as a place to learn how TEAACH Structured Teaching can be applied in a camp setting. Camp Awareness, Camp Discovery, and Camp Determination have developed programs to meet the needs of children with Asperger's Syndrome. Taken together, these camp programs have developed useful strategies and accommodations for individuals with ASD.

Chapter Eleven

Recreation Programs Initiated by Parents

Mary Lou Vandenburg, Phyllis Coyne, & Ann Fullerton

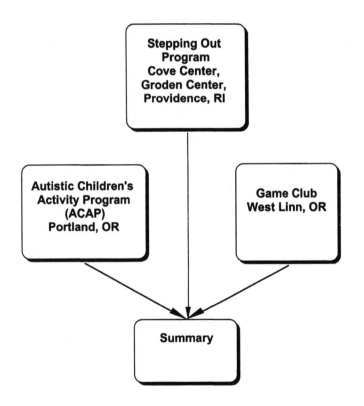

When children are young, most parents initiate and support their involvement in recreation activities. This may include developing groups, such as playgroups, for their child(ren). Parents of individuals with ASD may need to continue initiating and supporting their child's participation in recreation activities into adulthood. Parents frequently take leadership roles in existing programs, particularly youth service organizations, to enable their child to participate. Several examples of parent leadership in youth service organizations are presented in Chapter 9.

However, when parents look for recreation options for their child with ASD, an appropriate option may not be available or the amount of support that would be required to allow their child to participate in an already existing program may be too extensive. Because many recreation programs do not meet the unique needs of individuals with ASD, some parents have created new recreation programs specifically for their child(ren) with ASD.

Box 11.1

Christine Bruno has gone to great lengths to provide her four sons, three of whom have ASD, with opportunities to recreate. After many years of less than fully satisfactory experiences with generic recreation programs, she and her husband, Clifton, discovered that school districts could apply for funding for Indian Education (Title VII) and encouraged their district to write a grant application. Since their school district has received funding, Christine and Clifton have taken an active role in the Title VII program in their district as members of the parent advisory board and leaders of recreation activities. They have stayed involved expressly so that their sons could have meaningful leisure and recreation experiences with typical peers with their same Native American heritage. Now all four of their children along with 50 others in their school district regularly take part in activities that celebrate their heritage while having fun. Recently tribal elders taught the group to make a traditional drum, which was followed by a blessing ceremony. Through this experience they learned about leatherwork, art, music, dance and cooking of their culture. Two of Christine's sons with ASD have continued to pursue the art form that they were introduced to through this activity.

Parents of children with ASD are uniquely qualified to create programs. They know ASD intimately, know the needs of their children, frequently are motivated to have the most current information on ASD and bring diverse personal and professional skills. Many excellent programs have been developed or initiated by parents. The previous chapter, Chapter 10, features one camp that was initiated through parent effort.

This chapter highlights three programs that were initiated by parents to meet the recreational needs of their children. They include the Autistic Children's Activity Program (ACAP), Stepping Out Program at Groden Center, and Game Club.

Autistic Children's Activity Program (ACAP), Portland, Oregon

Autistic Children's Activity Program (ACAP) is a nonprofit organization that focuses on direct services needed for children with ASD. ACAP was founded in 1987 in Portland, Oregon by a group of parents who had met through the Autism Council of Oregon, an affiliate of the Autism Society of America. They shared a concern about the absence of services for their children during the summer. They hoped to remedy the interruption in their children's schedules and service delivery during holiday and school vacations. They were also aware that their children needed to learn more than what is addressed in most

school programs. They, therefore, focused on developing a program that
provided life skill training, community
integration and recreation experiences.

A major goal of the parents who
founded ACAP was to broaden access
and experience in the community for
their children. The primary program
that they began was the ACAP Summer Program.

The ACAP Summer Program is
a community-based education and recreation program specifically for children and adolescents with ASD ages 4
through 18 years of age. The focus is
to teach skills that are useful in the

Photo courtesy of ACAP

community through recreation, social, sensory and communication experiences. The intent is to integrate these children into their community as well as provide the structure and
supports these children must have to function in their community. It also provides opportunities for future educators and other professionals to gain firsthand experience with children with ASD.

Since its inception in 1987, the ACAP Summer Program has grown significantly.
The program began with one classroom serving seven children with ASD. In contrast, the
2002 ACAP Summer Program had nine classrooms at five sites throughout the Portland
metro area and Southwest Washington, which served a total of 100 children with ASD.
Most of these classrooms are in rented space in public schools. The children are placed in
classrooms based on their ages and needs.

Over time the ACAP staff has discovered that participants with similar interests and
abilities often enjoy being together. ACAP has tried classrooms that include children with
a variety of levels of ASD, but have found that higher functioning participants with ASD
often like to "hang out together." The unique needs of these participants can be addressed
when they are grouped together. Many of the participants have learned from each other
and many lasting friendships have been established because of shared experiences. Some of
these higher functioning participants also enjoy helping others.

> **Box 11.2** Harry works in a classroom with higher functioning children with ASD who
> are younger than he is as a role model and buddy two days a week. This
> "pays" for his tuition to the classroom with his same age peers two addi-
> tional days a week.

Funding

As in most private, nonprofit organizations, funding is an ongoing concern. Funding
comes from a variety of sources. Fees for the program paid by school districts as part of
Extended School Year, parents, Oregon Office of Developmental Disabilities, and private
sources only cover a portion of the program's actual cost. Additional funding comes from
foundation grants and fundraising events. As ACAP has built capacity, parents have been
relieved that they no longer have to do all the fundraising themselves.

Staffing

The staffing pattern of ACAP has changed over the years. For the first five years of the program, a dedicated parent volunteered to coordinate ACAP and the only paid staff were the teachers. Now ACAP has many paid staff. These include:

- Executive Director, who is responsible for administrative functions of the overall organization, such as contracts and funding.
- Human Relations Coordinator, who hires staff, gets substitute staff as needed, and ensures that the right number of staff are in each classroom. This person has the vital task of matching compatible personalities of staff and participants in each classroom.
- Program Supervisor, who provides staff training and supports classroom staff. This person oversees the classroom structure, develops behavior plans and problem solves needs of staff, parents and participants particularly during crisis.
- Assistant Program Supervisor, who designs and makes most of the visual supports and teaches staff how to use these supports.
- Teachers (certified special education teachers), who supervise and are responsible for the overall management of their class.
- Assistants, who facilitate the participation and learning of one or two of the participants and are with the child(ren) at all times. The assistants also develop visual supports on the spot, as needed.

Staffing is planned for the safety of both the child and staff, and varies from a one-to-one ratio to one-to-two ratio depending on the needs of the child. The average staffing ratio is two staff to three children.

Staff Training and Preparation

One of the key ingredients in making ACAP successful is staff training. Classroom staff are paid for five days of training and program preparation before the start of the Summer Program every year. This training is vital to the success of the program, since there is a high turnover of staff from year to year. The basic content of this training is presented in Figure 11.1.

Figure 11.1
Staff Training and Preparation for the ACAP Summer Program

Monday: Teachers only.
- Review how to run an ACAP classroom
- Review the ACAP Summer Program procedures notebook
- Discuss how to manage assistant staff

Tuesday:
- Basic information on ASD.
- Information on ACAP, its philosophy and vision.
- How to develop and use a variety of visuals, such as trip books and mini-schedules.

Wednesday:
- How to write and present social stories.
- Plan a sample community outing and put the visuals together for that trip. Take the trip, if there is time.

Thursday and Friday:
- Meet with parents to discuss expectations and any questions.
- Each ACAP participant meets his or her teacher and staff meet the child.
- Set up the physical environment of individual classrooms.
- Each classroom staff plan together for each child in their classroom.

The comprehensive procedures notebook for teachers, that is reviewed on the first day of training, is an ongoing resource for teachers at ACAP Summer Program. This notebook includes the requirements of the job, all the forms that the teacher will need, field trip ideas, recipes, examples of visuals, and resources.

The effectiveness of the training program is clear when trained staff are compared to untrained staff. Some staff may be hired after the beginning of ACAP Summer Program. Although attempts are made to give these staff adequate information, they consistently do not understand ASD as well and make more mistakes that lead to power struggles. They also do not use visual supports as consistently or effectively as the staff who have participated in the ACAP training. This is an ongoing issue addressed by the program administrators.

Schedule of the ACAP Summer Program

All the classrooms have similar schedules, which is represented in Figure 11.2. The consistency of the schedule facilitates learning for children with ASD. Because many school districts use this program as Extended School Year, approximately an hour in the morning is spent on Individualized Education Plan (IEP) academic goals and objectives to prevent regression.

Figure 11.2
A Typical Day at ACAP Summer Program

- 9:00 Free Time
- 9:15-10:15 Group time: Younger children review the trip books which are the schedules for the outings; higher functioning children plan the community outing for the day. Both groups also work on IEP goals.
- 10:30 - 2:00ish Community activity
- When the children return, at least three days a week they "journal" about their day.

Community Activities

Community outings are taken every day. The participants ride mass transit or walk to their destination. Because of this, the locations of classrooms must be near buslines and playgrounds. If the bus stop is too far, the participants get too tired walking or it causes safety issues. Also, if it is not a direct line to sites or at least a good transfer line, there are too many transitions.

Having a small class size is vital for safety and enjoyment during community activities. Usually no more than seven children should attend a class at one time. If the class is too large, it can be unmanageable in the community and call attention to the group. A variety of activities occur during community outings.

Activities. Children have many different experiences in the community during ACAP Summer Program. They go swimming one day a week and to a fast food restaurant one day a week. They take trips to various other locations in their community on the other three days of the week. These trips include activities, such as:

- Playing with local children at a variety of parks
- Going to free concerts or puppet shows in the parks
- Going to the zoo

- Going to museums that have hands on experience, such as the Oregon Museum of Science and Industry or the Children's Museum
- Going to county fairs
- Eating at pizza parlors and playing video games there
- Going to gyms featuring gymnastics equipment
- Playing miniature golf
- Horseback riding
- Bowling
- Roller skating
- Playing in water fountains
- Going to the public library
- In addition, higher functioning participants take tours of different places such as industries, two to three times a summer.

Box 11.3

"I would never have taken my son on mass transit to go to a destination, but ACAP did and they "stretched" my son more than I would have been able to."

—*Mother of boy who attended ACAP Summer Program*

Many appropriate behaviors are practiced and learned during community activities, such as learning to wait in line, wait for the bus and wait for food in a restaurant. Social and behavioral IEP goals are worked on during the community outings. Frequently these appropriate behaviors and structured experiences expand a participant's future opportunities to be in the community. In addition, these experiences provide exposure to activities that may continue to be developed as a leisure pursuit.

Box 11.4

One mother related the following story of how she used her son's experience planning community outings at ACAP Summer Program to move beyond isolating himself in his room:

Her son had been isolating himself and would not come out of his bedroom all weekend. She had tried offering more privileges, special food, and other rewards that had worked in the past, but nothing would motivate him. She finally remembered that he had to plan community outings at ACAP and thought she might be able to use the same approach with him. She told him they had to go on a community outing and he needed to help plan it. He immediately came out of his room and planned the outing. He had become very comfortable with the planning process and structure of the community outings at ACAP. Using this link to ACAP gave him the confidence and the motivation he needed to come out of his room and get out among people.

Individuals with ASD may do something in one environment but have difficulty transferring these skills to other settings. However, generalization can occur by using a similar approach in the new situation.

After the community outing, the individuals return to their classroom base. There, they review what happened during the community outing. They may do this by talking about what had happened, reviewing their "trip book," or they may write about what happened.

Supports

Many types of supports are used to make participants successful in ACAP Summer Program.

Preparation. Participants are prepared for what will be happening in a number of ways.

- *Calendar of events*. Before each two-week period of ACAP, every parent and child is given a written and/or picture calendar of activities for that period.
- *Trip books*. Trip books utilize line drawings, logos, and photos to provide a visual sequence of the community outing for the day. They are first presented in morning group time. The majority of the participants understand what line drawings represent, but real objects may be used if a participant needs a more concrete level of representation to understand. The trip book provides information about what bus the class will be taking, where they are going, what they will do when they get there, how long the outing will last, and what they will do when they get back. The trip books were developed by two dedicated parents to address the difficulty in organization and sequencing information for the ACAP participants. The trip books fit in the assistants' backpacks for review before each transition during the community activity. Each time an activity depicted is finished, the picture representing it is turned over. This helps participants track the steps in the outing. Parents can also check out the trip books.
- *Social Stories*. Social stories are developed to prepare the participants for some community activities. Social stories, as discussed in Chapter 6, are short stories written to provide social assistance. ACAP staff have developed a notebook of commonly needed Social stories that can be further individualized for a participant.
- *Preteaching*. For some community activities the staff preteach the steps of the activity. For instance, they may make a list of steps and have the participants practice all the steps in the classroom before going into the community.

> **Box 11.5**
>
> Miki was very hesitant to go swimming. The staff prepared her for the swimming activity by developing and presenting a social story about the upcoming swimming activity. In addition, they gave her a picture sequence of what to do in the locker room and answered her questions. The day arrived for her to go swimming and the activity went fine. When she got back someone asked her how it went. Her response was, "They didn't tell me I would get wet." The staff had forgotten to tell her what they thought was obvious. They had told her she would get in the pool, but did not tell her she would get wet. They had assumed if they told her or showed her in pictures that she would get in a pool, she would know that she would get wet. However, you cannot assume anything with individuals with ASD.

Staff cannot always anticipate all the information needed by an individual. The depth of detail needed by these participants has often taken even experienced staff by surprise. Even with verbal participants with ASD, what we may think is obvious needs to be taught directly.

Box 11.6

The teacher had carefully prepared her class to go to a local sit-down German restaurant. She had created checklists and practiced all the steps. Her class appropriately ordered and ate their meal together. However, when the waitress wanted to clear the table one of the boys got very agitated. Since it was not a step the participants would need to do, she had not included clearing the table in the checklist. The boy had only been to fast food restaurants previously and, therefore, thought clearing the table and putting his dishes in the trash was his job. He thought the waitress was doing something wrong.

Visual supports for participation. Visual supports are a cornerstone of ACAP. Without visual supports, community activities would be much more difficult, if not impossible. ACAP uses a variety of visual supports to help participants make sense of what is going on. Visual supports are used to prepare individuals for community activities (described in the preceding section), during the activity and to review what happened after the activity. Much time is spent creating visual systems for each participant. Some visual supports, like picture sequences of routines or a specific activity can be mass-produced. Other visual supports need to be developed for a specific participant for a specific activity.

For first-time participants in ACAP, these visual supports often need to be revised after staff know the participant better. When visual supports that are effective with the participants are described or sent by school districts, ACAP staff can implement the most effective visual supports sooner.

Trip books and social stories are used during the community activities, as well as to prepare the participants for these experiences. Some other visual supports used during community activities are:

- Expressive communication key rings: Even the most talkative participants with ASD have challenges in expressing themselves, particularly in new or otherwise stressful situations. Some participants may carry their own mobile communication system that was developed at school to express needs, wants and feelings. However, many do not have such a system. Staff carry individual picture and word representations of items participants may want to request on separate cards placed on key rings. These rings can be attached to backpacks or to an adult's belt loop. The line drawings and pictures are of frequently desired or needed items, such as drink, bathroom, wait, fidget toys, etc. If a child is having difficulties waiting for the bus, the staff member could hand him/her a key ring for the participant to request something that would help him/her wait, i.e., a fidget toy or a drink of water.
- Visual representations of routines: Routines such as dressing, taking showers, washing hands or toileting are presented in a sequence of pictures and/or words. This allows an individual to be as independent as possible without constant verbal directions from an adult. Figure 11.3 provides an example of a picture sequence for the locker room routine after swimming that is used with many of the participants. This version is for boys, and a similar sequence featuring a girl is used with the girls.

Figure 11.3
Boys Picture Sequence for the Locker Room

(Personal communication from S. Peters, November 18, 2002. Created with The Picture Communication Symbols©1981-2002 Mayer-Johnson, Inc. Used with permission).

- Universal "no" symbol: Although it is best to tell individuals with ASD what to do, rather than what not to do, some individuals respond well to the universal "no" symbol, a circle with a line through it. It can provide a very powerful message. Figure 11.4 shows the universal "no" sign to indicate, "no running."

Figure 11.4
"No Running"

(www.do2Learn.com)

- Other visuals supports: Some other visual supports that are used in ACAP include: money templates, visual boundaries, picture menus from fast food restaurants, checklists for what to bring on community outings, T-charts of what is okay to do and what is not okay to do, written rules, and cue cards. Figure 11.5 shows a sample checklist for community outings.

Figure 11.5
Checklist for Community Outings
S. Peters (personal communication, Novermber 18. 2002).

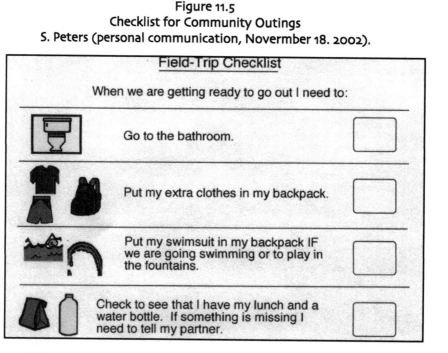

Created with The Picture Communication Symbols ©1981-2002 Mayer-Johnson, Inc. Used with permission.

Many visual supports are developed previous to activities, but not all the needs for visual supports can be anticipated ahead. Staff carry a backpack with some back up visual supports and keep yellow sticky notes or index cards with a pen in their pocket to provide visual information on the spot. An example of a picture sequence that was drawn on the spot is shown in Figure 11.6.

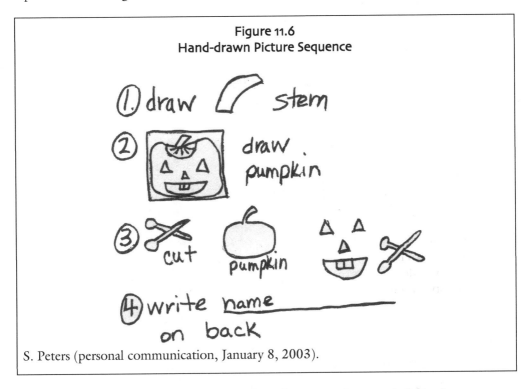

Figure 11.6
Hand-drawn Picture Sequence

S. Peters (personal communication, January 8, 2003).

If staff is caught without paper, they have been known to draw on their hands or arms to give participants the information that they need to be successful.

> **Box 11.7**
> The class had reviewed the trip book related to going to the zoo and was on the bus to the zoo. All was going smoothly until the bus went into a tunnel. Marty was confused and started screaming. His assistant immediately grabbed her pen and started drawing on her arm. Marty calmed down when he understood that there was only one tunnel and they were almost at the zoo.

Assistants: Many of the children require one-to-one assistants to ensure safety and learning. Other children can learn and be safe with one other child and one assistant.

ACAP Summer Program is an example of how a program developed by parents can offer opportunities and has a place in the array of options for participants with ASD. The founding parents and present ACAP staff have identified many successful strategies. Because of the success of ACAP, there is always pressure to have more classrooms and provide more programs. The staff realize that they cannot provide a program that meets everyone's needs. They have learned to accept that some children are too stressed by all the changes and sensory stimulation in the community to participate in the outings at this time in their life. ACAP staff continually assesses their resources and support so that they can be realistic about what they can do well. They believe that they need to maintain their present size to maintain quality.

Stepping Out Program at the Cove Center, a part of the Groden Center, East Providence, Rhode Island

The Groden Center in East Providence, Rhode Island is a nonprofit agency that provides a wide range of services to individuals with ASD and their families. Some of these services include assessment, intervention, education, residential programs, and research. One of the center's many programs is the Stepping Out Program. The Stepping Out Program is a social and recreation group for adults with ASD.

The program was initiated by parents of young adults with ASD in 1985, who asked the Groden Center to develop a program that would address the social, recreation, and community access needs of their adult children with ASD. The parents of the group members meet twice a year as an ad hoc parental board to oversee the program's operation. Annually, a barbecue is held for all family and group members.

Currently the Stepping Out Program has 34 adult members from 17 to 45 years of age. The purpose of the program is to provide a vehicle for the group members to discover and develop their leisure interests, explore and enjoy their community, and belong to a social support group.

The interests of the group members drive the selection of activities. The members meet quarterly to decide what activities they want to pursue. Some activities can be engaged in almost immediately, but others require more preparation and training. Once the activities are identified, the leader's goal is for each member to learn the skills necessary to engage in the chosen activity as independently and fully as possible. Thus, the members' recreation interests lead to other learning experiences that the leader provides to the group as a whole, to small groups or to individuals depending as needed. For example, the director might arrange an individual or small group lesson to learn a recreation skill that some members need before they can do an activity. She might teach members how to balance a checkbook, so that they can keep track of their money and/or save for a major trip.

Group Activities

The group meets regularly on Fridays and Saturdays and occasionally takes a weekend trip. Sailing lessons, parties, dances, and movie trips are some of the activities that the group has chosen. On weekends they have gone camping, horseback riding, sailing, etc. The group has also traveled to New York City for sightseeing, to Plymouth Plantations, and to amusement parks in Rhode Island and New Hampshire. The group is planning a vacation cruise to Bermuda and is currently in the process of learning how to save money and budget for this trip. Whatever the group members want to do or attempt, the leader tries to help them plan and do.

One regular activity of the group is exercise. Some members sign up for unified sporting events through the special recreation program of the local parks and recreation department. In this particular community, the local YMCA has generously given each individual a YMCA membership to use the pool and exercise equipment.

Group Size and Staffing

The number of participants in any particular outing depends on how many are interested in that activity. The group size for one event was 24. For a group this size, the leader brought along five to six staff members. When the group is large like this, they break up into small groups at the site. Two or more staff, depending on the complexity of the activity, accompany 12 to 14 members to an activity. For example, two leaders would accompany a group of this size to the movies.

Preparing Group Members for Outings and Activities

When the group has identified an activity or location that interests them, then the leader obtains pictures and information about the activity or site. These materials are used to prepare the group members for the activity. The leader and group members talk about what is involved in the activity and examine the pictures and descriptions together.

For all major trips, the leader puts together a brochure with key written information that explains what they will be doing. This customized trip brochure is sent out to all members and their families. Each member reads the brochure and parents provide additional information about the trip to their adult child. The brochure enables group members to make an informed choice about participation.

Changes Over Time

Over the past 15 years, the director has seen changes in the members' desire for their parents to be involved in their specific activities. When most of the group members were younger adults, they were not interested in their parents participating in their activities. The parents readily honored this desire for experiences separate from their family. But now, as group members have aged, these older adults are more interested in their parents joining them for some events and trips. If the group decides to invite parents on a trip with them, the trip is then made available to parents. The larger group can help reduce the cost of the trip.

Game Club, West Linn, Oregon

Box 11.8

"With our help, Dalton tried wrestling, trapeze, basketball, baseball and choir, but nothing worked out. Knowing how much he loved to swing, I enrolled Dalton in a trapeze and tumbling camp for kids. I thought he would really like the trapeze activities. He would not participate. In baseball, he would stand in the middle of the outfield and chase butterflies, put his mitt over his head, or look up at the clouds. Finally, when I asked him what he liked to do best, his answer was, 'Play videos games.' I was tired of forcing MY ideas of what activities kids his age like and started paying attention to what held Dalton's interest and brought him joy. Game Club was born."
Michelle Kuepker, mother of a boy with ASD and founder of Game Club

Game Club is a monthly video game club for children with higher functioning ASD five to 18 years of age, their siblings and parents. It was begun in 2000 to open "the doors of friendship through like interests." Michelle Kuepker and her husband, Steve, like many parents wanted their child to be part of a club or a group. Activities such as wrestling, basketball, baseball, and choir were all either a disaster for their son or for the other children involved. Michelle knew that her son needed to be involved in activities that interested him, if he was going to participate and potentially make friends. She decided it was up to her to develop a way for this to take place. Since her son liked to play games, especially video games, she decided to start a group that focused on these activities. Since she was part of a parent support group in her area, she knew that others with ASD shared these same interests. This was the beginning of a dream come true for Michelle and the many families who have participated in Game Club.

Game Club has grown considerably since it began in 2000. Approximately 25 people, including those with ASD, their siblings and parents, attended the first night of Game Club. The families were primarily from the parent support group that Michelle was part of. Word spread fast about this club. Now an average of 115 people attends each time. The highest attendance has been around 125 people, including those with ASD, their siblings and parents.

Parents have stated that this is a place where their son or daughter with ASD can shine when they may not have been able to fit in any other organized sport or activity. Interaction is encouraged in Game Club. However, some children may choose to be by themselves.

Community Support

Many people support Game Club. One reason that Game Club is successful is because of the support and the donation of West Linn Lutheran Church, community businesses and the parents. Game Club relies on donations, such as the use of the classrooms and TVs from West Linn Lutheran Church. The congregation and staff of the church are very supportive of this endeavor and have done many things to make it successful. The donation of the use of video projectors from InFocus Corporation means that the games can be projected on the walls for a larger group to enjoy. The donation of coffee and pastries from Burgerville USA enhance the experience for all. Parents bring additional games, snacks, portable fans during the hot summer months, and may contribute to the donation jar. All those involved donate their time.

Parent Involvement

Game Club is entirely organized and run by parents. Each parent is responsible for his or her own child(ren). Parents facilitate interactions, referee any disagreements and generally monitor what is happening in each of the rooms. Sometimes the parents join in; other times they read or let the children play on their own.

> Box 11.9 "When I walked into Game Club the first night, there was a sense of belonging. This was the place to be. My wife and I went home that evening and wrote all the dates for Game Club on our calendar so we wouldn't miss any."
>
> —*Parent of a child with ASD at Game Club*

Parents find support from each other at Game Club. When parents are not supervising in one of the rooms, they use Game Club as an informal support group. One parent stated that parent interaction was the best part. There are usually several conversations going on among parents at the same time. Some share stories about their child's experience at school. Others ask for advice on behavioral issues or names of doctors or dentists.

Many develop friendships through their interactions. The discussion is often so stimulating that parents try to simultaneously socialize and supervise from the open doorways to the game rooms. In addition, a resource table of information about support groups and upcoming events keeps parents informed of other opportunities.

Structure of Game Club

A different type of activity is set up in each room of the church building for Game Club. These include:

- One room with one or more Play Station and Super Nintendo systems connected to TVs or a projector that projects the games onto the wall.
- One room with two Nintendo 64 systems and a Sega Dreamcast. In the game rooms, several children play at a time. The other children usually watch as the game is being played or pace while they wait for a turn.
- One room with board games and trading cards, such as Pokemon or Yugio cards.
- One large room is used to project movies and Battlebot episodes. Recently, the main feature in the movie theater was old King Kong films with popcorn. Battlebots was added to make the activity even more interesting.
- A quiet room to calm down and/ or get away from stimulation. The quiet room has low lights and some materials that can provide tactile stimulation. Any individual who is overstimulated and needs to take a break from all the activity can use this room. During the evening, there is usually at least one individual in the quiet room. When there is more than one child in the room parents monitor the noise and activity level in the room.
- One room contains snacks that are donated or brought by the parents.
- A separate room for teenagers. After meeting for awhile, the parents discovered they needed a separate room for teenagers. This room has board games and card games more suited to teens. A handful of teens play Game Boy, Dungeons and Dragons and card games, such as Magic with each other. Some partner to play against another team and work together to try to win. The interaction between the teams is often lively with authoritative explanations of the game. Other teens in the room may be on their own, looking at or organizing their cards. Since Game Club does not allow teen-rated video games, no video games are played in this room.

| Box 11.10 | "It's a place to get away from the chaos...a place to unwind after a day's hard work...a place to hang out." |
| | —A Teenager at Game Club |

Rooms with Signs

Sign-up Board

Parents Talking

Resource Table

Game Room

Sign for Movie

Supports

Wait turn. Game Club has a procedure to help the children to wait their turn. The children are taught to write their name on the board under the last name on the board if they want a turn playing a video game. The names on the board provide a concrete cue to wait and a visual way to track whose turn it is. A timer is set and, when the timer goes off, the child who is playing knows it is time to get off the game and the child who is next knows that it is his or her turn to play. A parent generally facilitates this process of taking turns. Sometimes the child who is next has moved to another room, since it is hard for many to wait, and the parent has to find the child.

Visual supports. Visual supports are used at Game Club. Written expectations are posted on the walls. The name(s) of the activity(s) that takes place in a room is posted on the door of that room. Maps are posted to indicate the location of rooms.

Game Club provides an environment in which the visual-spatial strengths of youth with ASD can be used in enjoyable activities. It is a place where many find a fit that has eluded them elsewhere. In addition, some of the typically developing siblings see their brother or sister with ASD differently after they have enjoyed Game Club with them. In fact, it is often the youth with ASD who are helping others.

Many children thrive in this environment. However, Game Club is not for every child with higher functioning ASD. Many variables cannot be controlled at Game Club. Participants with ASD may become overstimulated or agitated by all the activity of people talking, occasional children yelling, potential crowding and simultaneous video games. A child may be prone to imitate what s/he sees in a game without being able to discern that it is pretend and may use what they have seen in other situations. Parents know their child best and usually know if their child might enjoy Game Club.

Box 11.11	"Do you know how to make Game Club better? Have it every Friday night." —*Participant at Game Club*

Some parents and children have expressed that they would like Game Club to meet more often. A Teen Game Club has already begun meeting on another night. Parents from other parts of Oregon are starting their own Game Clubs.

Summary

Parents initiate programs that are specific to the needs of their children. In this chapter, a summer program for children, a social recreation group for adults, and a club focused around games were described. Although all their children have ASD, the age, level of functioning and purpose of the program have lead to very different, but effective programs. Parents and staff use visual information to prepare, instruct and support individuals with ASD. Participants in the three programs reviewed in this chapter gain in leisure skills, as well as skills of daily living.

Appendix A

Resources

Appendix A contains selected resources for the following areas: program development, training of staff, visual supports, sensory supports, social supports, and behavioral supports. Some of the resources are annotated.

Personal Accounts Written by Individuals with Autism: A Partial Listing

Grandin, T. (1995). *Thinking in pictures.* New York: Doubleday.

Grandin, T., & Scariano, M. M. (1986) *Emergence: Labeled autistic.* Novato, CA: Arena Press.

Sinclair, J. (1992). Bridging the gaps: An inside-out view of autism (or, Do you know what I don't know?). In E. Schloper, & G. Mesibov (Eds.) *High-functioning individuals with autism* (pp. 294-302). New York: Plenum.

Ward, M., & Alar, N. (2000). Being autistic is part of who I am. *Focus on autism and other developmental disabilities.* 15(4), 232-235.

Williams, D. (1992). *Nobody nowhere.* New York:Times Books.

Williams, D. (1994). *Somebody somewhere.* New York:Times Books.

Willey, L. H. (1999). *Pretending to be normal.* London: Jessica Kingsley Publishers.

Resources for Program Development

Bullock, C., & Mahon, M. (1997). *Introduction to recreation services for people with disabilities: A person-centered approach.* Champaign, IL: Sagamore.

Center for Recreation and Disabilities Studies. (1993). *School-community leisure link: leisure education program.* Chapel Hill: University of North Carolina.

Center for Recreation and Disabilities Studies. (1991). *The wake leisure education program: An integral part of special education.* Chapel Hill: University of North Carolina.

Coyne, P., Nyberg, C., & Vandenburg, M.L. (1999). *Developing leisure time skills in persons with autism.* Arlington, TX: Future Horizons.

This book provides a comprehensive, structured approach for individuals with autism to develop leisure interests and skills for school, home and community. It provides practical information and guidelines to enable individuals with autism to develop competencies for choosing and engaging in enjoyable leisure activities.

Dalrymple, N. (1992). *Helpful responses to some of the behaviors of individuals with autism.* Bloomington, IN: Indiana Resource Center for Autism.

This 36-page booklet discusses comments that are often made about individuals with autism by people who do not understand the disability. After each comment, an explanation is provided based on an understanding of autism. Possible helpful responses for each comment are listed.

Dalrymple, N. (1989). *Learning to be independent and responsible.* Bloomington, IN: Indiana Resource Center for Autism.

This 11-page booklet discusses how people with autism build trust in people and environments through successful interactions, individualized support programs, utilizing positive instructional and environmental supports that lead to increased opportunities, choice, and motivation.

Dattilo, J. (1994). *Inclusive leisure services: Responding to the rights of individuals with disabilities.* State College, PA: Venture.

Department of Recreation and Leisure Studies (1997). *Project autism.* Chapel Hill: University of North Carolina.

Dodge, D.T., & Colker, L.J. (1988). *The creative curriculum (third ed.).* Washington, D.C.: Teaching Strategies, Inc.

Durand, V.M., & Crimmins, D. (1992). *Motivational assessment scale.* Topeka, KS: Monaco

Fine, A., & Fine, N. (1996). *Therapeutic recreation for exceptional children.* Springfield, IL.: Charles C. Thomas Publishers.

Howe-Murphy, R., & Charboneau, B.G. (1987). *Therapeutic recreation intervention: An ecological perspective.* Englewood Cliffs, NJ: Prentice-Hall.

Janzen, J. (1996). *Understanding the nature of autism.* San Antonio, TX: Therapy Skill Builders.

Moon, M.S. (1994). *Making school and community recreation fun for everyone: Places and ways to integrate.* Baltimore: Paul H. Brookes Publishing.

Prather, P. (2001). *Accessing recreation: Strategies for inclusion.* Portland, OR: The Arc of Multnomah County.

Rynders, J., & Schleien, S. (1991). *Together successfully: Creating recreation and education programs that integrate people with and without disabilities.* Arlington, TX: The Arc of the United States.

Schleien, S., Meyer, L., Heyne, L., & Brandt, B. (Eds.). (1995). *Lifelong leisure skills and lifestyles for persons with developmental disabilities.* Baltimore, MD: Paul H. Brookes.

Schleien, S., Ray, M., & Green, F. (1997). *Community recreation and people with disabilities: Struggles for inclusion.* Baltimore, MD: Paul H. Brookes.

Schmidt, G., McLaughlin, J., & Dalrymple, N. (1986). Teaching Students with Autism: A Sport Skill Specialist's Approach. *Journal of Physical Education, Recreation and Dance,* September 1986. pp. 37-48.

Sherrill, C. (1993). *Adapted physical activity, and recreation and sport: Crossdisciplinary and lifespan* (fourth ed.). Dubuque, IA: Brown.

Wagner, S. (1999). *Inclusive programs for elementary students with autism.* Arlington, TX: Future Horizons.

Walker, P., Edinger, B., Willis, C., & Kenney, M.E. (1988). *Beyond the classroom: Involving students with disabilities in extracurricular activities at levy middle school.* Syracuse, NY: Center of Human Policy.

Resources for Training

Autism Association of America

Scroggins, B., & Lewis, C. (1991). *Introduction to autism.* Bloomington, IN: Indiana Resource Center for Autism. Video. 30 minutes.

This tape covers key points from the Introduction to Autism: Self-Instructional Module. It is narrated specifically to provide a clear, accurate introduction to understanding the disability.

Resources for Visual Support

Do2learn, www.do2learn.com
This website provides over 1,000 pages of free printable visual material, as well as commercial products for making visual supports for children and adults with special needs.
Goosens, C., Crain, S.S., & Elder, P.S. (1994). *Communication displays for engineered preschool environments.* Solana Beach, CA.: Mayer-Johnson Company.
Gray, C. (1993). *Taming the recess jungle.* Arlington, TX: Future Horizons
Hodgdon, L. (1996). *Visual strategies for improving communication.* Troy, MI: Quirk Roberts Publishing.
This book highlights a multitude of tools using visual communication and supports, including samples of visual communication tools, aids to give effective direction and visual strategies to organize the environment.
Mayer-Johnson, R. (1994). *The picture communication symbols combination book.* Solana Beach, CA: Mayer-Johnson Co.
Schopler, E., Mesibov, G.B., & Heasey, K. (1995). Structured teaching in the TEACCH system. In E. Schopler, & G.B. Mesibov (Eds.), *Learning and cognition in autism* (pp. 243-268). New York: Plenum Press.
Structured Teaching and TEACCH can also be contacted at:
www.autism-info.com/teacch
TEACCH. (1992). *Visual Learners.* Chapel Hill, NC: University of North Carolina.

Web Sites for Visual Support:

http://www.Do2learn.com

http://www.news-2-you.com

http://roadmapsforautism.com

Software for Visual Supports:

There are software packages available that provide quick access and the opportunity to create customized symbols. Many examples of visual supports are provided in the book *Visual Strategies for Improving Communication* (Hogdon, 1995) and the Dotolearn website. For visual language boards, daily schedules, Social Stories:
Boardmaker, Mayer-Johnson Co. 1987-2000, PO Box 1579, Solana Beach, CA. 92975-7579. 800-588-4548. Mayer-Johnson.com
Inspiration, Inspiration Software, 7412 SW Beaverton-Hillsdale Hwy., Portland, OR. 97225-2167. 800-877-4292. www.inspiration.com
Kidspiration, Inspiration Software, 7412 SW Beaverton-Hillsdale Hwy., Portland, OR. 97225-2167. 800-877-4292. www.inspiration.com
PICTOCOM SE 1996. Zygo Industries, PO Box 1008, Portland, OR. 97207-1008. 503-684-6006. www.zygo-usa.com
Picture It, Pix-Writer & Pix-Reader, Slater Software, 351 Badger Lane, Griffey, CO. 80820. 877-306-6968. www.slatersoftware.com
Storybook Weaver, it is published by the The Learning Company, 6160 Summit Dr. No, Minneapolis, MN, copyright 1996.

Resources for Sensory Support

Anderson, E., & Emmons, P. (1996). *Unlocking the mysteries of sensory dysfunction: A resource for anyone who works with or lives with a child with sensory issues.* Austin, TX: Future Horizons.

Anderson. A. (1998). *Sensory motor issues in autism.* San Antonio, TX: Therapy Skill Builders.

Cautela, J.R., & Groden, J. (1978). *Relaxation: A comprehensive manual for adults, children and children with special needs.* Champaign, IL: Research Press.

Grandin, T. (1999). *Sensory challenges and answers.* Arlington, TX: Future Horizons. Video.

Haldy, M., & Haack, L. (1995). *Making it easy: Sensorimotor activities at home and school.* San Antonio, TX: Therapy Builders.

Huebner, R.A. (2001). *Autism: A sensorimotor approach to management.* Gaithersburg, MD: Aspen.

Kranowitz, C. (1998). *The out of sync child: Recognizing and coping with sensory integration dysfunction.* New York: Skylight Press.

Myles, B.S., Cook, K.T., Miller, N.E., Rinner, L., & Robbins, L.A. (2000). *Asperger's Syndrome and sensory issues.* Shawnee Mission, KS: AAPC.

Trott, M.L. (2002). *Oh behave! Sensory processing and behavioral strategies.* San Antonio, TX: Therapy Skill Builders.

Williams, M.W., & Shellenberger, S. (1996). *How does your engine run? A leader's guide to the alert program for self-regulation.* Albuquerque, NM: TherapyWorks.

Resources for Social Support

Gray, C. (1995). *Social stories unlimited: Social stories and comic strip conversations.* Jenison, MI: Jenison Public Schools.

Gray, C. (1994). *Comic strip conversations.* Arlington, TX: Future Horizons.

Gray, C. (2000). *The new social stories book: Illustrated edition.* Arlington, TX: Future Horizons.

This book details the author's concepts of writing and using social stories to increase social awareness and social understanding in children with Autism Spectrum Disorder.

Gray, C. (1994) Social assistance. In A. Fullerton (Ed.), *Higher-functioning adolescents and adults with autism: A teacher's guide.* TX: PRO-ED.

Gray, C. (1994). *The social story kit: Writing for students with autism and related disorders.* Arlington, TX: Future Horizons.

Gray, C. (2000). *Writing social stories with Carol Gray.* Three hour video. Arlington, TX: Future Horizons.

The Gray Center for Social Learning and Understanding
http://www.TheGrayCenter.org

Henning, J., Dalrymple, N., Davis, K., & Madeira, S. (1982). *Teaching social and leisure skills to youth with autism.* Bloomington, IN: Indiana University Developmental Training Center.

Heyne, L., Schleien, S., & McAvoy, L. (1996). *Making friends: Using recreation activities to promote friendships between children with and without disabilities.* Minneapolis: University of Minnesota.

Indiana Resource Center for Autism and Indiana University Public Television—WTIU (1991). Autism: Being Friends. Video. 8:08 minutes. Bloomington, IN: Indiana Resource Center for Autism.

This autism awareness videotape was produced specifically for use with young children. The program portrays the abilities of the child with autism and describes ways in which peers can help the child to be a part of the everyday world.

Johnson, A.M. (1998). *More social skills stories: Very personal pictures stories for readers and nonreaders K-12.* Solana Beach, CA: Mayer-Johnson Co.

Johnson, A.M. (1998). *Social skills stories: Functional picture stories for readers and nonreaders K-12.* Solana Beach, CA: Mayer-Johnson Co.

Quill, K. (1995). *Teaching children with autism: Strategies to enhance communication and socialization.* Albany, NY: Delmar Publishing Co.

Perske, R. (1988) *Circles of Friends: People with disabilities and their friends enrich the lives of one another.* Nashville, TN: Abingdon Press.

Reese. P.B., & Challenner, N.C. (1999). *Autism & PDD: Social skills lessons.* E. Moline, IL: LinguiSystems, Inc.

Snell, M., & Janney, R. (2000). *Social relationships and peer supports.* Paul H. Brookes.

Sprague, J., & Wilcox, B. (1984). *Organizing a social service club for handicapped and nonhandicapped students.* Bloomington, IN: Institute for the Study of Developmental Disabilities

Resources for Behavioral Support

Bambara, L.M., & Knoster, T.P. (1995). *Guidelines: Effective behavioral support.* Harrisburg, PA: Pennsylvania Department of Education, Bureau of Special Education.

Dalrymple, N. (1992). *Helpful responses to some of the behaviors of individuals with autism.* Bloomington, IN: Indiana Resource Center for Autism.

This 36-page booklet discusses comments that are often made about individuals with autism by people who do not understand the disability. After each comment, an explanation is provided based on an understanding of autism. Possible helpful responses for each comment are listed.

Dalrymple, N. (1988). *Managing behaviors in community settings.* Bloomington, IN: Indiana Resource Center for Autism. Video. 28 minutes.

This tape takes the viewer through the development of a philosophy, identification of the purpose of behaviors, and development of environmental and reactive plans. It includes individuals with autism visiting the dentist, working at Holiday Inn, and trips to ski slopes and lakes.

Davis, K. (1999). *Your attitude just might be my biggest barrier.* Article. Bloomington, IN: Indiana Resource Center for Autism.

Fouse, B., & Wheeler, M. (1997). *A treasure chest of behavioral strategies for individuals with autism.* Arlington, TX: Future Horizons.

Greene, R.W. (2001). *The explosive child.* New York: Harper Collins.

Hodgdon, L. (1999). *Solving behavior problems in autism.* Arlington, TX: Future Horizons.

This book highlights how to look for antecedents, understand common causes and how to use visual strategies to communicate expected behavior.

Horner, R.H., Carr, E.G., Strain, P.S., Todd, A.W., & Reed, H.K. (2000). *Problem behavior interventions for young children with autism: A research synthesis.* Paper presented at the Second Workshop of the Committee on Education Interventions for Children with Autism, National Research Council, April 12, 2000. Department of Special Education, University of Oregon.

Lovett, H. (1996). *Learning to listen: Positive approaches and people with difficult behavior.* Baltimore: Paul H. Brookes Publishing Co.

Myles, B.S., & Southwick, J. (1999). *Asperger's syndrome and difficult moments: Practical solutions for tantrums, rage and meltdowns.* Shawnee Mission, KS: AAPC.

O'Neill, R., Horner, R.H., Albin, R.W., Sprague, J.R., Storey, K., & Newton, J.S. (1997). *Functional assessment and program development for problem behavior: A practical handbook* (second ed.). Albany, NY: Brooks/Cole.

Pratt, C., & Buckmann, S. (2000). Supporting Students with Asperger's Syndrome. IRCA Articles, Access Autism www.lidc.indiana.edu/-irca/IRCAarticles/supporti.html

Center of Positive Behavioral Interventions & Support
http://www.ed.gov/offices/OSERS/IDEA/memo.html

Research & Training Positive Behavior Support Site
http://stpreos.uoregon.edu/stpweb/pbs/default.htm

Appendix B

Web sites

Below is a list of Internet sites that you might find of interest. This list is meant for informational use only and is not meant to be a comprehensive list. It is meant to be a helpful place to begin your search for current information related to autism. This should not be construed as an endorsement of any professionals, services, or facilities.

Note: When typing the web site addresses, unless otherwise specified, be sure to add the standard http:// before the www.

Autism and Asperger's Independent Living Association
http://www.amug.org/-a203/rec
Autism Center
http://www.patientcenters.com/autism/news/pdd47990601.htm
Autism Connection
http://www.autismconnect.org
Autism Intervention Movement
http://www.pitt.edu/'mrkool
Autism Network International
http://www.students.uiuc.edu/-bordner/ani.html
Autism Resources
http://www.autism-resources.com
Autism Society of America
http://www.autism-society.org/
see our web site for links to many ASA Chapters
Autism Research Institute
http://www.autism.com/ari
Center for the Study of Autism
http://www.autism.com/
Division TEACCH (Treatment and Education of Autistic and Related Communication
    Handicapped Children) University of North Carolina
http://www.teacch.com
Do2Learn
http://www.do2learn.com
Geneva Centre for Autism
http://www.autism.net
Indiana Resource Center for Autism
http://www.lidc.indiana.edu/-irca/IRCAarticles/supporti.html
Kentucky Department of Education's Technical Assistance Manual on Autism for
    Kentucky Schools
http://www.kde.state.ky.us/osis/children/autism/autismmanual.asp
MAAP (More Advanced Individuals with Autism, Asperger's Syndrome and Pervasive
    Developmental Disorder)
http://www.netnitco.net/users/chart/maap.html

National Alliance for Autism Research
http://www.naar.org
National Institute of Mental Health (NIMH)
http://www.nimh.nih.gov/publicat/autism.cfm
National Institute of Health and Human Development (NICHD)
http://www.nichd.nih.gov/autism/autism.cfm
NICHCY-National Information Center for Children
  and Youth with Disabilities
http://www.nichcy.org
O.A.S.I.S (On-line Asperger's Syndrome
Information & Support)
http://www.udel.edu/bkirby/asperger/
Oregon Department of Education's Technical Assistance Manual on Autism Spectrum
  Disorder
http://www.ode.state.or.us/sped/spedareas/autism/autres.htm
Syracuse University autism information
http://web.syr.edu/'jmwobus/autism
The Gray Center for Social Learning and Understanding
http://www.TheGrayCenter.org
University of North Carolina's Project Autism
http://www.unc.edu/depts/recre/crds/autism/three
Yale University: Asperger's Syndrome information
http://www.info.med.yale.edu

Appendix C

Organizations

Appendix C is organized into four sections:

- Contact information for the organizations described in this book by chapter.
- Selected organizations in the area of ASD
- Selected newsletters and journals in ASD
- Selected organizations in recreation

Some of the resources are annotated.

Organizations Described in this Book by Chapter

Chapter 1

The Autism and Asperger's Syndrome Independent Living Association
http://www.amug.org/-a203/rec

Chapter 2

National Recreation and Park Association
Address: 22377 Belmont Ridge Road
               Ashburn, VA 20148-4501
Phone: (713) 858-0784
Web site: http://www.nrpa.org

The Arc
Web site: http://www.thearc.org

The Arc of Multnomah County, Oregon
Address: 619 SW 11th
               Portland, OR 97205-2692
Phone: 503-223-7279

Chapter 7

Jay Nolan Community Services, Inc.
Address: 15501 San Fernando Mission Blvd
Suite 200
Mission Hills, CA 91345
Contact: Jennifer Lingell
Web site: http://www.jaynolan.org

Creative Living A Program of the Autism Society of North Carolina
Contact: Kelly Stone, CTRS, Recreation Therapist
Address: 1220 Nowell Rd.
Raleigh, North Carolina, 27607-5134
Phone: (919) 854-6161

Provincial Outreach Program for Autism and Related Disorders (POPARD)
Address: 4812 Georgia Street
Delta, British Columbia, Canada V4K2S9
Phone: (604) 946-3610
Contact: JoAnne Seip, Director

Provincial Resource Program (PRP) for Autism and Related Disorder
Address: 4615 - 51st
Delta, British Columbia, Canada, V4K2V8
Phone: (604) 946-4160
Contact: Kitty Doyle, Teacher in Charge

Gateway Society Services for Persons with Autism
Address: 4807 Georgia St.
Delta, British Colombia, Canada, V4K 2T1
Phone: (604) 946-0401

Chapter 8

Portland Bureau of Parks & Recreation, Portland, Oregon
Address: Disabled Citizens Recreation
Portland Bureau of Parks and Recreation
1120 SW 5th
Portland, OR 97232-2754
Contact: Kevin Mattias, Camp Director and Recreation Leader

Northern Suburban Special Recreation Program (NSSRA)
Address: 3105 MacArthur Blvd
Northbrook, IL 60062
Contact: Tracey Crawford, Superintendent of Recreation
Phone: (847) 509-9400
Web site: http://www.nssra.org
Email: info@nssra.org

Specialized Recreation Program, City of Eugene Recreation Services

Address: Hilyard Community Center
2580 Hilyard St.
Eugene, OR 97405
Contact: Molly Elliott, CTRS, Director
Phone: (541) 682-5311
Web site: http://www.ci.eugene.or.us/rec

Chapter 9

National 4-H Council

Address: 7100 Connecticut Ave.
Chevy Chase, MD 20815
Web site: http://www.n4h.org

4-H, Oregon Extension Service

Address: Oregon State University
Corvallis, OR 97331-3608
Phone: (541) 737-1737
Contact: Jim Rutledge, State Program Leader & Department Head
Email: Jim.Rutledge@orst.edu

Girl Scouts of the United States of America

Address: 420 Fifth Avenue
New York, New York 10018-2798
Phone: (800) 478-7248
Web site: http://www.girlscouts.org

Girl Scouts—Totem Council

Address: 3611 Woodland Park Ave. N.
Seattle, WA 98103-9704
Phone: (206) 633-5600
Web site: http://www.girlscouts.totem.org

Challenger Sports Division

Web site: http://www.challenger-sports.org

Lake Oswego Challenger Sports Division

Address: 2100 Hillside Dr.
Lake Oswego, OR 97034
Phone: (503) 635-9046
Contact: Joy Lee

Chapter 10

Camp Kyowa
Disabled Citizens Recreation, Portland Bureau of Parks and Recreation

Address: Disabled Citizens Recreation
Portland Bureau of Parks and Recreation
Portland, OR

Web site: http://www.parks.ci.portland.or.us
Contact: Kevin Mattias, Camp Director and Recreation Therapist

Operation Access Project
A Collaboration between San Francisco State University and
San Francisco Department of Parks and Recreation

Address: Department of Recreation and Leisure
                 San Francisco State University
                 1600 Holloway Ave
                 San Francisco, CA 94132
Contact: Allison Stewart, Program Coordinator, Operation Access

Camp Awareness

Location: Indianapolis, IN
Web site: http://www.campawareness.com
Contact: Susan C. Hansen, Director

Mt. Hood Kiwanis Camp for Children and Adults with Disabilities

Address: 9320 SW Barbur Blvd
                 Portland, OR 97219
Phone: (503) 452-7416
Email: mhkc@hevanet.com
Contact: Evelyn Coffey, Program Director

Camp Royall

Sponsored by Autism Society of North Carolina
Address: 250 Bill Ash Road
                 Moncure, North Carolina, 27605-1345
Phone: (919) 542-1033
Web site: http://www.autismsociety-nc.org/summer_camp.html
Contact: Becky Cable, Assistant Director

Camp Discovery

Address: 661 Ottowa Ave
                 St. Paul, MN 55107
Phone: Contact Autism Society of Minnesota at (651) 647-1083
                 for information. The camp serves members of the society.
Contact: Kari Dunn Buron

Camp Determination

Address: Autism Asperger Resource Center
                 4001 HC Miller Bldg
                 Kansas University Medical Center
                 3901 Rainbow Blvd.
                 Kansas City, Kansas 66160-7335
Phone: (913) 588-5988
Email: aarc@kumc.edu
Web site: http://www.autismasperger.org
Contact: Edna Smith

Chapter 11

ACAP (Autistic Children's Activity Program)
Address: P.O. Box 4606
            Portland, OR 97208
Phone: (503) 649-2066
Fax: (503) 649-9228
Contact: Rosemary Chapman, Executive Director

The Stepping Out Program at the Cove Center
Address: The Cove Center (part of Groden Center)
            866 Broadway
            East Providence, RI 02914
Phone: (401) 438-4994
Contact: Pat Fiske

Game Club
Phone: (503) 656-6026
Web site: http://www.gameclubonline.com
Contact: Michelle Kuepker

Selected Organizations in the Area of Autism Spectrum Disorder

Asperger's Syndrome Coalition of the United States
Address: PO Box 9267
            Jackson Beach, FL. 32240-9267
Phone: (904) 745-6741
Web site: http://www.asperger.org

Autism Society of America [ASA]
Address: 7910 Woodmont Avenue, Suite 650
            Bethesda, Maryland, USA 20814-3015
Phone: (301) 657-0881
            (800) 328-8476
Fax: (301) 657-0869
Web site: http://www.autism-society.org/

ASA promotes lifelong access and opportunity for all individuals within the autism spectrum, and their families, to be fully participating, included members of their community. Education, advocacy, public awareness efforts and the promotion of research are all goals of ASA. The society is the leading source of information and referral on autism to parents, professionals, and members of the general public who are concerned with this disability.

ASA has local chapters. A listing can be requested for individual states, and will assist with the start up of a local support chapter. They publish a bi-monthly newsletter, Advocate, that is free with membership and several brochures. There is a new parent packet, "Getting Started," that includes local sources of information, reading list, the Nichcy News Digest, and professional information. ASA also has a video, "Into The Light," from the International Conference in Toronto. Order forms are available.

Cure Autism Now

Address: 5455 Wilshire Blvd., Suite 715
                Los Angeles, CA 90036
Phone: (323) 549-0500
                (888) 8AUTISM
E-mail: info@cureautismnow.org
Web site: http://www.cureautismnow.org/

Cure Autism Now is an organization of parents, physicians, and researchers, dedicated to promoting and funding research with direct clinical implications for treatment and a cure for autism. The largest private funder of autism research, since its founding in 1995 Cure Autism Now has directed over $10 million to support research projects and a crucial scientific resource—the Autism Genetic Resource Exchange (AGRE). AGRE is the world's first collaborative gene bank that contains information on families with more than one child with autism.

Division TEACCH

Address: University of North Carolina
                310 Medical School, Wing E
                Chapel Hill, NC 27559-7180
Web site: http://www.teacch.com

Division TEACCH (Treatment and Education of Autistic and Related Communication Handicapped Children) is a statewide, state-funded, community-based program in North Carolina. TEACCH is known for its assessment instruments, structured teaching model, and comprehensive training for parents and professionals.

Families for Early Autism Treatment (FEAT)

Address: P.O.Box 255722
                Sacramento, California, 95865-5722
Phone: (916) 843-1536
Web site: http://www.feat.org/

FEAT (Families for Early Autism Treatment) is a nonprofit organization of parents and professionals, designed to help families with children who have received the diagnosis of Autism or Pervasive Developmental Disorder (PDD NOS). It offers a network of support where families can meet each other and discuss issues surrounding autism and treatment options. FEAT has a Board of Directors that meets monthly to discuss issues, establish priorities, and vote on the direction of the organization. Every other month, a newsletter is published which contains current news and events. It can be sent free via mail or e-mail. FEAT has a Lending Library, where families can get information about Autism and check out teaching materials for their therapy programs for free. FEAT also offers Support Meetings on the third Wednesday of each month which are designed to provide information to families whose children have been diagnosed with Autism and to provide emotional support to those who need it. Throughout the year, FEAT has parties, field trips and fundraising events. These activities are the most fun for the parents because this is when many friendships are formed.

Geneva Center for Autism

Address:	250 Davisville Ave., Suite 200
	Toronto, Ontario
	Canada M4S 1H2
Phone:	416-322-7877
Web site:	http://www.autism.net

Indiana Institute on Disability and Community
(Formerly: Indiana Resource Center for Autism [IRCA])
The Institute for the Study of Developmental Disabilities

Address:	2853 E. 10th St.
	Bloomington, IN 47408-2601
Phone:	(812) 855-6508

This institute offers many resources for teachers, parents, and other service providers. They offer a range of useful print and video materials.

MAAP (More Advanced Autistic People) Services Inc.

Address:	P.O. Box 524
	Crown Point, Indiana, USA, 46307
Phone/Fax:	(219) 662-1311

MAAP (More Advanced Autistic People) is dedicated to assisting family members of more advanced individuals with autism by offering information and advice on autism, and by providing the opportunity to network with others in similar circumstances. MAAP also works to inform professionals and the general public about more advanced individuals with autism and how to meet their needs.

MAAP produces a quarterly newsletter, *The MAAP*. The newsletter allows subscribers to exchange information, learn about issues related to autism, and share with others who face similar challenges. MAAP distributes print materials relevant to high-functioning individuals with autism, responds to phone calls and letters from family members, professionals, and individuals with autism who need support or advice, and presents information at conferences, workshops, and meetings of parent groups.

OAR - Organization for Autism Research

Address:	2111 Wilson Boulevard, Suite 600
	Arlington, VA 22201
Phone:	(703) 351-5031
E-mail:	OAR@autismorg.com
Website :	http://www.autismorg.com/

The Organization for Autism Research (OAR) is a nonprofit organization formed and led by parents and grandparents of children and adults with autism. Its purpose is to put applied science to work in providing answers to questions that parents, families, individuals with autism, teachers, and caregivers confront each day.

Online Asperger Syndrome Information and Support (O.A.S.I.S.)

Website:	http://www.udel.edu/kirby/asperger

Selected Newsletters and Journals in ASD

Advocate, Autism Society of America, 7910 Woodmont Ave., Suite 300, Bethesda, MD. 20814-3069

Autism/Asperger's Digest Magazine, Future Horizons, 721 W. Abram St., Arlington, TX. 76013

Autism: The International Journal of Research and Practice, SAGE Publications, PO Box 5096, Thousand Oaks, CA. 91359

Focus on Autism and Other Developmental Disabilities, PRO-ED, 8700 Shoal Creek Blvd., Austin, TX. 78757-6897

Journal of Autism and Developmental Disorders, Plenum Publishing Corp., 227 W. 17th St., New York, NY. 10011

Journal of Positive Behavior Interventions, PRO-ED, 8700 Shoal Creek Blvd., Austin, TX. 78757-6897

The Morning News. Published by Jenison Public Schools and the Gray Center for Social Learning and Understanding, Jenison High School, 2140 Bauer Rd, Jenison, MI. 49428. Phone: (616) 457-8955.

Selected Organizations in Recreation

ADVENTURE WITHOUT LIMITS
Address: 1341 Pacific Avenue
                  Forest Grove, OR 97116
Phone: (503) 359-2568

AMERICAN THERAPEUTIC RECREATION ASSOCIATION
Address: 1414 Prince St., Suite 204
                  Arlington, VA 22314
Phone: (703) 683-9420
Web site: http://www.atra-tr.org

BOY SCOUTS OF AMERICA
Address: 1325 West Walnut Hill Lane
                  Irving, TX 75038
Phone: (972) 580-2000
Scouting for the Handicapped Service. Referrals and assistance to local troops.

BRECKENRIDGE OUTDOOR EDUCATION CENTER
Address: P. 0. Box 697
                  Breckenridge, CO 80424
Phone: (970) 453-6422
Wilderness adventures for people with varying abilities, disabilities and special needs, skiing, rafting, rock climbing, etc.

GIRL SCOUTS OF THE USA
Address: 420 5th Avenue
                  New York, NY 10018
Phone: (212) 852-8000
Services for girls with disabilities. Referrals to local troops, training for leaders.

INTERNATIONAL LLAMA ASSOCIATION
Address: 7853 E. Arapahoe Court, #2100
                    Englewood, CO 80112
Phone: (303) 694-4728

NATIONAL SPORTS CENTER FOR THE DISABLED IN WINTER PARK
Address: P. O. Box 1290
                    Winter Park, CO 80482
Phone: (970) 726-1540
Summer (rafting, biking, hiking, sailing, camping) and winter (alpine and cross-country skiing, snow shoeing, snow boarding) recreation activities.

NATIONAL THERAPEUTIC RECREATION SOCIETY,
NATIONAL RECREATION AND PARK ASSOCIATION
Address: 22377 Belmont Ridge Road
                    Ashburn, VA 20148-4501
Phone: (713) 858-0784
Web site: http://www.nrpa.org

NORTH AMERICAN RIDING FOR THE HANDICAPPED ASSOCIATION
Address: P. O. Box 33150
                    Denver, CO 80233
                    12041 Tejon Street, Suite 510 Westminster, CO 80234
Phone: (303) 452-1212 or (800) 369-7433
Referral to local groups.

SPECIAL OLYMPICS NORTH AMERICA
Jim Schmutz   Managing Director
Address: 1325 G Street, NW, Suite 770
                    Washington, D.C. 20005
Phone: (202) 628-3630
E-mail: jschmutz@specialolympics.org

References

4-H (2003). Retrieved January 6, 2003, from www.4-H.org

American Camping Association. (2002). Retrieved December 10, 2002, from http://www.acacamps.org/aboutaca.htm

American with Disabilities Act of 1990 (ADA), PL 101-336 (July 26, 1990). Title 42, U.S.C. 12101 et seq.: U.S. Statutes at Large, 104. 327-328.

American Psychiatric Association (APA). (1994). *Diagnostic and statistical manual of mental disorders (DSM-IV)*. (4th ed.) Washington, D.C.: American Psychiatric Association.

The Autism and Asperger's Syndrome Independent Living Association. (2002). Retrieved on May 8, 2002, from www.amug.org/-a203/rec

The Arc of Multnomah County. (2002). *Inclusive Companion Project*. Brochure. Portland, OR: The Arc of Multnomah County.

Attwood, T., & Gray, C. (1999). The discovery of "Aspie": Criteria by Attwood and Gray. *The Morning News, 11*(3), 1-7.

Ayers, J., Marquardt, L., Tingstad, K., & Fullerton, A. (2001). *The development of visual communication systems to support persons with autism at a residential camp.* Unpublished masters project, Portland State University, Portland, OR.

Bambara, L.M., Spiegel-McGill, P., Shores, R.E., & Fox, J.J. (1984). A comparison of reactive and nonreactive toys on severely handicapped children's manipulative play. *Journal of the Association for Persons with Severe Handicaps, 9*(2), 142-149.

Bambara, L.M., & Knoster, T.P. (1995). *Guidelines: Effective behavioral support.* Harrisburg, PA: Pennsylvania Department of Education, Bureau of Special Education.

Bedini, L. (1993). Transition and integration in leisure for people with disabilities. *Parks and Recreation, 28*(11), 20-24.

Beppler, M.C., Bortz, F.E., & Leach, D.L. (1978). *Let's look at 4-H and handicapped youth: A leader's guide.* University Park, PA: Pennsylvania State University.

Beppler, M.C., Bortz, F.E., & Leach, D.L. (1978). *4-H recreation leader's guide: Recreation and handicapped youth.* University park, PA: Pennsylvania State University.

Beyer, J., & Gammeltoft, L. (2000). *Autism and play.* Shawnee Mission, KS: Autism Asperger Publishing Company.

Boucher, J. (1999). Interventions with children with autism-methods based on play (editorial). *Child Language Teaching and Therapy Journal, 15*(1), 1-5.

Brisotl-Powers, M. (2002). National Institute of Child Health and Human Development, presentation Autism Society of America National Conference.

Brannon, Steve A. (1999). Leisure and recreation. In deFur, S., & Patton, J. *Transition and school-based services.* Austin, TX: ProEd.

Brannan, S., Arick, J., & Fullerton, A. (1997). The national camp evaluation study: A national study on the effects of specialized camps. *Camping Magazine, 70*(1), 28-31.

Brannan, S., Arick, A., Fullerton, A., & Harris, J. (1997). Inclusionary practices: A nation wide survey of mainstream camps serving all youth. *Camping Magazine, 70*(1), 32-34.

Brannan, S., Arick, J., & Fullerton, A. (2003). Effective practices and participant outcomes for youth: Inclusive camps and outdoor schools. *Coalition for Education in the Outdoors Sixth Biennial Research Symposium Proceedings*, Bradford Woods, IN.

Brocket, S. (November-December, 1998). Developing successful play activities for individuals with autism. *Advocate*. (ASA) pp.15-17.

burlingame, j., & Blaschko, T. (2002). *Assessment tools for recreational therapy* (third ed.). Ravendale, WA: Idyll Arbor.

Carr, E.G., & Durand, V.M. (1985). Reducing behavior problems through functional communication training. Journal of Applied Behavior Analysis, 5, 443-454.

Carroll, M. (1998). *Focus on ability: Serving girls with special needs*. New York, NY: Girl Scouts of the USA.

Certo, N.J., Schleien, S.J., & Hunter, D. (1983). An ecological assessment inventory to facilitate community recreation participation by severely disabled individuals. *Therapeutic Recreation Journal, 17*(3), 29-38.

Challenger Sports Division. (2002). Retrieved February 2002, from www.challenger-sports.org

Clark, G. & Patton, J. (1997). Transition planning inventory. Austin, TX: Pre-Ed.

Commission of the Reorganization of Secondary Education. (1981). *Cardinal Principles of Secondary Education*. Paper. Washington, D.C.: U. S. Department of Education.

Coyne, P., Nyberg, C., & Vandenburg, M.L. (1999). *Developing leisure time skills in persons with autism*. Arlington, TX: Future Horizons.

Coyne, P. (1980). *Well-being for mentally retarded adolescents: A social, leisure, and nutrition education program*. Portland, OR: Oregon Health Sciences University.

Dalrymple, N.J. (1987). *Introduction to autism*. Bloomington, IN: Institute for the study of Developmental Disabilities.

Dattilo, J., & Mirenda, P. (1987). An application of a leisure preference assessment protocol for persons with severe handicaps. *Journal of the Association for Persons with Severe Handicaps, 12*(4), 306-311.

Dattilo, J., & Rusch, F. (1985). Effects of choice on leisure participation for persons with severe handicaps. *Journal of the Association for Persons with Severe Handicaps*, 10, 94-199.

Davis, K. (1999). *Your attitude just might be my biggest barrier.* Paper. Bloomington, IN: Indiana Resource Center for Autism.

Dawson, G., & Adams, A. (1984). Imitation and social responsiveness in autistic children. *Journal of Abnormal Child Psychology, 12*, 209-226.

Dawson, G., & Watling, R. (2000). Interventions to facilitate auditory, verbal, and motor integration in autism: A review of evidence. *Journal of Autism and Childhood Schizophrenia, 2*, 359-377.

Department of Recreation and Leisure Studies. (1997). *Project autism*. Chapel Hill: University of North Carolina.

Dunn, C. (1996). A status report on transition planning for individuals with learning disabilities. In J. Patton, & G. Blalock (Eds.), *Transition and students with learning disabilities* (pp. 19-41). Austin, TX: PRO-ED.

Edginton, C., Jordan, D., deGraaf, D. & Edginton, S. (1995). Leisure and life satisfaction: Foundation perspectives. Dubuque, IA: Brown & Benchmark.

Elkind, D. (1981). *The hurried child: Growing up too fast too soon*. Boston: Addison-Wesley.

Ermer, J., & Dunn, W. (1998). The sensory profile: A discriminant analysis of children with and without disabilities. *American Journal of Occupational Therapy, 52*, 283-90.

Falco, R., Janzen, J., Arick, J., & DeBoer, M. (1988). *Project quest inservice manual*. Portland State University, Portland, OR.

Favell, Judith E. (1973). Reduction of stereotypes by reinforcement of toy play. *Mental Retardation, 11*, 21-23.

Favell, J.E., McGimsey, J.F., & Schell, R.M. (1982). Treatment of self-injury by providing alternate sensory activities. *Analysis and Intervention in Developmental Disabilities, 2*(1),83-104.

Ferrara. C., & Hill, S.D. (1980). The responsiveness of autistic children to the predictability of social and non-social toys. *Journal of Autism and Developmental Disorders, 10*(1), 51-57.

Fine, A. (1991). Therapeutic Recreation for Exceptional Children. Springfield, IL.: Charles C. Thomas Publishers

Fullerton, A. (1996). Who are higher functioning young adults with autism? In Fullerton, A., Stratton, J., Coyne, P., & Gray, C. (Eds.), *Higher functioning adolescents and young adults with autism: A teachers guide.* (pp. 1 – 20). Austin, TX: Pro-Ed.

Fullerton, A., & Coyne, P. (1999). Developing skills and concepts for self-determination in young adults with autism. *Focus on autism and other developmental disabilities, 14*(1), 42-52, 63.

Fullerton, A., Stratton, J., Coyne, P., & Gray, C. (1994). *Higher functioning adolescents and young adults with autism: A teacher's guide.* Austin, TX: PRO-ED.

Fullerton, A., Brannan, S., & Arick, J. (2000). The impact of camp programs on children with disabilities: Opportunities for independence. *Coalition for Education in the Outdoors Fifth Biennial Research Symposium Proceedings*, Bradford Woods, IN:, 89-99.

Fullerton, A., Brannan, S., & Arick, J. (2003). Qualitative outcomes for youth who participate in inclusive programs: A multi-case analysis across 14 camps and outdoor schools. *Coalition for Education in the Outdoors Sixth Biennial Research Symposium Proceedings*, Bradford Woods, IN.

Girl Scouts of the USA. (1968). *Handicapped girls and Girl Scouting: A guide for leaders.* New York, NY: Girl Scouts of the USA.

Girl Scouts of the United States of America. (2002). Retrieved on February 9, 2002, from http://www.girlscouts.org

Girl Scouts—Totem Council. (2002). Where is the next generation of women leaders? Girl Scouts. Where girls grow strong. Pamphlet. Seattle, WA: Girl Scouts—Totem Council.

Gorn, S. (1997). *The answer book on special education law (second ed.).* Horsham, PA: LRP Publications.

Grandin, T., & Scariano, M.M. (1986). *Emergence: Labeled autistic.* Novato, CA: Arena Press.

Gray, C. (1994). *Comic strip conversations.* Arlington, TX: Future Horizons.

Gray, C. (2000). *The new social stories: Illustrated edition.* Arlington, TX: Future Horizons.

Gray, C. (1996). Social assistance. In A. Fullerton (Ed.), *Higher-functioning adolescents and adults with autism: A teacher's guide.* Austin, TX: PRO-ED

Gray, C. (2000). Gray's guide to bullying part I: The basics. *The Morning News, 12*(4), 1-15.

Gray, C. (2001). Gray's guide to bullying part II: The real world. *The Morning News, 13*(3), 1-39.

Gray, C. (2001). How to respond to a bullying attempt: A guide for parents and professionals. *The Morning News, 13*(2), 1-14.

Greene, D., & Miyake, J. (2002). In *Columbia Regional Program—Autism Services.* CD ROM. Portand, OR: Columbia Regional Program—Austism Services.

Gutierrez-Griep, R. (1984). Student preference of sensory reinforcers. *Education and Training of the Mentally Retarded, 19*, 108-113.

Hammel, M. (2002). Personal correspondence. Portland, OR.

Henning, J., Dalrymple, N., Davis, K., & Madeira, S. (1982). *Teaching social and leisure skills to youth with autism.* Bloomington, IN: Indiana University Developmental Training Center.

Hodgdon, L.A. (1996). *Visual strategies for improving communication.* Troy, MI: Quirk Roberts Publishing.

Hodgdon, L.A. (1999). *Solving behavior problems in autism: Improving communication with visual strategies.* Troy, MI: Quirk Roberts Publishing.

Horner, L. (1993). Some things which work and some which don't and why I'm happy being autistic. Our Voice: *The newsletter of the autism international network, 2,* 19-23.

Horner, R.H., Carr, E.G., Strain, P.S., Todd, A.W., & Reed, H.K. (2000). *Problem behavior interventions for young children with autism: A research synthesis.* Paper presented at the Second Workshop of the Committee on Education Interventions for Children with Autism, National Research Council, April 12, 2000. Department of Special Education, University of Oregon.

Individuals with Disabilities Act Amendments of 1997, 20 U.S.C. 1400 et seq.

Janzen, J.E. (1999). *Autism: Facts and strategies for parents.* San Antonio, TX: Therapy Skill Builders.

Janzen, J. (1996). *Understanding the nature of autism.* San Antonio, TX: Therapy Skill Builders.

Jarrold, C., Boucher, J., & Smith, P. (1993). Symbolic play in autism: A review. *Journal of Autism and Developmental Disorders, 23*(2), 281-307.

Johnson, D., Bullock, C., & Ashton-Schaeffer, C. (1997). Families and leisure: A context for learning. *Teaching Exceptional Children, 30*(2), 30-34.

Jones, M. L., Favell, James E., Lattimore, J., & Risley, T. R. (1984). Improving independent engagement of nonambulatory multihandicapped persons through the systematic analysis of leisure materials. *Analysis and Intervention in Developmental Disabilities, 4* (4), 313-332.

Kasari, C.M., & Yirmaya, N. (1993). Focused and social attention of autistic children in interactions with familiar and unfamiliar adults: A comparison of autistic, mentally retarded, and normal children. *Development and Psychopathology, 5*(3), 403-414.

Kashman, N. & Mora, J. (2001). An OT and SLP Team Approach: Sensory and Communication Strategies that WORK! Las Vegas, NV: Sensory Resources.

Kern, L., Koegel, L., & Dunlap, G. (1984). The influence of vigorous versus mild exercise on autistic stereotyped behavior. *Journal of Autism and Developmental Disabilities, 12*(1), 57-67.

Kientz, M.A., & Dunn, W. (1998). A comparison of the performance of children with and without autism on the Sensory Profile. *American Journal of Occupational Therapy, 51,* 530-537.

Klin, A., Volmar, F.R., & Sparrow, S.S. (1992). Autistic social dysfunction: Some limitations of the theory of mind hypothesis. *Journal of Child Psychology and Psychiatry, 33*(5), 861-876.

Keogel, L.K., Koegel, R.L., Harrower, J.K., & Carter, C.M. (1999). Pivotal response intervention I: Overview of approach. *Journal of the Association for the Severely Handicapped, 24,* 174-185.

Libby, S., Powell, S., Messer, D., & Jordan, R. (1998). Spontaneous play in children with autism: A reappraisal. *Journal of Autism and Developmental Disorders, 28*(6), 487-497.

Lord, C., & Paul, R. (1997). Language and communication in autism. In D. Cohen, & F. Volmar, (Eds.), *Handbook of autism and pervasive developmental disorders,* (pp. 195-225). New York, NY: John Wiley and Sons.

Lovett, H. (1996). *Learning to listen: Positive approaches and people with difficult behavior.* Baltimore: Paul H. Brookes Publishing Co.

Mayer-Johnson, R. (2000). *The picture communication symbols combination book.* Solana Beach, CA: Mayer-Johnson Co.

McCune-Nicholich, L. (1981). Toward symbolic functioning: Structure of early pretend games and potential parallels with language. *Child Development, 3,* 785-797.

McGee, G.G., & Daly, T. (1999). Prevention of problem behaviors in preschool children. In C. Repp, & R.H. Horner (Eds.), *From effective assessment to effective support: Functional analysis of problem behavior* (pp. 171-196). New York, NY: Wadesworth.

Mesibov, G. (1986). *Structured teaching training.* Paper presented at Autism Conference, Portland, Oregon.

Moon, M.S. (1994). *Making school and community recreation fun for everyone: Places and ways to integrate.* Baltimore: Paul H. Brookes Publishing.

National 4-H Council. (2002). Retrieved June 5, 2002, from www.n4h.org

National Center for Children and Youth with Disabilities. (1991). Related services for school-age children with disabilities. *National Center for Children and Youth with Disabilities News Digest. 1*(2), 5-7.

National Recreation and Park Association. (2002). Retrieved on April 13, 2002 from http://www.nrpa.org

National Therapeutic Recreation Society. (1990). Position statement. Paper. Arlington, VA: National Recreation and Parks Association.

National Research Council. (2001). *Educating children with autism.* Committee on Educational Interventions for Children with Autism. Division of Behavioral and Social Sciences and Education. Washington, D.C.: National Academy Press.

Nietupski, J., Hamre-Nietupski, S., & Ayres, B. (1984). Review of task analytic leisure skill training efforts: Practitioner implications and future research needs. *Journal of the Association for Persons with Severe Handicaps, 9*(2), 88-97.

Odom, S. & Strain, P. (1986). A comparison of peer-initiation and teacher-antecedent interventions for promoting reciprocal social interaction of autistic preschoolers. Journal of Applied Behavior Analysis, 19, 59-71.

Oregon Administrative Rules. (2000). Oregon Department of Education, Salem, OR, OAR 581-015-0005.

Perske, R. (1988). *Circles of friends: People with disabilities and their friends enrich the lives of one another.* Nashville, TN: Abingdon Press.

Peters, S. (2002). Personal correspondence. Portland, OR.

Peterson, C.A. (1981). *Leisure lifestyle and disabled individuals.* Paper presented at Horizons West Therapeutic Recreation Symposium, San Francisco, CA.

Quill, K. (1995). *Teaching children with autism: Strategies to enhance communication and socialization.* Albany, NY: Delmar Publishing Co.

Realon, R E., Favell, J.E., & Phillips, J. F. (1989). Adapted leisure materials vs. standard leisure materials: Evaluating several aspects of programming for profoundly handicapped persons. *Education and Training in Mental Retardation, 24*(2), 168-176.

Realon, R E., Favell, J.E., & Dayvault, K.A. (1988). Evaluating the use of adapted leisure materials on the engagement of persons who are profoundly, multiply handicapped. *Education and Training in Mental Retardation, 23*(3), 228-237.

Reynolds, R. (1995). A look towards the future in service delivery. In S. Schleien, L. Meyers, L. Heyne, & B. Brandt. (eds.). Lifelong leisure skills and lifestyles for persons with disabilities.

Riguet, C.B., Taylor, N.D., Benaroya, S., & Klein, L.S. (1981). Symbolic play in autistic, down's, and normal children of equivalent mental age. *Journal of Autism and Developmental Disorders, 11*(4), 439-449.

Rincover, A., Newson, C., Lovaas, I. O., & Koegel, R. (1977). Some motivational properties of sensory stimulation in psychotic children. *Journal of Experimental Child Psychology, 24*, 312-323.

Rivco, T., & Davis, W. (1993). Teaching lifetime recreation and leisure skills to individuals with disabilities. *Issues in Teacher Education, 2*(1), 27-35.

Robinson, J., & Godbey, G. (1997). *Time for life: The surprising ways Americans use their time.* University Park, PA: Pennsylvania University Press.

Roeyers, H. (1996). The influence of nonhandicapped peers on the social interaction of children with a pervasive developmental disorder. *Journal of Autism and Developmental Disorders, 26,* 303-320.

Romanczyk, R.G., Locksin, S.B., & Matey, L. (2000). The children's unit for treatment and evaluation. In J.S Handelman, & S. L. Harris (Eds.), *Preschool education programs for children with autism* (second ed., pp. 49-94). Austin, TX: ProEd.

Schleien, S., Krotes, M., & Musstonen, T. (2000). The effects on integration of children with autism into a physical activity and recreation setting. *Therapeutic Recreation Journal, 21*(4), 52-63.

Schleien, S., Meyer, L., Heyne, L., & Brandt, B. (Eds.). (1995). *Lifelong leisure skills and lifestyles for persons with developmental disabilities.* Baltimore, MD: Paul H. Brookes.

Schleien, S., Rynders, J., & Musstonen, T. (1997). Effects of social play activities on the play behavior of children with autism. *Journal of Leisure Research, 22*(4), 317-329.

Schleien, S., Olson, K. (1985). Integrating children with severe handicaps into recreation and physical education programs. *Journal of Park and Recreation Administration, 3*(1), 50-66.

Schmidt, G., McLaughlin, J., & Dalrymple, N. (1986). Teaching students with autism: A sport skill specialist's approach. *Journal of Physical Education, Recreation and Dance, 57*(7), 60-63.

Schopler, E., Mesibov, G.B., & Heasey, K. (1995). Structured teaching in the TEACCH system. In E. Schopler, & G.B. Mesibov (Eds.), *Learning and cognition in autism*(pp. 243-268). New York: Plenum Press.

Schultheis, S.F., Boswell, B. B., & Decker, J. (2000). Successful physical activity programming for students with autism. *Focus on autism and other developmental disabilities, 15*(3), 159-162.

SELF (Special Education for Leisure Fulfillment) Curriculum Guide (1979). Washington, D.C.: Institute for Career and Leisure Development.

Seigel, B., Hayes, C., & Tanquay, P. (2001). Treatment of pervasive developmental disorders. In E. Weller, J. McDermott, & G. Gabbard (Eds.), *Treatment of psychiatric disorders* (third ed.). Washington, D.C.: American Psychiatric Association Press.

Sherrill, C. (1993). *Adapted physical activity, and recreation and sport: Crossdisciplinary and lifespan (fourth ed.).* Dubuque, IA: Brown.

Sigman, M., & Ungerer, J. (1984). Cognitive and language skills in autistic, mentally retarded and normal children. *Developmental Psychology, 20,* 293-302.

Sigman, M., Mundy, P., Sherman, T., & Ungerer, J. (1986). Social interactions of autistic, mentally retarded, and normal children and their caregivers. *Journal of Child Psychology and Psychiatry, 27*(5),647-655.

Sinclair, J. (1992). Bridging the gaps: An inside-out view of autism (or, Do you know what I don't know?). In E. Schloper, & G. Mesibov (Eds.), *High-functioning individuals with autism* (pp. 294-302). New York: Plenum.

Smith, M. J. (2000). *Teaching playskills to children with autistic spectrum disorder.* Shawnee Mission, KS: Autism Asperger Publishing Company.

Staub, D., & Peck, C. (1995) What are the outcomes for nondisabled students? *Educational leadership, 52*(4), 36-40.

Stone, W.L., Lemanek, K.L., Fishel, P.T., Fernandez, M.C., & Altemeier, W.A. (1990). Play and imitation skills in the diagnosis of autism in young children. *Pediatrics, 86,* 267-272.

United Nations. (1948). Principle 7, New York, NY: United Nations

Vandercook, T. et. al. (1989). The McGill Action Planning System (MAPS): A strategy for building the vision. *Journal of the Association for Persons with Severe Handicaps (JASH), 14*(3), 205-215.

Voeltz, L.M., Wuerch, B.B., & Wilcox, B. (1982) Leisure and recreation: Preparation for independence, integration, and self-fulfillment. In B. Wilcox, & G. T. Bellamy (Eds.), *Design of high school programs for severely handicapped students.* Baltimore, MD: Paul H. Brookes.

Vygotsky, L.S. (2000). Play and its role in the mental development of the child. In J. Bruner, A. Jolly, & S. Sylva (Eds.), *Play: Its role in development and evolution.* New York: Basic Books.

Wacker, D.P., Berg, W.K., Wiggins, B., Muldoon, M., & Cavanaugh, J. (1985). Evaluation of reinforcer preferences for profoundly handicapped students. *Journal of Applied Behavior Analysis, 18,* 173-178.

Ward, M., & Alar, N. (2000). Being autistic is part of who I am. *Focus on autism and other developmental disabilities, 15*(4), 232-235.

Wehman, P. (1976) Selection of play materials for the severely handicapped: A continuing dilemma. *Education and Training of the Mentally Retarded, 11,* 46-50.

Wehman, P., & Kregel, J. (1997). *Functional curriculum for elementary, middle, and secondary age students with special needs.* Austin, TX: PRO-ED.

Wehman, P., & Moon, M.S. (1985). Designing and implementing leisure programs for individuals with severe handicaps. In Brady, M. P., & Gunter, P.L. (Eds.), *Integrating moderately and severely handicapped learners.* Springfield, IL: Charles C. Thomas Publisher.

Wehman, P., & Schleien, S.J. (1981). *Leisure programs for handicapped persons.* Baltimore: University Park Press.

Wetherby, A., & Prutting, C. (1984). Profiles of communicative and cognitive-social abilities in autistic children. *Journal of Speech and Hearing Research, 27,* 364-377.

Wetherby, A., Prizant, B., & Hutchison, T. (1998). Communicative, social-affective, and symbolic profiles of young children with autism and pervasive developmental disorder. *American Journal of Speech-Language Pathology, 7,* 79-91.

Whitaker, P., Barratt, P., Joy, H., Potter, M., & Thomas, G. (1998). Children with autism and peer group support: Using circles of friends. *British Journal of Special Education, 25*(2), 60-64.

Willey, L.H. (1999). *Pretending to be normal.* London: Jessica Kingsley Publishers.

Williams, M.W. & Shellenberger, S. (1996). *How does your engine run? A leader's guide to the alert program for self-regulation.* Albuquerque, NM: Therapy Works.

Wilkerson, J. (2002). *Activity stories for the Mt. Hood Kiwanis Camp.* Unpublished masters thesis, Portland State University, Portland, OR.

Wing, L. (1980). Foreword. In C. Webster, M. Lonstantareas, J. Oxman, & J. Mack (Eds.), *Autism : New directions in research and education.* Elmsford, NY: Pergamon Press.

Wolfberg, P.J. (1999). *Play and imagination in children with autism.* New York, NY: Teachers College Press.

Wooten, M., & Mesibov, G.B. (1986). Social skills training for elementary school autistic children with normal peers. In Schopler, E., & Mesibov, G.B. (Eds.), *Social behavior in autism.* New York: Plenum Publishing.

Wuerch, B.B., & Voeltz, L. (1982). *Longitudinal leisure skills for severely handicapped learners.* Baltimore: Paul H. Brookes Publishing Co.

Index